Digital Analytics for Marketing

This comprehensive book provides students with a "grand tour" of the tools needed to measure digital activity and implement best practices for using data to inform marketing strategy. It is the first text of its kind to introduce students to analytics platforms from a practical marketing perspective.

Demonstrating how to integrate large amounts of data from web, digital, social, and search platforms, this helpful guide offers actionable insights into data analysis, explaining how to "connect the dots" and "humanize" information to make effective marketing decisions. The authors cover timely topics, such as social media, web analytics, marketing analytics challenges, and dashboards, helping students to make sense of business measurement challenges, extract insights, and take effective actions. The book's experiential approach, combined with chapter objectives, summaries, and review questions, will engage readers, deepening learning by helping them to think outside the box.

Filled with engaging, interactive exercises and interesting insights from industry experts, this book will appeal to students of digital marketing, online marketing, and analytics. A companion website features an instructor's manual, test bank, and PowerPoint slides.

Marshall Sponder holds a dual appointment as a Faculty Lecturer at Zicklin School of Business, Baruch College, USA, where he teaches digital analytics, text analytics, and Internet marketing to graduate and undergraduate students, and as an Associate Professor of Professional Practice at Rutgers Business School, USA.

Gohar F. Khan is a Senior Lecturer at the University of Waikato, New Zealand. His research interests include social media analytics, social media adoption/use, and network analysis. His work on social media and information systems has appeared in several refereed journals, conference proceedings, and books.

"*Digital Analytics for Marketing* explores the increasingly murky world of social media data, providing a comprehensive and practical framework for understanding and analyzing data from a variety of social media marketing channels. A must-read for digital marketing enthusiasts."

Stuart Dillon, *University of Waikato, New Zealand*

"Data analytics is one of the most significant techniques for modern business organizations to attain and sustain their competitive advantages. This book deals deeply with various data analytics on the Internet including web, social media, and mobile analytics. This is a must-read for beginners as well as experts who are eager to learn the strategic use of data analytics for marketing."

Hangjung Zo, *Korea Advanced Institute of Science and Technology, South Korea*

"This book is an excellent survey of the digital analytics world, providing a solid foundation to the breadth of platforms, tools, and apps. Sponder and Khan demonstrate how digital analytics is used for research by public entities and businesses to understand population and consumer behavior, and how this leads to improvement in population, quality of life, and/or increasing market share and profit."

Alan Barnett, *Baruch College, USA*

"In order to have an informed perspective on where we are and where we're going, it's imperative that we know from where it is we came. In *Digital Analytics for Marketing*, Marshall Sponder and Gohar F. Khan tackle a meaty subject and condense it into salient, palatable chunks for all levels. Required reading for the digital practitioner and technologist."

Barry J. Fleming, *VP, Digital, MPA – The Association of Magazine Media, USA*

Digital Analytics for Marketing

Marshall Sponder and Gohar F. Khan

Routledge
Taylor & Francis Group

NEW YORK AND LONDON

First published 2018
by Routledge
711 Third Avenue, New York, NY 10017

and by Routledge
2 Park Square, Milton Park, Abingdon, Oxon, OX14 4RN

Routledge is an imprint of the Taylor & Francis Group, an informa business

Library of Congress Cataloging-in-Publication Data
A catalog record for this book has been requested

ISBN: 978-1-138-19067-2 (hbk)
ISBN: 978-1-138-19068-9 (pbk)
ISBN: 978-1-315-64091-4 (ebk)

Typeset in Helvetica Neue
by Apex CoVantage, LLC

Visit the companion website at www.routledge.com/cw/sponder.

Dedication

Special thanks to my wife JoAnn Lefebvre and my son Adam Sponder.

This book happened, partly due to my faculty chair at Zicklin School of Business, David Luna, introducing me to Sharon Golan, an acquisitions editor at Routledge/Taylor & Francis in March 2014. Professor David Luna has provided invaluable support, and helped to create a great working environment in the department of Marketing and International Business at Baruch College. Since April 2014 the idea this manuscript gradually developed into its final form. Alan Barnett, Karthik Sridhar, and the Dean of International Studies, Myung-Soo Lee—my marketing department colleagues at Baruch—provided valuable advice and support as I began to write this manuscript. And the contributions of my friends Adi Andrei and Hitomi Sakamoto in London helped me to cement the data methodologies used in various parts of this book. I would also like to thank my colleagues at Rutgers Business School, Jennifer Fine, Joseph Schaffer, Lei Lei, Yaw Mensah, Ashwani Mong Richard Metzger, Ruqqayya Maudoodi, and Peter Methot for the support they have provided in support of the Rutgers Business School/Mason Gross School of the Arts course "Social Media for the Arts" that I author and teach. Social Media for the Arts has been the crucible that merged many of ideas of the Art/Technology merger that makes this book so different than others about Analytics.

As the manuscript moved towards completion, I discovered the work of Professor Gohar F. Khan and his *Seven Layers of Social Media Analytics* book one summer night while searching on Google. I was impressed with what I saw and bought a copy of his book immediately. One thing led to another, and Gohar became the co-author of this book, and I am very grateful for that. Gohar's contributions broadened the scope of the manuscript and deepened its academic underpinnings—a win-win in the fullest sense of the term.

Finally, I want to think some of my most talented students at Baruch College and Rutgers University who provided valuable editorial support and insights, along with a window into the millennial mind, such as Nate Harris, Rachit Mehta, Taylor Frankel, Sierra Laney, and Sharon Clott. These students continued to support and inspire me to create a book aimed at the next generation of analysts, thinkers, and business leaders.

Contents

Tables

Manuscript Class Reviewers at Zicklin School of Business and Rutgers University, and Other Academic Chapter Reviewers

Many students acted as reviewers during the Summer and Fall of 2016, their contribution was invaluable in refining the manuscript. I cannot thank my students enough for the work and insights they provided.

We also thank the various Routledge academic reviewers who provided valuable feedback on selected chapters during the initial drafts of this publication.

Mayar Abdelmeguid, Samiul Abtahee, Anabel Acevedo Velasquez, Hussein Agiz, Bakhtawar Ahmad, Samir Ahmed, Shafkath Ahmed, Jorge Alfaro, Hufnagle Allison, Kaur Amarleen, Mariam Aminyar, Roy An, Kimberly Andresen, Sandy Anya, Alex Arnold, Alex Arnold, Sur Arushi, Akram Baig, Steven Bambico, Nikita Barde, Poonam Bavishi, Daniel Berlin, Tarakshaya Bhatia, Jeremy Blumenthal, Haley Bramble, Kayla Brantley, Nicole Brougham, David Busch, Brendan Byles, Ho Jun Cha, Mrudula Chakravarthy, Jessica Chang, Suryateja Chatakondu, Abdulnasser Chebly, Melanie Chen, Xijun Chen, Shah Chintankumar, Christina Cho, Sarah Choi, Michael Choi, Marcus Choi, Sarah Choi, Lucelia Chou Zheng, Ittihad Chowdhury, Andrew Chung, Cynthia Chung, Cayla Cook, Jillian Curwin, Marcel Czajkowski, George Dahdouh, Nicholas Dass, Sunny d'Ave, Julian Davis, Eric Deng, Nidhi Desai, Aditi Devrajan, Inderpreet Dhaliwal, Aatin Dhanda, Sandra DiBitetto, Sandra DiBitetto, Moredee Eang, Nicholas Eduardo, Yomna Elbeyali, Russell Epstein, Karen Fahim, Chadly Fakir, Mary Fam, Shelly Farez, Kristina Fari, Rebecca Feliciano, Honey Fender, Pamela Feng, Caitlyn Ford, Caitlyn Ford, Erica Frezza, Asiya Fricke, Andrea Gandolfo Macchiavello, Xiao Xia Gao, Tiffany Garnett, Andriy Gavrysh, Arvind Gayam, Sana Ghafoor, Sohyun Han, Songyee Han, Yilin Hao, JanYing He, Jacqueline Hernandez, Brianna Hernandez, Jacqueline Hernandez, Noelle Hickey, Daniel Hincapie, Hao-Yu Ho, Dingfan Hu, Zhiqian Huang, Shahzaib Hussain, Jonathan Ibrahim, Thomas Ippolito, Vishal Jain, Daniel Jimenez, Shannon Judson, Adham Kaawar, Rachel Kandyba, David Kanevsky, Manjyot Kaur, Michael Keane, Juhi Kharawala, Christine H Kim Kim, Hanna Kim, Yoon Mi Kim, Julia Klein, Sandra Kolakowski, Christian Kot, Michelle Kot, Natasha Kothare, Aanchal Kumar, Christy Kwok, Baback Lahijani, Jared Lal, Sierra Laney, Cherry Lau, Jung Hwan Lee, Rachel Li, Shannon Liao, Xin Lin, Fanzhuo Liu, Bryan Loh, Lynn Luong, Kevin Ma, Jillian Ma, Allison Maddock, Duha Magzoub, Zahid Mahmood, Rahyan Mahmud, Danielle Mainardi, Christine Mais, Jennifer Malvagna, Jamie Manalastas, Karina Margarian, Alexia Marrache, Jeffrey Marron, Michael Mayorga, Caelan McCarthy, Rushi Mehta, Yanhua Mei, Will Meisel, Caroline Mickowski, Penelope Min, Sara Mohamed, Brianna Moonsammy, Aitsana Moukaeva, Keirstyn Moyle, Osama Naim, Nateshwar Nauth, Ismel Nunez, Tugce Ozdemir, Sylvia

Pak, Somil Parekh, Seungjong Park, Chang Park, Yun Jin Park, Stephen Park, Ryan Park, Joseph Park, Hyunjoon Park, Palak Patel, Parth Patel, Sagar Patel, Radha Patel, Parth Patel, Nirali Patel, Kishan Patel, Mehal Patel, Nirali Patel, Arjun Pawar, Stephanie Peschiera, Marissa Petrullo, Julie Petulla, Alex Phung, Laraub Pirzada, Sonika Poudyal, Kavya Raghunath, Cristian Ramos, Jacqueline Ramos, Joseph Rizzo, Alexa Roemer, Julio Rojas, Scott Russell, Jacquelyn Samilow, Maria Paulina Samson, Sara Sayed, Tori Schober, Natalia Segovia, Maya Shanfeld, Jiawei Shen, Nitiben Sheth, Charles Sheu, Deveshwar Singh, Dattamanoj Sreedhara, Camille Suarez, Trenton Sweeney, Marisa Tedesco, Anuj Tevar, Benjamin Thieberger, Daniel Tobar, Olivia Tomie, Fiona Tran, Jennifer Tran, Michelle Umana, Hasan Usmani, Sara Vallejo, Elijah Martie Viola, Smitha Vivekanandan, Mohamed Vizam, David Vizcaino, Xin Wang, Megan Watt, Gwendolyn Weigelt, Eoin Wenger, Amanda Wisnack, Justin Yee, Christine Yen, Lin Yi, Victoria Yoffe, Jasmine You, Christian Zapata, Mahmoud Zayed, Jason Zhai, Xin Zhang, Lei Zhang, Xunqing Zheng, and Konrad Zielinski.

Preface

This textbook is not just another book about business or Digital Analytics.

In fact, we did not set up to write a Digital Analytics textbook, but rather, a guide book into the world of digital and social media analytics *as we see and experience it*. We are professors who teach Digital Marketing courses at our respective universities and have authored books on similar subjects (Social Media Analytics)[1] with similar titles before we knew of each other. I was first made aware of Gohar F. Khan and his book during the summer of 2016, well into the research for this textbook. One thing led to another, and Gohar became my co-author in this endeavor.

One roadblock to writing a textbook focusing on Digital Analytics is that there is no consensus on what should or should not be in it. We can treat the subject at a very high level (a better treatment for managers) or take a more granular approach; the latter would very likely be a boring textbook, while the former would work well for managers, but lack enough substance to be useful as a textbook. We went as far towards the middle as we could comfortably go. However, even between two co-authors, we're not experts on all aspects of digital marketing, and we can't cover everything in a way that will keep every reader happy; we're OK with that— we hope the readers are too. Consider that it is impossible to "know everything," especially within subjects that are constantly evolving and changing, such as social media. Just as in life, we can accomplish much more by having an open mind and a willingness to learn, we can learn a great deal by exploring digital marketing and its analytics. If we believe we can learn this material and it is interesting to us, we will. The rest are just details, some of these we cover, other aspects we may have left out or simply sketched out. If we have stimulated the readers' interest and enthusiasm to learn more about digital marketing, we've accomplished our purpose.

How This Book Was Written

This book is based on things analysts and stakeholders are trying to measure and are not sure how. Nonetheless, digital marketing and social media must be measured to be effective. As a lecturer at Baruch College and a Professor at Rutgers University, it was frustrating that there were not, in my opinion, good textbooks for subjects I teach. Several of the textbooks that have been published were not current or not focused in the direction needed for students' optimal learning (particularly in regards to retention). It was also clear that the subjects of Digital Marketing and Analytics are still forming, and are part of emerging media with a smattering of "Big Data."[2] Since there was no book that covered most of the material in my courses, I came up with the idea of writing this book in early 2014 (although it took another two years to write a proposal and find the right publisher, and finally, the right co-author).

The need for this book became its main premise. For instance, at Baruch College, I had spearheaded the initiative to start a Programmatic Advertising program (few are familiar with the term) over the last three years. Algorithmic marketing is a new concept to most students and faculty—there aren't many texts on the subject—and of those that do exist, within a year or two from publication, the industry has already been transformed.[3] Likewise, Text Analytics is rarely taught in academic intuitions, and when it is offered, it is from a CIS (Computer Information Systems) perspective rather than a marketing perspective. Moreover, what bothered us the most was that most of the textbooks were written by academics who often had not worked in the field. That is where Gohar F. Khan, my co-author, who is a Senior Business Analytics Lecturer at the University of Waikato, New Zealand, comes into the picture; his book, *Seven Layers of Social Media Analytics*,[4] has a chapter on Text Analytics in it. Gohar's book is a practical book with tutorials and case studies for platforms that are generally free to get a hold of (such as Lexalytics Semantria, NodeXL, VOSON, Google Fusion Tables, etc.). Gohar is a professor and has authored or co-authored more than 40 peer-reviewed papers covering some of the subjects we cover in the book.[5]

There is another elephant in the room that hampers almost all teaching efforts on these subjects—data and tools. The problem for many of us in the digital marketing space is there just is not enough of the right kind of business data that we are permitted to have access to. It is not so much what we ask students to do; it's the way the information is acted on by the student that is more important—do they really understand what the value is of what they are doing? As a result, we decided to write this book to encapsulate an experiential approach that would engage students, get them to think outside of the box, and deepen their learning.

Digital Analytics Simulations

There are some excellent platforms with simulations we have used in some of our classes such as Stukent Mimic Pro,[6] Adobe Education and the Adobe Analytics Sandbox,[7] the Google Analytics Sandbox (which launched in August 2016, with real data),[8] Brandwatch for Students,[9] IBM Watson Analytics for students,[10] the Google Analytics Marketing Challenge and Google Partners,[11] and comScore for Education.[12] They are all great learning platforms, some have real data, but getting students to use the tools together and formulate the insights from them, is missing. We are both platform independent. We deal with various platforms we have worked with (i.e., Adobe Analytics, Google Analytics, comScore, etc.) but our goal is to write about the opportunities that these platforms uncover for marketing insights.

A Grand Tour of Digital Analytics

This book was conceived as a "Grand Tour" of Web/Digital/Social/Search Analytics platforms along with ways to apply the information derived from them and best practices around applying and storing the data/reports. It's our belief that digital data should not be viewed apart from other marketing channels, or even other subjects, but the important thing to keep in mind is whether we can get actionable intelligence out of it or not. We want to train our students to be able to extract and combine data in an intelligent way, in their own way, so it can be acted on—and we want our students to own, retain and generalize their learnings. We want to come up with a program to stimulate extensible and long-lasting learning rather than write a purely academic textbook on the subject. Our book will leave students with the understandings needed to make sense of the current business measurement challenges, to extract insights, and to take strong, effective actions on the collected data. A caveat: While our subject of Digital Marketing is focused and deep, it is also vast, and we obviously didn't cover everything or every platform. But, it does not matter. We did not want to write another boring textbook (there are already too many of those!), and we are going for a more process-oriented approach instead.

Approaches to Digital Analytics

Industry Certifications

Although there is no scholarly consensus on what a Digital Marketing program or textbook must contain, there are several different frameworks and points of view on the subject area. For instance, the Digital Analytics Association created a competency framework with three levels,[13] and for Web and Digital Analytics that is as close to an industry consensus as we are going to get, based on the point of view of several practitioners and hiring managers.[14] The focus of the DAA's competency framework builds on a realistic assessment of what being an analyst boils down to, the eyes of many industry practitioners who work in the leading industries that use Digital Analytics. Also, the Internet Advertising Bureau (IAB) certification programs for Digital Advertising operations,[15] Digital Sales,[16] and the New Marketing Institute[17] have created training on subjects such as Programmatic Advertising. We decided to take our own approach rather than rehash what has already been written.

University—Data Science and CIS-Focused

Another way to approach Digital Analytics is as an applied science, much as physics and mathematics are treated and taught—this would seem to make sense from a from a CIS/Data Science perspective. For example, Northwestern runs a Master of Science in Analytics[18] with a focus on predictive analytics,[19] which can also be taken online. NYU SCPS offers an MS in Integrated Marketing[20] as well as new pathways professional diploma program[21] (a rebranding of their non-degree certificate courses for both for online and in-person); these programs tend to focus on software design, programming algorithms, and looking for patterns in the data that can be applied to marketing. The CIS approach, to be fair, is what is generally considered the proper training for this subject, but it raises a dilemma, of going too deep into the algorithmic weeds (a phrase we just coined) and comes at the cost of authentic ideation and synthesis (which is closer to the discipline of the arts and philosophy). After all, just about every statistics and data science schooled pundit who predicted the outcome of the US Presidential Election of 2016 and Brexit, were proven wrong, including the poster child of the 2012 Election, Nate Silver.[22]

Are We Living in a Data Analytics Bubble?

My belief is that there is a "bubble" in analytics and Big Data that has formed and it is already starting to pop[23]—specialized training in analytics thinking and technique are important, no doubt, but it's even more important to understand what is worth analyzing and what is worth doing, along with the best approach to take—making the best decisions, in short. Our book can help readers think outside of the box and form their own opinions (at least, through the book's teachings, the student can learn much of what they need to know on their own). A data science approach works best when business processes and outcomes are very well defined, which is not the case for many businesses when their data or operations are taken into consideration.[24]

A Third Way: The Web as an Organism— Web Science Trust

The Web Science Trust (WST), co-founded by Tim Berners-Lee (the founder of the World Wide Web), operates as a scientific and artistic brain trust that partners with universities all over the world to create programs in "Web Science"[25]—studying the web as an evolving organism that merges art and science—typified by programs running at the University of Southampton (UK).[26] One of the co-authors attended a WST event taking place at the Royal Society in London in 2011[27] where Berners-Lee spoke. In approach, our book is closer to the Web Science Trust philosophy, as we understand it, but we haven't partnered with them. In fact, the approach that the WST takes sounds like what my Rutgers Social Media for the Course is.

Connecting Curriculums

At the Zicklin School of Business, I teach a one-day Digital Marketing Bootcamp every January to students majoring in some aspect of Business who may want to study Digital Marketing and Analytics.

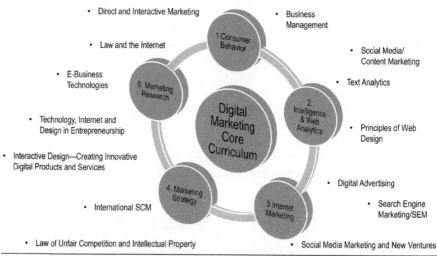

Figure PR1 Parts of the core curriculum and electives.
Source: Digital Marketing Program, Baruch College.

We offer five core courses in the Digital Marketing Curriculum at Baruch College, as shown in Figure PR1. When the Bootcamp was created, it seemed as if each course represented a different lens, examining marketing data in a different way. The curriculum prepares a student for the fundamentals of the digital world, and digital data. Yet the material in the courses was not interconnected as well as it could be. I think we should try do something and decided to help students to better connect the dots for themselves—by creating a book and a training program that, *at the very least*, informs students on our five core curriculum courses, and connect that foundation to our wide selection of elective courses, as shown in Figure PR1. That's why I came up with the idea for this book. It could be that we haven't yet succeeded in this textbook of connecting all the parts of our curriculum as well as it could be done. Perhaps we have too many "holes" where more could have been filled in. We will let the reader decide that for themselves. We believe that we're at the very beginning of a new frontier, linking the learnings from various courses in more efficient ways so students can use the curriculum information and internalize their learning.

Connecting the Dots

A few years ago, on one of my frequent visits to London, I took a close friend of mine, Adi Andrei, who is a data scientist, to lunch (please note that Adi Andrei contributed Chapter 17 to this book). I told Adi what I wanted to do and my idea for this book. We came up with the concept of the "Data Selfie" and "Online Presence Assessment," radar diagram, and self-assessments. Maybe I was dreaming about them all along, and just looking for the right circumstance, use case, set of data, or whatever. Or maybe it was talking to Adi that stimulated an idea in my mind—that all these disciplines could be combined if we could find the right framework and approach. Adi and I jotted down a few points that day at lunch:

1. Create an approach that shows the progress that a student and the class made from the beginning of the course until the end of the course.
2. Make the Connect the Dots Approach extensible and customizable to almost any subject.
3. Build the textbook around the first two points.
4. Come up with soft assessments that students could run on themselves or a business and come up with visualizations (the Data Selfie) that help them to understand how they are performing so they can take some action, make a change, shake things up.

The last part of my proposal had me stumped. My friend showed me how to create visualizations, but the questions around each assessment were not clear. For example, I didn't know the questions to ask or the right scale and evaluation criteria.

As soon as I got back from London, I experimented with my graduate Summer Web Analytics Class, having them evaluate what they wanted to achieve versus what I hoped they would learn in my course. I even published my thoughts at ClickZ, an online magazine that I wrote for at the time.[27]

I wasn't technically doing anything new with my study, as shown in Figure PR2, but I felt the concept was different, as were some of my questions. I wanted to know if my students had unrealistic expectations of what they would learn in my class, or not.

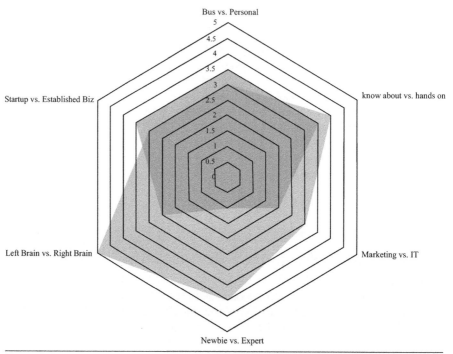

Figure PR2 The first Analytics Selfie, July 2014, Baruch College Web Analytics graduate class. *Source:* WebMetricsGuru Inc, published at ClickZ.com.

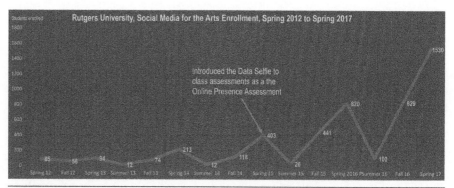

Figure PR3 Rutgers University, Social Media for the Arts course growth, 2012–2017. *Source:* Marshall Sponder, WebMetricsGuru Inc.

The Data Selfie showed that most graduate students were familiar with the Web/Data Analytics, and I had to find a way to connect with them, perhaps by humanizing the material, or making it more practical.

Success would be measured again at the end of the semester when students took the same assessment. The closer my expectations came to what they felt they achieved, the more successful the course would be. I didn't achieve the results I had hoped for the first time, but I kept at it. The focus was turning analytics inside—turn the student on themselves, make them look within for their own way to connect the data.

The following year, I added the Selfie methodology to the Rutgers course I authored and continue to teach. The classes continue to grow which show a need for the materials and approach we are presenting in this textbook.

The Online Presence Assessment

The easiest way to apply the Data Selfie was to use it to measure Social Media; the metrics were readily available via free third-party data platforms, even if the data wasn't perfect, and needed to be cleaned and normalized somewhat. I have changed the data sources several times over the past three years as some of the platforms have gone out of business, or changed their Terms of Service.

Table PR1 The Online Presence Assessment.

Social Media Benchmarking www.slideshare.net/webmeticsguru/online-presence-assessment-rutgers-social-media-for-the-arts			
Chanel	Metric	Third-Party Tools Used	Limitations (caveat)
Blogs	Domain Score	**Blog Analyzer** www. blog-analysis. com/	Public hosted Tumblr and WordPress can provide inaccurate readings.
Videos	SocialBlade	**Creators Grade** www. socialblade.com (use A+ through D- Grade)	Only works for YouTube Channels.
Twitter	SocialBlade	**SocialBlade Twitter grade** www. socialblade.com (use A through D Grade)	Fragmented and shallow metrics make it imperative to look past followers.

(Continued)

Table PR1 (Continued)

Social Media Benchmarking www.slideshare.net/webmeticsguru/online-presence-assessment-rutgers-social-media-for-the-arts			
Chanel	Metric	Third-Party Tools Used	Limitations (caveat)
Facebook	Likealyzer Score	**Likealyzer** www.likealyzer.com	Works on Facebook Business pages only, there is no measure for personal profiles.
LinkedIn	Connections ORfollowers	**LinkedIn** number of Connections (personal pages) or number of followers (Business Pages).	None, but LinkedIn other provides priority metrics for paid customers.
SEO	LXRSEO Overall Score	**LXRSEO** https://lxrseo.com Use the Overall Score of the domain.	We do not know the details of how grading is arrived at. Only lets users do one search a day.
Instagram	SocialBladeInstagram Score	**SocialBlade** Instagram grade http://socialblade.com/instagram	We don't know exactly how SocialBlade's ranking algorithm works.
Local Search Listings	MOZ Local	**MOZ Local** https://moz.com/local—creates a local score of any business that has a physical address	Local visibility does not include check in—geo-location data, which is left out for now.

Source: Marshall Sponder, WebMetricsGuru Inc.

Ideally, it would be great to have one platform that collected and charted everything, that tracked students' progress and made it available online (perhaps directly in the course shells of my online courses), but that was beyond the technical skill at my disposal at the time. The point of the Analytics Selfie (via the Online Presence

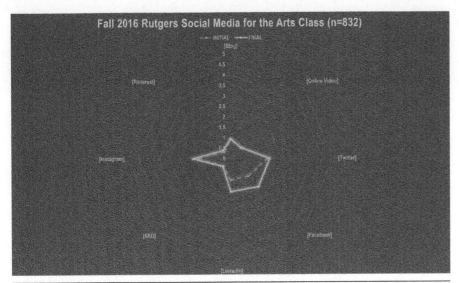

Figure PR4 Class growth in online presence in Social Media, Fall 2016.
Source: WebMetricsGuru Inc.

Assessment) was for students to see for themselves how the information they absorbed in my course made a difference in their lives and in their studies. In many cases, it changed what they wanted to study or their career choices, both before and after they graduated. While the Analytics Selfie was far from perfect, it was good enough.

Individually, many of my students made much bigger strides than is shown in Figure PR4—all I did for the class is average the beginning measurements with the final measurements that they performed at the end of the semester. I tried to throw those scores out, getting rid of outliers, which showed that the class, overall, grew the most in their Facebook and LinkedIn presence. Since LinkedIn is the main platform for business social networking, increasing their presence on LinkedIn very often led them to new opportunities they otherwise might not have discovered.

Extending the Data Selfie

My concept for connecting the dots was not as far along as I had hoped when the manuscript was reaching its final stages. Fortunately, I discovered that I did not need to come up with all the assessments as others have already done that for me, particularly a website called Demandmetric.com. Demand Metric is a performance marketing association that has almost 100,000 paid members—my co-author is among them.[28] Demandmetric.com contains many marketing assessments and tools that approximated what I had in mind when I drafted the proposal to Routledge. The Demand Metric Excel Templates discussed herein will be available as part of the Instructor's Guide that accompanies this textbook.

Marshall Sponder, June 2017

Preface Citations

1. "Amazon.com: *Social Media Analytics: Effective Tools for Building, Interpreting, and Using Metrics*." www.amazon.com/Social-Media-Analytics-Effective-Interpreting-ebook/dp/B005EPUAJC. Accessed April 15, 2017. "Amazon.com: *Seven Layers of Social Media Analytics*." www.amazon.com/Seven-Layers-Social-Media-Analytics/dp/1507823207. Accessed April 15, 2017.

2. At the Zicklin School of Business, lecturer Marshall Sponder authors and teaches courses on Web Analytics and Web Intelligence, Text Analytics and Social Media Analytics, Introduction Internet and Digital Marketing. At Rutgers Business School and Mason Gross School of the Arts, assistant professor Marshall Sponder authors and teaches a popular online course titled "Social Media for the Arts," which thousands of students take every semester. Social Media for the Arts may be the largest class at Rutgers University, across its 31 schools (see www.rutgers.edu/academics/schools-colleges).

3. The world is changing so quickly that many of the subjects of study we teach have significant and rapid updates. We need to come up with an approach to curating the shifts in the material and evolving a point of view on those changes. Connecting the dots, linking up the material is best done by the student, but as course designers and teachers, we need to do more to make the material easier to synthesize (to make one's own).

4. "Amazon.com: *Seven Layers of Social Media Analytics*." www.amazon.com/Seven-Layers-Social-Media-Analytics/dp/1507823207. Accessed April 15, 2017.

5. "Journal articles: Social is a business culture not just tools." https://gfkhan.wordpress.com/publications/journal-articles. Accessed April 15, 2017.

6. "Mimic Pro: The world's #1 Internet marketing simulation—Stukent." www.stukent.com/mimic-pro-simulation. Accessed April 15, 2017.

7. "Web analytics, website analysis and reporting: Adobe Analytics." www.adobe.com/marketing-cloud/web-analytics.html. Accessed April 15, 2017.

8. "Analytics demo account: Google Help." https://support.google.com/analytics/answer/6367342?hl=en. Accessed April 15, 2017.

9. "Brandwatch for students." www.brandwatch.com/students. Accessed April 15, 2017.

10. "Easy analytics for education: Industry—IBM Watson Analytics." www.ibm.com/analytics/watson-analytics/us-en/by-industry/education. Accessed April 15, 2017.

11. "Google online marketing challenge." www.google.com/onlinechallenge. Accessed April 15, 2017.

12. "Education—comScore, Inc." www.comscore.com/Industries/Education. Accessed April 15, 2017.

13. "Competency framework: Digital Analytics Association." www.digitalanalyticsassociation.org/competency-framework. Accessed April 15, 2017.

14. "About DAA competency framework: YouTube." www.youtube.com/watch?v=Bn4S0FH7xKA. Accessed April 15, 2017.

15. "IAB digital ad operations certification." www.iab.com/iab-ad-ops-certification-overview. Accessed April 15, 2017.

16. "IAB digital media sales certification—grow your media career." www.iab.com/iab-digital-media-sales-certification-overview. Accessed April 15, 2017.

17. "New Marketing Institute (NMI): MediaMath." http://nmi.mediamath.com. Accessed April 15, 2017.

18. "Home: Master of Science in Analytics—Northwestern's McCormick School of Engineering." www.mccormick.northwestern.edu/analytics. Accessed April 15, 2017.

19. "Masters in Predictive Analytics, MS Analytics Degree—Northwestern School of Professional Studies." http://sps.northwestern.edu/program-areas/graduate/predictive-analytics. Accessed April 15, 2017.

20. "MS in Integrated Marketing—NYU." www.scps.nyu.edu/academics/departments/marketing-and-pr/academic-offerings/graduate/ms-in-integrated-marketing.html. Accessed April 15, 2017.

21. "Diplomas—NYU SPS Professional Pathways." www.sps.nyu.edu/professional-pathways/diplomas.html. Accessed April 15, 2017.

22. "Why Nate Silver, Sam Wang and everyone else were wrong." www.quantamagazine.org/20161108-why-nate-silver-and-sam-wang-are-wrong. Accessed April 15, 2017.

23. "Is Big Data a bubble set to burst? Data Center Knowledge." March 30, 2015. www.datacenterknowledge.com/archives/2015/03/30/big-data-bubble-set-burst. Accessed April 15, 2017.

24. "The analytics advantage: We're just getting started—Deloitte." www2.deloitte.com/content/dam/Deloitte/global/Documents/Deloitte-Analytics/dttl-analytics-analytics-advantage-report-061913.pdf. Accessed April 15, 2017.

25. "Two globally-renowned research institutes join WST Network." October 24, 2016, www.webscience.org/2016/10/24/two-globally-renowned-research-institutes-join-wst-network/. Accessed April 15, 2017.

26. "Web Science: Free online course—FutureLearn." www.futurelearn.com/courses/web-science. Accessed April 15, 2017.

27. "Connecting data with the Analytics Selfie—ClickZ." July 28, 2014. www.clickz.com/connecting-data-with-the-analytics-selfie/30390. Accessed April 15, 2017.

28. "Resource finder: Select a topic to find research." www.demandmetric.com/resource-finder-select-topic-find-research-tools-and-expert-advice. Accessed April 15, 2017.

The Evolution of Digital Analytics and the Internet

CHAPTER OBJECTIVES

After reading this chapter, readers should understand:

- Structured and unstructured data
- Introduction to the Internet and the World Wide Web
- Evolution of the Web

In this chapter, we cover the fundamentals of digital marketing channels that are found in the online world, such as paid, mobile, search, social, and email. Our focus on digital marketing is a product of the changing marketing landscape. As technology progresses, consumers interact with people on a larger scale through websites and mobile applications. Through these connections, a business can harvest vast amounts of data to provide information on important matters, such as target consumers and business operations. Most data being created is observed online, within social media and Web services. Examples of this shift are present in online banking, news and commentary, lifestyle and fashion, travel and lodging sites, education, online dating services, and so on. As time progresses, the infrastructure supporting the Internet evolved to become more powerful and sophisticated as companies invest in more digital resources and increase their online business.

How Digital Analytics Began

Digital Analytics is the study of various forms of business data to improve the online experience of a business and its customers. The evolution of Digital Analytics took place simultaneously with the development of digital marketing. For our purposes, once Internet technology was developed, it was made to be accessible and extensible to the public. The Internet allowed search engines and social media to emerge as specific online marketing disciplines that students and practitioners could study and master. Also, the development of the Google search engine and its associated Web services supplemented this change and revolutionized the manner and ease with which we access and use data.

Structured versus Unstructured Data

More than 50 years ago, the data we had collected was mostly "structured." Structured data is data with a high level of organization, such as balance sheets (cash, accounts payable), medical devices (heart rate, blood pressure), or census records (birth, employment). The structure is provided in the collection of the data through certain objectives so that once the data is captured, it occupies a specified field. Nowadays, we capture a great deal of "unstructured" or "semi-structured" data. Structured data can be processed easily in a relational database or spreadsheet. Unstructured data is information that does not exist in a row and column database. To be able to capture unstructured data, we must modify and create special tools that manipulate the data into intelligible results. Otherwise, when left unmanaged, data can become overwhelming, making it difficult to organize and work with.

There are three types of data from this perspective—data that is easy for data scientists and perhaps business analysts to organize and extract meaning from, and *data that is not* (this is the main difference between structured and unstructured data). There is an additional state of data that is termed "semi-structured." It consists of information that is nearly prepared and ready to be organized, but it lacks the cleaning and organization necessary for it to be processed; for example, resolving misspellings and spacing errors in a column of data.

Businesses are interested in mining unstructured data because of the possible benefits of the data-driven insights, such as reducing operation costs, responding more quickly to changing market conditions, and innovative market research. Once the unstructured and semi-structured data is organized for analysts to use, the applications created with the newly structured data can be organized and shared across the various business, nonprofit and educational enterprises.

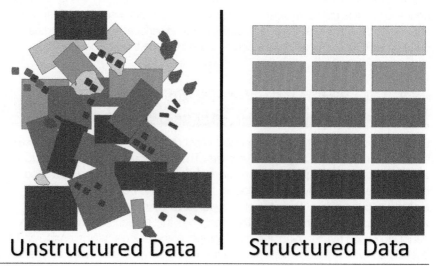

Figure 1.1 Structured vs. unstructured data.
Source: WebMetricsGuru Inc.

The Evolution of the Internet

The Internet, formerly called Arpanet by the Department of Defense (DOD), is a global network of interconnected networks that was created in 1983 as a way for researchers to quickly and freely communicate. In 1990, the now famous computer scientist Tim Berners-Lee created the World Wide Web, which opened the network for everyone, nationally and internationally.

Tim Berners-Lee and the World Wide Web

Tim Berners-Lee is most famous for his creation of the World Wide Web. When Berners-Lee worked at CERN (the European Organization for Nuclear Research, founded in 1954, which operates the largest particle physics laboratory in the world), he encountered a problem: physicists from all over the world came to CERN, worked for a period, and then left. To fix the disorganization between the multitude of platforms and protocols, Berners-Lee created the World Wide Web: a universal medium to link information (and people) together. In November 1989, he created the three protocols—HTTP, URL, and HTML—that we now know as the "Web," which brought him global fame. With the rise of mobile devices, the World Wide Web continues to maintain its level of significance in the modern world, much as it did in the early 1990s. Berners-Lee recently[1] commented on the growing trend of Internet users to favor native applications (that are experienced by users individually) instead of Web apps that can sustain a wider conversation and community. Berners-Lee would like to see companies and developers focusing on building Web apps using HTML5, so content and experiences are more shareable than dedicated Web apps designed to run exclusively on mobile devices. HTML5 pages render faster and identically across all Web browsers (mobile and desktop) while requiring less coding.

Network Types

Web networks are "logical constructs" or ways of representing and simplifying complexity that help both humans and computers understand how data spreads across several interconnected devices. The data is moved over phone lines, cables, and satellites and sent to the intended devices via intelligent network devices, such as switches, hubs, and routers. For the most part, the communications infrastructure remains invisible to the average user, unless it breaks. Once that happens, interruptions and error messages become more noticeable and cryptic, uncovering a vast group of protocols and interconnections that are often difficult to troubleshoot. Today, there are at least five methods to connect to the Internet and the World Wide Web, including:

- Public Internet
- Intranet: network that runs internally in an organization
- Extranet: two or more joined networks that share information
- Mobile: the mobile Internet used by our handheld devices connecting through Internet providers
- Internet of Things—devices talking to devices—creates Intelligent Web

Internet Timeline

- 1950s: After WWII, the Cold War spawns the need for new ways to communicate more quickly, hence Arpanet originated for military uses.
- 1960s: Arpanet became available to researchers around the world.
- 1970s: Apple and IBM developed personal computers in the late 1970s, which appeal to a new audience who can run simple word processing and spreadsheet applications on them.
- 1980s: Transmission Control Protocol/Internet Protocol (TCP/IP) created as a basic communication language for the Internet. The National Science Foundation operated the backbone and banned commercial traffic.
- 1980s: Web 1.0, or the first stage in the World Wide Web, developed, which was entirely made up of static, non-interactive Web pages connected by hyperlinks.
- 1990s: Venture capital funding poured into untried and uniquely individual business models.
- 1991: Gopher developed as a TCP/IP for searching and distributing documents over the Internet. Hyper Text Markup Language (HTML) developed for creating Web pages and Web applications.
- 1993: Mosaic was the first freely available browser, which soon spawned Netscape. Mosaic supported Gopher, file transfer protocol, and network news transfer protocol.
- 1995: Yahoo! Search Engine debuted and initially used Google algorithms up until 2004 where it began investing in its algorithms.
- 1998: Google Search founded on September 4, 1998 by Larry Page and Sergey Brin. Google Search differentiated itself from other search engines by focusing on the relevance of pages based on patterns formed in hyperlinks.
- 2000–2002: Businesses failed during the 2000s, which led to the disappearance of venture capital funding.
- 2004–2009: The popularity of the WWW equated to a rapid growth in users, content, and sales, both B2C and B2B. As a result of the popularity, there is an emergence of new players, such as Facebook, Twitter, Foursquare, YouTube, and LinkedIn—the social networks we are familiar with today.

An Introduction to the World Wide Web and How It Works

The World Wide Web is a set of protocols and services enabling devices to communicate with each other, and it provides the basis for the study of Digital Analytics, whereas the Internet is the global network of interconnected devices, such as personal computers, smartphones, switches, routers, satellites, and cables. Through the interrelationships, the Internet is composed of several technologies, and one of the underlying software technologies is the WWW, or simply, "the Web." In its simplest form, the Web is composed of interlinked hypertext documents (e.g., websites) that can be accessed through Web browsers such as Google Chrome, Apple Safari, Firefox, and Microsoft Edge/Internet Explorer. The Internet functions as a large phone book or digital directory that can translate an almost infinite number of names into numbers as well as numbers into names.[2] The numbers point back to logical network addresses. These networks point to nodes on the network using Internet routing protocols. Computers and software require the logical address of the port numbers that communications are directed to and from. Services communicate with each other, on the same computer and other computers connected to the network. However, the rest of the underlying communication that powers the web is transparent to users.

Note: The World Wide Web represents only 1% of the entire Internet; the Dark Web, Deep Web and their vast ecosystem make up the rest. The Dark Web is part of the World Wide Web content existing on overlay networks that use the public Internet but require specific software, configurations or authorization to access.[3] The Deep Web is the part of the World Wide Web whose contents are not indexed by standard search engines for many reasons. The Deep Web is opposite to the World Wide Web.[4]

The Seven-Layer OSI Model

The most common way to visualize communications on the Web is by using the operating systems interconnection (OSI) seven-layer model. Data packet communications are broken down from a physical layer device, such as an Ethernet or wireless port of a network node, which is usually a computer or mobile device. Communications are transformed from the physical level all the way up to the application level, where users interact with the communications and reply. The process of traversing the seven layers of connectivity happens several times each second, and the result is the Web that we interact with.

The Evolution of the Web

The Web has radically evolved since it was first created, the earliest version being referred to as Web 1.0. As Table 1.1 shows, the Web has three distinct phases, and we cover each of them in this chapter.

Table 1.1 Web 1.0 to Web 4.0.

Web 1.0	Web 2.0	Web 3.0	Web 4.0
Read-Only	Read–Write	Personal, Portable, Extensible	Converged
Company & Business focused	Community, Social focused	Focused on the Individual	Personal Assistants (Siri/Google Now Cortana)
Home Page	Blogs, Blogging, Wikis	Streaming media, Live streaming, Data Waves	Bots/Intelligent Agents/Drones

(Continued)

Table 1.1 (Continued)

Web 1.0	Web 2.0	Web 3.0	Web 4.0
Own your content	Share your content	Collect & Content	Programmable Content & Content on Demand
Web Forms	Web Applications	Smart/ Autonomous Applications	Artificial Intelligence/ Algorithms
Web Directories and Folders	Content Tagging	User Behavior / Quantified Self	Private Cloud, Internet of Things
Page Views	Cost Per Click (CPC)	User Engagement via collected metrics	Cross Channel Measurement
Banner Ads	Interactive Ads	Behavioral Ads & Targeting	Programmatic Advertising
Britannica Online	Wikipedia	Semantic Web	Transparent Web/WikiLeaks
HTML and Web Portals	XML / RSS	RDF/RDFS/OWL	Quantum Computing, AI

Source: WebMetricsGuru Inc.

Web 1.0

Web 1.0, "read-only web," is an early version of the Internet and is static in nature. It has a one-to-many fashion of sharing information. In Web 1.0, Web developers and designers create websites and content for users to consume. The design of the site prevents users from contributing to the content or crafting a response. Web 1.0 users are only passive recipients of the information and content, which means they would be considered the readers, not contributors, of the content. Web 1.0 is another channel of narrow information distribution like other conventional one-to-many technologies, such as radio and television. Web 1.0 websites are only used for information presentation purposes and not used for generating information or content.

Web 2.0

Web 2.0 is the version of the World Wide Web that most of us have experience of. It is characterized by the shift from static webpages to user-generated content and the emergence of social media and mobile technologies. Web 2.0 alters the WWW landscape by turning the Web into a collaborative ecosystem where users could create content, share ideas, and offer actual products and services. Web 2.0 allows two-way and many-to-many information flow and user-generated content.[5] The content generated by users over social media platforms is known as user-generated content (UGC). Some tools of this collaborative ecosystem are podcasts, blogs, tags, social bookmarks, social networks, wikis, etc. One thing to note is that Web 2.0 is not a technical standard or an update to the first standard, Web 1.0. However, it reflects the changes in the way people use the Web and how programmers design websites. Due to changing societal norms, webmasters and programmers develop platforms allowing users to create, monetize, and share their content.

Features of Web 2.0

- **Scalability of software:** This refers to the ability to gather behavioral data via cookies and clickstream analytics. A clickstream is a path or order of pages that visitors choose when navigating through a site. (Note: clickstreams, when applied to the Web, are the categories of websites that users visit on a regular basis—the clickstream is used for retargeting purposes.) Users emerge as co-developers, and software begins harnessing the collective intelligence of developers and users.
- **Long tail:** This is a term popularized by *Wired Magazine* editor Chris Anderson in 2004. It refers to many products that sell in small quantities and is contrasted with the limited number of bestselling products. New platforms and revenue models are tailored to an individual's needs and desires. For example, Amazon and eBay are powered by organic and paid search engines to serve individuals better. Businesses begin to make a living by serving people in a micro-audience but at a global level. People could also build their personal brand easier now because artists could find their niches earlier and invest in a small, but a constant number of patrons. As an effect, businesses are currently focused on a long tail keyword strategy and specific keyword phrases to capture and guide interested Web users to their products and services.
- **New business models:** Collaborative economy business models, such as Airbnb and Uber, begin to threaten the survival of older business models, such as hotels and cabs.
- **Device agnostic software development:** Mobile software development toolkits, such as the Android SDK, aid in the development of programs that run on the largest number of devices possible.
- **Web Analytics:** Web Analytics matures as a platform to measure Web 1.0 and Web 2.0 digital activities.
- **Search engines:** These pick up specific keywords that when used in a search, and can narrow down results from the infinite amounts of unstructured data.
- **Semantic Web:** This is an extension of the Internet which makes the Web intuitive and intelligent by separating the presentation of content from its meaning. The Semantic Web simplifies the way in which we can customize and personalize communications.
- **Social media:** Social media are websites and applications that focus on communicating and sharing through mobile devices and stimulate social networking.
- **Anywhere Internet:** This speaks to the expansion of the Internet to nearly half of the global population in the 2010s. In turn, there is a rise of automated advertising, also known as Programmatic, which would have been impossible without Web 2.0.
- **Geo-location:** Mobile devices broadcast their location to Internet Service Providers via global positioning system (GPS), near field communication (NFC), and geofencing. GPS simplifies navigation by eliminating the need for physical maps, which saves time and energy.

Web 3.0

Web 3.0 is the next iteration of the World Wide Web. Web 3.0 marks the era of a connected Web operating system where most software components (e.g., application programs and operating systems) and data processing reside on the Internet. Web 3.0 is smarter, quicker, and more reliable at connecting data, concepts, applications, and people. A critical dimension of Web 3.0 is the Semantic Web or Linked Data. The Semantic Web is known as the "web of data" (W3 2015) and aims to make huge amounts of data and the relationship among the datasets Web-available in a machine-readable format, such as Resource Description Framework (RDF) format, for applications to query it. RDF is a general-purpose language for representing information on the web (W3 2015).[6] The World Wide Web became more personalized with an "on demand" approach. Below are examples of the changes the World Wide Web experienced:

- **Democratization:** Everyone can become a content creator and content consumer. Most businesses are transforming to align with the new capabilities developed through Web 1.0 and Web 2.0 with the extensibility and automation of Web 3.0. For example, bloggers can create their blog, post public content to their blogs, and collaborate with other content creators to promote virality in their posts.
- **Intelligent applications:** Intelligent applications customize and personalize the user's web experience with insights forged by geo-location services, predictive analytics, and Big Data. Through the invention of intelligent devices and software, the Internet of Things was produced.
- **Collaborative economy:** Business models that leverage network and Internet technology to satisfy needs, such as Uber and Airbnb.
- **Smart fabric:** Smart fabric refers to processed and shared information and its location, whether it is in cloud computing, Hadoop, iBeacons, mesh networks, intelligent devices, or data lakes.

Recent Examples of Web 3.0-Driven Business Acquisitions

In 2015, IBM purchased the Weather Company to predict consumers' purchase behavior based on weather changes.[7] Because of the acquisition, IBM collects billions of sensors' data from around the world while releasing real-time information and insights to tens of millions of users via Watson Analytics.

Also, in 2015, Verizon acquired AOL. Verizon created a synergy as an ISP and coupled it with the large content publisher, AOL. Verizon's acquisition allowed it to combine viewer's programming preferences collected from set-top boxes and cellular communications of Verizon subscribers. About a year later, Verizon acquired Yahoo! to shape the digital advertising marketplace. With these insights, the programmatic advertising and targeting technologies that AOL developed could be deployed to create competent advertising solutions against Google and Facebook.[8]

Web 4.0

Web 4.0 is relatively new and directed to emerging technologies such as the Internet of Things, quantified self, private clouds, intelligent computing, embedded intelligence, predictive analytics, and artificial intelligence.[9] There are many interesting Web 4.0 developments, and we will cover the subject in the next edition of this textbook.

Common Internet Terms

URL (Uniform Resource Locator)

The basic building block of the World Wide Web is webpages. Webpages are assigned a virtual "address" defined as an URL. A Uniform Resource Locator (URL), also known as a Uniform Resource Identifier (URI), is a web address specifying its location on a computer network and a mechanism for retrieving it. An URL is the representation of a URI, although many people use the two terms interchangeably. Note that URN refers to the Uniform Resource Name, which is a means to call a network regardless of its numerical address or URI (which often changes on a regular basis). A typical URL could have the form http://www.example.com/index.html, which indicates a protocol (HTTP), a hostname (www.example.com), and a file name (index.html). URLs occur most commonly to reference web pages (HTTP), for file transfer (FTP), email (email to), database access (JDBC), and many other applications.[10] Tim Berners-Lee defined URLs with Request for Comments (RFC) 1738 in 1994 to the URI working group of the Internet Engineering Task Force (IETF).

Domain Name

Simply, a domain name is a location where a collection of pages live or can live, and when there is a topology or map of a domain. For example, the domain ESPN.com provides visitors with popular sports scores while nytimes.com provides news reporting and commentary. Domain names are an extension of our concept of location: we live on the Earth, in a country, in a city, and at a physical address. To send and receive mail, we must specify the address we are sending it to, and usually we want to include our address, just in case the mail cannot be delivered. Moreover, we built a system on the Web that operates the same way, except it is for computers, networks, and services. The naming and address resolution system in place is called the Domain Name Services (DNS) and has existed since the Internet, or World Wide Web appeared.

- Root domains are set to apply universally.
- Once a web domain is set up, "subdomains" are created within their domain.
- Administration of subdomains is set up within an organization's Domain Name Service.

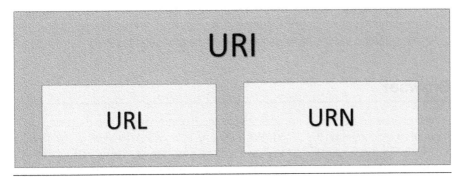

Figure 1.2 URI structure.
Source: Marshall Sponder, WebMetricsGuru Inc.

DNS Servers

The Domain Name Service is a distributed global registry that resolves domain names to Internet IP addresses and vice-versa. One of the hallmarks of the Domain Name Service is its scalability and extensibility—DNS can resolve every domain and subdomain to the correct IP address on the planet! DNS is extensible because network administrators can control the names and IP addresses of all the devices on their internal networks, also called Intranets, with full confidence that the designations are propagated across the entire global DNS network. DNS servers communicate with each other so the mapping and routing of messages can reach their destinations and vice-versa. The "network map" is both resilient and easy-to-update. It is also one of the most successful examples of democratized control of resources. Local network administrators can handle the details of addresses in subdomains they oversee.

Servers

Servers are computer programs or machines capable of accepting requests from clients and responding to them. When a server is running on hardware, it can usually be accessed over a network. A server can run unattended without a computer monitor, input device, and USB interfaces. Many systems and user "processes" are called "servers" and work with "clients" that are programs and individual addresses (or identities) that work.

IP Address (Internet Protocol)

The IP address is the key aspect of how Internet traffic goes back and forth from an address to the rest of the Web (which includes Intranets or organization internal domain). Internet Protocol address (IP address) is a numerical label assigned to each device (e.g., computer, printer) participating in a computer network that uses the Internet Protocol for communication. There are two versions in use: IP Version 4 and IP Version 6. Each version defines an IP address differently. IP address typically still refers to the addresses defined by IPv4.

- An IP address is written out in both numeric forms (Version 4 & Version 6) so that we can understand it.
- Hexadecimal addressing is used for computer programming so that the address can be computed and operated on by the various routing mechanisms (e.g., routers, intelligent switches). Routers move information back and forth throughout the Internet or Intranet (Note: The Intranet is a "private" Internet that allows communication with an organization without going through the Web).

Browser

A Web browser is a software application for retrieving, presenting, and traversing information resources on the World Wide Web. An information resource is identified by a Uniform Resource Identifier (URI/URL); it may be a webpage, image, video, or other content. Modern browsers, however, go beyond surfing the Web through the addition of plugin applications that extend the capabilities of the browser.

Transport Layer Security (TLS)

Transport Layer Security (TLS) is a protocol that ensures privacy between communicating applications and their users on the Internet. When a server and client communicate, TLS ensures that no third party may eavesdrop or tamper with any message. TLS is the successor to the Secure Sockets Layer (SSL).

Web Hosting

Web hosting is a type of Internet hosting service that allows individuals and organizations to make their website accessible via the World Wide Web. Web hosts are companies that provide space on a server owned or leased for use by clients, as well as providing Internet connectivity, typically in a data center. The location of web hosting services varies widely. The most basic are webpages and small-scale file hosting, where files are uploaded via file transfer protocol (FTP) or a web interface. The files are usually delivered to the web "as is" or with minimal processing. Many Internet service providers (ISPs) offer this service free to subscribers. Personal website hosting is typically free, advertisement-sponsored, or inexpensive. Business website hosting has a higher expense depending on the size and type of the site.

Cloud Computing

Computing and data storage on public clouds, private clouds, or hybrid clouds has revolutionized data processing and brought the era of Big Data to fruition. Public and private cloud suppliers, such as Amazon, Apple, Salesforce, and Backspace, are used by corporations and government agencies to keep and process data. Cloud computing may have conceptually been possible before its start date in 2008, but it did not take off until programming stacks were created alongside with virtual storage systems and virtual processing to leverage it.[11] Cloud resources are often shared by multiple users and dynamically reallocated according to demand. This reallocation makes sense, as the data is often processed where it is located rather than moved to another data repository first. Clouds allow economies of scale and rapid updates of the data, which is faster than previously thought possible. For the user and application developer, no hardware is needed for cloud computing. The cloud provider handles the hardware, so there are no upfront charges for purchasing and maintaining servers. In turn, organizations only use and pay for the resources they need.

Cloud Computing Uses
- Web-based email
- Mobile apps
- Real-time geo-location systems (Google Waze, Google Maps)
- Store photos or videos online
- Use apps like Google Docs, Google Analytics, Adobe Creative Suite
- Store or backup files online with Dropbox or similar platform
- Customer intelligence (e.g., Salesforce, Oracle, and Adobe Marketing and Sales Clouds)

Cloud Computing Issues

- Certain types of input and output operations are much slower (e.g., copying a file system to Dropbox may take several hours).
- Usage charges can creep up when data processing needs rapidly increase.
- Clouds occasionally crash. Vital services and applications can suddenly stop functioning. Even applications that do not directly pull from the cloud may be vulnerable. It occurs when a component references software or data located in the cloud. Clouds are complex constructs with high fault tolerance, but they are also susceptible to errors that are difficult to troubleshoot.
- Clouds provided by different vendors or platforms are usually not interoperable. Some organizations have high security and continuity of service requirements and want to avoid a single point of failure. Having multiple clouds with different vendors or providers would be desirable to ensure a quality product or service with no failures but could be incredibly costly.
- Information stored in a cloud environment may be insecure, even when it is encrypted.

Introduction to First-Party and Third-Party Data

We are approaching a time when a complete curation of the customer experience is within our sights. Barriers in C2B information-sharing are slowly fading as the initial privacy concern shock begins to fade away. Soon, a customer driving past Walmart will be shown an ad in their self-driving vehicle reminding them that the TV they were searching for on Amazon is available for a discount. As they enter to pull up or to park, they could be informed of the benefits of installing the Walmart app. Once they enter the store, the app could then guide them towards the TV, but only after exposing them to curated ads via iBeacon technology from their favorite brands. As they then leave the store, they will be given incentives to review their experience so that this whole process can be optimized. The landscape of marketing has changed quite a bit. There was once not enough information about clients, but now there is too much.

- Marketers collect more customer data than they can act on. Conversely, from a customer perspective, customers should turn off geo-location notifications broadcast from applications on their mobile devices when they are not needed.
- First-party data is data collected by the website for use in tools, such as Adobe, Google Analytics, or customer relationship management (CRM). The CRM data can be very useful and tell many things about websites. For example, it can tell how many visited a site, pageviews, time spent on a page, bounce rate, and conversion funnels among many other things. The CRM data can be segmented to show what is valuable to stakeholders. For example, stakeholders may want to segment by demographics (age and gender) and affinities to gain a better understanding of consumers, along with the type of advertising campaign that would be helpful to run.

Consider all the avenues of interaction with a person that can now be quantified and stored, knowingly or not: mobile app, social, on site, blog, in person, and on the phone. There is much uproar over the sharing of "personal" data for marketing purposes, based on first-, second-, and third-party data or cookies. These marketing efforts could be considered by some to be an invasion of stranger's personal privacy. Most consumers are unaware their information is being examined at this level and they have not given their permission.

Text Analytics

Text analytics did not formally exist until about 1975. The simplest way to explain text analytics is the method of turning text into numbers, similar in structure to a spreadsheet so that statistics and other types of analysis can be run on the data. In the "What's the Big Data?" infographic,[12] text analytics evolved with other data science disciplines since its inception. The public awareness of text analytics is low, although organizations have been examining text for some time. In fact, the Google search engine—and all search engines—is powered by text analytics. Most people do not realize the rich intelligence that can be extracted from text documents (refer to Chapter 10 for more details on this subject).

Digital Analytics History

Digital Analytics is as old as the Internet, see Figure 1.3. Web Analytics is a solution for businesses that want to gather behavioral data from their websites. Web data helps businesses gain a better understanding of their customers and thus improve customer experience, which leads to benefits, such as more sales or conversions.

The existing platforms were developed for webmasters and IT professionals in the early to mid-1990s to keep track of downloads, file input or output, etc. The first Web Analytics platforms were developed to analyze Web server logs and provide diagnostic readouts.

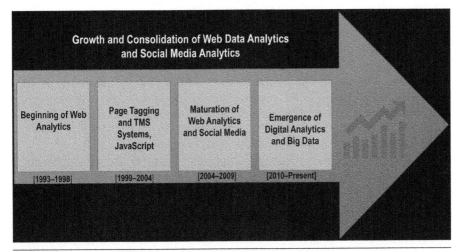

Figure 1.3 Evolution of Digital Analytics.
Source: WebMetricsGuru Inc.

With the advent of JavaScript in the late 1990s, newer and more adaptive tracking methods using Web cookies evolved. A Web cookie is a small piece of data sent from a website and stored on the user's computer by the user's Web browser while the user is browsing. Cookies are chosen by the Web server to identify users, prepare customized webpages, or to save site login information about users, so they do not need to re-enter the same login information every time they visit a website.

Web tracking shifted away from installing software to a third-party hosted solution. Web Analytics no longer needed dedicated servers to collect or process the data. It became the basis of a new page-tagging approach using JavaScript beacon scripts.

However, the broad adoption of JavaScript and remotely hosted analytics software turned out to be a mixed bag that came with several positives and negatives. While the JavaScript improved tracking of some web activities, it missed tracking others, such as file downloads. Tracking rich media required more analytics enablement and was often neglected. Thus, JavaScript tracking led to gaps in basic data collection.

The Era of Massive Data Growth— Data is the New Oil

Every year, the amount of information being generated surpasses almost all the information humanity has created in its entire history, and most of the data being generated is unstructured. Welcome to the world of Big Data! Structured data is what we have in spreadsheets with rows and columns and the information already organized. Unstructured data is becoming just about everything else. Data is created so massively and quickly that new ways to process and store it have become necessary. Data growth requires individuals who know how to work with the data.

Massive Growth of Unstructured Data

Turning information from its unstructured form and providing it with structure has been compared to alchemy, the ancient science claiming it was possible to turn lead into gold. The term "data is the new oil" reflects the current consensus that the most valuable asset an organization has is its data.

Examples of turning data into dollars:

- Credit card companies detect unusual spending patterns of their customers using sophisticated algorithms that examine massive datasets. Customers are immediately alerted of the suspicious activities by phone or email. This activity saves customers and credit card companies billions of dollars a year.
- Major retailers use unstructured data collected for customer transactions to refine their online search engines and to encourage customers to buy more products.
- Food and beverage suppliers merge customers, logistics, and manufacturing data to improve their plant operations significantly.

As the Internet and its capabilities evolved, it became the driving force behind decisions about what makes sense now, along with the data and analytics to both power and understand these new abilities and their impact and implications.

Rise of Online Advertising

As popularity is increased with the Internet, online marketing and advertising rose to match with businesses' new strategy of "staying connected" by increasing the resources and capabilities a consumer could perform. In this context, "staying connected" refers to the emphasis we place on being reachable through online communications or various messaging applications at any given time.

Overall, the amount of digital advertising spending in 2015 is projected to double by 2020. Spending is expected to increase in developed countries, including the United States, parts of Europe and Asia, and in small pockets of Latin America and the Middle East. Digital advertising as a percentage of total advertising is continuing to grow, which highlights the need for increasing the analytics around the sector, especially in the United States.[13]

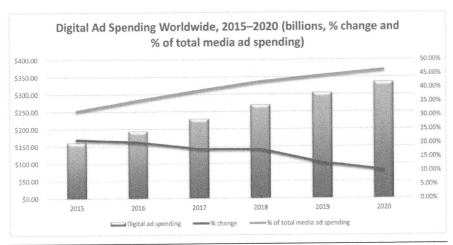

Figure 1.4 Digital ad spending worldwide, 2015–2020. Data derived from eMarketer.
Source: WebMetricsGuru LLC

The Digital Industrial Economy

It is imperative as a business leader to understand the digital space and marketing within it. "By the 2020s, every organization will be an IT organization, and every leader will be a digital leader," said Peter Sondergaard, Gartner SVP and head of research, at the opening of the annual Gartner Symposium. By 2020, he predicts, "digital is the business; the business is digital." Sondergaard creates the analogy in the argument that businesses will be synonymous to their online counterparts. It could be concluded that his beliefs are a product of observing globalization in the Digital Age where businesses strive to compete with their competition and establish market share through online conversions. By increasing digital efforts, businesses may have the opportunity to tap into new segments, create greater brand awareness, or defend their business against competitors.

Other points from Sondergaard at the Gartner Symposium include:

- The Internet is changing how business is conducted. It is also vastly increasing the opportunities and precision of business communications and operations.
- Marketing communications have become more complex and streamlined, with many more touchpoints, as well as opportunities to acquire, retain, and convert customers.
- Technological advancement is constant, making it necessary and challenging to keep pace with these changes.
- Business models and their economics are rapidly changing and evolving.[14]

Review Questions

1. What are the main differences between Web 1.0, 2.0, and 3.0?
2. Explain the difference between Web clients and Web servers.
3. What is cloud computing?
4. What are the seven stages of the OSI model?

Summary

In this chapter, we introduced the reader to some of the essential constructs that make Digital Analytics possible, such as the development of the Internet and World Wide Web. The technology that powers our digital experience is invisible to us until it breaks. At that point, we are painfully aware of the mechanisms for communicating information, such as clients and servers, Internet routing protocols, and so on.

The technology becomes useful to us when we run applications such as search engines, that help us organize and find information on the Web. As new technologies, such as search engines and social media, evolved, analytics have developed to help us understand the data and optimize our efforts. Through the effective use of technology, we improve marketing, which sets the stage for the rest of this book.

Chapter 1 Citations

1. "Is the Web dead? 'No,' says Tim Berners-Lee, but native apps are 'boring.'" December 10, 2014. http://venturebeat.com/2014/12/10/is-the-web-dead-no-says-tim-berners-lee-but-native-apps-are-boring/. Accessed April 15, 2017.
2. "Would you like to know how the web works? BusinessProgrammer.com." April 16, 2015. www.businessprogrammer.com/how-the-web-works. Accessed April 15, 2017.
3. "Hacker lexicon: What is the Dark Web? WIRED." November 19, 2014. www.wired.com/2014/11/hacker-lexicon-whats-dark-web. Accessed April 15, 2017.
4. "Invisible Web: What it is, why it exists, how to find it, and its inherent ambiguity." August 1, 2006. http://yunus.hacettepe.edu.tr/~soydal/bby216_2011/4/InvisibleWebWhatitis.htm. Accessed April 15, 2017.

5. O'Reilly, T. (2007). "What is Web 2.0: Design Patterns and Business Models for the Next Generation of Software." *Communications & Strategies* 1:17. www. oreilly.com/pub/a/web2/archive/what-is-web-20.html. Accessed April 15, 2017; Kaplan, A.M. and M. Haenlein (2010). "Users of the World, Unite! The Challenges and Opportunities of Social Media." *Business Horizons* 53(1): 59–68; Kietzmann, J.H., K. Hermkens, I.P. McCarthy and B.S. Silvestre (2011). "Social Media? Get Serious! Understanding the Functional Building Blocks of Social Media." *Business Horizons* 54(3): 241–251.

6. "Data." W3C. www.w3.org/standards/semanticweb/data. Accessed April 15, 2017.

7. "IBM buys Weather Company's digital assets, expanding move into data crunching." October 28, 2015. www.wsj.com/articles/ibm-buys-weather-companys-digital-assets-expanding-move-into-data-crunching-1446069911. Accessed April 15, 2017.

8. "How Verizon's Yahoo buy will reshape the digital ad marketplace." August 8, 2016. http://marketingland.com/verizon-yahoo-reshape-digital-ad-marketplace-186713. Accessed April 15, 2017.

9. "Web 4.0: The ultra-intelligent electronic agent is coming—Big Think." http://bigthink.com/big-think-tv/web-40-the-ultra-intelligent-electronic-agent-is-coming. Accessed April 15, 2017.

10. "Uniform Resource Locator—Wikipedia." https://en.wikipedia.org/wiki/Uniform_Resource_Locator. Accessed April 15, 2017.

11. "Who coined 'cloud computing'?—MIT Technology Review." October 31, 2011. www.technologyreview.com/s/425970/who-coined-cloud-computing. Accessed April 15, 2017.

12. "History of data science (infographic): What's the Big Data?" February 17, 2015. https://whatsthebigdata.com/2015/02/17/history-of-data-science-infographic. Accessed April 15, 2017.

13. "Digital Ad Spending Worldwide to Hit $137.53 Billion in 2014—eMarketer." April 3, 2014. www.emarketer.com/Article/Digital-Ad-Spending-Worldwide-Hit-3613753-Billion-2014/1010736. Accessed April 15, 2017.

14. "Gartner: Get ready for 2020's 'Digital Industrial Economy'—PCMag.com." October 7, 2013. http://forwardthinking.pcmag.com/show-reports/316608-gartner-get-ready-for-2020-s-digital-industrial-economy. Accessed April 15, 2017.

Search Engines and the Internet

CHAPTER OBJECTIVES

After reading this chapter, readers should understand:

- Search engines and search results
- SEO, SEM, and search engine analytics
- Viral media

In this chapter, we cover the development of Internet search engines and the analytics behind Search Engine Optimization and Search Engine Marketing. Advances in search engine technology spawned a new era of individualized content creation, content sharing, and social media. Some content tended to be shared more often than most, leading to the emergence of viral media (media that is rapidly shared at no additional cost to the content creator via "network effects").

Search Engines

A search engine serves as the gateway to social media and helps find information. Search engines yield two types of search results: organic and paid. Businesses use marketing to optimize the search results to their advantage. Search engines rank organic results based on more than 200 ranking factors in an algorithm. Based on organic search ranking factors, businesses primarily focus on Search Engine Optimization (SEO), the process of optimizing a website to receive the most visitors through a search engine. By contrast, Search Engine Marketing (SEM) focuses on paid search business solutions. SEM involves the process of buying traffic through paid search listing paired to specific keywords that are being searched for on the search engine. SEO and SEM have their advantages and marketers should combine both, as most organizations have several initiatives that can benefit from both types of search.

Search engines are Internet services or software designed to search information on the Web that corresponds to a request (e.g., keywords) specified by the user. Considering that there are billions of websites on the Internet, search engines play a crucial role in helping us find the right information in a limited amount of time. Before

Table 2.1 Differences between paid and organic search.

Factor	SEO	SEM
Triggered by	Keywords	Keywords
Control of Search Results Ranking	No control on search results (search engine algorithms control this).	Almost total control over where and when search results (paid advertising) appears.
Cost	Free	Paid
Measurement (impressions, clicks, etc.)	Web Analytics, search consoles	Web Analytics and paid search advertising tools.
Best Use Cases	Brand awareness, advocacy, education, and support	Time- and location-sensitive marketing campaigns.

Source: Marshall Sponder, WebMetricsGuru Inc.

shifting our focus to search engine analytics, let's understand different types of search engines.

Types of Search Engines

Based on the mechanisms they operate; search engines can be divided into three categories:

- Crawler-based
- Directories
- Meta search engines

Crawler-Based Search Engines

As the name suggests, crawler-based search engines create their databases or lists automatically without any human intervention. Examples of crawler-based search engines are Google.com and Bing.com. Crawler-based search engines are widely used to find and access content over the Internet. They operate in three steps:

1. Web crawling
2. Indexing
3. Searching

Web Crawling

Search engines start by collecting and storing information about webpages. This mechanism is termed Web crawling. A Web crawler, also known as a Web spider or bot, is a computer program or software specifically designed to collect and store data about websites for indexing.

Indexing

Indexing helps classify a site correctly for searching purposes. The data crawled or extracted is then indexed and stored in a database for quick access. Every search engine may follow different techniques for indexing webpage data. Common indexing techniques include storing meta tags, which are used in the header of a webpage and provide descriptions of the website and keywords related to a website.

Searching

Searching is the final step in search engine operations. When a user requests specific information by entering keywords in a search engine, the search engine queries the index and provides a list of the most relevant webpages by matching it with the indexed keywords.

However, it may not be that simple. Search engines use a variety of factors to rank and provide a list of matching websites based on:

- **On page:** Content quality as determined by search algorithms.
- **Off page**: Links from other websites, search engines, social media, and email.
- **Metadata and usability:** Title, description, keywords, alternative text, custom meta tags, mobile accessibility, page display speed, etc.

A takeaway here is that to achieve good search results; an organization must place keywords in section titles, images, and in the general content of its website.

Main Organic Search Factors

1. **Keyword hierarchy:** Alignment of keywords with specific webpages throughout the site.
2. **Keyword layout:** Location of the keywords on the webpage.
3. **Website design:** Usability and page loading speed.
4. **URL:** The main keywords contained in the URL.

SEO can be improved through the introduction and maintenance of certain habits. Over time, we have been able to create general guidelines that enhance SEO. The following are examples of the guidelines and how to implement them. One insight is to have relevant keywords embedded in a website to aid a search engine robot. Search engines use relevant keywords to evaluate the Internet site against the searched term. Internet sites with high keyword relevancy will, in turn, show up higher in the results for a searched term. A search engine may use keyword density, which means the percentage of times the searched term(s) are located on a website. An average keyword density a marketer may strive for would be 5–8%, which equates to five or eight words out of every 100 words.

A few other tips are as follows:

- If one repeatedly uses the same keywords or definitions in page content, it may be perceived as spam.[1]
- Keywords added to the page title impacts webpage visibility in a search engine.[2]

- High title and full-text keyword frequency can increase site visibility.
- Flash animations may not impact the SEO results because they cannot be indexed as easily by web crawlers and bots, as the more simply structured HTML content.[3]

For a corporation to better understand its Internet presence, its website statistics should also be checked on a regular basis to understand both how users access and utilize the site and also what impact site changes may have on these behaviors. Also, the overall design of a website should be created alongside the corporation's Search Engine Optimization strategy.

Directories

The directory listings are manually compiled and created by human editors. People who want to be listed in a directory submit an address, title, and brief description of their website, which is then reviewed by the editor and included in it. Some good examples of human-created directories are Yahoo Directory, Open Directory, and LookSmart.

Meta Search Engines

Meta search engines compile and display results from other search engines. When a user enters a query, the meta search engine submits the query to several individual search engines, and results returned from all the search engines are integrated, ranked, and displayed to the user. Examples of meta search engines include Metacrawler, Mamma, and Dogpile. By integrating results from several search engines, meta search engines are capable of handling large amounts of data and can save time by focusing on one meta search engine.

Local and Global Search Engines

Based on their scope, search engines can be divided into two types: local and global.

Local Search Engines

Local Search has a few different meanings, depending on the context of what we are searching on. For example, a search engine can be local in the sense that it is embedded with a website and only indexes and searches the content of that site. Amazon's CloudSearch or any other search engine embedded within a website is an example of a local search engine.

Local Search Optimization
When we are searching for nearby locations to us, neighborhood and street-level information can appear as local search results. However, optimizing Web content for local search is a deliberate task. Until recently, local search was hard to do by keywords alone because it required multiple versions of Web copy for each locality, which would require millions of Web copies. However, the world is changing, and SEO can now target specific audiences and specific localities using a variety of local search marketing tools.

Global Search Engines

Global search engines are used to search for content on the Web. Google.com and Bing.com are examples of global search engines. However, note that global search engines can be localized. Google Search, for instance, can also be embedded within your website to help users find information on your site although Google is phasing out its site search platform as of April 1st, 2017.

Essential Functions of Search Engines

Digital marketers use search engines for:

- **Brand awareness**: A brand is seen and recognized by consumers in a top search result once a branded search term or the name of the brand is searched for.
- **Online sales**: Search engines drive traffic to webpages to purchase a product or service.
- **Lead generation**: Organic search can acquire potential consumers through the content or targeted keywords used. Paid search aids in search and Web Analytics, which can be employed in Return on Investment (ROI) calculations.

Essential Functions of Web Search Engines

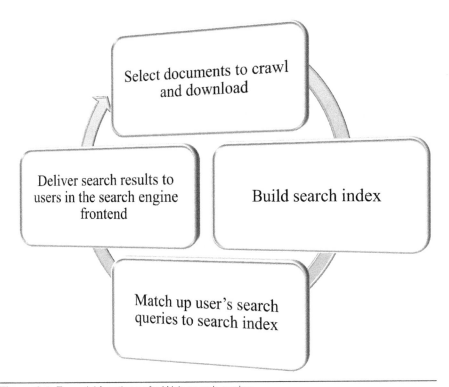

Figure 2.1 Essential functions of a Web search engine.
Source: WebMetricsGuru Inc.

How Search Engines Work

While the heavy reliance on Web links seems somewhat crude and overused today, Google's PageRank algorithm was revolutionary in its time, for finding and ranking quality content over inferior content (i.e., websites and pages) for a specific search term or query. As time went on, judging the quality of a site based on its links became much less useful as search marketers developed methods to manipulate the search results. Because of this activity, subtle and complex methods were used to determine the order of ranking of pages for a specific search term(s). By the mid-1990s, the Internet quickly became crowded. Internet routers, servers, and bandwidth were strained by the capabilities of the devices until Web caching emerged to cut down Internet traffic. Web caching saves local copies of time-stamped Web data on a local server, so instead of going to the data source, a Web server connects with a local Web cached version, which remains in place until the source of information is updated. Once the change is detected, Web caching propagates, and the local copies are updated, so they stay in sync with the original.

The Three-Step Search Engine Process

1. Search indexes evolved as a sorted "master list" of the websites and pages of each website currently available on the World Wide Web, found by the Internet crawlers a search engine employs to get the data in the first place.
2. Once a user enters a search term or phrase, it is evaluated by the search engine, which tries to understand what the term means and identify any misspellings present.
3. The most relevant pages in the search index are matched with the query and served up to the user by the search engine, operating on its unique set of search algorithms.

Search Engine Analytics

When we talk about search engine analytics, we mean two things:

1. Search Engine Optimization (SEO)
2. Search engine trends analysis

Search Engine Optimization and Search Engine Marketing

Search Engine Optimization (SEO) is the set of techniques used to improve a website's ranking on a Search Engine Result Page (SERP).[4] A SERP is the list of the results returned by a search engine in response to a user's query.

Organic and Paid Search Results

There are a couple of main differences between organic (unpaid) and paid search results. Paid search results are tailored to the searcher. For example, if you search

Table 2.2 CTR based on SERP position.

Position in Search Results	1st result	2nd result	3rd result	4th result	5th result	6 to 10th results	2nd page of results	3rd page and beyond of results
Search Click-Through Rate (CTR)	31 %	14 %	9.9 %	7 %	6 %	4 %	4 %	2 %

Source: WebMetricsGuru Inc. based on data from Marketingland.com.[6]

'cars' frequently, you will see more ads for cars as then your paid search results will be related to that as well. Organic results appear mainly because of their relevance to the user's query. Lastly, paid search results are paid advertisements. A study tested the effect of sponsored ad ranks on the click-through and conversion rates for an online retailer and found that top positions usually had higher click-through rates, but not necessarily higher conversion rates.[5] Conversion rates depend on the searcher's experience on the landing page(s) and are not under the search engine's direct control. Search engines are becoming more intelligent and successful in matching search results with a searcher's experience on landing pages via algorithms and analytics.

Social media marketers strive to develop search engine strategies to make their websites appear at the top of search results. When a site appears on the first page of the search results, users are more likely to pay attention to it.[7] Search engine ranking is even more crucial to the business owners when the website is selling products or services. High rankings on SERPs can mean more Internet traffic to a website, which in some cases converts to more paying clients and higher return on investment.[8] For social media marketers, it is important to understand the mechanism behind the SERP ranking. There may be a variety of factors search engines consider to rank websites, such as keywords and relevance. However, the most important factor that determines SERP ranking is the PageRank. PageRank is an algorithm used by Google search engines to rank websites' SERPs. The higher-ranking websites are displayed on the top of the search results page. Google's PageRank algorithm predominantly relies on the quality of incoming hyperlinks, in-links, to rank websites. A website, for example, with in-links from some famous Internet sites (e.g., CNN.com) will appear on the top of the SERP if compared with a site that has no quality in-links or low-quality in-links. To understand the in-link quality and number argument, consider Figure 2.2, where nodes represent webpages, and lines represent in-links (arrowhead pointing to a page) and out-links (arrowhead pointing away from a page). The PageRank algorithm will place page B higher on the SERP, even though there are fewer in-links to B when compared to D. The ranking exists because the in-links to website B are from a more credible or higher quality website (Page A). Bottom line, your objective is to increase the number of quality in-links to your site.

Users can access SEO metrics by using free SEO tools such as Open SEO Stats; an extension for Google Chrome is available at http://pagerank.chromefans.org. With Open SEO Stats, users can determine the ranking of a website based on Google PageRank. Google PageRank uses a scale of zero to ten to indicate the importance the Google search engine allocates to the page. In addition to page ranking, Open SEO Stats also provides information about website traffic, hyperlink status, the speed of the page, etc. It should be noted that Google no longer shows the PageRank of a page, and the calculation of the PageRank of a page involves many more factors today, than it did 20 years ago.

Search Trend Analytics

Search engine trends analytics deals with analyzing and understanding the keywords people use in a search engine against a timeline, such as a month or year, or even across several years. Consequently, search engine data is a gateway into the minds of customers. Through search engines, customers find what they want. Thus, search trend analysis can provide valuable information to the social marketers. Google Trends is one of the most insightful trend analysis tools. Google Trends uses massive amounts of search engine data to analyze the world's interests and predict trends. For

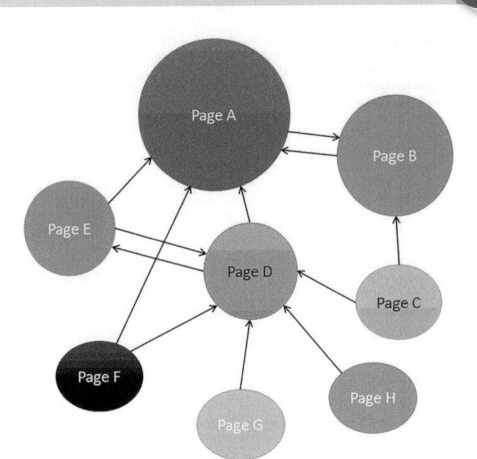

Figure 2.2 PageRank algorithm ranking example.
Source: Gohar F. Khan.

example, in the financial sector, Google Trends data has been used to detect "early warning signs" of stock market moves.[9] In the health sector, Google Trends data has helped predict world flu epidemics.[10] Engineers at Google.org, for instance, using Google Trends data, found a strong correlation between the searches for flu-related topics and the numbers of actual flu cases circulating in different countries and regions around the world.[11] From a business perspective, Google Trends can help also answer a variety of questions, including the following:

- How do people search for your brand?
- When does interest spike in your products or services?
- Which keywords are driving more traffic?
- Which regions are interested in your brand?
- What are trending topics over the Internet?
- How are your competitors performing?

Search Engine Analytics Tools
The following are commonly used social media analytics tools; most of them are also free to use.

- **Google Trends** is a search engine analytics tool. More information is available at http://trends.google.com.

- **Canopy** is a multimedia analytics tool designed to support deep investigation of large multimedia collections, such as images, videos, and documents. More information on Canopy is available at www.vacommunity.org/article[32].
- **Google Alerts** is a content detection and notification service that automatically notifies users when new content appears on the Internet (e.g., social media, the Web, blogs, video, and discussion groups) matches a set of search terms based on user queries. Users are alerted through email. More information is available at www.google.com/alerts.
- **Icerocket** specializes in blog searches and captures activity on Facebook, Twitter, and Flickr. More information is found at www.icerocket.com.
- **TweetBeep** is like Google Alerts for Twitter. Users choose keywords and receive daily search results via email. More information is available at http://tweetbeep.com.

Best Practices for Doing SEO for Digital Marketing (Inbound and Outbound)

Basic SEO involves following the examples below, leveraging content, and creating additional content when analytics inform stakeholders and analysts that there is a content gap. Content gaps occur when visitors and searchers are looking for a specific keyword or phrase, but the term is not located on the website.

Strategies That Work the Best for SEO

For an effective SEO strategy, keyword research has the most value, but there are no shortcuts to developing SEO as an effective marketing channel. The general guidelines suggest that choosing the right "words" or "keywords" seems to be the best strategy, but that keyword should be supplemented with compelling content geared to your audience. Spending time creating interesting content for specific website visitors is the most effective SEO tactic, but it is also one of the most difficult to do effectively or to scale since content creation is time-consuming and the results are incalculable. On the other hand, keyword research takes less effort and is effective. In fact, the process of creating new content and choosing the best keywords for it takes so much time and effort that a marketer must make informed choices as to best allocate their time and resources.

Page Tag Elements of SEO

Page tag elements are optimized metadata, or sets of data that give information about other data, which distinguishes to search engines what the page is about.

Building Blocks of SEO

URLs

Uniform Resource Locator (URL) is used to specify addresses on the World Wide Web. A URL is the fundamental network identification for any resource connected to the Internet (e.g., hypertext pages, images, and sound files). URLs have the following format: protocol://hostname/other_information.

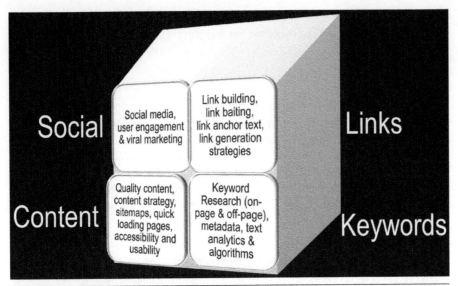

Figure 2.3 Building blocks of Search Engine Optimization.
Source: WebMetricsGuru Inc.

While URLs should be unique to a site, they are carefully considered before they are assigned. For example, a URL should include the most relevant keywords because search engines still consider keywords within URLs as a ranking factor. Additionally, relevant keywords in URLs help target audiences recall the website. Keywords strategically placed in the URL help search engines, via the use of text analytics (covered later in this book), to understand the meaning within the content of webpages and websites. Thus, searchers are provided with more relevant content, based on what they are searching for. The same considerations impact title tags, header tags, body text, alt text, and anchor text.

Title Tag
The title tag is an HTML element critical to both SEO and user experience. It briefly and accurately describes the topic and theme of an online document. The title tag is displayed in the top bar of Internet browsers.[12]

Header Tags
The header tag, or the <h1> tag in HTML, will usually be the title of a post, or other emphasized text on the page. It will usually be the largest text that stands out. There are other header tags in HTML like an h2, h3, h4, etc.[13]

Main Content (Body Text)
- The main content is not usually the first item on a webpage. Users must navigate through an extensive list of navigation links, sub-lists of links, corporate icons, site searches, etc. before arriving at the main content.[14]

Alt Text
Alternative text (alt text) is a word or phrase inserted as an attribute in an HTML document to tell website viewers the nature or contents of an image. The alt text appears in a blank box that would normally contain the picture.[15]

Anchor Text

Anchor text is highlighted in a hypertext link and can be clicked on to open the target webpage.[16]

Organic Search

Organic search engine optimization involves creating or changing website copy and site links for high search engine results. When websites have optimized content and keyword meta tags, search engines know how to categorize the site more efficiently. Organic search is still considered "free visibility." Any business or blog can rank highly on an organic search result, but the amount of work put into SEO may still not result in achieving the top result. Results can be imprecise. However, it is usually a profitable investment over the long term.

Principles of SEO

- Design for relevant and popular content
- Optimize content
- Spread content for the entirety of the Web
- Adjust site to changing search algorithms

SEO as Customer Acquisition

Figure 2.4 Online and offline customer acquisition strategies.
Source: WebMetricsGuru Inc.

Search Engine Optimization as Owned Media

SEO is a process of working on pages or websites that a stakeholder has access to (i.e., a webmaster or business owner/operator). SEO is an owned media channel. One controls and leverages organic content to capture and keep consumers. Owned media content is improved through optimization techniques. The result of effective SEO is more visibility or higher ranking in search results and more search referrals to the site. However, effective search engine optimization is not easy to do. Business and site owners are being told by search engines to focus on the quality of their content and user experience instead of focusing on the manipulation of Internet search capabilities. Now, businesses are spending time and energy on specialized marketing analytics by channel. Marketing analytics is specialized because no single analytics platform captures all the readouts on all marketing channels as per Figure 2.4

Internal Search Considerations

Website search is an internal search engine that indexes the entire website and allows visitors to search within the site. Many websites have deployed Google's customized free site search services, now being discontinued, or employ other free and paid alternatives. Using internal search engine query logs for analysis, stakeholders can create need assessments and help determine areas where content is missing that would better serve customers and potential customers. One of the significant advantages of having internal site search set up and running on a website is that the site owner can understand the unmet needs of visitors. External search engine referral traffic reflects only those searchers who decided to click on the search engine result that led to the website page. Searches that the website appeared on as an impression, a link that was seen but not clicked on by a user, are not captured in Web Analytics, but search impressions are captured by platforms such as the Google Search Console, and ported to Google Analytics, when properly configured.

Other Types of Internal or Custom Search Engines

Besides using popular public internal search engines, such as Google and Bing, there are other ways to utilize search technology to organize information. Many websites have their search engines that enable searchers to find specific information hosted within a site. However, Google is not the only custom search engine provider around. Third-party vendors and types of search engines can be used on images, videos, and audio files. We will not go into the uses of custom search engines in depth, but assisting searchers to find what they are searching for helps your business and consumers' satisfaction.

- Google custom search engine: Site administrators use Google's search technology to set up their search engines for a selected index of pages on their website or a collection of any websites on the Web. Custom search engine users configure how search queries are processed.[17]

- **Free third-party search engines:** Many third-party search engines are installed on a website via a script or Web API call.[18]
- **Google Search Console:** Formally called Google Webmaster Tools, Google Search Console provides information on search analytics, such as impression data from the Google search engine and crawling performance and messages from Google-bot and other Google services. Google Search Console serves as the communication between webmasters and Google about the health and performance of their websites.[19]

Search Console Authentication Methods[20]

- Uploading a Google file to the Web server
- Adding a meta tag to the HTML of the website
- Adding a new domain name system (DNS) record referring to the search console address
- Using their Google Analytics or Google Tag Manager account

Enterprise search engines: Many organizations have their own industrial-strength search engines, which require a different set of data algorithms compared to popular search engines. In these search engines, marketers search queries of potential and actual customers as they navigate through their website. Armed with this information, marketers find out what customers are looking for on their sites and whether or not they found it. Marketers use this information to improve their offerings to meet consumer's expectations.[21]

Video search engines, such as YouTube and Vimeo, are becoming increasingly valuable as a form of market intelligence. YouTube is the second largest search engine in the world—after Google.

Vertical search engines, such as Career Services, LinkedIn, and Monster.com, and dating search engines Match.com and eHarmony, are customized search engines with specific listings of jobs, products, and services, partners, etc. Consequently, a customized search engine can be created around any subject.

Understanding and Optimizing Search Engine Performance

While there are several books on this subject, performing SEO on a site comes down to having a defined need to improve the business performance of a website or group of websites and using various tools and methods employed to achieve that purpose. Some tools used are:

- First-party data is provided by various Digital Analytics platforms. The default data collection provided is sufficient for small businesses, but larger organizations will have more sophisticated reporting needs.
- Organic and paid search term and referral reports work well enough with the default settings but can be customized to increase their efficiency and effectiveness, particularly for enterprise reporting.

- The third-party search engine optimization tools help website owners improve the search engine ranking and performance of their website properties. One of the tool's capabilities is the ability to crawl a site to index pages and their appearance in other search engines. The tool eliminates issues affecting search engine website ranking for specific user search queries. Organic search tools improve the quality and number of backlinks to their sites. Some of them also provide competitive research capabilities that could be useful for website optimization and business performance.

Offsite SEO

Offsite search engine optimization, or backlink optimization, creates more attractive websites for search engines by having sites more easily found in Web searches. "Link building" or "reputation building" is considered the primary offsite SEO tactic. Core aspects of offsite SEO are the following:

Links and Link Building

It is extremely cumbersome to find quality links from other websites and most reciprocal linking schemes have little effect on website rankings. In turn, website traffic referrals are preferred by search engines.

- Number of backlinks
- Backlinks from related and relevant websites
- Links to relevant competitors
- New content creation may attract links from other websites. Link bait, or links whose purpose is to drive clicks, falls into this category
- Anchor text
- Link neighborhood
- Link freshness
- Search engines can detect abnormal linking strategies and penalize it. When it looks like a website is getting new backlinks too quickly based on its size and update activity, the search engine decides if the link growth is abnormal and acts accordingly.
- Link diversity
- Social sharing

Popularity Metrics' Role in SEO

PageRank, Author Rank, Trust Rank, MozRank, and Authority Rank are another way of ranking content based on its quality. PageRank is a measure of the quality of a page or site in the Google search engine based on webpage copy and incoming or outgoing links on the page. Author Rank rates the authority of the author of the content in the search engine, while Trust Rank rates the trustworthiness of the backlinks from the websites pointing to the website or webpage. Authority ranking is an alternative metric calculated by Moz for PageRank indicating how likely a domain or website will rank highly in Google's search results. Popularity metrics are easy for search engines and analytics vendors to generate. They serve as directional indicators that optimization changes are having a positive effect on search engine ranking. However, search engines and their constantly updated algorithms are the only true authority from their ranking algorithm. The most successful strategy for SEO is providing content that the audience finds valuable.

Generating Search Engine Traffic

- **Online press releases:** Generate links and traffic that might temporarily impact the quality and popularity score.
- **User engagement data from Web Analytics platforms** (e.g. Google Analytics): Helps site owners understand how users experience their website content.
- **Photos, art, video, and music sharing via social media:** May generate online discussion, engagement with the website, and ultimately, a higher quality score.
- **Wikis allows users to post, edit, and organize content:** Engages online users.
- **Link building:** Creates online reputation through links. Should be earned and not falsely manufactured.

SEO professionals agree that content marketing is the most efficient strategy for website owners who want to rank high in search engines.

Summarizing Organic SEO

Many third-party tools can be used in conjunction with Google Analytics, or other Web Analytics, to better understand and improve the SEO of websites or blogs. SEO is an "owned media" acquisition and customer intelligence strategy as well as a content creation strategy.

SEO Features

- Success with SEO depends on upon understanding the consumer's "voice" and creating content that addresses what customers and potential customers are searching for.
- Web usability is the ease of use of a website. Search engines will assign higher ranking in the search results to content when it has more Web usability or UX.
- High quality link-building that leads to higher quality scores, popularity, Trust Rank, and PageRank.
- Every piece of data reflects an activity, and all search activity is trackable.
- Search engines are getting much better at detecting signals—they are used to process text, but now they find patterns in other mediums, creating more sophisticated ranking methods.

Use Cases for Search Engines

- Branding
- Online sales
- Lead generation
- Traffic generation
- Content generation and consumption

Ranking Scores and Algorithms

Algorithms are trending greatly in the modern world as we try to systemize our daily lives mathematically. Algorithms could be simplified as invisible rule books that are programmed to process and act on data as a human might. The oldest algorithms are embedded in search engines and control how content is rated and ranked for search results. We will have more on algorithms in later chapters, but our first real introduction to the subject is in this chapter.

Note: The Google search engine runs several hundred algorithms in a single instance globally. The algorithms in different regions have elements unique to their region because language and lexicons are different across regions or at the local city level.

Therefore, even if a searcher figures out a way to outsmart a set of Google algorithms to provide higher rankings for chosen keywords, it does not necessarily mean those results will be persistent, or even representative of what the current state of algorithms will be in other regions at any given time.

Additional Points to Keep in Mind about Search Engine Algorithms

- Search engines are an early application of document classification and the core algorithmic methods applied to Web documents gathered by Google from the World Wide Web, internal documents, and file types gathered within organizations (Intranet).
- Furthermore, information retrieval and text mining are almost identical, regardless of the kind of application (e.g., Internet search and retrieval, image retrieval, and classification) that we are talking about.
- Search engines define relevance by using classification and weighting elements within the website content, or web page.
- PageRank was an algorithm invented to improve search results. Currently, it is largely obsolete, but at the time of its appearance in 1998, it was a major factor in the emergence of Google as the leading search engine, a place it still holds today. Recently mobile websites were given more weight as a ranking signal in Google's algorithm when mobile traffic from search surpassed desktop and laptop share. PageRank considers many factors, both on the page and off the page and currently, while Google still calculates it, it is not normally visible for a score.

The metadata, arrangement, and markup of data turn out to be more valuable than the raw data it describes. For example, when searching for a video, the metadata, the topic of the video, and the time and place it was created allows the search engine to find the video. Conversely, the video content would not be helpful to search engines because they cannot understand the video's raw footage (although that situation is changing with Google's development of deep learning algorithms, such as Google Deepmind, that allows it to learn on its own, without user intervention). It may be necessary to adjust the scoring and distribution of webpages and document files manually when the results are not optimal. Such adjustments are the subject of much debate in many domains of knowledge, from a purist sense of perspective, where, if the information were perfectly structured and algorithms were perfectly written and applied, the need for manual scoring and patching would and should not need to exist. We do not live in a perfect world, and we cannot know everyone who will search or the ways that information is used. No matter how clear and concise we are in structuring information for one purpose, when it is employed in another context, or found by someone else, it may need to be modified to be useful.[22]

Search Engine Updates

It can take a lot of work to update Web content for better visibility with higher search engine results. Google generates user reviews of search results produced by human testers. The reviews are compared against two sets of algorithmic results on a prepared index of search engine listings.[23] The large datasets require cleaning up at a janitorial level of detail before they are useful for analysis. The transformation is complicated by the increasing velocity of data generated.

In the search engine domain, many of the patches are related to the way users have manipulated search engine results. In any case, there will always be a need to "fix" or patch things, including search engine results.[24]

Local Search Engine Ranking Factors

A significant search engine ranking factor is the number of words in the search term; a term with one word (e.g., "water") is going to be very common in several billion documents or pages and be tough to rank in the top search results in any conceivable way. On the other hand, "carbonated water," while still a difficult term to rank for, is infinitely easier to get a top ranking for than "water." Finally, a term such as "carbonated water in Newport, Jersey City, New Jersey" could pull a high search ranking because there are few viable competitors for that term in the search results. The more words in a search query, the more likely there will be less competition for the top ranking. The audience for that result might be much, much smaller—perhaps only a few people will be searching for "carbonated water in Newport, Jersey City, New Jersey." There is less competition and less demand in a local search than in searches not restricted by location. If the audience is highly valued and highly segmented, say a millionaire's club located in a town where several of the members are looking for carbonated water for their drinks, then you might have hit a valuable niche. To test this, you could do search results in a local vicinity matched against some businesses that might require "carbonated water" in other analytics tools like comScore QSearch, when they are available to the search analyst.

Paid Search—Growth in the Size and Value of Search Marketing is Rising

Overall, between 2014 to 2018, Search Ad spending will increase by approximately 6% per year worldwide, as reported by eMarketer.[25]

Types of Search Marketing

- Directory listings
- Search engine marketing
- Search Engine Optimization (SEO), also known as natural or organic search
- Pay-per-click (PPC), also known as paid search

Each type of search has its role that it is better suited for.

Organic Search vs. Paid Search

Both are needed and have different purposes and capabilities.

How Organic Search Works

Keywords: Selected words or phrases when doing a search.
Meta name: Known as a meta tag or meta element, usually located in the header portion of a site's HTML code.
Algorithm: Displays the search engine's "best guess" as to which pages are most relevant.
Title tag: Title in blue bar at the top of webpage, which is important for SEO Rankings.

How Webpages Are Evaluated by Search Engines

Google Search evaluates more than 200 signals on webpages and backlinks to determine the search engine ranking of any website. Businesses focus on the elements of their websites directly under their control, such as the page or website title and the standard meta-tags. By providing quality and frequent Web content, businesses gain more quality traffic from search engines.[26]

Paid Search

In this subsection, we examine the world of paid search briefly, in which we will:

- identify the various types of search engine advertisements and their parts;
- analyze the effectiveness of search engine advertising campaigns;
- determine ways to improve an ad's position without increasing the bid amount; and
- create a categorized list of keywords from which to advertise on a search engine.

Where Paid Search Fits within the Digital Marketing Mix

One form of paid search is called "pay for click" or known better as "text ads." Text ads appear in search engines' results. In Figure 2.5, pay for click is a small part of the overall marketing mix that is now part of digital marketing—anyone can participate, and there is virtually no barrier to entry.

Paid Search Overview

Keywords: Words and phrases are triggering ads to display in the search engine results (paid).

Ads: Short sales pitches in text or images.

Bids: How much advertisers are willing to spend to show their ads, get clicks and conversions.

Landing page: The first page that searchers see after they click an ad and often where the conversion takes place.

Conversions: Actions that visitors take on a website such as leads, orders, downloads, or phone calls.

Process: Tracking results, conversions, return on ad spends with testing, improving web content, tools and resources.

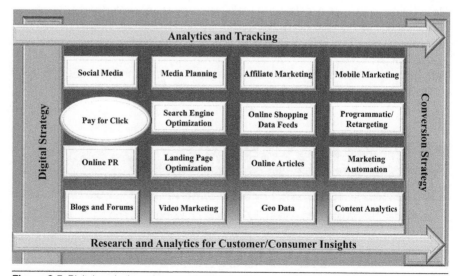

Figure 2.5 Digital marketing mix process and strategy.
Source: WebMetricsGuru Inc.

In general, the higher that ads appear on the website page or the search result page, the more clicks they get, and the more advertisers pay for those ads. There are also targeting methods (broad versus narrow) in matching up keywords and phrases to searchers and what they are searching for online (based on their search queries). The overall performance of advertising campaigns has more to do with the targeting used than what is in the ad. Paid advertising is not a total marketing solution for most businesses, but advertising can be extremely useful for short-term campaign events (such as a sale or time-sensitive offering) as they offer precision targeting (or at least the illusion of it). For the long term, paid advertising can address branding needs if done within a strategic plan. Users view impressions of a brand ad several times. They could be influenced by what they see, even if they do not click on it. Thus, brand managers measure branding using a longer timeframe than most commonly used conversion metrics.

Specifically, let's examine the following parts of paid search.

- Pay per click (PPC)
- Search Engine Marketing (SEM)
- AdWords and Bing Ads
- Campaign, ad groups, keywords, and ads
- Impressions
- Click-through rate (CTR)
- Cost per click (CPC)
- Conversions and conversion rate
- Cost per acquisition (CPA)
- Quality score
- Display URLs and destination URLs

Paid Search Tactics Most Commonly used by Marketers

To run effective paid search campaigns, most search marketers collect an abundance of first-party data from their websites with the help of Web Analytics reporting. Paid search marketers generate and run several keyword variations, which means they typically have a large list of keywords to run on paid search engines on a regular basis. Usually, this task alone is someone's full-time job. Paid search advertising involves content that has images, the most common type of paid search ad is a text ad. Text ads require the advertiser to define the title, description lines, and display URL as part of the ad—A/B testing eliminates the guesswork of successful design of a text ad or paid search landing page. A/B testing compares two or more versions of a webpage to see which one performs better.

Text Ad Effectiveness

Paid search impressions are defined by the possibility of seeing the ad, like how a Twitter impression is defined. The cost per click and average position of an ad is a function of the bidding strategy along with the actual quality of the text link ad to be clicked on. Click-through rate is the number of instances an ad is displayed divided by the number of times the ad is clicked. Paid search metrics are now able to be imported into a Web Analytics platform or reside within the paid search campaign platform, usually Google AdWords, Bing Ads, or some other third-party Ad Network platform running the ads across ad exchanges. Paid text ads are more effective in some industries than others.[27] From a business perspective, it is no secret that every transaction does not happen in a vacuum; there are clearly buyers and sellers of a product or service, and this is often best symbolized with the "exchange" or "auction" model. Nothing in this transaction has an actual fixed price and the price of the keywords associated with the text ad varies based on supply and demand. In that light, it might be more illuminating to look at the number of people searching for products or services in each industry online and the value to the user of what is being offered to evaluate better whether the campaigns are profitable or not. The metrics provided do not say if "targeting" or "creative" is effective or not or by how much. Intermediate metrics such as CPC, CPA, CTR provided by the advertising platforms are unable to measure the advertising quality (although Google AdWords does have a "quality score" that is performance-based but doesn't go far enough because Google cannot yet read the mind or emotions of the viewer). If we go further down the rabbit hole, most significant transactions (organizations running several thousand ads a day) are running with automation and bidding strategies along with programmatic advertising.

Do Platform Vendors Provide Accurate Metrics?

The intermediate metrics provided by most analytics platforms do not address "ad blocking" (and they may not be able to provide the number of blocked ads on a mobile device), which became an issue in 2015 when Apple built in Ad Blocking to iOS 9. We can only control a part of the "equation" of search engine ranking, and imperfectly at that, since Google and other search engines are changing the ranking factors and weightings while keeping the exact algorithms as trade secrets. On the other hand, even of the elements we control, it is possible for malicious code to infect our websites and impact our rankings and even inclusion in the search engine index. For that reason, it is better to keep Search Engine Optimization as simple and straightforward as possible, perhaps even being more conservative in implementing adaptive features (such as an infinite scroll feature), because they may impact how search engines process and rank websites in search results.

The Search Query Formulation Process

There is a generic process that is repeated when a user searches the Internet using a search engine. This process continues until the searcher finds what they are looking for, or gives up searching.

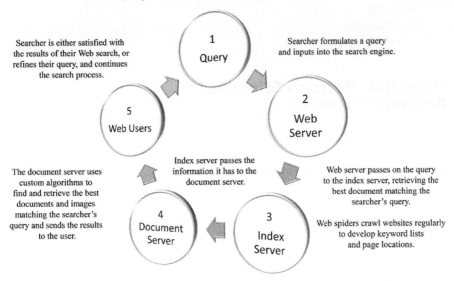

Figure 2.6 Search formulation process.
Source: WebMetricsGuru Inc.

Developing and Implementing a Search Optimization Strategy

From an analytics perspective, the best way to go about marketing campaigns is to try it first and wait a few weeks before making any changes (exploratory approach), collect the analytics and feedback, and use the "cycle of improvement" approach (Figure 2.6) to understand the gaps and strengths of your website. At a certain point, when there is enough data to know what things need to be changed or added, then it is time to define and implement SEO strategy.

Using Paid and Organic Search Together

Businesses often rely on a single strategy to succeed. However, in search and social media, it is better not to. While Search Engine Optimization is ideal for overall long-term growth, site owners cannot get consistent results that way. Consider combining paid and organic search marketing for the best marketing results.

Running a Paid Search Campaign

1. Investigate broad search categories and trends
2. Narrow down keywords
3. Determine traffic and cost

4. Select terms and match criteria
5. Design ads
6. Run campaigns
7. Measure and refine

Objective: Perform Effective Keyword Research

To effectively use keywords which are essential for effective organic and paid search:

- define the audience being targeted and
- decide what kind of site, or blog, to create or maintain.

Several free tools for keyword research are "good enough," such as Semrush.com or Moz.com. Google Analytics can also help with SEO/SEM traffic and research related to a website. Once results come back from the campaigns, the data should be used to improve the campaign while it is running.

Leading Search Engines

Google attained its position as the leading search engine by the turn of the century. The only place it does not dominate is in China, where Baidu is preferred.[28]

Other Types of Search Engines

- Local
- Vertical
- Specialty/industry
- Topical
- Image
- Mobile
- Universal search

Google is not the only search engine that matters for marketing; in fact, it may not even be the best search engine for certain things such as social media and industry-specific searches. Marketers could take a few different approaches to determine the best search engine for a given type of search (i.e., interior design).[29] Defining the desired information expected as an outcome of the search is necessary to decide which search engine is the best for a given task.

Referral traffic: Find the top search engine referring organic search traffic to top interior design sites by using a third-party analytics platform such as Alexa Analytics or SimilarWeb.[30] Sometimes another service, such as Pinterest.com, or even a website such as businessinsider.com sends the most traffic. Paid analytics platforms such as comScore and Nielsen can also provide visualizations and reports of incoming traffic to a category or a specific website.

Conversions: Most websites exist to serve an audience. The end of a search is the searcher or visitor finding what they are looking for and taking action on the site (i.e., a conversion event). By this criterion, a business can determine the best search engine for their organization.

Online Advertising

Online advertising is a part of digital marketing, and the primary goal is to acquire new customers.

Types of Online Advertising

The purpose of online display advertising is to deliver various advertising and brand messages to website visitors, on demand and with precision; there are several types of advertisements as well as commonly used formats for them. For example, a company running a sale might run ads that appear to specific targeted audiences on at specific sites and at specific times of day. If an advertiser wants to deliver their message in a precise way, they are going to have to pay for it in one way or another.

Display (Banner) Ads
Display or banner ads refers to advertising that takes place on digital websites. It includes many different formats and contains items such as text, images, Flash, video, and audio. The primary purpose of display advertising is to deliver general advertisements and brand messages to site visitors.[31] Several studies show the impact of display advertising on search behavior. Display advertising drives search clicks for up to two weeks after searchers see the ad.[32] The impact of display advertising on searchers is highest immediately after the ad is viewed, but persists for some time (at least a week).[33]

Standard Pixel Sizes for Digital Advertising
- Banner 728 × 90
- Big box 300 × 250
- Skyscraper 160 × 600
- Square 250 × 250

Types of Display Ads
- **Video ads**
- **Rich media ads (expendable ads):** Flash files that may expand when the user interacts on mouse over (polite) or auto-initiated (non-polite).
- **Overlays:** Ads that appear above content and that are possible to remove by clicking on a close button.
- **Interstitials:** Ads displayed on webpages before expected content is loaded onto the webpage.
- **Sponsorships:** Advertising that includes a logo or adds a brand to the design of a website.
- **Ads that appear on a sidebar or top bar:** These ads stay on the page unless the viewer marks it as uninteresting or offensive.

Display advertising has robust targeting and analytics; ads can be targeted based on customer type, location, time and—in some cases—the target audience's behavioral activities.

Text Search Ads

Search advertising is a method of placing online advertisements on webpages displaying results from search engine queries on the desktop or mobile devices. Keywords typed into the search engine by a searcher trigger text ads to be displayed by the search engine (this is called an advertising impression). The most common search engines that run text advertising are Google, Bing, and Yahoo, but there are many more specialty search engines, along with many websites that run their search engines and display advertising based on the searches that visitors make on the site.

Types of Search Ads
- **Paid search ads** are what we typically see when we type search queries in Google, Yahoo, and Bing.
- **Contextual ads** are a type of online search ad based on context. When a searcher lands on a travel-themed page of a website, a search ad is triggered. Searchers might see luggage, local restaurant, or hotel ads based on the content of the page.

Targeting on Social and Mobile Networks

Ads on social and mobile networks can be targeted to specific audiences based on several characteristics such as:

- Keyword based
- Interest based
- Demographics and psychographics based
- Location based
- Affinity based
- Activity based
- Behavioral based
- Recommendation based

Social network advertising, also known as social media targeting is a way to describe forms of online advertising that focus on social networking services such as Twitter, Facebook, Instagram, LinkedIn, Pinterest and so on. There are many types of ad units and options, and some of these differ based on the social network involved. Because the members of a social network store information about themselves such as their age, gender, interests, and location, advertising can be hyper-targeted to them. Also, advertising can become subtle and powerful as social networks store members' activities and can run sophisticated algorithms to better understand what members are interested in seeing, which they can in turn offer to advertisers. Another aspect of social media advertising that is absent in search marketing is the concept of the "social graph," which is a representation of the interconnection of relationships in an online social network. Search marketing targets *searchers* based on what they are searching for. Social media advertising targets *users* based on what they like and who their friends are.

Visitor and Customer Acquisition

Event Marketing

Events can be used to acquire new customers/audience. A marketing event can take place online (such as an email signup, virtual conference, virtual trade show, webinar or even a podcast/vidcast) or offline (an event that happens in the 3D world, such as a trade show at a convention center or hotel).

A new type of "event" that can be the basis of marketing is called "pop-up" or "flash" based, mainly to showcase or sell a new product; the store is said to "pop-up" in the park for a certain number of hours during a specified day (period). Pop-up events usually are much less expensive to run, and with current e-commerce, wireless, near-field, iBeacon/Bluetooth, and GPS services can be highly effective at reaching targeted audiences and communities when they are properly planned and executed.

Optimized Social Media Press Releases

While hardly a new concept, the technology behind search engines and social media is identical and lends itself not only to Search Engine Marketing and display advertising but also to the dissemination of targeted news stories that an interested organization, company or individual might want to run that targets news media outlets. However, the press releases also show up in search engine results (SERPs) on search engines and, occasionally, on social media sites (which usually run their own search engines). Optimizing press releases is much less relevant now than it was five years ago (search engines have "devalued" these links somewhat as it is overused).

Web Portals

Portal advertising deals such as placements on Yahoo's home page have become less prevalent as portals. However, they can still be an effective way to reach a targeted audience.

Viral Marketing

Viral marketing has changed a lot since the days of the dancing babies and funny cat videos that became popular on YouTube circa 2006. Initially thought of as the most sought-after form of marketing, it is inexpensive and very efficient and rapidly disseminated across social media channels (hence the word "viral"). Viral marketing is not something to depend on, but is now becoming much closer to a "science" and is just another form of "paid media." Emotions are at the root of viral marketing, one of the characteristics of viral media is that those who will share it feel strongly about some aspect of the content (or the way the content makes them feel). In fact, the ALS bucket challenge and Wear Yellow for Seth viral campaigns were both able to raise awareness due to their emotional components! Online videos are the easiest form of content to spread (and largely where the term originated in regards to social media). Videos provoking a strong positive response are 30% more likely to be shared.[34] Viral media might as well be "paid media," and in many cases the advertisers pay for the viral. For example, at the 2014 Academy Awards, Ellen's selfie was purported to be worth $1 billion of "earned media" for Samsung, an Academy Awards 2014 sponsor, but was arranged (and paid for) before the Academy Awards took place. Clearly, there is an element of "leveraging opportunity" in generating viral content, but excepting for rare spontaneous accidents, viral media (as a marketing tactic) is anything but spontaneous.[35]

Ellen DeGeneres ✔
@TheEllenShow

⚙ [Following]

If only Bradley's arm was longer. Best photo ever. #oscars

RETWEETS	LIKES	
3,297,555	2,292,379	

10:06 PM - 2 Mar 2014

↩ 221K   ♻ 3.3M   ♥ 2.3M   •••

Figure 2.7 Ellen's selfie at the 2014 Academy Awards.
Source: Twitter.[36]

Social Media Advertising

Four primary objectives for paid branded content on social media sites:

1. Build brand awareness
2. Engage existing customers
3. Increase size of community
4. Drive traffic to an online destination

Facebook Advertising

Advertisers on Facebook can potentially reach more than 1 billion members.

- Facebook ads offer narrow targeting with more than 70 different languages, interactive features, ease of creation, and excellent metrics.
- Facebook has continued to innovate and broaden its ad units and targeting capabilities in and out of Facebook.

Twitter and LinkedIn Ads

Twitter launched promoted tweets or ads that appear as content at the top of a page or timeline in 2010 and attribution targeting in 2014. As Twitter, Facebook, and LinkedIn are all public companies, there has been much pressure to monetize content better via advertising offerings. Within Twitter, for example, advertisers can target Twitter users by 350 narrow interests.[37] However, users can opt out of being targeted by advertisers by changing their profile settings. LinkedIn introduced targeting via specific goals by using direct ads and sponsored listings to target by job title and function, industry or company size, seniority or age, and LinkedIn Group membership. Both Twitter, LinkedIn, and Facebook offer "custom audience" targeting where marketers upload a list of names, accounts, email addresses, phone numbers, and so on, to run ads targeting the people in their customer list, online.

Video Advertising

Marketers can place ads before, during, or after videos on sites such as YouTube and Vimeo. Each ad platform has its own analytics that report on how many views and clicks paid advertising generates for the advertiser. YouTube and Vimeo have their analytics platform for video views; when advertisers use YouTube, reporting is merged. However, unlike Google AdWords and the Google Search Console, YouTube analytics reports are not yet imported into Google Universal Analytics.

- In-stream videos are 15–30 seconds and can be pre-roll, mid-roll, and video takeovers; the videos may also have interactive banners, buttons, branded player skins, and/or in-text video ads.
- Streaming video ads are becoming more prevalent as Facebook and Twitter made it easier to create and share videos on their networks.

Mobile Advertising

eMarketer predicted that mobile ads would reach $2.61 billion in 2012.[38] Attribution remained a problem in 2014, but mobile advertising is acting as a disruptive influence on many business models. Several issues affect the future of mobile ads:

- Wireless bandwidth is currently small, which affects downloads.
- Limited ad-size due to small screens.
- Advertising tracking requires different techniques.
- Many mobile users are opposed to paying for ad time.
- Despite the issues, content-sponsored ads on a mobile device are likely to increase in the future.
- Mobile ads are not as popular as those seen on a TV screen or computer because they often force the viewer to leave the page they are on.

Mobile advertising formats available to marketers include:

- Paid search
- Display ads
- Post-call advertising (a user sees digital ads right after placing a phone call)
- Full-screen takeovers
- Messaging
- Location-based ads
- Video
- Voice
- Apps

There are many audience acquisition tools, but they are not all equally effective. With online ads, most sites offer a limited number of formats for which to create and serve ads on their sites. Marketers can use newer advertising technologies to do precision targeting of an audience, but the accuracy is still questionable.[39] The main issue with interest-based targeting is the purchased third-party data provided by identity brokers have proven to be of uneven quality. However, retargeting does suffer from the same quality issue because the visitor was served the first-party cookie previously when visiting a website and is later targeted by the same site/advertiser. Other acquisition techniques include events, publicity, affiliate, portal, and viral marketing.

Landing Page Optimization

Optimizing landing pages is more commonly called "conversion optimization" to improve the percentage of visitors to the website that becomes sales leads and customers as measured by Web Analytics. In other words, the measures of landing page optimization are usually behavioral and measurable. The concept of "landing pages" implies that a campaign of some kind is running that drives traffic to it (the landing page). Consider that any page of a website could be a page that visitors land on or see when they reach a site, especially in the age of social media and deep linking. On the other hand, most visits to a page of a website will not necessarily be driven by a campaign, so the term "landing page" might not be the best description (unless you want to envision all traffic coming to a website as driven by some campaign, clearly stated or not).[40] Much of what marketers look for in landing page optimization (LPO) is clear metrics like conversion rate, and every one of the metrics cited above is measurable via Web Analytics. Finding the right metrics to measure the performance of landing pages depends on the goals of the campaign(s) that are driving visitors to the landing page along with the type of business running the campaign.

Qualitative Considerations about Landing Pages

The content owner or stakeholder of a landing page should consider what is going to help the page draw attention from desired Web visitors. Landing pages should include the following elements:

- value propositions
- calls to action (can be determined via analytics)
- demographics (can be determined via analytics, although the intended audience demographics may not be as easy to learn if it is not stated on the Web or by the business owner)
- intended purpose of the landing page

Optimizing Landing Pages with Testing

Define the goals and targeting for a landing page including the audience segment, possible improvements, changes, and desired outcomes.

- Set up analytics tracking that includes statistics, data and designated metrics that will be used to evaluate the effectiveness of the landing page(s) for the purposes or goals it serves.
- Many marketers also run paid advertising tests on their pages, mostly to check Web copy and headlines, along with calls to action. The idea here is to fail fast and furiously to get at optimal campaign settings and landing pages sooner.

Use "on page"/"on-site" metrics to monitor in Web Analytics:

- Time on site
- Pages per visit
- % new visitors
- Bounce rate
- Goals
- Revenue
- Exit pages

Visitation metrics to track (referrals):

- Location
- Device
- Browser/OS
- Domain/provider

Typical goal setup (Google Analytics Goals, Adobe Analytics "Conversion Event"):

- % of visits to a landing page that result in a conversion (typically ~2%).
- % of visits to a landing page that lead to capturing a lead (lead generation) (usually ~8%, can vary based on some factors).

However, landing page optimization is not always done consistently or well enough, per eMarketer. LPO has some significant hurdles in implementation that is similar in complexity to Tag Management—but even simple systems like Google's can become complex. The more stringent the testing, the more likely a company will run into issues, such as limited technical resources that are trained or have the time and focus on implementing LPO. Content creation and testing process need to be in alignment—and that is not an easy thing to accomplish (which is why so many organizations fail to do it well). Up to 18% of marketers, per eMarketer, employ LPO consistently and thoroughly (which improves conversion rates and customer experience with the website).[41] The rest of the marketers do not use analytics for landing page optimization because LPO is hard to integrate into existing creative and production processes. A/B testing is one of the easiest LPO operations to set up (multivariate testing is much more challenging, but most organizations do not require it, either—in any case, having enough Web content is necessary for this to be a worthwhile investment of time and energy). Interestingly, A/B testing is one of the most efficient ways to test and improve landing pages, but marketers do not use it as much as they should.[42] A/B testing of landing pages is relatively straightforward; the marketer has two versions of the same page, and the version that rates higher (based on the above metrics) will be selected, whereas marketers will drop the lower ranking page. Multivariate testing (MVT) is a bit more complicated, as it allows marketers to test multiple variables on a webpage. The goal of multivariate testing is to determine which combination of variations performs the best out of all the possible combinations. Whereas A/B testing does not require many visitors to determine which version of the webpage works better with a chosen audience, MVT takes considerably more visits to determine the optimal combination of elements. MVT requires much more skill in setting up, and it also needs more creative content to alternate; there are also several possible combinations of page elements to test. MVT will take longer to execute.

Platform Tools used in Landing Page Optimization and Testing

- Optimizely
- Unbounce
- Google content experiments
- Crazyegg
- Clicktale
- Kampyle
- Ethnio
- Qualroo
- Surveymonkey

We are just skimming the surface here, as there is a lot more that goes into landing page optimization, but most of it includes details in the testing implementation, which is beyond the scope of this textbook.

Connecting the Dots

The SEO Maturity Assessment

Some of the topics we cover in this chapter are the evolution of the Internet, the World Wide Web, and search engines. Ultimately, the development of the Web is impossible for organizations to leverage without search engines.

Evaluating Search Engine Optimization Maturity

Readers who have access to the Search Engine Optimization Maturity Assessment by Demandmetric.com can self-evaluate their own organization's Search Engine Optimization (SEO) maturity. Use the SEO Maturity Assessment to help measure an organization's SEO maturity across four key success drivers:

1. Strategy, Buy-in, & Skills
2. Process Definition, Automation, & Systems
3. Keyword Management
4. Results Reporting & Metrics

Utilizing the Excel Spreadsheet

Download the Digital Analytics for Marketing SEO Maturity Assessment (available from Demandmetrics.com for paid members) and examine the first tab (instructions). Next, fill out the second tab (maturity assessment); this may take up to two hours to complete. When done, an SEO Maturity Index Diamond (radar chart) will be populated along with an SEO Maturity Index tabulated score. Use the radar chart and score to gauge one's SEO maturity; the same assessment can be adapted to gauge other websites, including competitors.

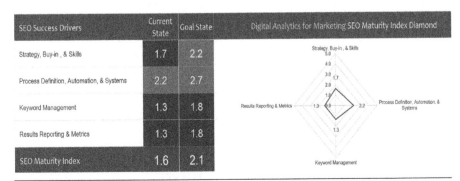

SEO Success Drivers	Current State	Goal State	Digital Analytics for Marketing SEO Maturity Index Diamond
Strategy, Buy-in , & Skills	1.7	2.2	
Process Definition, Automation, & Systems	2.2	2.7	
Keyword Management	1.3	1.8	
Results Reporting & Metrics	1.3	1.8	
SEO Maturity Index	1.6	2.1	

Figure 2.8 Demandmetrics Digital Analytics for Marketing SEO Maturity Assessment.
Source: WebMetricsGuru Inc. and Demandmetrics.com.

Interpretation

Once the assessment is filled out, then consult the results and recommendations tab to gain insight and act on the assessment. Leveraging digital marketing requires an awareness of the technologies as well as an alignment with business processes. Based on the assessment, the organization needs to take concrete steps to develop its business strategy and define its Digital Analytics and SEO initiatives. Take the SEO Maturity Assessment on a periodic basis to observe the changes in strategy and outcomes that result from acting on the assessment and its recommendations.

Summary

In this chapter, we took a deep dive into search engine technologies and how they operate at a functional level for digital marketing.

Review Questions

1. What does the acronym "SEO" stand for?
2. What is the difference between paid search and organic search?
3. What are the two aspects of search engine analytics?
4. What is the function of a search engine?
5. Explain different types of search engines.
6. Differentiate between local and global search engines.
7. What is search engine analytics?
8. Explain the two main categories of search engine analytics.
9. What is the purpose of Search Engine Optimization?
10. What is the purpose of search engine trend analysis?

Chapter 2 Citations

1. "What is search engine optimization: SEO?" Utku Köse and Nursel Yalçın. www.academia.edu/521384/What_is_search_engine_optimization_SEO. Accessed April 15, 2017.
2. "The impact of webpage content characteristics on webpage visibility in search engine results (part I)". ACM Digital Library. May 1, 2005. http://dl.acm.org/citation.cfm?id=1063282. Accessed April 15, 2017.
3. "What is search engine optimization: SEO?" Utku Köse and Nursel Yalçın. www.academia.edu/521384/What_is_search_engine_optimization_SEO. Accessed April 15, 2017.
4. Pan, B. (2015). The power of search engine ranking for tourist destinations. *Tourism Management* 47: 79–87.
5. "Does social influence work?" Krannert School of Management. www.krannert.purdue.edu/faculty/kkarthik/wise12/papers/wise12_submission_143.pdf. Accessed April 15, 2017.

6. "A new click through rate study for Google organic results." October 1, 2014. http://marketingland.com/new-click-rate-study-google-organic-results-102149. Accessed April 15, 2017.

7. "In Google we trust: Users' decisions on rank, position, and relevance." http://onlinelibrary.wiley.com/doi/10.1111/j.1083–6101.2007.00351.x/full. Accessed April 15, 2017.

8. "Comparative analysis of homepage website visibility and academic rankings for UK universities." December 4, 2013. www.informationr.net/ir/18–4/paper599.html. Accessed April 15, 2017.

9. "Quantifying trading behavior in financial markets using Google Trends." April 25, 2013. www.nature.com/articles/srep01684. Accessed April 15, 2017.

10. "Detecting influenza epidemics using search engine query data." November 19, 2008. www.nature.com/articles/nature07634. Accessed April 15, 2017.

11. "Detecting influenza epidemics using search engine query data." November 19, 2008. www.nature.com/articles/nature07634. Accessed April 15, 2017.

12. "SEO Basics: What is a title tag and why is it important?" InsideView Blog. August 19, 2010. https://blog.insideview.com/2010/08/19/what-is-a-title-tag. Accessed April 15, 2017.

13. "How to write a header tag (h1) for SEO." Pear Analytics. http://pearanalytics.com/blog/2014/how-to-write-a-header-tag-h1-for-seo. Accessed April 15, 2017.

14. "WebAIM: 'Skip Navigation' Links." October 25, 2013. http://webaim.org/techniques/skipnav. Accessed April 15, 2017.

15. "What is alt text (alternative text)? Definition from WhatIs.com." http://whatis.techtarget.com/definition/alt-text-alternative-text. Accessed April 15, 2017.

16. "Anchor text—learn SEO." Moz. https://moz.com/learn/seo/anchor-text. Accessed April 15, 2017.

17. "Sign in—Google Accounts." https://cse.google.com/cse/all. Accessed April 15, 2017.

18. "Free site search engines." April 11, 2015, www.thefreecountry.com/scripthosting/searchengines.shtml. Accessed April 15, 2017.

19. "Webmaster tools." Google. www.google.com/webmasters/tools/dashboard. Accessed April 15, 2017.

20. "3.1 Set up your search console account." Google Help. https://support.google.com/webmasters/answer/6001104?hl=en. Accessed April 15, 2017.

21. "List of enterprise search vendors." Wikipedia. https://en.wikipedia.org/wiki/List_of_enterprise_search_vendors. Accessed April 15, 2017.

22. "Weekly infographic: Google algorithm updates from 2003 to 2015!" PageTraffic Buzz. September 4, 2015. www.pagetrafficbuzz.com/google-algorithm-updates-2003–2015/21359. Accessed April 15, 2017.

23. "Matt Cutts on how Google tests its algorithms." Search Engine Watch. April 3, 2014. https://searchenginewatch.com/sew/news/2337829/matt-cutts-on-how-google-tests-its-algorithms. Accessed April 15, 2017.

24. "The fundamental guide to SEO in 2016." Forbes. November 10, 2015. www.forbes.com/sites/jaysondemers/2015/11/10/the-fundamental-guide-to-seo-in-2016. Accessed April 15, 2017.

25. "Global ad spending growth to double this year." eMarketer. July 9, 2014. www.emarketer.com/Article/Global-Ad-Spending-Growth-Double-This-Year/1010997. Accessed April 15, 2017.

26. "Algorithms—inside search." Google. www.google.com/insidesearch/howsearchworks/algorithms.html. Accessed April 15, 2017.

27. "Average click-through rate (CTR): Learn how your average CTR compares." www.wordstream.com/average-ctr. Accessed April 15, 2017.

28. "Why has Baidu, rather than Google, succeeded in China?" Quora. www.quora.com/Why-has-Baidu-rather-than-Google-succeeded-in-China. Accessed April 15, 2017.

29. "Alexa—top sites by category: Arts/design/interior design." www.alexa.com/topsites/category/Arts/Design/Interior_Design. Accessed April 15, 2017.

30. "Alexa—top sites by category: Arts/design/interior design." www.alexa.com/topsites/category/Arts/Design/Interior_Design. Accessed April 15, 2017.

31. "Display Advertising Guide." IAB UK. www.iabuk.net/disciplines/display-advertising/guide. Accessed April 15, 2017.

32. "Study: Display ads drive search clicks after two weeks." January 22, 2014, http://searchengineland.com/study-display-ads-have-delayed-impact-on-search-182320. Accessed April 15, 2017.

33. "Display advertising impact: Search lift and social influence." http://ilpubs.stanford.edu/993/2/displayadinfluenceTR.pdf. Accessed April 15, 2017.

34. "*Viral Marketing: The Science of Sharing* (9780195527988)." www.amazon.com/Viral-Marketing-Science-Karen-Nelson-Field/dp/0195527984. Accessed April 15, 2017.

35. "Samsung won $1b in earned media from Ellen's selfie." Odwyerpr.com. April 9, 2014. www.odwyerpr.com/story/public/2220/2014–04–09/samsung-won-1b-earned-media-from-ellens-selfie.html. Accessed April 15, 2017.

36. "Ellen DeGeneres on Twitter." https://twitter.com/theellenshow/status/440322224407314432. Accessed April 15, 2017.

37. "The AdStage blog: Twitter targeting tactics that get results." November 5, 2015. http://blog.adstage.io/2015/11/05/twitter-targeting-tactics-that-get-results-2. Accessed April 15, 2017.

38. "New forecast: US mobile ad spending soars past expectations." eMarketer. January 5, 2012. www.emarketer.com/newsroom/index.php/forecast-mobile-ad-spending-soars-expectations. Accessed April 15, 2017.

39. "Predictably inaccurate: Big data brokers." November 18, 2014. www.linkedin.com/pulse/20141118145642–24928192-predictably-inaccurate-big-data-brokers. Accessed April 15, 2017.

40. "The anatomy of a perfect landing page." Kissmetrics. https://blog.kissmetrics.com/landing-page-design-infographic/. Accessed April 15, 2017.

41. "How can marketers improve landing page optimization?" eMarketer. April 23, 2015. www.emarketer.com/Article/How-Marketers-Improve-Landing-Page-Optimization/1012390. Accessed April 15, 2017.

42. "How to test your landing pages #infographic." Visualistan. March 16, 2015. www.visualistan.com/2015/03/how-to-test-your-landing-pages.html. Accessed April 15, 2017.

Social Media History

There are countless stories related to the role of social media in contemporary society. For example, in the entertainment industry, a Korean, pop performer Park Jae-sang who goes by the pseudo name of Psy made his claim to worldwide fame through the spread of his "Gangnam Style" on YouTube video.[1] The effect of his catchy beats and relentless chorus allowed a unknown genre to reach our Top 40 stations and expose K-pop to the masses. Yet, not all viral media is upbeat and light-hearted, the political uprising commonly called the "Arab Spring" took place due to the use of social media.[2] From the Arab Spring, the world experienced an uprising over a highly controversial issue through what was later called the "Twitter Revolution" or "Facebook Revolution." Protestors took to social media to share their experiences, plan demonstrations and protests, and voice their opinion during political turmoil. Modern technology facilitated the conversation among them as a collaborative think tank to help paint the political atmosphere and create a united front for the people.

Through these examples, we see how malleable social media is to the needs of the population, whether it is political or entertaining by nature. Since social media is reliant on the content generated by users, users are encouraged to share their interests, passion, and insights within social media. With posts from specific users, marketers can peer into consumer behavior at an individual or group level, but they are not limited to passive research. When users are engaged, marketers can use these connections to build and collaborate with the users on subjects they are passionate about. The use of social media and the impact of its diffusion in contemporary society have reached epic proportions. Billions of people flock to social media platforms such as Facebook, Twitter, and YouTube, where they share, tweet, like, and post content. Social media analytics is based on the underlying tools, measures, and technologies of a social media platform. To begin the

Table 3.1 Share of digital media time by platform from comScore Media Matrix.

Total Time Spent Per Day on Media (Average)	2010	2018	%Change
Desktop/laptop	22%	17%	−20%
Magazines	3%	2%	−54%
Mobile (nonvoice)	4%	28%	666%
Mobile video	0%	9%	1939%
Newspapers	5%	2%	−63%
Print	8%	3%	−59%
Radio	15%	12%	−22%
Smartphones	2%	17%	1039%
Tablets	0%	11%	N/A
TV	41%	32%	−22%

Source: WebMetricsGuru Inc.

discussion of social media analytics, we will examine past technological trends as our foundation.

For instance, society has shifted from viewing smartphones as a luxury to owning them being the new standard of living. Consequently, mobile Internet usage has grown to make up 65% of all digital media time spent.[3] Mobile apps dominate due to the rapid growth of iOS and Android mobile devices. By replacing the personal computer with a smartphone, a user had the freedom to document what is happening around them and share it in real-time. Beyond devices, the evolution of deep learning systems opens new capabilities for content creators and social media users. Stanford University and Google researchers are building neural networks or computer systems that function like the human brain. The neural nets are used to analyze footage from live webcams and mobile camera devices (refer to Chapter 10 for more details). Deep learning systems are powered by text and image-based algorithms and used to curate our social media news feeds. In layman's terms, while using social media, the platform learns and adapts to what users post, watch, or like, and provides additional content, advertisements, people to follow, or content that the platform believes will appeal to the individual.

Social Media and Web 2.0

Built on the Web 2.0 philosophy (i.e., to give more control to the user over the content), social media can be defined as an Internet-based platform with capabilities to allow users to upload text, videos, audio, and graphics. Social media and Web 2.0 are often used interchangeably, but they can be slightly differentiated by their "back to the roots of the Web" or "forward-looking, futuristic" direction.[4]

Core Characteristics of Social Media

The best way to understand social media is through the core features that set it apart from other forms of communication.

Peer-To-Peer

Social media enables interaction among the users in a peer-to-peer fashion, unlike conventional media such as print, radio, telephone, and television that use a top-down, broadcast communications model. The effect of a peer-to-peer medium is the exchange is provided to all users so that every voice has a platform.

Participatory

Unlike conventional technologies, social media enables and encourages users to participate in it and provide feedback. Users can engage in online discourse through blogging, commenting, tagging, and sharing content, etc.

User-Generated Content

Users generate social media content that is published on various social media platforms.

Conversational

People can freely express their views and opinions on an equal footing in social media due to its built-in peer-to-peer conversation capabilities. Conversations often take place between celebrities, politicians, companies, and individuals in real time. The peer-to-peer conversation characteristics of social media make it possible for members to communicate and collaborate in real time, regardless of their location, wealth, occupation, or beliefs.

Relationship Oriented

Most social media tools allow users to establish and maintain social and professional relationships easily. For instance, LinkedIn members can leverage their profile page to forge new business relationships and expand their professional connections. Facebook page administrators can use their pages to gain traffic and spread the word about their personal or business project. As the same time, users can share what is going on or how they feel.

Social Media Timeline and Brief History

Social media is not limited to the most common platforms, such as Facebook, Twitter, YouTube, and blogs. In this book we consider social media to be any online platform (proprietary or purpose built, public or private) that enables users to participate, collaborate, create, and share content in a many-to-many context.

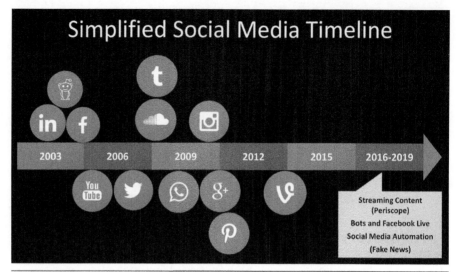

Figure 3.1 Social media timeline.
Source: WebMetricsGuru Inc.

Social media platforms began to emerge around 2004, and specialized analytics platforms to examine social media began to appear around the same time (covered in detail in Chapter 9). Because social media platforms were just coming into existence, there was a small audience using these platforms initially. Since then, there has been a steady rise in adoption, and now most people who are online have at least one social media account.

Blogs

Blogs are one of the first forms of social media that evolved; the first blogs appeared in the early 1990s and became popular after the turn of the century. Blogs quickly became the choice channel for reputation and brand-building. A blog is a type of online personal space or website where an individual (or organization) posts content (text, images, videos, and links to other sites) and expresses opinions on matters of personal (or organizational) interest on a regular basis. Many blogs may have a theme that interests its followers. Common types of blogs focus on travel, cooking, fashion, art, music, parenting, etc. Businesses may also have blogs to cater to their consumers. For example, the clothing brand Free People (see www.freepeople.com for more information about this fashion brand) is considered a lifestyle blog and provides interesting content on design, activities, and travel spots that its free-spirited readers would enjoy visiting. The most popular blogging platforms are WordPress, Tumblr, and Blogger. Blogging does not require technical know-how or programming skills. Ordinary users can easily build and manage a professional-looking blog (technological aspects of blogging are covered in greater detail in Chapter 9).

WordPress

WordPress was founded in 2003 as a self-hosted blogging tool. It is powered by open-source software and independently owned, unlike Tumblr and Blogger (owned by Yahoo and Google, respectively). WordPress is the platform of choice for many popular online magazines, such as Quartz, The New Yorker, and Time. com.[5] WordPress uses various software modularized platforms created by open-source developers (called plugins) to provide a steady stream of new services. Matt Mullenweg is the founder of WordPress. His purpose for WordPress was to democratize and monetize online publishing for content creators and blog authors.[6] He designed WordPress as a blog tool that would alleviate work for content creators while still providing quality content to readers. His philosophy focused on finding the right ratio between time spent reading blog content versus time spent creating the content. The widespread use of blog posts allowed the masses to create and create more easily content and ideas to be read and shared.

Tumblr

David Karp,[7] the founder of Tumblr, created a platform that made it easy for creative people like him to post anything, easily. Karp was not satisfied with the blog alternatives available in the 2004–2006 timeframe. He believed that other blog platforms were built to service publishers or to replace websites. Thus, Tumblr became the most lightweight cousin of the other platforms such as WordPress and Movable Type, an advantage for creative artists to post their thoughts and images. Tumblr created its first "Artist in Residence" program to encourage the use of Tumblr for creativity as a differentiation point.[8] Tumblr imitated some of the features of other social media platforms such as Twitter. Like Twitter, Tumblr has a version of the retweet called a "reblog." Tumblr gained a noticeable following, and in December 2014 was named the Fastest Growing Social Media Platform,[9] even though Yahoo acquired Tumblr in 2013.[10] Tumblr's audience used the platform for years without advertisements and disapproved of Yahoo's introduction of paid advertising, which created issues for all accounts.[11] The future for Tumblr is unclear since Verizon acquired Yahoo in 2016.[12]

Tumblr's Advertising Miss

In November 2016, Yahoo introduced a profit-sharing program with Tumblr bloggers.[13] The program suffered, and many Tumblr users expressed discontentment and shied away from the advertisements. One of the reasons that Yahoo failed to reap a return on their investment is that Tumblr's audience is composed mostly of millennials (who are predisposed to be distrustful of most advertising). Besides, millennials are hard to target with online advertising and avoid websites and applications that use excessive advertising on their sites.[14]

YouTube

The introduction of YouTube marks the beginning of the viral video era. While other video sites, such as Facebook, are quickly gaining market share, nothing comes even close to YouTube in the sheer size of the audience, because it shares the same data as the owner, Google. YouTube users have an advantage because they can use its shared links to convert video posted on YouTube into mp3 format and store it on their smartphones. YouTube is a video-sharing website on which users can upload, view, and share videos. It was created in February 2005 and has been owned by Google since late 2006. YouTube eliminated the need for recording on VCR, CD, DVR devices, and Cable TV networks. It is the third most visited website on the Internet. YouTube users watched more than 7 billion hours of video every month in 2015. Due to its popularity, it is the second largest search engine, next to Google. In 2016, YouTube introduced YouTube Red, a paid-for subscription service. YouTube Red eliminates the advertisements that distract from its videos and introduced YouTube Red originals.

Three former PayPal employees and coworkers of Elon Musk created YouTube: Chad Hurley, Steve Chen, and Jawed Karim. It originated as a new online dating site called "Tune in Hook Up."[15] While online dating videos failed, the technology and interface fit a marketing need to share content. The service was renamed YouTube and acquired by Google in 2006. The world of online video has changed dramatically. Five years ago, YouTube was receiving 3 billion video views per day. YouTube provided its users with the first 720p HD video, which was new to the mass-market handheld device world. Users quickly latched on to the HD user-generated revolution. In 2015, users were recording and uploading 4k videos from their smartphones[16] (note: 4k is the resolution standard designed for digital cinema and computer graphics). The increasing sophistication of devices, coupled with more powerful and inexpensive software, allows anyone to become an accomplished content creator. The content creator's world continues to expand with the introduction of streaming live video. Mobile device users can now broadcast a live video stream of their choosing, for free with Twitter's Periscope, Amazon's Twitch, and Facebook Live. A marketer has options to track the performance of live-streamed video. For example, with Twitter Periscope live video streaming, marketers can track their success using analytics platforms, such as Keyhole, or by creating their own using the Twitter API.[17]

YouTube for Business

An important feature of YouTube is the YouTube channel. A YouTube channel is an online public space (or page) on YouTube. A YouTube channel allows channel owners to upload videos, leave comments, or make playlists. Businesses from around the world use their YouTube channels in a variety of ways such as advertising their products and services, educating customers, posting training materials, etc. YouTube is a great advertising channel and offers a variety of ad types and formats. Marketers utilize YouTube influencers by sponsoring these users and using their network of subscribers.

Twitter (Microblogging)

Twitter is an online microblogging service that allows users to post and read short messages called "tweets." A tweet is a text message limited to 140 characters. In fact, microblogging is a miniature version of blogging that allows users to exchange and publish brief messages, including text, images, or links to other websites.

Jack Dorsey, a well-known entrepreneur, was one of the original founders of Twitter and is the CEO of Twitter and a point-of-sale platform called Square. Dorsey was an undergraduate student at New York University, where he introduced the idea of an individual using an SMS service to communicate with a small group. The tipping point for Twitter's popularity was the 2007 South by Southwest Interactive (SXSWi) conference. During the event, Twitter usage increased from 20,000 tweets per day to 60,000, with hundreds of conference-goers keeping tabs on each other via constant tweets. Panelists and speakers mentioned the service, and the bloggers in attendance touted it. Over time the business world has adopted Twitter as a marketing communications channel: only 20 of the Fortune 500 companies engage with their customers on Facebook, while 83% have a presence on Twitter. It remains a favored means of communications for business,[18] news,[19] and politics,[20] but Twitter's future as an independent social media channel is uncertain.[21]

Fundamentals of Twitter

- **Followers:** Followers are people who follow a user on Twitter. If another user follows someone, it means that:

  - Another user will show up in that person's follower list.
  - Another user will see that person's tweets in his or her timeline whenever he or she logs in to Twitter.
  - The person can send the other user direct messages—although there is an option to send direct messages to anyone based on the receiver's account settings.

- **Following:** A follow on Twitter is a subscription to an account. Those tweets will appear on the follower's Twitter feed. Following another on Twitter means:

  - A user is subscribing to another user's tweets indefinitely.
  - Another user's updates, retweets, and favorites will appear in the home tab.
  - Another user can send the user direct messages.
  - Private accounts must provide their permission to be followed.

- **Tweet:** A tweet is a 140-character message. It can include a video, picture or link.
- **Retweet (RT):** A retweet is a repost of someone else's tweet. One way to gauge the popularity of tweets is by measuring retweets. Popular tweets can get many retweets, and several celebrities are paid for their tweets.[22] It is important to note that only the tweets from public accounts can be retweeted.

One of the objectives of a Twitter user should be to increase their followers. Research suggests that the number of followers and following strongly correlated, meaning that people who follow Twitter accounts more often end up getting more followers, and vice-versa.

Direct Messages

Unlike a tweet, which is public and seen by everyone, a direct message is a private message seen only by the sender and the recipient. However, a direct message can only be sent to followers unless the recipient has updated their account settings.

Mention

When another user includes a username preceded by the @ symbol in a tweet, it is called a "mention." The mentions tab on the notifications page collects tweets that mention a user by his or her username so he or she can keep track of conversations others have about him or her. Some mentions are an indication of influence or popularity.

Hashtags

The hashtag (#) symbol is used to mark and categorize keywords or topics in a tweet. Twitter shows trending hashtags in the left navigation of a member's Twitter page. Trends can be tailored based on algorithms that measure the activities of those accounts that the user is following, or can be manually set to a locality, such as New York City. In short, trends can be adjusted to focus on local or global activities. Hashtags are used on Twitter, Facebook, and Instagram. Hashtags knit loose structures into social media interactions and allow public conversations around the subject that can be decoded and gleaned for insights on public sentiment. For instance, the Twitter hashtag #WikiLeaks can be clicked on to see commentary on the subject. Analytics, such as Tweet Archivist, examine the statistics around the hashtag.[23]

Using Twitter for Business Purposes

Twitter is a thought-sharing website, but not every business can thrive there. Certain verticals, such as real estate, would be better off focusing on more visual media-sharing sites, such as Facebook or Instagram. Twitter users can use tweets, sponsored tweets, and right-hand rail ads to communicate to customers and potential audiences.

Facebook

Founded in 2004 by Mark Zuckerberg, Facebook is an online social network service where users can create profiles, upload photos, and video, send messages and keep in touch with family, friends, and colleagues. As of October 2016, Facebook has more than 1.8 billion registered users.[24] Apart from its primary function as an online social network site, Facebook has become an important marketing and outreach channel for all sorts of organizations including governments. Also, Facebook groups and Facebook events can advertise business events.

Facebook Pages

Any business can benefit from having a Facebook page, where page administrators can build audience, and target followers using Facebook advertising. However, Facebook pages have many rules, regulations, and laws surrounding their use for businesses.

Facebook Messenger

Facebook Messenger is a mobile application created for friends and family to communicate and is also an innovative tool for shopping, marketing, productivity, and personal improvement. Facebook Messenger uses "bots" to automate messaging. Bots and social media seem like they should be polar opposites, but with half of humanity using social media, it may serve to create a necessary counterbalance to the massive amount of online communications, as well as a scaling mechanism for twenty-first century digital marketing.[25]

Bots have the following capabilities:

1. Send and receive API text, image, and rich bubbles with call-to-action statements.
2. Use generic message templates.
3. Create welcome screens and "get started" buttons.

Bots exist for many business types and categories. To fully understand the power of Facebook bots, a marketer should experiment with them. Common bots include Babun (for startups—http://babun.github.io), Growthbot (for marketing and sales—https://growthbot.org), Surveybot (for creating surveys on Facebook—https://surveybot.io), and Kukie (recommends free tools).[26] Facebook page administrators can also make use of Facebook Live. Facebook Live includes live video scheduling, scheduled broadcast sharing, and pre-broadcast lobbies to verified pages (for more information, see https://techcrunch.com/2016/10/18/facebook-live-unlocks-scheduling-and-pre-stream-lobby-first-for-verified-pages). By scheduling a broadcast, viewers get a one-time notification in their news feed reminding them that the stream is starting. Page administrators can write an announcement post for the scheduled broadcast and publish the announcement to the news feed.[27]

Reddit

Founded in 2005 by UVA roommates Alexis Ohanian and Steve Huffman, Reddit has become a major entertainment, news, and social networking website where community members can submit their content and share other content, like an online bulletin board system. In 2014, Reddit became the "respectable" online venue for brand conversations, due to the community's honesty and marketers' need for authentic conversations around brands.[28] Reddit.com is a combination of hundreds of "forums" that are each centered on certain topics (i.e., sports teams, funny videos, and movies).

Reddit's unique contribution to social media is the invention of the "SubReddit," which acts as a bulletin board around a subject and can include collaborative efforts (covered in more detail in Chapter 9). In each forum, which is dubbed a "SubReddit," users can submit his or her content (i.e., photos, video, direct text) or share content (i.e., website articles). Registered Reddit users can vote on any submission, which alters its ranking on the SubReddit. The more positive votes a submission gets, the higher up on the SubReddit it is. If a submission from a SubReddit gets a lot of net positive votes (positive votes minus negative votes), then it may end up on the "front page" of Reddit, which shows all the top submissions from across all its various SubReddits.

Yelp

Yelp was founded in 2004 as a restaurant and retail review site; it grew quickly and went public in 2011. Yelp revenues come from businesses advertising. By 2010 Yelp had published more than 4.5 million user-generated reviews. At the same time, Yelp expanded throughout Europe and Asia; in 2016, Yelp.com had 135 million monthly visitors and 95 million reviews. By using Yelp, a member can rate restaurants, stores, or an activity, on a scale of one to five and can also include pictures and comments with the ratings.

Snapchat

Snapchat is one of the newest social media platforms catering for the younger generation where it "snaps" their day, what they are doing, and more. Snapchat has become one of the top three social media platforms, especially for millennials, who favor it over all others.[29] Founded in 2011, Snapchat's founder, Evan Spiegel, came up with the idea for the platform while attending a class at Stanford; he wanted an easier way to communicate with his friends than the other social platforms offered. With Snapchat, photos sent to individuals are intended to last up to ten seconds depending on the sender. Snapchat Stories are a feature of Snapchat that allow users to post multiple pictures to their "My Story" feed. The My Story feed is intended for friends or everyone to see, depending on a member's settings. A year after launching, Facebook unsuccessfully tried to buy Snapchat for $3 billion.

Snapchat gained popularity by adding filters, geo-filters, and chat sessions to enhance the user experience. A chat section is like live video chatting. Snapchat has "live stories" to allow users to view people's stories from around the world. Many organizations are paying Snapchat for personalized filters. For example, RayBans, a well-known brand of sunglasses, has a filter where Snapchat users could appear to be wearing a pair of sunglasses. Other types of filters, such as fun filters, allow a person to appear as a dog or have a flower crown. Filters enhance the Snapchat experience and indicate why the platform has become so popular for millennials. Users can save the pictures they take with the fun filters, and share them on other social media sites like Twitter, Instagram, and Facebook, increasing the audience for their posts. With the gaining popularity, Snapchat is leveraging their features into new and innovative marketing strategies for organizations. Consequently, due to the popularity of these newer Snapchat features, most have been extensively copied by Facebook and Instagram, recently.

Viral Media

Viral media has changed over time, and the dynamics of which content will go "viral" is constantly evolving (examined in more detail in Chapter 9). The rise of viral media has fundamentally redefined the way information is spread and consumed. If a marketer wants his or her content to be shared or "go viral," they should target like-minded individuals, along with their family and friends.

Influence

Influence and influencers are marketing concepts established when Gabriel Tarde who wrote his book, *L'opinion et la foule*, in 1898.[30] Tarde said that there was a full cycle to conversations like the news. This meant that individuals who knew information, would talk about it with others, and sway public opinion through their charisma. In 1944, sociologist Paul Lazarsfeld published his seminal book, *The People's Choice*, which examined the 1940 presidential election and the factors that shaped voter behavior and action in Ohio.[31] Until this study, the media was viewed as a magic bullet, able to directly sway the mass population very effectively. In fact, during the Second World War, this theory was put to work in various governmental propaganda efforts. In contrast, however, *The People's Choice* discussed a two-step flow of information from the media to the masses. In Lazarsfeld's theory, "opinion leaders" were directly involved in the dissemination of information and distribution of that information to the masses. These opinion leaders read what the media said and then repeated it via conversations to their followers—not unlike what occurs in social media today. Publishers and marketing professionals had a keen interest in forming relationships with influencers after realizing the economic benefits of these friendships. Influencers are further discussed in Chapter 9.

LinkedIn

LinkedIn is a social media platform for professionals to network with each other and is also used as a recruiting tool for many large companies. LinkedIn has more than

400 million members, and its membership seems to be growing at ~100 million new users each year. LinkedIn created an infographic of its history spanning 2003 through 2017.[32] In June 2016, Microsoft acquired LinkedIn for $26 billion; but it is too early to determine the impact of the Microsoft acquisition on LinkedIn.[33]

Search Engine Optimization

Search Engine Optimization (SEO) developed during the first half of the 1990s. Once websites were easily created, they began to proliferate rapidly, consisting of text content and links to and from other websites. Soon, websites and texts accumulated at such a high rate that it became hard to find relevant information. The first search engines used "text analytics," "semantic analysis," and a rudimentary form of backlink analysis to determine what pages and websites to show at the top of search results. SEO studies how people use search engines and how to improve websites. Determining the right keywords to use is one of the most challenging aspects of SEO.

Visual Social Media (Instagram and VSCO)

Visual social media platforms serve various purposes and are included here because of their focus on media sharing. Instagram is a mobile photo-sharing app and social network created in 2010. It provides easy upload service, which allows instant feedback from the community of users. Instagram has a crowd-sourced, self-maintaining feedback loop built into the platform that curates creativity and interest for an individual. Initially, Facebook feared Instagram, due to its dominance in the photo-uploading service. In 2012, to combat competition, Facebook bought Instagram for $1 billion. VSCO is a new shooting and editing photo app. Many of its users edit the photo before uploading it to Instagram or other social networks, but it has developed into a photo-sharing service for those keen on photography.

Social Networking Sites

Social networking sites or services (SNS) are social media platforms that are focused on online social relationships among users. Some examples of SNS include Facebook, Google+, etc. SNS allow users to build and maintain social relationships among people who share interests, activities, backgrounds, or real-life connections.

Most SNS allow users to:

- Construct a public or semipublic profile
- Establish links (friendship) and relationships with other SNS users
- View and converse with their list of connections and those made by others within the network.[34]

In addition to its public version, Facebook recently released a business social networking site, "Facebook at Work," aimed at cooperating users and allowing them to create social networks and collaborate.

Content Communities

Content communities, such as YouTube and Flickr, are defined as "a group of people coalescing online around a common activity or interest. The object can be about anything, for example, photos, videos, links, topic or issue, and is often organized and developed in a way that either includes social network elements or makes them central to the content."[35] The most popular content community site is YouTube.

Online Collaborative Projects (Wikis)

Online collaborative projects or tools allow people to plan, coordinate, add, control and monitor content in collaboration with others. At the core of the online collaborative projects is the concept of wiki. A wiki is a type online content management system that allows users to add, modify, or delete content simultaneously in collaboration with others. Famous examples of wiki-based platforms are Wikipedia and Wiki-spaces. Ward Cunningham conceived the concept of the wiki.

Using Wikis for Business Purposes
Wikis are an excellent way to communicate and collaboratively work on projects with other people. A very good example of a collaborative wiki is www.wikipedia.com. Wikipedia has more than 30 million articles in 287 languages written collaboratively by volunteers around the world. However, Wikipedia is just one type of website built on the wiki model. There are several other notable wikis. Google (www.sites.google.com) provides project wikis that can be configured for business purposes. Wikis are also helpful in SEO or product display websites.

Folksonomies — Tagging

The term folksonomy, also known as social tagging, social indexing, and collaborative tagging, is attributed to Thomas Vander Wal.[36] The phrase is a fusion of the words "folk" and "taxonomy". In simpler words, it is the method of organizing data and content (through tagging) from a user's perspective. For example, del.icio.us, a social bookmarking system, allows users to tag, organize, classify, and share content (web addresses or sites) in their unique ways. Since the Wiki content is tagged with useful keywords, it speeds up searching and finding relevant content.

Virtual Worlds, Augmented Reality and Virtual Reality

Virtual worlds are computer-generated online environments. They can take the form of a three-dimensional (3D) virtual social world (e.g., Second Life) where people digitally represent themselves in the form of avatars and interact with others through text and voice messaging. Or, it can consist of interactive virtual games, such as Minecraft where users do create the virtual world around them.

Virtual reality is another dimension of virtual worlds, where real and virtual are fused together. Virtual reality uses computer software and hardware tools to simulate physical presence the virtual world. Some virtual worlds do not necessarily require computer software, such as *Gaia Online* or *Club Penguin*. Virtual Reality (VR) is part of a technology and lifestyle trend of creating technology that places the humans in a "virtual world," rather than using a character or avatar to represent themselves in cyberspace.

Mobile Apps

Mobile apps are becoming an integral part of our lives. Mobile apps are special-purpose tools developed to perform a variety of activities we do every day while on the move, such as communicating, social networking, sharing information, and shopping. Tinder and Skout, for example, are designed to facilitate social relations, and Viber aims to facilitate communication.

Mobile Apps

Social media is not only limited to the types above, but any online platform, including purposely built mobile apps, that enable us to participate, collaborate, create, and share content in a many-to-many context while using our mobile devices. Content can be anything, including information, audio/video, profiles, photographs, text, etc. Organizations are increasingly creating purpose-built social media apps for collaboration activities. A good example of such a platform is the Enterprise 2.0,[37] which uses social media tools, such as blogs, wikis, and group messaging software to allow employees, suppliers, and customers to network together and share information.

Social Media Takeaways

According to *Wired Magazine*, the average American spends nine hours a day glued to one or more screens creating and/or consuming social media content.[38] Consequently, we will study social media and its analytics in depth in later chapters of this book.

Review Questions

1. What is social media? Moreover, what makes it different from the traditional media?
2. What are some core characteristics of social media?
3. Briefly explain different social media types with examples.
4. Briefly explain how businesses can leverage Facebook, YouTube, Twitter, blogs, and wikis?
5. Differentiate among social media, Web 2.0, and social network sites.

Chapter 3 Citations

1. "Get to know K-Pop Rapper PSY and his viral hit song 'Gangnam Style'." MetroLyrics. September 7, 2012. www.metrolyrics.com/news-story-get-to-know-k-pop-rapper-psy-and-his-viral-hit-song-gangnam-style.html. Accessed April 15, 2017.

2. Brown, F.P. "Twitter's impact on the news and media cycle." February 27, 2013. www.westernjournalism.com/twitters-impact-on-the-news-and-media-cycle. Accessed April 15, 2017.

3. Sterling, G. "All digital growth now coming from mobile usage." comScore. April 4, 2016. http://marketingland.com/digital-growth-now-coming-mobile-usage-comscore-171505. Accessed April 15, 2017.

4. "Social media: back to the roots and back to the future: Michael Haenlein." www.michaelhaenlein.eu/Publications/Kaplan,%20Andreas%20-%20Back%20to%20the%20roots%20and%20back%20to%20the%20future.pdf. Accessed April 15, 2017.

5. "30 top websites & blogs that are powered by WordPress." Colorlib. January 19, 2016. https://colorlib.com/wp/most-popular-websites-powered-by-wordpress. Accessed April 15, 2017.

6. "Matt Mullenweg." Wikipedia. https://en.wikipedia.org/wiki/Matt_Mullenweg. Accessed April 15, 2017.

7. "David Karp." https://en.wikipedia.org/wiki/David_Karp. Accessed April 15, 2017.

8. "David Karp: Why I started Tumblr—founder stories." March 2, 2011. www.youtube.com/watch?v=nbNxvY6nuTs. Accessed April 15, 2017.

9. Southern, M. "Tumblr is now the fastest growing social media platform, edging out Instagram and Pinterest." November 28, 2014. www.searchenginejournal.com/tumblr-now-fastest-growing-social-media-platform-edging-instagram-pinterest/121008. Accessed April 15, 2017.

10. Isidore, C. "Yahoo buys Tumblr in $1.1 billion deal." May 20, 2013. http://money.cnn.com/2013/05/20/technology/yahoo-buys-tumblr. Accessed April 15, 2017.

11. Romano, A. "Tumblr's advertising problem summed up in 1 orange cat." May 22, 2013. www.dailydot.com/business/tumblr-yahoo-native-advertising-problem. Accessed April 15, 2017.

12. Morris, D.Z. "Is getting rid of fake news bad for Facebook's business?" November 20, 2016. http://fortune.com/2016/11/20/facebook-fake-news-business. Accessed April 15, 2017.

13. "Tumblr." July 26, 2016. https://staff.tumblr.com/post/148012671115/money. Accessed April 15, 2017.

14. Lang, M. "Millennials really hate advertising, study finds—here's why." May 5, 2016. www.sfgate.com/business/article/Millennials-really-hate-advertising-study-finds-7393642.php. Accessed April 15, 2017.

15. "YouTube's origin story." *National Geographic*. 28 July, 2016. http://channel.nationalgeographic.com/videos/youtubes-origin-story. Accessed April 15, 2017.

16. Morrison, K. "From YouTube to Periscope: The evolution of web video (infographic)." November 30, 2015. www.adweek.com/socialtimes/from-youtube-to-periscope-the-evolution-of-web-video-infographic/630757. Accessed April 15, 2017.

17. Contrini, M. "How to use the public Periscope stream API.", July 7, 2016. https://medium.com/@matteocontrini/how-to-use-the-public-periscope-stream-api-8dfedc7fe872#.swhpxe6jr. Accessed April 15, 2017.

18. "Consumers will punish brands that fail to respond on Twitter quickly." October 29, 2013. www.lithium.com/company/news-room/press-releases/2013/

consumers-will-punish-brands-that-fail-to-respond-on-twitter-quickly. Accessed April 15, 2017.

19. Brown, F.P. "Twitter's impact on the news and media cycle." February 27, 2013. www.westernjournalism.com/twitters-impact-on-the-news-and-media-cycle. Accessed April 15, 2017.

20. Kapko, M. "Twitter's impact on 2016 presidential election is unmistakable." November 3, 2016. www.cio.com/article/3137513/social-networking/twitters-impact-on-2016-presidential-election-is-unmistakable.html. Accessed April 15, 2017.

21. Adams, P. "What Twitter's uncertain future means for marketers." November 2, 2016. www.marketingdive.com/news/what-twitters-uncertain-future-means-for-marketers/429505. Accessed April 15, 2017.

22. Case, L. "How much do celebrities get paid to tweet?" July 20, 2016. www.wetpaint.com/how-much-do-celebrities-get-paid-to-tweet-663232. Accessed April 15, 2017.

23. www.tweetarchivist.com/79c0cf74/51353. Accessed April 15, 2017.

24. "Number of Facebook users worldwide 2008–2016: Statistic." www.statista.com/statistics/264810/number-of-monthly-active-facebook-users-worldwide. Accessed April 15, 2017.

25. "25 Stellar Facebook chat bots digital marketers must use now." December 27, 2016. https://blog.startafire.com/facebook-bots-digital-marketers/Startafire. Accessed April 15, 2017.

26. "25 Stellar Facebook chat bots digital marketers must use now." December 27, 2016. https://blog.startafire.com/facebook-bots-digital-marketers/Startafire. Accessed April 15, 2017.

27. Constine, J. "Facebook Live unlocks scheduling and pre-stream lobby, first for verified Pages." October 18, 2016. https://techcrunch.com/2016/10/18/facebook-live-unlocks-scheduling-and-pre-stream-lobby-first-for-verified-pages. Accessed April 15, 2017.

28. Ingram, M. "Reddit to brands: You say you want a conversation? Put your money where your mouth is." August 7, 2014. https://gigaom.com/2014/08/07/reddit-to-brands-you-say-you-want-a-conversation-put-your-money-where-your-mouth-is. Accessed April 15, 2017.

29. "U.S. Snapchat users demographics 2016." www.statista.com/statistics/326452/snapchat-age-group-usa. Accessed April 15, 2017.

30. "*L'opinion et la foule*: Tarde, Gabriel de, 1843–1904." July 17, 2008. https://archive.org/details/lopinionetlafoul00tarduoft. Accessed April 15, 2017.

31. "*The People's Choice: How the Voter Makes Up His Mind in a Presidential Campaign.*" Amazon. www.amazon.com/Peoples-Choice-Voter-Presidential-Campaign/dp/0231085834. Accessed April 15, 2017.

32. www.agency2.co.uk/b2b-marketing-evolution-linkedin/.

33. Greene, J. "Microsoft to acquire LinkedIn for $26.2 billion." June 14, 2016. www.wsj.com/articles/microsoft-to-acquire-linkedin-in-deal-valued-at-26–2-billion-1465821523. Accessed April 15, 2017.

34. Boyd, d.m. and Ellison, N.B. (2007) "Social Network Sites: Definition, History, and Scholarship." *Journal of Computer-Mediated Communication* 13(1): 210–230.

35. "Content Communities." Technology in Prevention. http://ww38.
    technologyinprevention.wiki-spaces.com/Content+Communities. Accessed
    April 15, 2017.

36. "Thomas Vander Wal." Wikipedia. https://en.wikipedia.org/wiki/Thomas_Vander_
    Wal. Accessed April 15, 2017.

37. McAfee, A.P. (2006) "Enterprise 2.0: The Dawn of Emergent Collaboration." *MIT
    Sloan Management Review* 47(3): 21–28.

38. Leckhart, S. "Balance your media diet." July 15, 2009. www.wired.com/2009/07/
    by-media-diet. Accessed April 15, 2017.

Digital Analytics Industry Players

The Digital Analytics Ecosystem

This chapter covers the Digital Analytics industry at a very high level. We cannot discuss the Digital Analytics industry without briefly examining the data these platforms produce alongside with how data is acquired and processed.

Three Types of Data

First-Party Data

First-party data focuses on the concepts of ownership, control, and privacy. It is an extension of the types of operational and customer information organizations already collect. It is extremely valuable data for mining consumer insights because it is the relevant information that a marketer has collected from his or her audience. First-party data is collected on past actions taken by consumers, so it is limited to current or past consumers. Examples of first-party data include email lists, customer relationship management, purchasing data stored within in-house databases, data on social media channels, such as Facebook pages, Twitter accounts, LinkedIn company pages, Instagram, Pinterest, and Snapchat. Marketers use first-party data to retarget visitors who came to their websites or are connected on Facebook with display ad campaigns. As more information is extracted from consumers, the content became more personalized and website conversion rates increase.

Second-Party Data

Second-party data is data collected through other organizations, companies, or individuals and shared with other marketers. The marketer may have little or no control of the relevance or depth of the information collected with the second-party data which is being shared with them from their business partners and affiliates. An example of second-party data is seen in banking and credit card agreements. In the small print of most banking and credit card agreements, statements detail the permitted uses of customer data. Among the clauses, there is usually a statement about the information gathered from customer activities and shared with affiliates and business partners. Sometimes, customers can opt out of these second party arrangements, but often they cannot.

Third-Party Data

Third-party data covers the data available to marketers that is aggregated, and sold by market research companies.

Many third-party data companies use predictive modeling via sampling and other statistical methods to prepare their data sets.

Third-Party data provides intelligence that could be used for behavioral and contextual targeting. Ideally, marketers use first-party data in their strategies, but third-party data can supplement the strategy or provide groundwork when first-party data is insufficient.

Stories about Converging First-, Second- and Third-Party Data

Macy's

Suppose a shopper is looking for a new dress shirt. The shopper enters his or her requirements for the shirt into a Google search. The shopper lands on a website, such as Macys.com, and looks for available dress shirts. Through Macy's point of view, they would not have enough information to identify the shopper, but they can recognize their past behavior if the consumer visited the website previously, or suggest styles based on in-house, first-party data previously collected about the customer. However, if Macy's combined third-party data collected by the vendors—i.e., data brokers, demand-side platforms, and data management platforms—with Macy's first-party data collected by Web Analytics, information may converge and provide insights, such as hovering activity on different shirts and shirt colors and point-of-sale (POS) data. Macy gains knowledge of who to prospect to (i.e., demographics and psychographic information) and the other merchandise the individual may be interested in purchasing. It may also use its intelligence to predict time-sensitive purchases and price adjustments for the shopper.

Thus, Macy's can create an engagement strategy that meets the needs of a specific customer, while using the same technologies to handle thousands of customers with similar needs every moment. To include second-party data, this information may be purchased from AMEX and Citibank on credit card activities of Macy's online shoppers. Then, it can be combined with local store POS data to predict what shirts to show a shopper from a specific region, such as Jersey City, New Jersey. Ultimately, Macy's needs partners in the Digital Analytics ecosystem to help it align its internal data with third-party data.

Metropolitan Museum of Art

One of the authors is a frequent museum-goer and is a member of the Metropolitan Museum of Art.[1] The Met (a term the museum is commonly known by) has been trying to figure out who its customers are but falls short of achieving its goal, despite its best efforts. Most of the visitors—83%, based on the co-author's research—are tourists and visit the museum just one time (refer to Chapter 9, Figure 9.3, where other aspects of this case study are covered). However, it becomes problematic to collect sustainable revenues with museum visitors when the suggested museum admission is $25, but visitors can pay whatever they like. The museum wants to know what attracts visitors to come to the museum and what would keep them coming back. Its goal is to convert more visitors into members and better establish loyalty with its audience.

Challenges

Most of the visitors to the Met were paying the $25 MET admission price due to their inexperience with the museum. However, unless they pay with a credit card, the Met will know nothing about its visitors, as it does not collect an email address, mobile phone number, or social media handle, such as a Twitter or Facebook account. So, what can the Met do to find out more about who its customer is, and what they might want from the museum?

Opportunities to Collect Data

There are some things that the Met could do to collect data, but most of these require contracting with outside vendors.

- Each time a museum visitor uses the free Internet that the museum provides, the device ID of the mobile device is collected and saved in application logs of the vendor who maintains the Met's wireless networks. Should the visitor return to the museum, based on the application server logs, it can determine the number of times that device has accessed its network, thereby gaining an understanding of whom the customer is, based on their device (including the ISP, such as Verizon or T-Mobile or Sprint).
- By partnering with the ISPs, the Met could look up the device ID and, perhaps, determine who the customer is (i.e., demographics, clickstream behavior, income bracket, cable viewing habits) via ComScore, Nielsen, and the ISPs who have been selling their anonymized first-party data to clients,[2] and applications that run on the mobile devices. The ISP contains the addressable audience data, a term frequently used with programmatic advertising, connected with the mobile device that was detected at the museum. When the mobile device ISP is the same as the cable/FIOS ISP provider (via the wireless hub in the household that registers all the device IDs in the home that use the Internet), the ISP also captures the data of all wireless connections/devices to the household or business. Other times, the addressable audience can be

determined, somewhat, by third-party data provided by external vendors, such as Simulmedia, who deliver business outcomes for marketers through the power of audience targeted television.

- Visitors to the museum typically take several "selfies" and/or tweet, post, or create videos at the museum, or soon after.[3] Much of this data is public and can be captured on the Internet, along with the locations within 20 feet, in the museum, when the visitor posted the content. The data can be collected into real-time heat maps, showing the most popular parts of the museum along with the most popular times to visit and post at the Met. Furthermore, more than 1% of the total foot traffic to the museum can be collected from platforms such as Picodash.com, Geofeedia.com, Welink.com, along with many others. This data can be matched up with names, addresses, phone numbers, approximate income, to name a few, by external vendors such as Spokeo and Salesforce.com. In fact, many selfies were being taken in the Met's bathrooms, along with a certain number that appeared outside the museum, right on the steps using the hashtags #gossipgirl and #xoxo.
- iBeacons have been set up at the Met, but not in every exhibition (not yet, at least). The Met launched a mobile app a few years back that can be made to work with iBeacons (we discuss Bluetooth technology/iBeacons later in this book) to assist museum goers on the art they are viewing while running the Met app.

The Metropolitan Museum may not collect and align its data to these suggestions—to be fair, hardly anyone does. But, this example shows that through implementation, the MET could derive all the information it would need to get much closer to a full, 360-degree view of their visitors. For more information on data continuity through first-, second-, and third-party data, please refer to the following co-author's Slideshare presentation—Merging Geo Social Data & Web Analytics at the Metropolitan Museum of ART.[4]

Third-Party Data and Analytics

Web Analytics, an example of first-party data, provides data on what is happening in the organization or business website by placing cookies into a visitor's browser. Web Analytics often lacks competitive or industry data outside of the tracked website. Most organizations would like to know how well they are competing in the major areas connected to their business goals and revenue with a few exceptions (see below). Taking competitive analysis information into consideration, Google Analytics provides anonymous benchmark data collected that can be useful to provide some idea of how well a website is performing against others in similar industries and locations. It also provides second- and third-party data from the DoubleClick Ad Network. Other platforms, such as IBM Coremetrics and Adobe Analytics, include industry-wide metrics gathered from customers running the analytics platform. Third-Party audience data from ComScore and Nielsen has been combined with Adobe Analytics in some customer implementations.

Digital Analytics Maturity Model

Several proposed models have been put forward for years as the "right" way to conceptualize the development of this marketing discipline such as the Digital Analytics Maturity Model (see Table 4.1)[5].

Table 4.1 Digital Analytics Maturity Model.

Phase 1 Planning & Research	Phase 2 Web Analytics & KPI Formulation	Phase 3 Behavioral Analytics	Phase 4 Digital Marketing	Phase 5 Enterprise Strategy
Select analytics platform	Visitor acquisition reporting	Funnel/clickstream analysis	E-commerce reporting	Analytics powered content servers
Infrastructure planning	Top level dashboard reporting	Visitor and behavioral segmentation	Automated alerts	Omnichannel marketing
Center for excellence consulting	Entry and exit page reporting	Digital campaign measurement	Visitor tracking via Web Analytics	Enterprise governance and data democratization
Train stakeholder on Web Analytics reporting	Basic reporting for line of business and stakeholders	Search Engine Optimization and Search Engine Marketing	Customer lifetime value optimization	Determining return on investment
Defining requirements for analytics implementation	Customized reporting and instrumentation	Personalized and customized content	Persona generation and scoring models	Participation scoring and activity-based costing
Define and lockdown business goals/objectives	Finalize enterprise dashboards	A/B and MVT Testing	Multi-channel tracking/call tracking	Predictive analytics
Define and lock down KPIs	Set up/configure tag management systems	Social media analytics	Email/CRM/Web Analytics integration	Prescriptive analytics and strategic planning

Source: WebMetricsGuru Inc.

Everything encountered in within Web/data analytics falls into one of these columns and slots.

Third-Party Data Ecosystem

To provide more depth, Table 4.2 introduces the new concepts before going into detail regarding what is necessary to understand and utilize the information.

Table 4.2 Digital data landscape.

Digital Ecosystem		Role
Publishers		Attract visitors to a site by providing relevant content marketing to a target audience. Site owners can monetize their website through selling advertising and providing anonymous user profiles to data brokers.
Data Owners		Have a direct relationship with digital consumers based on their own first-party data, perhaps using third-party data from Acxiom and Experian.
Data Aggregators		Set up and sign deals with publishers and other data providers that allows customized data segmentation and targeting, via advertising.
Data Exchanges		Platform for storing, purchasing and combining first-, second-, and third-party data from multiple sources. Use the combined data for precise targeting and programmatic/retargeting.
Networks		Identify and purchase audience segments as part of a media buy (typically using programmatic advertising/retargeting).

Source: WebMetricsGuru Inc.

Third-Party Data Aggregators—What They Do

1. Aggregate behavioral data of audience members from online publishers, such as the *New York Times*, and Web portals, such as Yahoo, that repackage and resell them to other organizations.
2. Provide data collection scripts for publishers to run on their sites, allowing third-party data aggregators to collect data from publishers and portals as part of an ad network (e.g., Audience Science) or revenue share agreement (e.g., BlueKai).
3. Provide third-party cookie lists for sale to advertisers and agencies that are used for ad targeting. The cookie list is available for bidding within minutes (particularly for in-market audiences) and has a shelf-life of up to two months.

Every third-party data aggregator has their way of combining data—that is why it is better to assemble the data side by side *but not intermix it*, which will degrade data quality. Third-party data collection is similar to an "uncontrolled laboratory" where platform vendors are mixing up their formulations of data, interpretations, and context with no regulation authority to monitor them, and there is no way to cover the cornucopia in any textbook. Rather, we present an experience of connecting the dots using third-party data and leave the cornucopia conundrum to other writers.

> This book provides a combination of digital marketing concepts, definitions, case studies, examples, peer-reviewed research, and exercises or assignments that foster personal observation of data, ideation, and connecting the dots.

As the data can be modeled and interpreted in many ways, it is hard to separate opinion from fact in what vendors want to highlight about their platforms (and for readers to see) versus the business value delivered by the platform. What Big Data offers is the process of separating the collection from the use of it. Collecting data for one purpose can be reused for another (creating "network effects"—much as we have seen in the last decade with certain aspects of social media), looking for patterns, clustering, and correlations in near real-time that we might otherwise miss. However, in the rest of this chapter, it becomes clear that it is almost impossible to take the data out of the data collection platform without losing its context, validity, and exposing all kinds of bias in the collection and data shaping process that usually remain unseen. Perhaps data curation is what we need to be investing time in exploring and limiting our discussion here to a few platforms that are known to be more "reliable." In this book we examine a limited number of data platforms we have used, as authors and practioners, considering their strengths and limitations as representative of the overall first- and third-party data ecosystem. From the information we covered, readers can generalize the insights and apply them across several industry use cases along with a much larger platform collection.[6]

Analytics Platforms vs. Data Integration Software

Combining Digital Analytics with media measurement and attribution has become on of the hottest trends in digital marketing and analytics. According to Gartner, traditional Web Analytics is a mature discipline dominated by a few players such as Adobe, Google, and IBM.[7] The need for much more accurate measurement led to a vast influx of analytical talent moving into marketing departments and led to an evolutionary change in these tools, so they provided what stakeholders needed. Prime examples are Adobe Analytics and Google Analytics. Both are working hard to combine Digital Analytics with media measurement and attribution. One weakness of all the Web Analytics platforms: they are narrowly focused on the presentation layer of the Web that depends on JavaScript. Web Analytics platforms are not adaptive enough to integrate comfortably with a rapidly evolving marketing stack. Case in point, many of the activities that marketers want to measure on websites are not based on a page rendering. Instead, customer behavior is often asynchronous and omni-channel based, in nature, and the JavaScript beacon model is not ideally suited to capture those activities.

Table 4.3 Digital data landscape.

Third-Party Data Providers

	Specialty Compilers for Lifestyle Events	Credit Score, Credit Card Data, Purchase Data	Segmentation Tool Providers for Geodemographics	International Data Providers	Compilers, Demographics and Firmographics	Digital and Web Data aimed at Data Aggregators and Analytics Vendors	Syndicated Research focused on Third-Party Consumer Data	List Management for Direct Marketing and Response Data
First American Core Logic, Home Data		Equifax	Claritas, True Strategic Solutions	Assesso, ABase	Experian	BlueKai	Simmons, Arbitron	Millard Group, Walter Karl Company, Infinite Media
Fidelity Data, Epsilon, iBehavior		Experian	Experian, Acxiom, Equifax	Dataminer, NewDbase	Acxiom	Exelate, Lotame	NPD	Direct Media INC, MeritDirect, Take5
Student Marketing		Transunion	IXI, Nielsen	Bertelsmann, Callcredit	Epsilon, Knowledgebase Publishing	Targus Info	Comscore	BeachList Direct, Noble Ventures, WorldData
Wiland Direct		Visa	Spectra Intelligent Marketing	Veda, Tangram, Infocore	D&B, Compass Marketing Group	Experian and Epsilon	Scarborough Research	MediaSource Solutions, Fasano, The List Experts
Datalogix		American Express		Experian	INFOusa, V12 Group	Datalogix, Comscore, Nielsen, PeekYou	MRI	Edith Roman

Source: WebMetricsGuru INC.

Table 4.4 Web Analytics comparison chart.

Feature	Google Analytics	Adobe Analytics	WebTrends
Cost	Free	Costly	Activity based on pageview usage
Site Limits	Profile (one account can have several profiles)—(rollups are available)	Reporting suite (rollups are available)	Profile/site
Real Time Data	Limited/otherwise 24-hour latency	Most reports have short latency. Calculated metrics are subject to delays in real-time data	Limited
Social and Mobile Tracking	Yes	Yes	Yes
Dashboards	Customizable	Customizable	Customizable
Segmentation	Customizable	Customizable and logic-based/programmable	Customizable
Internal Search, Paid Search and SEO Reporting	Yes	Yes	Yes

Source: WebMetricsGuru Inc.

Adobe provides some benchmarking information on a yearly basis that customers can use to determine how well their websites are performing related to the rest of the industry or category they are in. For most users, the free version of Google Analytics is more than enough. However, many organizations have specific needs that dictate other choices.

Demographics Data

comScore MyMetrix provides a wealth of data on many of the top websites in a region. comScore gains its data through a panel comprising millions of users who agree to run metering software on their Internet-connected devices. Once the data is collected and de-duplicated, it can be applied against official census numbers in a location/geography. comScore publishes an estimation of the actual traffic, behavior, geographic, psychographic, income/gender, and cross-visiting behavior. This third-party information can be valuable to businesses, particularly for advertisers and publishers, who are otherwise unable to gather the data. Other providers of information are similar, but have a different cut or view of the data (and different methods to collect and tabulate it) including Quantcast and SimilarWeb, to name a few. Some of this third-party data is surfacing in newer analytics platforms such as IBM Watson Analytics along with the different marketing clouds from Salesforce, Adobe, Oracle, and IBM.

Types of Web Analytics Roles

Web Analytics requires a diverse set of roles.[8] Web Analysts are involved in interpreting online data aggregated through tools such as Google Analytics, Adobe Analytics, WebTrends and third-party data aggregation platforms such as comScore Media Metrix. Often, content is optimized using A/B and multivariate testing. Web Analytics can be applied to almost any industry and is not unique to any industry. The data analyst needs to know how to interpret and implement the data the abovementioned platforms provide and is expected to create modeling solutions and tactical analysis based on that data.

Analysts should have good domain knowledge along with a detailed business background within specific industries where the analytics are deployed. Analysts often have earned Master's degree in a marketing-related field combined with related work experience (of five years, on average). They should be proficient in Web Analytics, JavaScript, R programming, HTML, data visualization tools, SEO and SEM. Analysts are often employed to monitor, analyze, derive insight and report on specific key performance indicators (KPIs), Return on Investment (ROI), marketing dashboards, A/B and MVT testing, finding and reporting new insights based on data. Common roles include:

- **Data capture (analyst):** Web/data analytics setup, tagging, checking that the data capture is working, ensuring reports inform stakeholders, etc. Usually, someone has 1–2 years of experience, with supervision, can perform this set of tasks.[9] Systems involved with data capture need a lot of custom configuration to be effective.
- **Reporting and forecasting engineer:** Engineers connect industry and company data so they can interpret the data being captured.[10]
- **Business culture consultant:** The consultant gathers information on how the organization functions and how to best improve it by making sense of what the data is saying, and then aligning those insights with defined business goals.
- **Site/content optimization vendor:** Vendors configure the appropriate systems and connect them together.
- **Marketing optimization vendors and analysts:** The analysts configure marketing automation systems such as Marketo or programmatic advertising systems such as MediaMath and Appnexus.

As web/data analytics continues to evolve, the roles above may change.

Web Data Collection Issues

There are some problems with web data collection such as:

- Users in Web Analytics platforms are not identical to people. Users are cookie value (first-party data), and an accurate count of Web users is not the same as actual users—as the same user might be accessing the website through multiple devices (each having its own IP address and cookies). The remedy for this problem is to have users log in to the site, so it is counted accurately, but that is not always possible.[11]

- Web Analytics can no longer capture the variety of traffic produced by the customer's journey.[12] In fact, no single piece of software does it all in one place.
- Meaningful information is hard to isolate due to excessive amounts of generated data (refer to the Metropolitan Museum example earlier in this chapter). It is also tempting to use the wrong key performance indicators, such as likes, shares, and followers, because they are easier to gather than others—which might be better suited but are harder to collect.[13]

  - To reinforce the confusion about which metrics to use, there is no consensus on the right metrics for consumer activities on the Web.[14]

Review Questions

1. What is the difference between first-party data and third-party data?
2. Is there such a thing as a "second-party cookie?"
3. What are the five main elements of the third-party data ecosystem?
4. What are the most common Web Analytics roles?
5. What are the main data collection issues covered in this chapter?

Chapter 4 Citations

1. Sponder, M. "Enrich your data to increase converged analytics effectiveness." November 17, 2014. www.clickz.com/enrich-your-data-to-increase-converged-analytics-effectiveness/28712. Accessed April 15, 2017.

2. "The $24 billion data business Telcos don't want to discuss." October 26, 2015. http://adage.com/article/datadriven-marketing/24-billion-data-business-telcos-discuss/301058. Accessed April 15, 2017.

3. One of the authors counted approximately 500 Instagram selfies posted to social media over a three-day period from 1/20/17–1/22/17 (from 2,540 Instagram posts) at the Metropolitan Museum. Just a few used the hashtag "selfie," the rest had to be discovered by manually viewing and counting them. No doubt, AI could be trained to do this, also—see www.screencast.com/t/NxkcVjF9. For more information on how the reader can capture this type of information refer to www.picodash.com. The specific Picodash location to perform this search is www.picodash.com/explore/map#/40.7795,-73.9635/200/-. Accessed April 15, 2017.

4. www.screencast.com/t/NxkcVjF9.

5. "immeria: Review of Maturity Models." September 1, 2009. http://blog.immeria.net/2009/09/review-of-maturity-models.html. Accessed April 15, 2017.

6. "LUMAscapes: LUMA Partners." www.lumapartners.com/resource-center/lumascapes-2. Accessed April 15, 2017.

7. "Gartner says these vendors lead in digital customer analytics." October 1, 2015. www.cmswire.com/digital-experience/gartner-says-these-vendors-lead-in-digital-customer-analytics. Accessed April 15, 2017.

8. "The changing role of the Web Analyst." Econsultancy. February 3, 2012. https://econsultancy.com/blog/8793-the-changing-role-of-the-web-analyst. Accessed April 15, 2017.

9. Wilson, T. "All Web Analytics tools are the same (when it comes to data capture)." http://analyticsdemystified.com/analytics-strategy/all-web-analytics-tools-are-the-same-at-least-when-it-comes-to-data-capture. Accessed April 15, 2017.

10. Kiss, M. "How to deliver better recommendations: Forecast the impact!" March 23, 2015. http://analyticsdemystified.com/analysis/how-to-deliver-better-recommendations-forecast-the-impact. Accessed April 15, 2017.

11. Cushing, A. "Why Google analytics' user metrics are BS (for most sites)." September 12, 2016. www.annielytics.com/blog/analytics/google-analytics-user-metrics-bs-sites. Accessed April 15, 2017.

12. SEOMOZ. "Why visitor analytics aren't enough for modern marketers." October 16, 2013. www.olmblog.com/2013/10/search-engine-optimization/why-visitor-analytics-arent-enough-for-modern-marketers. Accessed April 15, 2017.

13. Ingram, M. "When it comes to media, not everything that counts can be counted." January 6, 2015. https://gigaom.com/2015/01/06/when-it-comes-to-media-not-everything-that-counts-can-be-counted. Accessed April 15, 2017.

14. Ingram, M. "We are drowning in data about readers and attention, but which metrics really matter? You won't like the answer." April 15, 2014. https://gigaom.com/2014/04/15/we-are-drowning-in-data-about-readers-and-attention-but-which-metrics-really-matter-you-wont-like-the-answer. Accessed April 15, 2017.

Basic Web Analytics and Web Intelligence

CHAPTER OBJECTIVES

After reading this chapter, readers should understand:

- Web Analytics versus Big Data
- Common tools used for analytics
- Intermediate Metrics and Web Analytics
- Web Analytics attribution models

Web Analytics

This chapter provides students with a basic understanding of how digital Web Analytics platforms work and covers how to set them up effectively. One goal of this book is to familiarize readers with current measurement systems and how they can be leveraged (going deep enough into the material, but broad enough that we avoid getting into the weeds). It leaves the details to the reader to explore further as the media measurement stack is evolving. Web Analytics is the measurement and analysis of website traffic and site conversion, and it is used to understand visitor behavior, in order to optimize the site (conversion processes, navigation, campaigns, aesthetics).

Web Analytics Use Cases

- Optimize websites.
- Maximize the marketing placed on websites.
- Learn how site navigation, content, and aesthetics affect the bottom line, which should align with business goals.
- Learn from past marketing efforts on a website.
- Optimize future campaigns to increase conversion on a website.
- Recommend website or marketing changes based on an analysis of website behavior.
- Implement site changes or recommend changes to those in authority to do so.

Why Study Web Analytics?

According to Avinash Kaushik, a prominent analytics evangelist for Google and co-founder of MarketMotive, a digital training consultancy, marketers use online data to address fundamental business problems by leveraging data relevant to their business.[1] Below is information about Web Analytics that marketers use to help them understand its foundation and capabilities:

- In the past, business owners and stakeholders depended on "interpretative" and "proxy-driven" success measurements. An example of a proxy success measure would be a click. It is often used as a measure that shows interest in a digital campaign. Using Web Analytics, business users can use data to measure success, instead of blind faith because the amount of capturable data has grown significantly.[2]
- The Web provides access to an infinite amount of data at a low cost. By adding a tag to a website, anyone can collect an enormous amount of consumer behavioral data from a site, which provides a thorough understanding of successful and poor digital marketing strategies.
- Web and data analytics provides qualitative and quantitative data about monitored websites and customers, including customer intent for the company and, at times, competition and desired outcomes for online and offline business goals. With these insights, there can be continuous improvement aligning websites with stated business goals.
- Web and Digital Analytics is a broad field that covers more than websites. It is no longer sufficient to group people into segments based on the Web Analytic supplied demographics or behaviors (via DoubleClick). Analysts are expanding their skill set to include R, Python, statistical programs such as IBM SPSS, and visualization platforms such as Tableau.
- Web and Digital Analytics are not part of "Big Data."[3] Web Analytics databases are structured by the platform vendors (via a consensus that evolved as the first Web Analytics appeared in the mid-1990s as illustrated in Figure 1.3 in Chapter 1—it has been extended as the platforms take on more capabilities) to allow business owners and data analysts to understand a business better and to report their findings clearly and more efficiently to the right people. Conversely, Big Data must be cleaned, organized and structured before it becomes useful for most applications.

When people speak about Big Data, it is usually unstructured or semi-structured data (refer to Figure 1.1 in Chapter 1). Web Analytics takes the raw data collected from a visitors' Web browser and structures it into reporting suites (considered part of an organization's first-party data) for easy access and use for analysts and stakeholders, as illustrated in Figure 5.7 later in this chapter. Web analysts operate on structured data in reporting suites and produce detailed reports of website and marketing performance using segmentation against preset business and website goals. Web analysts do not need to be programmers whereas, with Big Data, it is a requirement.

In comparison, data scientists work with large sets of semi-structured and unstructured data (Big Data) to create interactive and predictive analytics intelligence against marketing goals, Data scientists must program in Python, R, or use IBM SPSS, SAS or another high-end statistical platform. In addition to the programming skills, data scientists need massive amounts of data to work with and run algorithms on. Web analysts work with the first-party data that is collected and structured for them and requires a different skillset, including business knowledge and business communications skills. However, web analysts and data scientists share a passion for "data"; it's just a different set of data.

Web Analytics and Big Data are closely related. Both are solutions that deal with the complexity of data that is being generated and collected and provide stakeholders with information that leads to actionable results. Ideally, an analyst should be able to operate across the spectrum of analytics (see Figure 5.1).

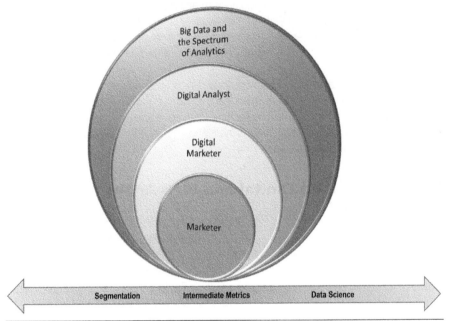

Figure 5.1 The spectrum of Web Analytics.
Source: Marshall Sponder, WebMetricsGuru Inc.

Commonly Used Software Platforms Supporting Web Analytics

There are several free or inexpensive platform tools commonly used with Web Analytics. These tools are modular and easy to learn (for those who like to program). Below are commonly used platform tools for digital analytical projects:

- **R:** Statisticians and data miners use the R programming language for developing statistical software and data analysis. R's popularity has increased substantially in recent years. It has become one of the most commonly used languages for data analytics and Big Data projects.
- **Python:** Python is a high-level dynamic programming language that allows programmers to create software with a minimum of programming code.
- **IBM SPSS:** SPSS (Statistical Package for Social Science) is a statistical package that can perform highly complex data manipulation and analysis with simple instructions.

- **Tableau:** Tableau is a standard data visualization platform for enterprise data.
- **Perl:** Perl is a high-level, general-purpose programming language that is used especially for developing Web applications.

The Evolving Data Analytics Curriculum

The massive growth of online business has created the need for individuals that can measure the impact of digital marketing initiatives. Web Analytics is expanding to cover more courses in the marketing curriculum at colleges and universities, including new courses that focus on Big Data and innovative uses of technology to improve business results. Many universities are adding Digital Analytics curriculum. Overall, in the workplace and at educational institutions, the consensus is that:

- Web Analytics as a crucial skill for marketers in today's market.
- Digital marketing is a framework that needs to remain flexible enough to change and grow as digital and marketing technologies advance.
- With the right exposure, skills, and understandings, students have a better shot at finding great jobs and careers.

Focusing Just on Digital and Web Analytics is Too Narrow

In a 2017 LinkedIn query study (see Table 5.1), the size of the potential audience for a Web Analytics position was searched through LinkedIn's databases. The result was that "Web analysts" and/or "Web analysis" on a search was too narrow at 0.1% based on LinkedIn queries. The LinkedIn results in Table 5.1 suggest Digital Analytics is a much broader discipline than Web Analytics. "Marketing analyst" returned a

Table 5.1 Data from a LinkedIn search query executed in January 2017.

Type of Analyst	How Many (Worldwide, 1/2017) Source: LinkedIn	Percentage
Anyone on LinkedIn who has the word "analyst" in their title (current or past)	9,496,380	100%
Financial Analysts	854,254	9.0%
Marketing Analysts	435,832	4.6%
Web Analysts (broad match)	132,337	1.4%
Database Analysts	94,382	1.0%
Media Analysts	87,879	0.9%
"Web Analysts" (narrow match)	12,892	0.1% (probably, too narrow a focus)

Source: WebMetricsGuru Inc.

higher yield at 4.6%, which should be used by those entering the workplace. The findings suggest that Web analysts are often tasked with extended organizational responsibilities (and, we have discovered a statistically relevant percentage of profiles listed multilingual communication and business communications skills). Essentially, the job market requires candidates to be well-balanced with diverse skills, such as database programming, business communications, and management, to perform jobs that would be included in Web Analytics roles.

Requirements for Effective Web Analytics Deployments

To be effective with Web Analytics, it takes specific, organizational business context at a detailed level, combined with an understanding of how to use the analytics for high performance. Deep knowledge of business operations is required to harvest accurate analytics reporting that generates desired business results.

Guidelines to keep in mind when solving analytical problems include:

- Obtaining the right data to answer defined business questions.
- Understanding a company's operation at a detailed enough level so that its data can be correlated with the business's digital activities.
- Delivering the reporting and insights to the right people, along with the right visualizations and language to garner the best responses.

Web Analytics: Path of Value

Some have envisioned the field of Web Analytics as being functionally like a stack of dominos. One of the co-authors built his Web Analytics course on the Domino or Gartner model[4] as it seemed to be the most comprehensive of those examined.[5] However, new maturity models appear with regularity, and there may be better ways to organize Web Analytics topics in the future. According to David Loshin, who writes at Data-Informed on issues related to evaluating and implementing big data analytics in business: "Executing this sequence in alignment with organizational needs requires people who can champion new technologies while also retaining a critical eye to differentiate between hype and reality."[6]

Defining the Five-Step Web Analytics Process

According to Avinash Kaushik, failure in digital marketing campaigns occurs when the real purpose of the campaign is not clear. Too often, business goals are unclear or are missing, so the success or failure of a campaign is undeterminable.[7]

Below are the guidelines marketers need when creating a campaign:

1. Identify the business objectives at the beginning of a project.
2. Associate goals for each business objective.
3. Define key performance indicators (KPIs) related to each business objective.
4. Identify target values for each KPI.
5. Determine the segments of people/behavior/outcomes to analyze why the project succeeded or failed.

Web Analytics implementations in organizations that already have distinct business processes in place are usually more successful. The reason is obvious: when business processes are poorly defined, they are much harder to instrument and measure.

Focusing on Strategy—Deciding What is Worth Counting (and How to Count)

As shown in Figure 5.2, a successful Web Analytics implementation moves down a path beginning with an overall strategy to lower level tactical business targets that can be measured. Later, the results are contemplated and communicated with mid-level managers, generating digital strategies and key performance indicators that impact stated business objectives. Finally, once the measurements are defined and campaigns implemented, analysts define behavior segments and business targets, as part of their day-to-day operations, to achieve the larger, stated goals.

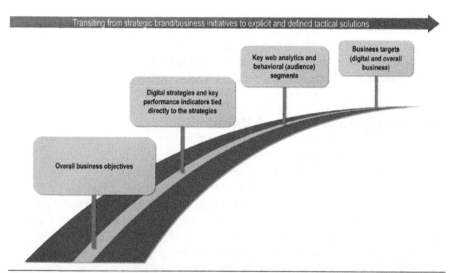

Figure 5.2 Moving from objectives to digital strategies.
Source: WebMetricsGuru Inc.

Figure 5.2 is an example of a well-defined analytics and business strategy for a voter registration drive that an organization in that activity can operate with.

The Cycle of Improvement

The "Cycle of Improvement" (refer to Figure 5.3) is the continuous improvement cycle that businesses operate in, as market conditions, competition, and technology change. There are cycle charts for Search Engine Optimization and Search Engine Marketing that work in a similar way. The digital measurement process involved in the Cycle of Improvement includes mobile, social, campaign, survey, competitive, and offline data, such as closed sales from online leads (see Figure 5.4).

Table 5.2 Measuring a voter marketing initiative from start to finish.

	Strategy A: Generate Awareness	Strategy B: Sign up Volunteers who are, or plan to be, likely Voters	Strategy C: Generate Donations to enact "Get out the Vote"
Overall business objective: Improve the relationship between voters and representative government in the United States.	Objective A: Launch a website dedicated to reaching active voters	Objective B: Use the website to recruit likely voters (get them on a consumer, customer list)	Objective C: Increase the collection of donations on the website
	KPIs: Frequency, recency and time spent from Web Analytics	KPI: # of potential voters who signed up (via Web Analytics)	KPI: Revenue collected in USD (via shopping cart)
	KPIs: Social media metrics such as shares, followers, fans, pins, etc.	KPI: # of potential voters who respond (via webform/email)	KPI: Donation size (goal is to increase it)
	KPI: Watch specific videos created to generate awareness and buzz	KPI: # of potential voters who have signed up by specific state voting districts	KPI: Respond to an email pledging to vote in the next election

Source: WebMetricsGuru Inc.

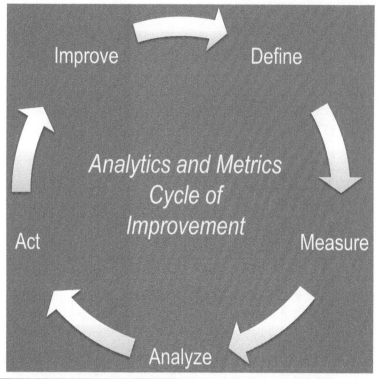

Figure 5.3 Analytics Cycle of Improvement.
Source: WebMetricsGuru Inc.

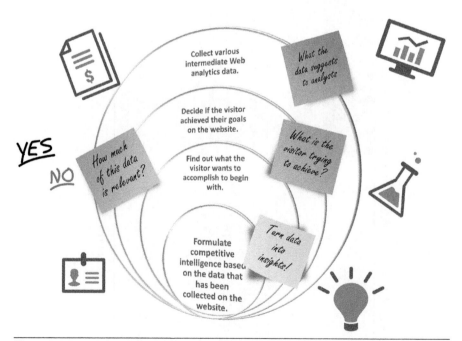

Figure 5.4 Moving from Web Analytics data to business insights.
Source: WebMetricsGuru Inc.

Key Business Requirements (KBR) vs. Key Performance Indicators (KPIs)

People working in any specialty tend to get involved with the terminology and lexicon commonly used in that community. For marketers, individuals involved in analytics planning and implementation tend to communicate using certain terms such as KBRs and KPIs. Key performance indicators (KPIs) are the digital measurements marketers use to track progress, whereas key business requirements (KBRs) reflect the business requirement or goal that the processes are meant to realize. For instance, referring to the schema shown in Figure 5.5, if KBR 1 is a business requirement to encourage types of member content to be shared more often, then the implementation of the "share button" and the number of times it is clicked on becomes one of the KPIs that informs KBR 1.

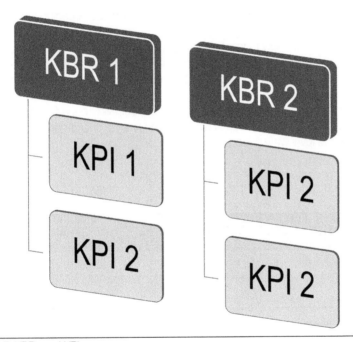

Figure 5.5 KBRs and KPIs.
Source: WebMetricsGuru Inc.

People have strong opinions about these lexicons. Gary Angel, author of *Measuring the Digital World: Using Digital Analytics to Drive Better Digital Experiences*, expresses his opinion about traditional KPIs many marketers use: "The challenge with KPIs is *most of the standard digital metrics are almost useless* to make marketing decisions because they were designed to measure the wrong things and do it in the wrong way."[8]

Angel stated his belief that "our reality is constrained by the tools we experience it with," and addresses his concerns about the accuracy of Web Analytics platforms. He is brazen about his opinion because Web Analytics platforms do not represent the activities or outcomes most marketers care about. Instead, they provide diagnostic readouts. Marketers should be skeptical of various marketing platform analytics because most do not reflect the true needs of most marketers or customers.

Below are reasons why Web Analytics fall short of marketers' standards:

- The first Digital Analytics tools were built to read weblogs, not to measure the digital world. Though the capabilities of the tools have improved the basic views they provide, have not changed much, according to Angel.[9]
- Humans build the websites for specific purposes. Web Analytics tools are not able to determine the purpose of a website. If they could, analytics reports would be more useful.

Mapping KBRs to KPIs (as shown in Figure 5.5) is an essential part of getting the value from Web Analytics deployments. Using Web Analytics effectively requires that stakeholders and analysts exercise a degree of "introspection"—to understand what the real needs are and a useful way to measure the process of getting those needs met (refer to Table 5.3).

Table 5.3 illustrates how to formulate the goals or KBRs shown on the left, for the website (which should include mobile apps), along with the specific conversion events (that happen on the website or app) smack in the center of the chart. The final part is how the activities on the website or app will be measured (on the right). However, the specific KPIs used to measure conversions will depend on the capabilities and implementation of the analytics platform (which an analyst or strategist ought to know well—this is the level we will focus on in this section).

Table 5.3 Mapping key business requirements to key performance indicators in Web Analytics.

Key Business Requirement	Conversion Event	Key Performance Indicators
Increase revenues (online)	Finish checkout process	Purchase, checkout initiation rate, buyer conversion rate, order conversion rate
Increase revenues (online)	Add products or services to shopping cart	Product browse to cart add ratio, category browse to cart ratio, shopping cart addition
Decrease customer support costs	Decrease traffic to "contact us" pages	Percent of visitors viewing "contact us" pages, percent of visitors searching for "contact related" content
Decrease customer support costs	Drive traffic to "self service" pages	FAQ/service document take rate, percent of visitors using site search, site search yield rate, CSAT scores

Source: WebMetricsGuru Inc.

Note: In Adobe Analytics, conversion events are set up by administrators. Google Analytics does the same by limiting goal setup to users with administrative access

Web metrics (i.e.: pageviews, visitors, time spent on page, etc.) are, too often, called KPIs and used to measure marketing, the designation is misleading for the following reasons:

- Most of these so-called KPIs are Intermediate Metrics that are produced by the platforms at their convenience, and they have almost nothing to do with any real business marketing outcome. They are indicators, much like the dashboard of a car indicates diagnostics about the speed and health of the vehicle.
- KPIs presented out of context have little meaning for marketers. By connecting KPIs with circumstances and business goals, they become actionable.
- Most of the metrics/KPIs commonly used by digital marketers are outdated— particularly those commonly related to top SEO rankings.[10]

Table 5.4 KBRs and KPIs by industry.

	Media/ Advertising	Technology	Retail	Personal
KBR	Draw repeat visitors deeper into site content	Generate leads	Draw more visits to product pages	Lose 20 lbs.
Conversion Events	How content is consumed	Complete a form	Product view, cart addition, checkout	Weight on scale (being 20 lbs. less)
KPI 1	Pageviews	Leads generated	Revenue	Weight (lbs.)
KPI 2	Monthly uniques	Lead conversion rate	Average revenue per visit	Weight (lbs.) trend
KPI 3	Pageviews per visit	Cost per lead	Orders/order conversion rate	HDL
KPI 4	Visits per visitor	Web inquiries	Average order value	LDL
KPI 5	# of subscriptions	Inquiry failure rate		

Source: WebMetricsGuru Inc.

The best metrics for an organization will almost always be customized to an organization's most valuable business requirements and goals.

We created an example of the KBRs and KPIs that well-known brand Starbucks might have used.

Example: Starbucks.com

The first Starbucks store opened in 1971 in Seattle. Upon creation, its self-proclaimed goals were to "share great coffee with our friends and help make the world a little better." The goal surpassed being a company of passionate purveyors of coffee but also achieving a replicable franchise with a full and rewarding coffeehouse experience, regardless of its location. If Starbucks were interested in creating a strategy that included KBRs and KPIs for their digital marketing efforts, it might look like the one in Table 5.5.

Table 5.6 shows important KPIs that could be used by Starbucks across different industries and channels.

Calculated Metrics

Most Web Analytics platforms provide out of the box metrics by default. They have variables/dimensions that can be customized: users configure the platform to collect the data they want, they can create a calculated metric to include in dashboard visualizations and custom reports. Table 5.7 shows general types of metrics.

Table 5.5 KBRs and KPIs by digital marketing initiative.

KBRs	Increase Brand Awareness	Increase use of Rewards Cards	Grow Mailing List	Increase Online Product Sales
KPI 1	Unique visitors	Click path	Click path	Unique visitors
KPI 2	Click path	Sign-up rate	Mailing list joins rate	Purchase rate
KPI 3	Pageview count	Login rate		
KPI 4	Page depth	Card member page view count		
KPI 5	Organic search keywords			
KPI 6	Click-through rate on online ads.			

Source: WebMetricsGuru Inc.

Table 5.6 Common KPIs by industry and channel.

Industry	E-Comm	Social Media	B2B	Content Marketing	SEO	Facebook	Twitter	Instagram	Pinterest	YouTube
KPI 1	Conversion rate	Follower Growth	Total cost savings	Unique visits	Return on investment	Likes	Followers	Followers	Pins	Subscribers
KPI 2	AOV	Link Clickthrough	Quality of service	Geography	Keyword ranking	Reach	Follower	Total media	Pinners	Views
KPI 3	Days to purchase	Shares	On-time delivery	Mobile readership	SERPs	Impressions	Impressions	Likes	Repins	Likes/dislike
KPI 4	Visitor loyalty	Referrals	Inventory availability	Bounce rate	CTR	Engaged Users (page)	Engagement rate	Total reach	Impressions	Playback source
KPI 5	Visitor recency	Publishing volume	Contact compliance	Clickstream	Goal conversion rate	Engaged Users (post)	retweet	Impressions	Clicks	Comments
KPI 6	Task completion rate			Pageviews	Backlinks	PTAT	favorite	Engagement rate	Engagement rate	Sharing
KPI 7	Share or search					Edgerank				Estimated time watching

Source: WebMetricsGuru Inc.

Table 5.7 Comparing traffic and conversion-based metrics and KPIs.

	Site-Wide Metrics	Report-Specific Metrics
Traffic Metrics (out of the box)	Pageviews, visits (sessions), visitors	Reloads (page specific), time spent on page, and others
Conversion Metrics (requires deliberate setup)	Revenue, orders, units, shopping cart events (e-commerce events in Google analytics), custom events	Product views, any configured campaign reporting, and conversions (goals and events in Google Analytics)

Source: WebMetricsGuru Inc.

Traffic metrics, such as those shown in Table 5.7, usually do not need any setup by users or platform administrators—they are out of the box reporting that the platform vendor sets up, but they are also Intermediate Metrics that don't provide much business value, when they are taken literally (out of context). The conversion metrics shown in Table 5.7 must be configured manually, by an administrator of the Web Analytics platform, and are intended to represent events that have tangible business value, such as the view of a brand's product page (perhaps, by a prospective purchaser).

- Adobe Analytics supports Calculated Metrics that are numeric, percentages, currency-based, and time-based. For example, a "time to complete" calculated metric can be created that counts the elapsed time in hours and minutes between the beginning of an event and the end of it.
- Creating a Calculated Metrics called average order value (AOV) is quickly set up by driving revenue/orders (both conversion events are configured by administrators).

In Adobe Analytics, conversion rates and Calculated Metrics are automatically updated in the Funnel Reports. Users can configure several Calculated Metrics in Adobe while the free version of Google Analytics allows five Calculated Metrics per profile (GA Premium probably allows far more).

Web Metrics Breakdowns

Breaking down Web Analytics data to very accurate reporting is done in a few different ways. Each platform has a slightly different name and procedure. The more specific the question, the better the report can be (when the data and context are available to inform it).

Adobe Analytics Breakdowns

Table 5.8 illustrates how certain Web Analytics platforms, such as Adobe Analytics, allows analysts and stakeholders to get report readouts that are specific to what they are interested in knowing about (i.e., a certain page, device, location, etc.).

Table 5.8 How Adobe Analytics classifies behavioral data collected on a website by the platform.

	Correlations (traffic)	Sub-relations (conversions)
Definition	Breaks down traffic reports by other traffic reports to show pageview distribution.	Break down conversion reports by other conversion reports to show success events.
Reports	Pages, site sections, custom traffic.	Products, campaigns and custom conversion events.

Source: WebMetricsGuru Inc., derived from Adobe Education.

Types of Web Metrics

There are two kinds of web metrics, activity based traffic versus conversion event-based metrics. Depending on which Web Analytics platform used, the reports may have different names, but the same functionality exists on almost every Web Analytics platform.[11] Readers are encouraged to compare Table 5.8 and Table 5.9—they are very similar. Both tables indicate that a base set of Web metrics are provided with every Web Analytics profile or reporting suite (left column), but the real business value comes from defining and configuring custom metrics (right column). Consequently, setting up useful Calculated Metrics requires introspection and experimentation to determine what should be measured, and multiple iterations for a successful implementation.

Traffic Metrics vs. Conversion Metrics

All Web Analytics platforms make a distinction between "activity metrics," such as entries and exits, time spent, pageviews and visits that focus on the presence of activity by a visitor (during a visit or session) versus actual destination metrics such

Table 5.9 Activity (out of the box) metrics vs. milestone metrics (configured).

Activity/Traffic Metrics		Events/Milestones/Conversion Metrics
Pageviews		Purchase metrics (revenue, orders, units, etc.)
Visits		Cart metrics (opens, adds, checkouts, etc.)
Unique visitors (daily, weekly, monthly, etc.)		Custom events (registrations, form completion, etc.)
Path related metrics (entries & exits, single access, reloads, time spent on page, average page depth)		Report-specific metrics (product views, campaign click-throughs, instances, etc.)

Source: WebMetricsGuru Inc., inspired by Adobe Education.

as a purchase, registration, form completion, and so on. Traffic or activity metrics are "out of the box" data, unconfigured Web Analytics platforms. Conversion/milestone metrics must be set up deliberately and customized (by someone who has the necessary admin permissions in the Web Analytics platform) and depend on the use of custom variables and program memory to run. Web Analytics platforms, such as Adobe Analytics, do not allow administrators to combine traffic breakdowns with event breakdowns due to their different nature and purposes.

Correlation Filters

Adobe Analytics and Google Analytics offer report filtering, but they are evoked in various ways. Adobe Analytics has secondary dimensions but calls them "correlations." Analysts select several correlations at one time if desired. For example, a correlation filter can be configured that shows how many confirmed registrations took place from 25–29-year old visitors to a fashion retail website during a given period. If the data is collected in the Web Analytics platform, there is probably a breakdown or correlation filter report that will be able to inform a specific business question.

Metrics Configuration

In Adobe Analytics, the following metrics are set up by administrators:

- **Props:** Used to track page-by-page site traffic activity in Adobe Analytics (they do not persist between pages of the website)—props capture the value of pageviews, visits, new and repeat visitors connected to a specific page. Using props is a way to save memory usage in Adobe Analytics as well as speed up processing.
- **eVars:** Used to track conversion events and traffic activity in Adobe Analytics; most implementations come with a standard set of eVars that can be configured and more can be added (for additional cost), and these variables are enduring (they track events across visits).
- **Events (conversions):** Custom events set up by administrators in Adobe Analytics to track conversions—the event tracking is at the core of Web Analytics (together with the integration with the Adobe Marketing Cloud), as without a custom set of events that are measured stakeholders might as well run Google Analytics for free.
- **Products:** Track products that are viewed, sold, added to a shopping cart, or removed from a shopping cart. Adobe Analytics assumes that retailers will want to sell products and track them, thereby creating a variable class and reports to support it built around just that function (no doubt it made the platform more popular with publishers, retailers and financial organizations that are bottom line sales focused).

Both Adobe Analytics and Google Analytics allow users to create custom dimensions. Adobe Analytics' custom reporting requires the specialized setup of props, eVars, events (conversions) and products to deliver business value to stakeholders. One fundamental difference between both platforms: Google Analytics is free to use (so using resources does not generate a charge), but there are limits to how many custom dimensions and reporting are allowed.

What is the Best KPI for a Website?

Start by determining the questions that Web Analytics is put in place by a business to answer—this line of inquiry will drive organizations to find data and metrics that will best inform their question(s).

- The KPIs are going to differ from organization to organization, although industries generally focus on similar sets of metrics.
- KPIs and KBRs demand a very well-defined set of business processes that have key entry points where Web Analytics systems can be deployed.

Choosing Relevant Web Metrics

Metrics are the currency of Web Analytics, which is an excellent "bean counter" containing much built-in intelligence about Web traffic and conversions taking place on a monitored website. Some of the more common metrics are visits, unique visitors, pageviews, revenue, and time spent.

- Each business is unique, and KPIs should be tailored to the company's needs.
- Knowing how an industry or organization operates makes it easier to determine what to look for and benchmark.

Intermediate Web and Social Media Metrics

Intermediate Metrics are marketing data that falls within the range from impression to purchase, such as bookmarks, views, recall, the number of followers, shares, clicks, retweets, likes, pins or downloads (note: the authors refer to Intermediate Metrics as "Action Metrics" in several other chapters of this book). Google convinced the world to believe in the "click." Facebook has done the same with the "like," Twitter with the "follower," and Pinterest has with the "pin." Web Analytics did the same thing with "visits," "visitors," "pageviews," "hits," and "bounce rate," to name a few of the better-known metrics. From the authors' perspective, Figure 5.6 and Figure 9.2 in Chapter 9 are two sides of the same coin; Web Analytics, and social media analytics have created their own currencies but they are not interchangeable, and they should not be combined in a single metric with integrity (because they measure different behaviors from different audiences). Consequently, they are not very useful as a proxy for business analytics metrics. Unfortunately, Intermediate Metrics are too often used by stakeholders as a proxy for business activity metrics (likely by uninformed stakeholders or their analysts.)

Consequently, while Intermediate Metrics are useful as a measure of audience engagement, they should not be considered the endpoint of a "Return on Investment" calculation. Perhaps, the only use case we can think of offhand where Intermediate Metrics work as ROI is a publisher or advertiser who is paying for clicks on their ads or content, outright, as part of a campaign, with designated landing pages and e-commerce transactions. As marketers learn to deliberately instrument their goals, strategies, tactics, and KPIs (refer to Figure 16.3 in Chapter 16), they

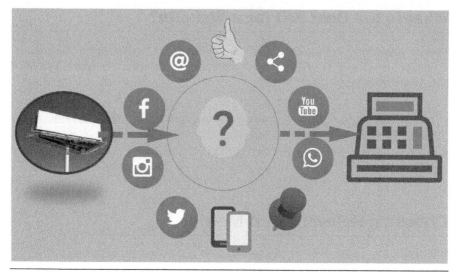

Figure 5.6 Intermediate Metrics and their impact on Return on Investment. *Source*: WebMetricsGuru Inc.

are more likely to be successful aligning their KPIs as Intermediate Metrics, to their stated business goals.

This much we can say about most Intermediate Metrics:

- They are *not* the end goal of most businesses, and they rarely correlate to estab-lished business outcomes *in and of themselves*.
- Analytics platforms are incapable of doing attribution from Intermediate Metrics alone.

  - Example: Domino's Pizza—how many of those people who "liked" Domino's Pizza have placed an order online or been to the store? Intermediate metrics such as a Facebook "like" provide much useful information but are not a proxy for actual sales data, and while advertising efforts are effective, they do not always inform fundamental business questions.

One of the issues with social media is that brands are incorrectly basing their successes on increasing metrics such as "page likes" and "account followers," which are too simplistic to inform their actual business initiatives or tell enough of the story to be that useful. Often, there are many subsequent actions connected to Intermediate Metrics that can't currently be tracked (or, at least, cannot easily be tracked).

Where Intermediate Metrics could be Useful

- Startups.
- Any organization building brand awareness.
- Individuals who are building their personal brand (i.e., blogger, publisher, celebrity, politician, etc.).
- Advertisers and publishers.
- Situations where measuring sales and revenue is almost impossible to determine.

Table 5.10 Custom variables in Google vs. Adobe vs. Webtrends Analytics.

	Pre-Configured Variables	Semi-Free Custom Variables	Free Custom Variables
Definition:	No influence on how variables are filled or called, and are provided out of the box by the platform provider (Google, WebTrends, Adobe, etc.).	Reporting context is limited in scope, often come out of the box but need to be configured.	Totally configurable, can be used in any context and are open to all admins.
Examples:	Technology, URL/page, geography, referring sites, search keywords.	Adobe "pageName", GA on-site search terms, ecom variables, custom events, props, success events.	GA and WT Custom dimensions and metrics, Adobe eVars.

Source: WebMetricsGuru Inc.

Viewpoints on Intermediate Metrics

- Intermediate Metrics act more as barometers for interested parties on commonly intangible attitudes of a potential or *de facto* online audience, while they are not perfect, just like the weather forecast, they show the trend. Intermediate Metrics should be treated as characteristic data points that measure aspects of Web performance but aren't comprehensive.
- Intermediate Metrics produced by social media platforms such as Twitter and Facebook are publicly available and often free to collect, and perhaps that is why they are so popular. The Intermediate Metrics are *tangentially indicative* of how a website/Web presence performed in the past and how it is currently performing.
- Connect Intermediate Metrics with a campaign—it is a mistake to apply them more broadly.

Custom Variables

The value of analytics implementation comes from precisely setting up conversion metrics using custom variables, which is a step many business owners fail to do well, or at all (also refer to Tables 5.7, 5.8, and 5.9 in this chapter).

Designing KPIs That Work

There is an art to developing a useful KPI, and here is one approach:[12]

- Define the business problem (what are the main issues the organization faces?).
- Chose a single issue (per KPI), at least one designated stakeholder, and a designed KPI indicator that would be useful to that stakeholder.

- Define three or four processes associated with the matter around the KPI (but don't get too specific, yet).
- Define a statistical measure that will be linked to each of the processes related to the KPI. By "instrumenting" an indicator and setting thresholds with a high/low action for each process, it becomes possible to place the KPI in a dashboard and act on it. In a nutshell, connect each business process with a data source that will inform it.
- Define the measurement algorithm for the KPI as a formula when possible.
- Define the procedure to conduct/measure the KPI.

Many of our students have created KPIs of their own (KPI creation is one of the Web Analytics course assignments and will also be included in the Instructor's Guide to this book, as a student resource).

Please note that many businesses create KPIs that are not based on Web Analytics. For example, many universities create KPIs that are meant to measure the effectiveness of the instructors and course quality. The metrics used in KPIs are diverse; most have nothing to do with Web Analytics; this chapter focuses only on the metrics that are used to formulate Web Analytics KPIs.

The Promise and Failure of Web Analytics for Stakeholders

The KPI approach appears to be both mechanical and logical, and akin to decision support systems that are common in many industries, such as automotive, aerospace, construction, etc.[13] Web Analytics works best in organizations that have very defined business processes—the same kind of processes that facilitate KPI development. Incidentally, Web Analytics was created to satisfy tactical measures that business owners defined (before proceeding to instrument Web Analytics in their businesses—if they have not done that, the analytics reporting will not be very helpful). That is because Web Analytics was created (or, at least initially sold to users/subscribers) based on the idea that it would help mature business organizations solve their problems, activities or issues with more actionable data. As it turned out, many organizations—that have not done the necessary set up work, in this sense, they are "immature"—are not ready or able to spend the time or resources to set up analytics well enough to benefit from it.

Common Use Cases for Web/Data Analytics

Use cases are examples of where an organization uses Web Analytics to perform a business function.[14]

Below are the most common for Web Analytics:

- Collect visitor data to owned media websites (to better understand customers or potential customers).
- Performance measurement (against KPIs).
- Marketing optimization (measure and understand, through analysis, how campaigns are performing and improve the performance by making changes based on the data obtained).

- Content optimization (understanding why the website exists and whether the content on the monitored site contributes to that purpose, making changes based on the collected data to improve the content).

How Web Analytics Track User Web Data

Internet data is primarily gathered from Web server log files or JavaScript tags (third-party APIs to external data sources are an additional method, they are discussed in more depth in later chapters). Most platforms use the JavaScript method because it requires less overhead and is considered superior for most situations (but not all).

- **Server log file analysis:** Web server log files contain information on file downloads and search engine crawlers not tracked by Web beacons.
- **Web beacons:** Every page tracked by Web Analytics has a small snippet of JavaScript code that executes when the page is loaded by a Web browser. The JavaScript code on the webpage is customized by the marketer to capture the exact information marketers need for their Web Analytic and financial business reports.

Web Beacon Tracking (Most Common Method)

When a visitor visits a site, the Web server sends page information while the page displays in the browser.

As the page loads in the Web browser and the Web Analytics JavaScript Beacon code on the page executes, it sends a request to the analytics server as

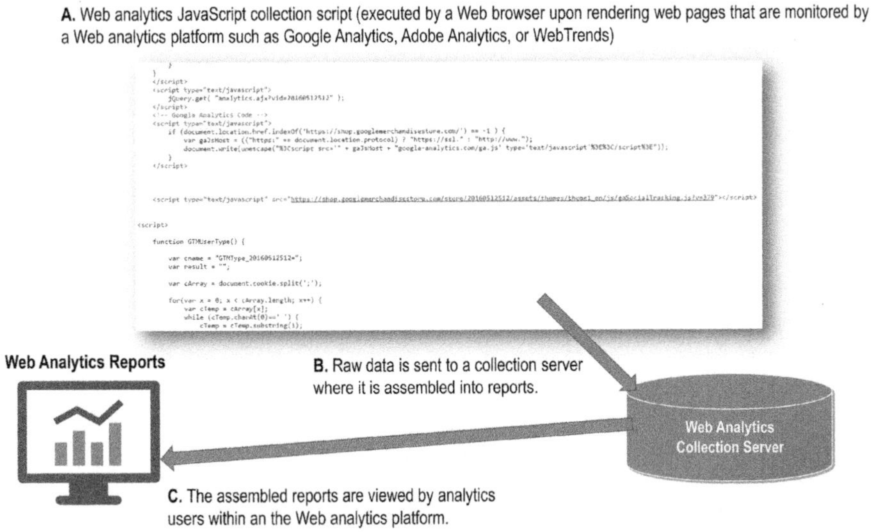

A. Web analytics JavaScript collection script (executed by a Web browser upon rendering web pages that are monitored by a Web analytics platform such as Google Analytics, Adobe Analytics, or WebTrends)

Web Analytics Reports

B. Raw data is sent to a collection server where it is assembled into reports.

Web Analytics Collection Server

C. The assembled reports are viewed by analytics users within an the Web analytics platform.

Figure 5.7 Web Analytics tracking pixel and data collection mechanism.
Source: WebMetricsGuru Inc.

a transparent 1-pixel-sized image along with various raw data that is captured from the visitor's session (visit).

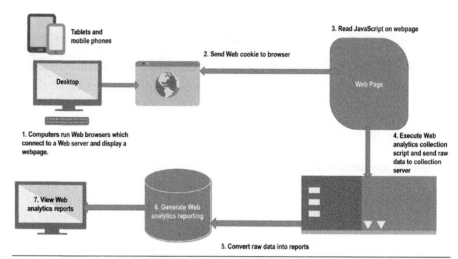

Figure 5.8 Web Analytics tracking process.
Source: WebMetricsGuru Inc.

By installing Web Analytics tracking code on a website, the visitor's browser activity on the site is tracked by an analytics server in parallel with the website's Web server. When a page loads in a browser, the JavaScript code on the page is executed as the page renders. All following activity on the page in question is tracked by the Web Analytics collection server as raw data where it is processed into reports. Once the data is fully processed, the raw data is dumped (to save on system resources and data storage). We believe that many organizations are not entirely informed of the drawbacks of Web beacon (JavaScript) tracking, that is why we are highlighting many of the disadvantages first. Drawbacks to JavaScript tracking include:

- Analytics tracking that is improperly implemented is not recoverable once the analytics server creates the reporting from the raw data that is collected from visitors' browsers. Consequently, potential data loss should be a concern organizations must address because of using JavaScript tracking.
- Some visitor behavioral activities (such as file downloads, video views, Flash and Shockwave files, mouse hovering movements, Ajax web code, pageviews, podcasts, vidcasts, and streaming media, in general, etc.) on the website that are being measured using Web Analytics, are not normally trackable using the default configurations of all Web Analytics platforms. However, Web Analytics can track virtually all visitor activity on the website—but it takes a significant cost in time, effort and business expense (ultimately).

The advantages of using JavaScript tracking are evident:

- Reduced infrastructure costs—most of the raw data is processed and stored in the cloud and can be scaled on demand (Google Analytics has successfully done this) and offered to users at a reduced price (for many, such as those who use the free version of Google Analytics, the platform is free).

- Superior tracking of many (but not all) visitor activities that can be merged with third-party data (such as DoubleClick)
- Extensibility of the analytics implementations. There is literally no limit to the number of websites that can be tracked with this method.
- The analytics providers (particularly Google) have an enormous swath of humanity they are tracking via their websites—the collected data can be used for industry and site benchmarking, behavioral targeting, and market intelligence (second and third-party data) for analytics users, advertisers, and publishers.

To deploy Web Analytics effectively, it should be part of a company's strategic initiative and team (occasionally dubbed the "Center of Excellence") to receive requests and funnel the insights to the rest of the organization. Well-defined business processes and business strategies are a prerequisite to getting substantial value out of Web Analytics platforms.

For example, if a company wants to increase visitation to a page on their site by 25% next month, they should take steps beforehand to be sure they can collect all the data necessary to measure their progress, before beginning the advertising campaign. While it is possible to implement processes in analytics as one goes, it is better to set up the analytics before launching a new program or campaign.

The Digital Analytics Maturity Model

When deploying Web Analytics, consider the model outlined in Table 5.11 (i.e., organizations must choose a solution, set it up and train users in Phase 1 to be able to do basic and advanced reporting in phases 2 and 3).

No one is perfect. No organization (or individual) *always* acts sequentially—we are all inconsistent frequently; in real life, we learn from our mistakes, improvising, integrating, and improving our actions and insights as we go along.

Table 5.11 Defining the Digital Analytics Maturity Model.

Phase	Functional Definitions of the Digital Analytics Maturity Model
1	Strategic consulting to establish the right framework for an organization.
2	Basic training on how to use the analytics platform to run and refine is reporting.
3	Advanced consulting to customize analytics measurement to the very specific needs of each client.
4	Visitor intelligence to connect the dots and make sense of the collected data to further business goals.
5	Integrating and converging data collection and reporting, which is very hard to do, expensive and time-consuming.

Source: WebMetricsGuru INC.

Iteration and Learning from Mistakes

The Digital Analytics Maturity Model presented in this chapter is not mutually exclusive with learning how to deploy Web Analytics by making several iterations and mistakes to discover what works (in real life both processes can take place simultaneously) — our takeaways depend on the context of the learning. Since no one is perfect (even a machine or a program as both are fashioned by humans), no one is going to have a perfect implementation of Web Analytics, ever. Nothing is a mistake if we learn something valuable from it — the biggest mistake we make in life (and Web Analytics) is not learning anything from our mistakes, and by extension, over time, not recognizing what our mistake was.

If we do not make mistakes and continue to iterate off those errors, there is no progress. Nothing we put forward in this book should be taken as the only acceptable way to accomplish the subjects we cover in this book.

The Role of Iteration within the Digital Analytics Maturity Model

Perhaps, a better way of conceptualizing Table 5.11 is to add in a more iterative component — most organizations will move back and forth between the Maturity Model phases.

- **Phase 1/Phase 2:** Many organizations will move to Phase 1 and Phase 2 (perhaps forever) until they reach a fulcrum point of a well-informed stakeholder and management consensus, thereby allowing the organization to move on to Phase 3 (where useful standalone applications are developed for stakeholders).
- **Phase 3:** At Phase 3, standalone analytics insights are successfully developed for departments and lines of business (LOBs), but the data produced by the applications cannot be used extensible or easily combined. Analytics data and insights are usually effective because they are localized and contextual. At this stage, the data cannot be combined with other information within the organization. Eventually, organizations find that stalling at Phase 3 in the analytics implementation creates too many reporting silos and analytics vendors (duplicating the same functions) that cannot be combined.
- **Phase 4/5**: Phases 4 and 5 require a significant commitment to business alignment, along with the necessary resources to instrument and implement the business technology alignment. Consequently, few organizations are receiving the full benefit of their analytics investment because they are unable to progress to Phase 4 or mature into Phase 5.

There is no universal and extensible list of companies that are functioning at Phase 4 or 5 in the Digital Analytics Maturity Model, as far as we can tell (although we can guess that organizations such as Amazon and Google are probably right up there, at Phase 5.) What is more troubling is that many organizations are skipping the necessary first two phases, which guarantees an epic analytics implementation failure (for example, if we suddenly find ourselves behind the wheel of a moving car, but we do not know how to drive).

To sum up, the sequence of the Digital Analytics Maturity Model Phases that an organization goes through is far less important than skipping the early phases, or beginning of Phase 3 (i.e., skipping Phases 1 and 2 and suddenly purchasing an off-the-shelf third-party application to solve a critical, yet under-defined business problem.)

Two Case Studies about Web/ Data Analytics Implementation

1. Caesars Entertainment invested in an Adobe Analytics implementation (Adobe's Digital Marketing Suite) to manage their numerous online properties of more than 60 websites for various properties and services. Caesars also had 40 Facebook pages by 2013 to be more data-driven as an organization and collect data in a usable, actionable form.[15]

   - Two main customer segments were identified consisting of Frequent Independent Travelers (FITs) and Total Rewards Members (TRMs) that were driven by different needs and behaviors. Using A/B testing, content was tested and optimized for both segments, which increased conversion rate by up to 70%.
   - Caesars used Web Analytics to measure the impact of social media across FIT and TRM segments.

2. Motor Insurers Bureau created as a microsite to generate awareness of motor insurance in specific geographical locations across the UK (House of Kaizen) and used Google Analytics to provide an integrated view of a multichannel marketing campaign with site interaction metrics.

   - A custom implementation of Google Analytics provided an in-depth understanding of their location data with custom dashboards reflecting KPIs showing what content was most effective.

Most Web Analytics platforms have several different ways to customize data collection and reporting.

Defining What to Measure and How to Measure It

The best way to deploy Web Analytics is to begin with an "introspection process" that business leaders and stakeholders within the organization go through (see Table 5.11, Phase 1) to determine what the company cares about or wants to accomplish (this is typically conducted by strategic business consultants such as McKinsey & Co, or a Web Analytics vendor such as Adobe). At the start of Phase 1, business leaders and stakeholders provide input about everything they want to know more about, defined and matched up with analytics capabilities and the costs that are involved in obtaining the information. After this process is concluded, an initial Web Analytics implementation can be mapped and approved with a few clear deliverables that make sense to instrument.

Helpful Questions for Phase 1 (Discovery Process)

- **What is the business paying for?** For simple businesses, it is easy to figure out where the time, energy, and money are being spent. A simple implementation of Google Analytics (free) is more than enough for small businesses. For more complex organizations, a highly customized Web Analytics implementation is necessary.

- **Where does the business spend most of its time?** There is an old saying that "time is money"; to find out what is important, determine how organizations or businesses focus their time. Web Analytics requires that business value (of a process or activity) to be defined in a way that the analytics can measure.
- **What is "driving" the focus on money, resources or time?** For example, consider the key business requirement of losing weight could be remaining fit and attractive. One of the KPIs is the weight of the person on a scale from day to day, as measured in pounds, kilograms, or stones (in the UK).

When an organization, business, or individual defines what drives their main metrics of value, Web Analytics can provide most of them. Having said that, as shown in Figure 5.9, the most important business goal of B2B marketers appears to be an Intermediate Metric that Web Analytics can provide: Web traffic. Web traffic is an activity metric and should never be the end-point of a business goal (although it can be considered a campaign goal), suggesting that marketers need more clarity regarding what they really want to accomplish before they define their goals. Once the business goals are defined, they can be instrumented using a DSS (Decision Support Services) approach.[16]

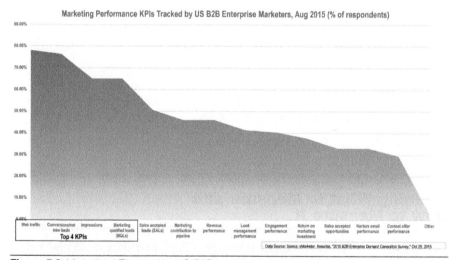

Figure 5.9 Marketing KPIs used by US B2B marketers.
Source: WebMetricsGuru INC with data sourced from eMarketer.com

As an instrumentation example: "If we knew that [KPIs] were consistently rising/falling over the last week/ month, we would [ACTION]."

Once we can define the driver of change in a business metric, we can begin to instrument the Key Performance Indicator—so the change can be measured. The next step is finding out what actions are needed and who takes them.

- A weather alert flashes on the iPhone of an umbrella street vendor that there is a 95% chance of heavy rain in the next 15 minutes nearby.
- If the umbrella street vendor is well-positioned for a lot of foot-traffic and well-prepared, they could act based on this signal and quickly sell their entire stock of umbrellas. The retailer would arrive at a busy intersection in their city with several umbrellas to sell to pedestrians whose goal is staying dry.

- Both the umbrella vendor and the pedestrians passing by (who don't have an umbrella and do not want to get wet) achieve their goals.
- Acting on the weather alert while it is raining creates measurable value for the umbrella retailer and the pedestrian. We used this example to highlight that DSS systems using Web and data analytics should lead to outcomes that are mutually beneficial to all parties involved. Conversely, we should, on principle, examine that our business goals and initiatives provide measurable value to both sides of the equation (the seller and the buyer).

Data Can Be Applied in Different Contexts

If we strayed inadvertently into the realm of economics with the umbrella vendor example, forgive us. In our view, all subjects we study in universities are interrelated—the more we can create interrelationships on the various topics studied, the better. It's also more likely students will retain the information they read about and study if they can apply it in different contexts. The best way to start on that path (interrelationships of the curriculum in the context of digital marketing) is to think of applications where Web Analytics and Text Analytics (Chapter 10) can illuminate market strategy, consumer behavior, economics, public affairs, environmental policies, and vice-versa.

For too long, in our view, universities have focused on their own program curricula, or businesses their own business context. It is a common saying that if we are going to catch more fish, we need to cast a wider net, and to begin to think more broadly.

Types of Data Marketers Value the Most

Figure 5.10 illustrates a well-known desire of many digital marketers to harness the power of the Internet to gather "first-party data" from their digital properties, perhaps combining it with third-party data from data brokers or other third-party applications, business partners or affiliates.

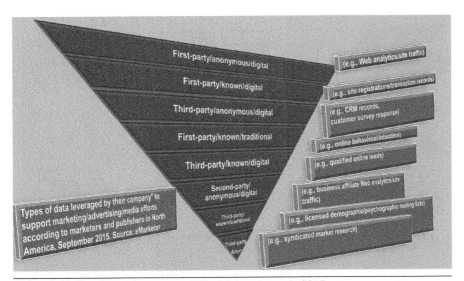

Figure 5.10 Top eight data sources of US digital marketers in 2015.
Source: WebMetricsGuru Inc. from data provided by eMarketer.com.

Web Analytics Attribution Methods and Algorithms

The path the customer takes to find out about a product or service and purchase it is commonly referred to as the "customer journey." Due to the fragmentation of media the customer or consumer can discover and engage with digital content via many touchpoints, perhaps in a circular or zig-zag process that is rarely linear (except with direct marketing campaigns such as PPC ad appearing on Google Search).

Because of the rise of social media, mobile devices and media fragmentation (not to mention audience fragmentation), the customer journey is much more complex than the digital activities Web Analytics platforms can track out of the box.[17] It is much harder to get a complete picture of the customer journey using Web Analytics even with newer additions such as Adobe Social, various CRM additions coming from Google, Adobe, and IBM. The Third-Party Marketing Clouds from Salesforce, Oracle, IBM, and Adobe have evolved to capture and harness customer data, but they are expensive to deploy and manage. There are methods that Web Analytics platforms use to determine the attribution of web visitation and to evaluate or "weight" it, from an ROI (Return on Investment) perspective. Most of these methods take additional configuration, although some are in place by default, such as last-click attribution modeling.

Attribution Models

Attribution models are a method that Web Analytics platforms decide which sources of traffic are making a bigger contribution to a conversion event (such as a Web purchase, file download, etc.) For example, Figure 5.11 is sourced from a standard Google Analytics report showing how Web Analytics determines the origins of Web traffic that leads to a conversion event. The top referral patterns of online visitors to an e-commerce website are presented in Figure 5.11.

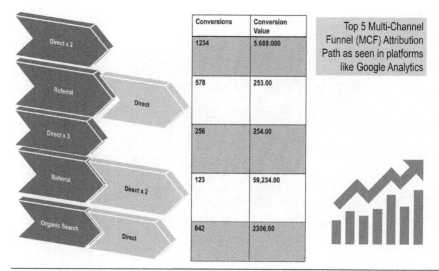

Figure 5.11 Visualization of Google Analytics multi-channel funnel attribution and ROI.
Source: WebMetricsGuru Inc. from Anonymized Google Analytics Data.

Site Pathing Analysis

Up to this point, we have examined how a business acquires a visitor—now will we talk about how to track the visitors' behavior once they arrive on the website. Web Analytics tracks visitors' movements as they transverse a website visitors arrive on a site—this is called site pathing analysis. Figure 5.12 shows two pathing methods that Web Analytics uses to track visitors on a website (based on the first page browsed during a session/visit).

- **Point to point:** Used when businesses are more interested in knowing if the customer reaches the endpoint (i.e., that a user purchases an item is all that matters).
- **Direct path:** Used to optimize the visitor flow on the website (i.e., visitors are dropping out and leaving the site before purchasing anything, and we can track the pages where this occurs more frequently).

Depending on what the goal of the Web Analytics analysis is, point-based analysis might be all that is needed, whereas, if site performance is going to considered then direct path analysis might make more sense, providing it is set up in a fair and equitable way.

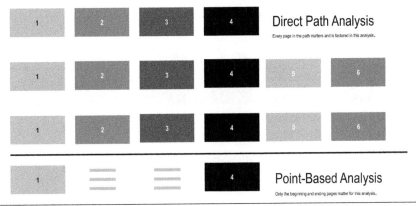

Figure 5.12 Comparing direct-path and point-based path analysis.
Source: WebMetricsGuru Inc. from concepts taught by Adobe Education.

Providing Actionable Web Analytics Reporting for Stakeholders

Web Analytics collects a lot of website data (some believe Web Analytics collects too much data), but it is diagnostic in nature. Figure 5.13 illustrates four types of interested parties that require different analytics reporting. One reason data lakes, data marts, and data warehouses exist is to allow the information produced by analytics platforms to be more atomic, so it can be broken apart, reassembled, and messaged into different types of reporting that are stored in the cloud or private data repositories. In the schema shown in Figure 5.13, it is extremely unlikely that stakeholders who are marketers are going to benefit from a website data performance report provided to the

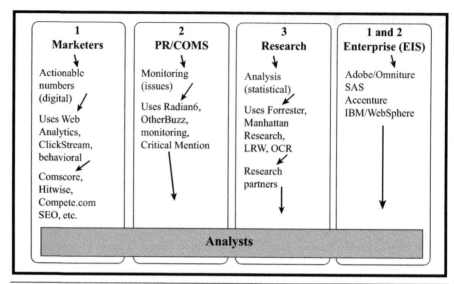

Figure 5.13 Customizing reports for different types of stakeholders.
Source: WebMetricsGuru Inc.

Enterprise team, or vice-versa. Making the data more atomic seems to make sense, if the necessary business context can be created, or added in, when reporting is created and/or delivered.

Review Questions

1. Define what Web Analytics is typically used for? What are some "non-typical" applications of Web Analytics? (Try to think of a few.)
2. Define the Five-Step Web Analytics Process. Do you think there could be more steps to add to this process?
3. What do the terms KBR and KPI stand for? Who defines them?
4. What is a Calculated Metric? Does Google Analytics allow Calculated Metrics? What about Adobe Analytics—do they enable users to create Calculated Metrics?
5. Define the difference between point-based analysis and path-based analysis (for pathing/attribution).

Chapter 5 Citations

1. "Simplilearn." August 26, 2015. www.youtube.com/watch?v=BuEYkl2_b5I. Accessed April 15, 2017.
2. "Simplilearn." August 26, 2015. www.youtube.com/watch?v=BuEYkl2_b5I. Accessed April 15, 2017.
3. Nerney, C. "Soon, everybody will be a data scientist." August 29, 2014. www.cio.com/article/2600624/big-data-analytics/soon-everybody-will-be-a-data-scientist.html. Accessed April 15, 2017.

4. Dykes, B. "Analytics: 5 key steps to generate value." October 3, 2012. www. analyticshero.com/2012/10/03/analytics-5-key-steps-to-generate-value. Accessed April 15, 2017.

5. Hamel, S. "Review of maturity models." September 1, 2009. http://blog.immeria. net/2009/09/review-of-maturity-models.html. Accessed April 15, 2017.

6. Loshin, D. "Achieving organizational alignment for Big Data analytics." July 17, 2013. http://data-informed.com/achieving-organizational-alignment-for-big-data-analytics. Accessed April 15, 2017.

7. Kaushik, A. "Multi-channel attribution modeling: The good, bad and ugly models." November 8, 2013. www.kaushik.net/avinash/multi-channel-attribution-modeling-good-bad-ugly-models. Accessed April 15, 2017.

8. Angel, G. (2016) *Measuring the Digital World: Using Digital Analytics to Drive Better Digital Experiences*. Upper Saddle River, NJ: Pearson Education, Inc. Emphasis added.

9. Angel, G. (2016) *Measuring the Digital World: Using Digital Analytics to Drive Better Digital Experiences*. Upper Saddle River, NJ: Pearson Education, Inc.

10. Spiegel, B. "Ditch your digital top 10 metrics now!" August 1, 2013. http:// marketingland.com/ditch-your-top-10-metrics-now-53525. Accessed April 15, 2017.

11. Sandhu, A. "Web Analytics comparison." March 11, 2013. www.slideshare.net/ maverickaman/ga-wt-omtr. Accessed April 15, 2017.

12. Savkin Follow, A. "Design KPI." June 20, 2010. www.slideshare.net/asavkin/ design-kpi. Accessed April 15, 2017.

13. *"Pulse."* www.amazon.com/Pulse-Science-Harnessing-Internet-Opportunities/ dp/0470932368. Accessed April 15, 2017.

14. Smith, S. "How do companies use Web Analytics?" http://smallbusiness.chron. com/companies-use-analytics-54630.html. Accessed April 15, 2017.

15. "At Caesars, digital marketing is no crap shoot." February 1, 2013. www. dmnews.com/marketing-strategy/at-caesars-digital-marketing-is-no-crap-shoot/ article/277685. Accessed April 15, 2017.

16. *"Pulse."* www.amazon.com/Pulse-Science-Harnessing-Internet-Opportunities/ dp/0470932368. Accessed April 15, 2017.

17. "Marketers struggle to map multichannel customers' journeys." April 24, 2015. www.emarketer.com/Article/Marketers-Struggle-Map-Multichannel-Customers-Journeys/1012398. Accessed April 15, 2017.

Advanced Web Analytics and Web Intelligence

CHAPTER OBJECTIVES

After reading this chapter, readers should understand

- Web Analytics stakeholders
- Basic and advanced segmentation in Web Analytics
- Goal-setting and conversions

Once Web Analytics platforms are deployed, they should be configured to capture all the information needed to make business decisions concerning the website that is being measured. The information Web Analytics platforms collect also need to be communicated to stakeholders and decision-makers within the organization/ enterprise.

Stakeholders

The Stakeholder Ecosystem

The business stakeholder has become an interesting brew, so to speak, in many organizations. Everyone seems to want the data that Web Analytics produces, but hardly anyone knows what to do with it. The reaction of most business owners is that the data readouts are too technical, and were created for analysts (which is true). But, Web Analytics contains a wealth of information that could inform any business function, once the data is taken out of the platform and put into the context the extended stakeholder needs it to be in. In this regard, it's worth spending a few paragraphs discussing whom the extended stakeholder might be, as illustrated in Figure 6.1. Some of the more advanced thinking about stakeholders comes from companies like IBM. Per IBM, Big Data & Analytics Hub[1] presents a newer way to group stakeholders that it terms a "data hub." The data hub encourages enterprise data collaboration, something that a siloed stakeholder-based organization inhibits.

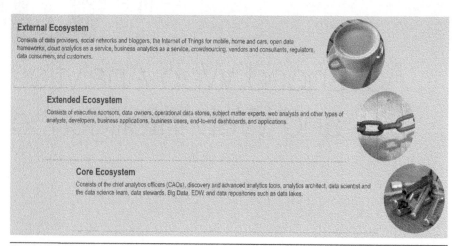

Figure 6.1 Web data analytics ecosystem.
Source: WebMetricsGuru Inc.

Three interacting spheres define the *data hub* analytics ecosystem:

- **Core ecosystem:** Individuals and technologies assemble the data that is required, analyze the data to generate insights, and determine actions based on these ideas to achieve business outcomes. In this grouping, Web Analytics and the Centers of Excellence should be placed—because analytics has become a critical business function.
- **Extended ecosystem:** Individuals, groups, and systems direct the analytics projects, collaborate with the core team, provide raw data, consume the outputs, and act on the insights. In this grouping, LOBs (lines of business) and various departments within an organization should be placed who need critical business data but do not have the means to gather it directly.
- **External ecosystem:** Customers, business partners, vendors, data providers, and consumers interact with the organization to help deliver the full potential of big data goals. Many organizations have business partners—even competitors can be business partners in some arrangements, and certain data can be shared between parties, which should be considered the "external ecosystem."

The old way of dividing stakeholders into separate constituencies created mediocre results because the needs of different stakeholders were too often not aligned. Unless Web Analytics data can be put in the proper context, it is unlikely to be useful to anyone—usually requiring an analyst to interpret the data readouts.

Stakeholders' Roles are Key

The most important characteristic a stakeholder has is what kind of actions they can take in an organization—their very specific roles will determine the kind of Web Analytics reporting they need.

Questions to ask stakeholders before delivering Web Analytics reports:

1. What is your role in the organization?
2. In the interest of providing you with actionable information to inform your decision-making, what types of actions do you take in your role(s)?
3. What information do you need from the Web Analytics team?

Advice: Let Stakeholders Believe That They Are Driving the Reporting

Typically, stakeholders have a very limited, stereotypical view of what Web Analytics data contains and how it can be used; they need to be educated. The best way to generate actionable Web Analytics reporting is to present a series of options of the data they can have in their readouts and reports (i.e., do you want A, B, or C?). Caveat, when presented with the specific reporting deliverables that were chosen, the stakeholder(s) may push back, and respond that the report they received was not what they asked for. That is due to the nature of reporting, in general, which is iterative in nature.

Avoiding Becoming a Report Monkey

When stakeholders receive the reporting that they asked for, it is often different than what they claim they requested. This disconnect could arise from the analyst or the stakeholder, or an imprecise way of defining what is to be delivered. In this case, analysts are invited to redo the report, tying up Web Analytics in an endless stream of report revisions and late working hours. Analysts can streamline their workload by delaying reporting until the stakeholder requirements are nailed down; when that is not possible, just produce an ad hoc, one-time report. We also want to put forward a point of view that repeating analytics reporting due to constant revisions and omissions may sap any time or energy left to discover new and exciting insights into the organization. Becoming a report monkey is the fastest way to burn out of the analytics industry. We all need some to time to play with these platforms and discover something new, especially if industry believes in the mantra of data being the "new oil." Consequently, all analysts should spend time discovering new patterns in the data (whatever data they are asked to examine), and not exclusively focus on daily, weekly, and monthly deliverables, support tickets, and ad hoc requests. In other words, there needs to be some room for discovery and play in the analytics process or else we burn out quickly.

The Type of Information Stakeholders Want

We examined the extended stakeholder ecosystem in Figure 6.1; let's examine what kind of data the recipients in the ecosystem want to know (that Web Analytics platforms can illuminate.) Organizations purchase and deploy digital analytics platforms to fulfill several business priorities such as targeting, content optimization, and social engagement, as shown in Table 6.1. However, Web Analytics usually does not contain information on real-time marketing, social media analytics, programmatic optimization, mobile optimization, content optimization and social media engagement in a ready-to-use format for stakeholders.

Examples of marketing operations Web Analytics can/can't inform:

- **Multi-channel campaign management:** Omnichannel analytics requires proper JavaScript tagging of all digital assets. Web Analytics reporting supports this schema, but it must be set up beforehand and be regularly maintained.
- **Marketing automation:** Usually handled by third-party platform services rather than Web Analytics platforms. However, Web Analytics reporting informs customer targeting, digital advertising, and email marketing, when configured to track those activities.

- **Customer scoring:** Customer scoring is not usually in Web Analytics platforms (although content scoring is).
- **Mobile optimization:** Web Analytics platforms possesses a wealth of data originating from the mobile devices of visitors to the tracked website.

Table 6.1 Top digital priorities of client-side marketers worldwide 2015–2016.

Top Digital Priorities for Their Company According to Client-Side Marketers Worldwide, 2015 & 2016 (% of respondents)			
Digital Priorities	2015	2016	Y2Y Diff
Targeting and personalization	**30%**	**31%**	**+3.33%**
Content optimization	29%	29%	0.00%
Social media engagement	27%	25%	−7.41%
Multichannel campaign management	**22%**	**24%**	**+9.09%**
Brand building/viral marketing	24%	23%	−4.17%
Conversion rate optimization	20%	19%	−5.00%
Marketing automation	**15%**	**18%**	**+20.00%**
Mobile optimization	**16%**	**17%**	**+6.25%**
Search engine marketing	17%	16%	−5.88%
Video content	15%	15%	0.00%
Mobile app engagement	13%	13%	0.00%
Joining up online and offline data	12%	11%	−8.33%
Cust scoring & predictive marketing	**9%**	**10%**	**+11.11%**
Social media analytics	9%	9%	0.00%
Real-time marketing	9%	8%	−11.11%
Programmatic buying/optimization	na	6%	n/a

Source: WebMetricsGuru Inc. and eMarketer data.

Methodology: Data is from the January 2016 Econsultancy report titled "Quarterly Digital Intelligence Briefing: 2016 Digital Trends" in association with Adobe.

7,002 marketing, digital and e-commerce professionals worldwide were surveyed in December 2015.

Note: 2015 n = 2,748; 2016 n = 3,167; respondents chose their top 3

Top Growing Digital Priorities are:

1. Marketing Automation
2. Customer Scoring and Predictive Marketing
3. Multichannel Campaign Management
4. Mobile Optimization
5. Targeting and Personalization

Enriching Web Analytics Reporting with External Data Sources

Web Analytics captures the actions of visitors that take place on tracked websites, but not the marketing activity happening in other locations, outside of the site or offline (although there are other ways to extend the data and reporting contained in Web Analytics platforms via analytics APIs, custom variables, and database writes — aspects of external data capture are examined briefly in previous chapters).

We have established so far that to get a fuller, more actionable picture of consumer activity, Web Analytics alone is not sufficient — we must add other data, such as weather information and road traffic data (listed in Table 6.2) and merge it with tracked website behavior (which informs user/customer behaviors).

In the example of the umbrella street vendor in Chapter 5, it was easy enough to get climate data pulled from the Weather Channel/IBM Watson, which informed a direct action, capitalizing on an impending rainstorm in a nearby outdoor pedestrian area. If the vendors were working for a single company who controlled all such operations around the city, they would need to be alerted and supplied with enough umbrellas before it rains to make it worthwhile to stand out in the rain and sell them to interested pedestrians. Such an application needs website data via Web Analytics, combined with geo-data and climate data. While this example may seem somewhat far-fetched and whimsical, it's a very tactical example of what combining first-, second- and third-party data can accomplish.

The Web Analytics Ecosystem

The world of Digital Analytics may seem complicated, but it is not so complex — Google Analytics evangelist Avinash Kaushik[2] did a splendid job of simplifying it, as shown in Table 6.3.

We think Table 6.3 covers Phases 1, 2 and 3 of the Digital Analytics Maturity Model shown in Table 5.11, in Chapter 5. Avinash deals with a simple Web Analytics implementation that deploys structured data to several departmental and enterprise

Table 6.2 Comparing unstructured, structured and internal house data types.

Unstructured External Data	Structured External Data	Internal Data
Utility Usage	Census Data	Sales Transactions
Search Terms	Partner Data	Web Analytics
Financial Market Data	Some Geo-Data	Product Shipments and Returns
Travel Traffic Data	Social Profiles	Inventory Data
Climate Data		Call/Contact Center Data
Geo-Data		Invoices
Blog Comments		CRM Data
Social Media Data		Employee Data
News		Marketing Campaigns

Source: WebMetricsGuru Inc.

Table 6.3 Parts of the Web Analytics ecosystem, detailed.

Step	Element of Web Analytics	Analytics Ecosystem Definition
1	Choose the Web Analytics platform/tool vendor	Google Analytics (several versions now), Adobe Analytics, etc.
2	Choose the metrics to track (this may take some introspection/trial and error and experimentation to settle on the right set of metrics)	Metrics are simply numbers.
3	Define business goals	Increase revenue by 20% in the current quarter from the last quarter.
4	Develop/choose Key Performance Indicators (KPIs)	A KPI is a metric that helps you understand how you are doing against your objectives (such as bounce rate).
5	Set Dimensions for measurement	A dimension is an attribute of visitors to the website such as traffic sources, search keywords, referring sites, campaigns, countries, etc.
6	Pure data pukes (customize reporting)	Find analysts that enjoy looking at the data.
7	Analysts/big brains	Hire the right people to live with the data and interpret it for stakeholders.
8	Custom reporting	Reporting is further developed, and new reports (and metrics) are created as needed.
9	Custom data pukes	Develop analysts that know how to find the relevant data needed.
10	Set up advanced segmentation	Advanced segmentation, looking at the entire universe of website data to focusing on micro-clusters for actionable insights.
11	Develop Insights	From the data form a concept of what is happening on the website and why.
12	Take action(s)	Implement changes to improve performance and measure the results.
13	Competitive realities	Perform a SWOT analysis using your Web Analytics (and third-party data).
14	Business impacts	Quantifying what will happen once the actions are taken.
15	New opportunities	Opportunities that are developed by using the collected data.

Source: WebMetricsGuru Inc. from Avinash Kaushik.

business requests—that is as far as Web Analytics can illuminate, by itself. To reach Phases 4 and 5 of the Digital Analytics Maturity, we must go past Web Analytics and explore all the kinds of data that exist or would be useful and put them in a Data Lake or Data Warehouse. But if we just confine ourselves to Web Analytics implementation, Tables 6.3 and 6.4 serves us well.

Kaushik breaks down the implementation of Web Analytics into three phases as described in Table 6.4, which will take up to three years from start to finish to complete. However, we do not have independent research to support this view, and it is presented as bespoke findings from Avinash Kaushik, based on his writings. Perhaps companies will jump through Phases 1–3 of Table 6.4 faster, or maybe they get stuck in Phase 2 (the most frequent outcome).

Notwithstanding the above, the duration of the stages of Web/Data Analytics implementation will probably take closer to three years, per Kaushik.[3] Implementing the technology is part of the reason; the way the organization communicates internally with its stakeholders and customers is the other part.

Organizations who are not committed to analytics improvement will also have a hard time progressing beyond the first three steps of analytics projects as shown in Figure 6.2. Incidentally, Kaushik's Implementation Phases 1–3 in Table 6.4 line up very

Table 6.4 Phases of implementation of a Web Analytics ecosystem, detailed.

Phase	Characteristic	Description	Time Frame
1	Data Capture	Putting tools in place and identifying the first set of metrics; this will quickly be followed by an effort to understand business priorities.	First six months
2	Data Reporting	Many reports generated but not much business value from them (yet).	Months 7–12
3	Data Insights	Generate actionable reporting that moves organizations forward.	1–3 years

Source: WebMetricsGuru Inc. from Avinash Kaushik.

Developing and Managing Big Data Analytics Projects

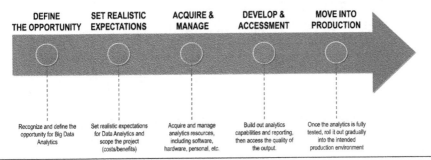

DEFINE THE OPPORTUNITY	SET REALISTIC EXPECTATIONS	ACQUIRE & MANAGE	DEVELOP & ACCESSMENT	MOVE INTO PRODUCTION
Recognize and define the opportunity for Big Data Analytics	Set realistic expectations for Data Analytics and scope the project (costs/benefits)	Acquire and manage analytics resources, including software, hardware, personal, etc.	Build out analytics capabilities and reporting, then access the quality of the output.	Once the analytics is fully tested, roll it out gradually into the intended production environment

Figure 6.2 Managing the process for Big Data Analytics adoption.
Source: WebMetricsGuru Inc.

nicely with the first three stages of Big Data adoption presented in Figure 6.2—that's because they are common measures in any data implementation, regardless of the data or tools we are discussing.

Evaluating Websites

Web Analytics platforms are designed to measure the behavior of visitors on a website, and website design (UX) on visitors. Once website KBRs are defined and matched to appropriate KBRs, it is possible to determine whether the site is fulfilling its intended purpose or not. In fact, evaluating the impact of website design and functionality on visitors is one of the main use cases for Web Analytics as shown in Figure 6.3.

Pragmatic Web Analytics

The following questions can serve as a rough guide when looking at any website's Web Analytics for the first time, and every Web Analytics platform should be able to shed light on the following:

- Which pages are working well for the purposes they are intended?
- Which pages get low or no traffic?
- Which areas in a website do visitors drop off /leave?
- Which pages are high exit pages?
- Which campaigns are driving success on a site, and which ones are just costing us money but not providing business value?
- Which products or services are selling and which are not?

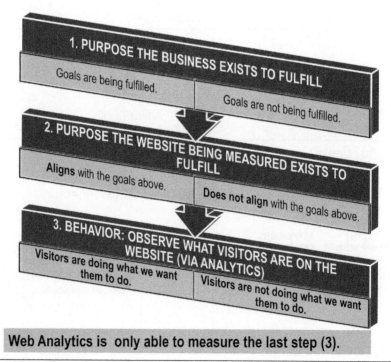

Figure 6.3 Questions to ask when understanding if a website implementation is successful. *Source*: WebMetricsGuru Inc.

Table 6.5 How Google Analytics defines conversion actions.

Type	Description	Example
Destination	A specific page location loads	A thank you page, webpage or application screen
Duration	Sessions that last a specific amount of time, or longer	Ten or more minutes spent on a support website
Pages/ pageviews per session	A user views a specific number of pages or pageviews	Five or more pages or pageviews have been loaded
Event	An action defined as an EVENT is triggered	Social share, video play, ad click, etc.

Source: WebMetricsGuru Inc. from information provided by Google Analytics Developers Portal.

This series of questions helps to deliver practical, diagnostic mini-insights that can help an organization optimize their websites, especially if they have first defined what each page is intended to do and how they would like visitors to interact and move around the site.

Goals and Conversion Events

Goals can be KPIs, often these are defined ahead of knowing what would be best to track. Fortunately, most analytics platforms allow stakeholders to define several goals, so it is usually possible to add new targets and/or refine the goals that are already in place.

There is always something unique in every business. It is likely that custom metrics and Key Performance Indicators will be more useful than the standard, out of the box "Intermediate Metrics" that analytics platforms provide. Business value arises from how the data is customized, that seems to be a universal for every subject we deal with in this book.

Key Performance Indicators (KPIs)

In Chapter 5 we mentioned that Key Business Requirements (KBRs) are informed by specific Key Performance Indicators (KPIs). Certain types of KPIs, such as "request a quote" are commonly used in certain types of businesses (i.e., automotive dealers).

Typical KPI Metrics Used by Industry

This is just a sample, there is lots of variety, customization, and creativity that can be applied here.

- **Retail:** product view, checkout, purchase
- **Media:** subscription, contest sign-up, page view, video view

- **Finance:** application submission, login, self-service tools usage
- **Travel:** booking (purchase), internal campaign (click-through), search (pricing itinerary)
- **Telecommunications:** purchase, leads, self-service tools usage
- **High-tech:** whitepaper download, RFP, form completion, support requests
- **Automotive:** lead submission, request a quote, brochure download

Definition of Good KPI

The perfect metric is the one the stakeholder or business user can understand and act on. A Key Performance Indicator is chosen because it informs business strategy and measures business growth.

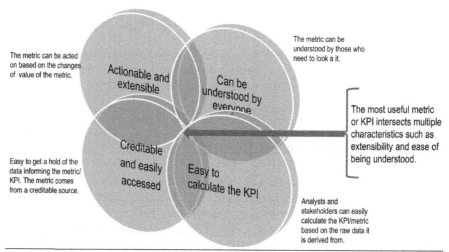

The metric can be acted on based on the changes of value of the metric.

The metric can be understood by those who need to look a it.

Actionable and extensible

Can be understood by everyone

The most useful metric or KPI intersects multiple characteristics such as extensibility and ease of being understood.

Easy to get a hold of the data informing the metric/KPI. The metric comes from a creditable source.

Creditable and easily accessed

Easy to calculate the KPI

Analysts and stakeholders can easily calculate the KPI/metric based on the raw data it is derived from.

Figure 6.4 Defining the "perfect metric."
Source: WebMetricsGuru Inc.

Data Segmentation

Web Analytics platforms provide customized segmentation (slices of data) that can inform business decisions—and in this respect, they excel over other types of analytics platforms.

The behavioral segmentation shown in Figure 6.5 illustrates three custom customer segments to an e-commerce website. Custom segments are available for most reports and provide analysts and stakeholders with unique insights. Even free platforms such as Google Analytics provide amazing segmentations based on such visitor demographics, zip code, or neighborhood, and the sky is the limit for what Web Analytics can track provided extra coding and enablement are in place. Web Analytics collects custom traffic metrics administrators define and configure such as newspaper signups, spend velocity, or anything else stakeholders and analysts define, once the data is captured in the analytics platform, and assigned to the metric. However, in the clear majority of websites, almost no instrumentation is done. Analysts should educate stakeholders about what insights it is possible to get with these systems.

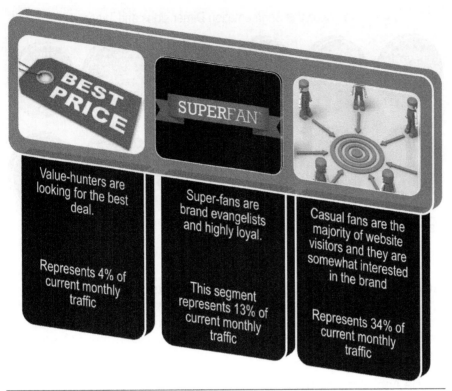

Figure 6.5 Example of behavioral segmentation on an e-commerce website.
Source: WebMetricsGuru Inc.

Custom Segmentation

Web Analytics platforms can divide visitors into different groupings, called segments.

What Can Go Into a Custom Segment

Web Analytics tracks visitor location (usually at the city level) including where visitors are coming from, what device they used, the browser, connection, time of day, day of the week, and so on. No doubt, server Web logs also contain similar information about location, date, time, etc.

Segments are comprised of many kinds of data (as per Figure 6.6) or a combination of them (provided the data be available/captured by the platform). It is best to focus on the characteristics and needs of the organization being analyzed and specific stakeholders when creating a custom segment. While Web Analytics allow analysts and administrators to create custom segmentations they should be validated against any stated or implied marketing task/goal by analysts and stakeholders. Segments exist for a specific marketing purpose; segments should be tested and validated against the intended goal for that segment, before using it for reporting. If the segment is not capturing the intended data, it should be improved until it does, or discarded.

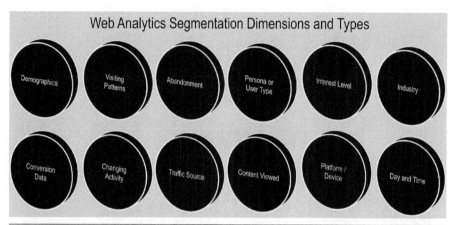

Figure 6.6 Segmentation types in Web Analytics.
Source: WebMetricsGuru Inc.

Adobe Analytics Custom Segments

Adobe Analytics has enhanced segmentation shared across multiple groups in the same organization, and similar segmentations capabilities exist in most Web Analytics platforms.

Adobe Analytics Segmentation Types

There are three basic types of segmentation, along with a new enhanced "programmable" segmentation type that were released in the spring of 2015. You can create programmable segments when certain defined Boolean logic conditions occur. Boolean segmentation (programmable segments) are a hybrid grouping type we have not seen in the other Web Analytics platforms we have used. More likely, if they don't exist in Google Analytics today, they probably will be added, eventually.

Analysts can define and reuse segments when needed and even build segments from other segments along with preset segment templates (Adobe Analytics). Also, multiple segments can be applied at the same time and compared with other segments. In Google Analytics, custom segments are even easier to create and apply than Adobe Analytics (the user interface is easier to manipulate and more intuitive). However, it is far more challenging to define the best segment to build (and then test it). According to Gary Angel:

> Segmentations divide people into interestingly differentiated groups. Every business has segments, and for every business, they are potentially infinite and unique. There's no single right segmentation, but segmentation is always useful. I have never studied a digital property that can't or shouldn't be segmented.[4]

Usually, there is a business need to examine the behavior of a heterogeneous group of visitors or visits, and that reason drives the creation and iteration of the segment.

Custom Segment Examples

By now readers should have an idea that segments are created to examine situations where stakeholders and analysts want to know more about certain visitors. Web

Table 6.6 Adobe Analytics segmentation types.

Segmentation Type	Definition	Example
Hit Based	Actions happening on a specific page or a specific resource such as a link to a page	Clicks on links on a specific page—a conversion event that exists only on a specific page (i.e., shopping cart checkout might be one example).
Visit Based	Visits occurring due to a campaign, or anything that happens during a specific visit	Paid search campaigns, tracking if a visitor is logged in or not during their visit (when authentication is present) and viewing specific content during a visit are some examples.
Visitor Based	Information about the state of visitors to the website (over a series of visits).	New vs. repeat visitors, registered vs. non-registered visitors, new customers vs. loyal customers and any geo-demographics such as age, gender, location.
Programmable (Logic Group)	Boolean logic triggered, exists if certain conditions are met (using "IF THEN" statements).	Visitor contribution goes beyond a certain value trigger, creates a segment and stores information about the visitor.

Source: WebMetricsGuru Inc. based on material from Adobe Education.

Table 6.7 Adobe Analytics segmentation examples.

Segment Example	Segment Type
Anyone who spent more than $600 on the retail website	VISITOR (set Revenue > 600 US)
A specific visit where $600 or more was spent	VISITOR (set Revenue >= 600 US)
Visitors that hand spent more than $600 over the lifetime of their visits to the website	VISITOR (set Revenue >= 600 US)
Males in the United States who purchased an item during a visit	VISITOR (set Gender = Male AND Country = the United States)
All visitors to specific sections of the website	VISITOR (set Site Section = Men AND Site Section = Woman)
Collect all the visits to the Men's Apparel page AND viewed two specific Men's Wallet pages (leather AND snakeskin) within 16 pages of each other (uses a logic group)	VISIT (set Page = Men's Apparel) THEN (within 16 pages of each other) (Page = Men's leather wallet AND Page = Men's snakeskin wallet)
Collect visitors that have more than ten visits to the website OR visitors from a specific campaign and spent at least $110 during that visit.	VISIT (Visit number >= 10) OR ((Campaign = Snakeskin Wallets paid ads AND Campaign Clickthroughs = True) AND Revenue >= 110 USD))

Source: WebMetricsGuru Inc. based on material from Adobe Education.

Analytics platforms support various kinds of segmentations (these could be set up with Google Analytics free version as well—anyone could create segments, even without administrative access, when needed).

Goal-Setting

The most important reason to implement Web Analytics is to gather the data regarding a website's chosen KPIs to provide the standard from which to compare changes in values over time. When starting with KPI measurement, take a baseline measurement of the metrics that comprise the KPIs—this will usually be an amount or percentage to gauge progress. Note that KPI ideation and formation should come first, but more often it happens the other way around because it is hard to know what to measure until you know what Web Analytics is capable of measuring. In other words, we do not know what we do not know...until we learn about it firsthand or hear about it secondhand and go ahead and experiment (try something new). When looking at deploying Web Analytics as a constantly evolving process, there is no perfect way to implement it in the complex business environment that most organizations operate in, and there will always be something done that should be better. As mentioned earlier, when beginning a new Web Analytics implementation, it is likely some of it may be changed later, as more information surfaces. The Web Analytics iteration process supports our belief that Web Analytics is a process, rather than a deliverable product.

Measuring Customer Acquisition

When a visitor visits a website, they generate data. Marketers can measure the impact of visitor activities as they happen on the site.

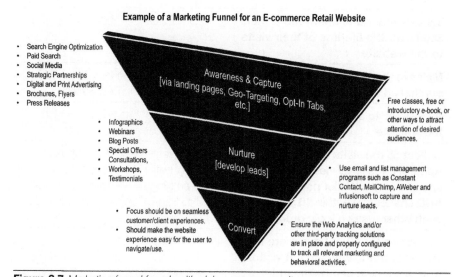

Figure 6.7 Marketing funnel for a health club e-commerce site.
Source: WebMetricsGuru Inc.

As we covered earlier in this section, while the customer journey is not truly a funnel; the visualization of a funnel is closer to how marketers envision the traffic traversing through their websites.

Traffic Sources

Except for the origin of the traffic the reports for each traffic source, are similar.

- **Organic search:** All the Web Analytics platforms report on a search engine, search keyword, and website referrals (links) by domain and pages. Search engine reports show the exact keywords that visitors type into their browsers (in search engines) that lead to a visit to the website.
- **Website referrals:** When a visitor arrives at the website by clicking on a link to the site that is on another site (as opposed to a search engine), this is called a site referral or link referral. Some platforms report Web domain referrals as well as page referrals; there may be a reason for this involving revenue allocation (when e-commerce is present), and it may also tie into attribution tracking that Google Analytics has become quite adept at providing over the past five years or so. Adobe Analytics (but not Google Analytics) provides the "original referring domain" reporting for attribution tracking. When a visitor returns to the website over several sessions but doesn't arrive from the same source, the analytics platform records all the sourced from which the visitor arrived (via cookie tracking). When the visitor makes a purchase (or conversion), it can be compared based on the attribution model of the last source or the very first source, in any case, the Web Analytics platform records the source of a visit.

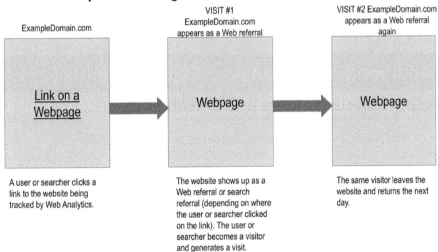

Example of Tracking Web Referrals in Web Analytics

Figure 6.8 How Web Analytics records Web referrals.
Source: WebMetricsGuru Inc.

Other referral sources

- **Direct traffic:** This type of traffic comes from people (visitors) who have already been to the website before *or* who know the name of the business/URL and simply type it into their browser address bar.
- **Paid search traffic:** When an advertiser runs paid search ads (i.e., using Google AdWords) they can set up their advertising along with the landing page. The URLs must be "tagged" properly with campaign parameters so that Web Analytics systems can tell the difference between an organic search referral and a paid one.
- **Other types of campaign traffic:** Can include email campaigns (which also need to be tagged so that the Analytics platform can tell what kind of traffic it is—where it originates) as the email client does not usually supply that data to the Web Analytics platform.
- **Social media:** Twitter, Facebook, LinkedIn et al. send traffic to websites, but the Web Analytics might not always be able to tell much more than the channel. Unfortunately, most social media sources of traffic to websites are walled gardens—they supply few details to the analytics platform of the actions that led to the visit. Google Analytics has a "data hub" that some social media channels participate in allowing for more details of the visitor referral (for example, a visit from Google Blogger provides the exact blog post the visit came from). Meetup.com (a data hub partner) provides the specific meetup group that resulted in a visit, but a session originating from Facebook, Twitter or LinkedIn does not have that level of data. The sharing of user identity information is a subject in and of itself, not covered in depth in this book. However, it is evident that social media users want to feel confident that they can use these sites/apps without having their privacy violated, channels such as Twitter and Facebook limit how much they share of this content.

There are other sources of traffic including mobile visits; most Web traffic comes from mobile devices, and, since 2015, Google evaluates websites as mobile friendly or not. Web Analytics treats mobile sessions as a separate set of reports that doesn't get bundled in with the sources we discussed so far in this section.

Additional Web Analytics Platform Features

Report Visualizations and Dashboards

The commonly used metrics produced by Web/Data Analytics platform are intermediate metrics; to turn the standardized outputs into actionable KPIs, they almost always are customized or transformed. Regardless of the platform, Web data is usually displayed in a few standard formats. Metrics have line items that give context and definition to the data along with graphic elements (bar graphs, pie charts, and trends are the most common visual elements). The information imparted is almost identical and has been moving towards having a more standard functionality as an analyst dashboard of sorts that is configurable and extensible (dashboards can be created on the fly, customized, and shared with co-workers with little effort).

Rollups

Web Analytics platforms can roll up multiple websites monitored to one comprehensive view, especially useful for large organizations that have many sites tracked by Web Analytics in separate profiles that also want to compare the performance of each next to one another using the rollup property, in this case (see Figure 6.9).

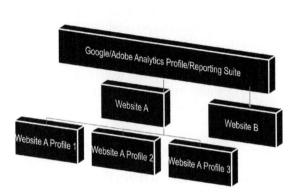

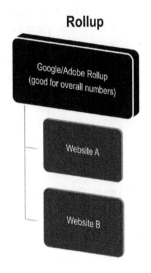

Cross domain tracking in Web Analytics: Sometimes it is more efficient to roll up numbers (which effectively "de-duplicates" traffic counts between different owned media digital properties).

Figure 6.9 Cross domain tracking in Web Analytics.
Source: WebMetricsGuru Inc.

Report Filtering

The text within analytics reports can be filtered by characters, regular expressions, or Boolean equations to find pages that have the exact or similar patterns. However, filtering can be applied at the profile level in Google Analytics.[5] Filtering is done to include or exclude certain data; typically, this is done to exclude traffic coming from the same domain as the website that is being monitored via Web Analytics or to exclude referrer spam that has become much more common in analytics reports of late.[6] However, one capability that is lacking from all Web Analytics platforms is filtering at the content level of a page/website, although this precisely what Web search engines provide.

Standard Reporting

There are standard reports that are very similar across platforms—we will not go over them here as there are several books and online videos/tutorials on them. There are differences between Adobe Analytics and Google Analytics regarding the details of setup and details of how the reports are displayed, but at a basic user level they are identical. However, as installations become more customized and higher-end (more expensive and complicated), there may be workflow, feature, and pricing differences (along with financing and license usage rights) that give one platform an advantage over the other.

Real-Time Data

Almost all Web Analytics platforms provide "real-time" readouts of traffic with little or no latency. However, standard and custom reports should be assembled from raw data sent over to the analytics server. Thus, it is reasonable to expect some delay of anywhere from a few hours to a day for standard reports. In most cases, it does not matter if the data is real-time or not, as organizations rarely act quickly to make changes on their websites. In some cases, having real-time data makes a meaningful difference and is worth having (i.e., a large publisher of the New York Times website[7] or a larger retailer like Amazon.com[8]). Analytics platforms that include near- or real-time reporting of Web data for organizations are appropriate for those who are willing to pay a significant amount for the real-time data.

"Time Spent" Calculations in Web Analytics

When it comes to calculating how long the visit to a page lasts (called a pageview); when a visit results in a single pageview, it is referred to as a "bounce (bounce rate)." The "time spent" on a page is not calculated when the visitor does not visit another page. The "average time spent" is calculated by dividing the total minutes spent on a page from all visits divided by the number of pageviews for that page; the same calculations are done at the site level as well.

Time spent is a metric calculated by comparing the time a visitor spends on a page with the time spent on the next page the user visits during their visit (as shown in Figure 6.10).

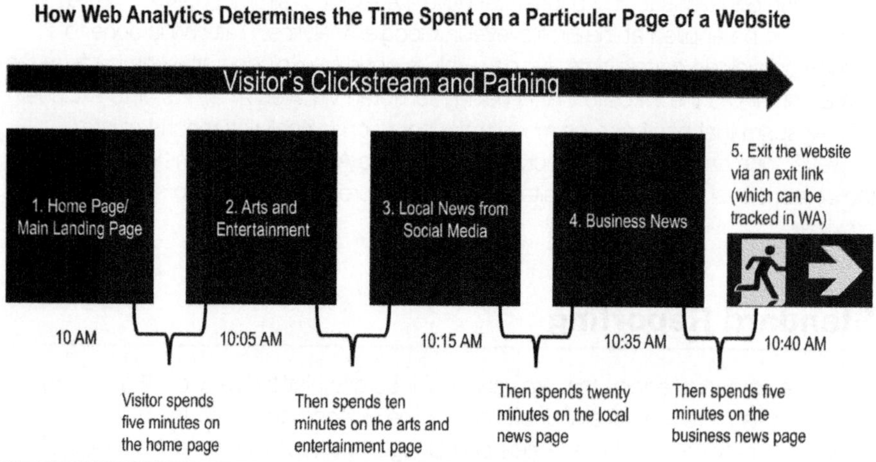

How Web Analytics Determines the Time Spent on a Particular Page of a Website

Figure 6.10 Web Analytics method of calculating time spent on a page (and of a visit/session). *Source*: WebMetricsGuru Inc., inspired by Adobe Education.

Participation/Contribution/Unique Page Value

Most Web Analytics platforms assign specific values to pages on the website (for engagement tracking), and when a user lands on that page in their path through the site, the value is added to the counter to calculate how engaged the user is in the website experience (during a visit).

Participation Grade/Page Scoring Grade
(All Web Analytics platforms have some method of weighting the value of a page towards a particular goal or purpose).

Figure 6.11 Adding page scoring to specific pages of a website.
Source: WebMetricsGuru Inc., informed by Adobe Education.

Setting up page scoring (the best name we can come up with for this feature) administrative access to analytics platform is needed.

Designing Dashboards

Reports are created, configured, and annotated so they can be seen in virtually any context that an analyst or stakeholder wants (dashboards are often hard for end users to grapple with unless they are annotated). Every major Web Analytics platform has configurable and standard dashboards as well as mobile applications where analytics reports can be viewed. Dashboards are standard fare for Web Analytics, and they can even be delivered by email and set up to be updated on a regular basis. Certainly, segmentation (custom segments) combined with dashboards makes them more efficient, because you can take a magnifying glass and blow up a specific group of visitors (or visits) in the context that a dashboard can highlight (such as geo-location, purchases, etc.). Dashboards can be made up of whatever the analyst or stakeholder wants them to be. If the data is present in the reporting suite or profile (what it is called is depends on the platform) it should be able to be added to a dashboard, especially if there is a defined business need to see the information in a defined context).

Geo-Segmentation

Web Analytics platforms can collect as much information about visitors as organizations, and particularly stakeholders desire. The one segmentation most analytics platforms have *without any customization* is the ability to geo-locate web traffic down to the city level (with additional enablement geo-segmentation can be further refined to focus on lat/long codes, zip codes, election districts, neighborhoods, and DMAs, or any custom combination thereof). Geo-segmentation reports can be broken down in several ways including designated marketing areas (such as greater NYC DMA), and Web Analytics platforms are flexible in how location is defined, and an analyst (administrator) could even make their own "DMA" or election district, if desired. Google Analytics allows users to visualize geo-location against almost any metric.

Technologies/Network Segmentation

Another type of segmentation that exists out of the box is the one associated with the service provider that allows visitors to access the Internet. The information from the Internet service provider (ISP) is often taken for granted but it is much richer as almost any business has its ISP/network address registered in its name. The Technologies/Network Segmentation report, for example, is a standard feature provided by Google Analytics and made available to analytics users. This report provides actual business names of a significant percentage of the website visitors to a website (useful information for generating business leads). Depending on the organization and their goals, knowledge of other businesses visiting the website can provide lead generation information and even drive some degree of content automation.

Campaign Tracking

Campaign tracking is a way to track specific actions that happen on a website with Web Analytics. Events on websites are assigned by administrators with a campaign code to make it easier to track (usually a link, could be a video or even file download). Campaign tracking requires coordination between stakeholders and administrators. The tracking codes can be set up by the administrator using unique identifiers that are chosen by the marketers, so they are easy to identify within the analytics reports.

Campaign Performance

Like any other URL on a website, a campaign can be examined using the "funnel" construct (or user flow diagram as shown in Figure 6.7) to see the impact of the campaign (or specific campaign code). Campaign codes with conversion funnels (or user flow diagrams) are a powerful means to track campaign performance. Funnels are useful when there are set ideas of what paths should be traversed by the customer (and in what order) for a campaign to be successful. Funnels work best for organizations with defined business processes and marketing campaigns. Most analytics platforms allow comparisons between two periods of time in most reports they provide; campaign funnels.

Attribution Models

When a visitor comes to a website the first time from a paid search ad and buys something (conversion event), it is evident the attribution is from a paid search campaign (that brought this visitor to the website/landing page).

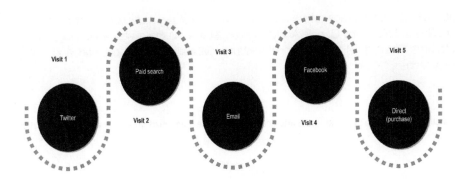

ATTRIBUTION METHODS: DEPENDING ON THE MODEL USED, DIFFERENT PARTS OF A VISITOR'S CLICKSTREAM BECOME MORE OR LESS IMPORTANT FOR DETERMING MARKETING ROI

Figure 6.12 Marketing attribution.
Source: WebMetricsGuru Inc.

However, what about when it is not?

What happens when a visitor returns to a site several times (not always by the same channel) before deciding if they engage in a conversion event (buy something, most often)—how do we count it? Do we give all the credit to the "first touch" attribution (paid search) or "last touch" attribution (say, Facebook)? How organizations decide to count success is more a marketing, and perhaps even a political decision, but it has profound implications in an omnichannel world where the customer journey often is not linear, as illustrated in Figure 6.13.

In Figure 6.13, paid search generated a different weighting depending on the last touch (default), first touch, or linear (each channel in the conversion process is assigned equal weight).

There are several types of attribution beyond the first touch, as shown in Figure 6.13, such as last touch attribution, linear, time decay, position-based, and custom attribution that can be set up using Web Analytics. Rather than discuss each type of

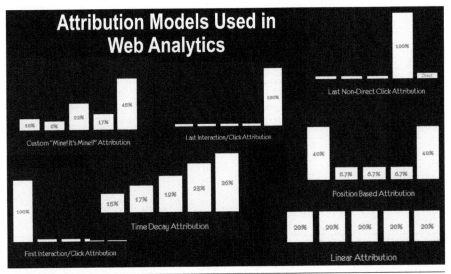

Figure 6.13 Various attribution models commonly used in Web Analytics reporting.
Source: WebMetricsGuru Inc.

attribution in detail, readers who want to know more about multichannel attribution should read a post by Google Analytics Evangelist Avinash Kaushik at his blog, *Occam's Razor*, titled "Multi-Channel Attribution Modeling: The Good, Bad, and Ugly Models."[9]

Calculating the value of social media Interactions is possible using platforms such as Google Analytics

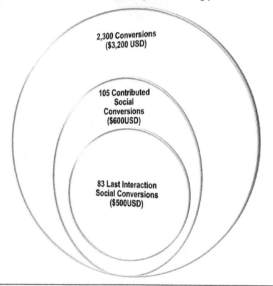

Figure 6.14 Google Analytics—social value report.
Source: WebMetricsGuru Inc.

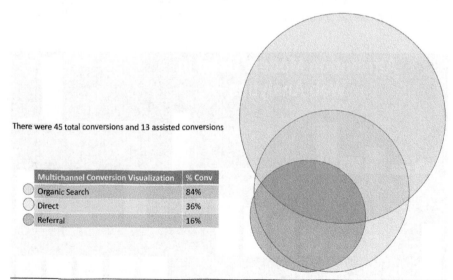

Figure 6.15 Google Analytics—multichannel conversion visualization.
Source: WebMetricsGuru Inc., referencing Google Analytics.

Which metrics are agreed upon and put in place has profound implications for how organizations function; the subject could be a book in and of itself. Metrics simplify complex situations but often come with a cost, losing sight of the real end goals.[10]

Assisted Conversions

Google Analytics has a type of visualization report called "assisted conversions" to help business owners and analysts better understand conversions taking place over more than one channel. By now most Web Analytics platforms have reporting similar to assisted conversions that include something like assisted conversions.

Tracking Mobile Traffic

Mobile Web traffic is vital. Mobile traffic makes up most Web activity that websites receive and is now a Google Search Ranking Factor as of April 21, 2015. The whole idea of what a website is has changed mirroring the development of Web 1.0, 2.0, 3.0 and 4.0 that we studied earlier. How can we ever be sure that Web Analytics platforms ever track all that activity? We cannot.

There have been several improvements to mobile device tracking in the Web Analytics platforms since smartphones became so dominant as communications and Web browsing medium including improved visitor identification, better mobile device-specific data collection, and reporting.

Table 6.9 shows the variety of reporting on a mobile device that is available in Adobe Analytics, and much the same functionality exists in Google Analytics although the specific reports might have different names. The key lies in mapping business

Table 6.8 Similarities and differences between the mobile Web vs. mobile apps.

	Mobile Web	Mobile Apps
DIFFERENT	• Unique mobile reports/dimensions • GPS locations (HTML5) • Smaller and more diverse form factors • Touch and Gesture Interactions	• Cohort analysis • SDKs for tracking code • Version fragmentation • Screen views and similar metrics • Offline usage • Shorter session timeout
SIMILAR	• JavaScript tagging • Conversion, traffic, and engagement KPIs	• Campaign tracking • Event tracking • Engagement and conversion metrics

Source: WebMetricsGuru Inc.

Table 6.9 Mobile device reports that Web Analytics platforms typically provide.

Report Type		Device data that is reported on in Web Analytics
Mobile Devices		By vendor, by device model
Device Type		Is the device a phone, tablet, gaming console or e-reader, etc.
Device Manufacturer		The vendor that manufactured the device such as Samsung, Apple, etc.
Screen Size		Display width x display height for all the devices detected by the Web Analytics platform
Screen Height		Hight of the mobile device display
Screen Width		Width of the mobile device display
Cookie Support		Display the cookies that are/aren't supported by the device model/operating system of the device
Image Support		Various types of image display times such as GIF, PNG, JPG, etc.
Audio Format		Various types of audio files that the mobile device accessing the website is able store such as MP3, etc.
Screen Color Depth		The number of colors a device can display
Video Format		Various video file formats that are able to be stored and played by the mobile device.

Source: WebMetricsGuru Inc. from Adobe Education.

needs with reporting capabilities (and then reporting it back to stakeholders in a language they understand).

Visitor Retention

Determining the activity of "loyal" customers (those who have made a purchase or registered on the website) in Web Analytics is commonly defined by the frequency with which a customer returns to the site, how long they spend during their visit, and how many pages they view. The number of products or services purchased on a recurring basis is examined in customer loyalty reports as well.

Return/Frequency

Adobe and Google Analytics provide similar readouts and segments showing the days between the last visit/session where the user took a specific action; in Google Analytics, this report is generated by running the "days since last session" report.

Visit Number Reports

Visit numbers, when combined with additional conversion metrics, can be very useful readouts. By combining visit numbers with other custom metrics, such as registrations, stakeholders can find the moment of maximum profitability for a marketing activity.

Sales Cycle Report (Adobe)

This report is unique to Adobe Analytics (platforms often have unique features and reports) but can be replicated in most other Web Analytics platforms. In this report, the variable "**s. Purchase**" needs to be set up to track consumer purchases by the administrator of the system and is best suited for retail sites. There are a couple of variations of the report, one for new, repeat, and loyal customers, and others that relate to the days before and after the first or last purchase.

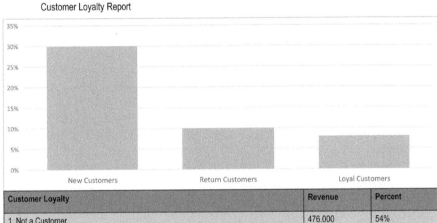

Customer Loyalty	Revenue	Percent
1. Not a Customer	476.000	54%
2. New Customers	331.000	28%
3. Return Customers	450.000	10%
4. Loyal Customers	250.000	8%

Figure 6.16 Customer loyalty report.
Source: WebMetricsGuru Inc., deriving information from Adobe Education.

Customer loyalty reports provides site owners with a good idea of how much of the revenue collected on the website is happening on the first visit versus subsequent visits. However, the real question is how a loyal customer is defined.

- New customers = first purchase on the website.
- Return customers = second purchase on the site.
- Loyal customers = third purchase and more on the site.

Metrics definition could be tweaked to say that loyal customers are only those who buy more than four or five times, but that is a marketing decision, not an analytics decision.

Setting Targets

Adobe Analytics can report how website performance measures stated goals. Targets enable stakeholders to track the progress of each site goal they create, and targets can be added to any dashboard. Adobe Analytics allows additional flexibility in how targets are set up. The analyst or stakeholder set up the targets, so any value over zero would have been "above the target." Google Analytics does not have targets (at least, not in this sense) but there are other third-party integrations such as Klipfolio that provide report targets appropriate for dashboard reports.

Academic Research Synopsis: "Journalism is Twerking? How Web Analytics is Changing the Process of Gatekeeping"[11]

Most online publishers also use Web Analytics to monitor the performance of their website/publishing portal, they can also use the data to evaluate the performance of specific news stories and articles along with the specific journalists who create the information is available as first-party data to the publisher. As news and magazine publishers have seen vast changes in their industries due to the Internet and social media, there have been many attempts to reward journalists for creating content that draws many page views and visits. Advertising can be displayed, and the publisher makes revenue based on the advertising and subscriptions.

Twerking, as mentioned in the title of the paper refers to an incident in 2013, when Miley Cyrus shocked people with her performance at the *MTV Video Music Awards*. MTV uploaded a story about the stunt and CNN used the article as a story on their homepage. It was an attempt to drive up their Web traffic, which in turn would allow CNN to increase their advertising revenue.

Measuring Web traffic via Web Analytics is now common, and in newsrooms traffic generation has become a requirement of the job—if the journalist does not generate enough relevant traffic because of their articles they may lose their job. Publishers are using Web Analytics (along with search engine optimization) to choose the subjects, phrases, and keywords that the journalist is asked to write. The following is a summary of a research paper on the way newsroom publishers use Web Analytics to decide what to publish (and what not to publish).

Questions/Hypothesis

- How do journalists use Web Analytics in their news work? (Restated—there are several use cases where Web Analytics is used for news work, and it has influenced journalism.)
- What factors influence journalists to use Web Analytics in their news work?

Gatekeeping: Content Curation

This paper uses the term "gatekeeping" rather than another that we prefer called "content *curation*." Gatekeeping is "the process of selecting, writing, editing, positioning, scheduling, repeating, and otherwise massaging information to become news," both terms are synonymous for this peer-research review.

Caveat, as more news aggregators/publishers use "clickbait" titles. It could be difficult to determine if the audience enjoyed the content. In such instances, other metrics such as session duration and time spent on page (collected by Web Analytics) can be deployed to get a better understanding of content effectiveness.

Using Web Analytics in Newsrooms

Publishers and newsrooms use Web Analytics to understand how their published content is being received by their online audience. The Intermediate Metrics produced by Web Analytics are used to determine, in many cases, how compelling a news story is. Not all writers or editors write for audience impact, but increasingly (to the researcher's alarm) more are doing so.

Ethnographic Research Methodology

The researcher conducted 30 interviews with three news publishers in Singapore. The observations from the interviews were coded into a text analytics platform called Nvivo. The paper cites a case where the editor of one of the three newsrooms chose a story about the Pope to run over the weekend. Their story was published because Web Analytics reports indicated it was receiving more traffic.

> "There's much interest over the weekend about the Pope being a 'regular' guy," the editor said, adding that stories on the new Pope did well on Chartbeat. "It was resonating over the weekend."[12]

Web Analytics Platforms Referred to in the Study

- **Adobe Analytics:** Omniture—essentially "Web Analytics." Adobe Analytics provides basic Web statistics and clickstream data on articles, column pages, and the overall online publication—it may also provide advertising and revenue reports.
- **Chartbeat:** Web Analytics with real-time visual diagrams—closer to heat maps with analytics data superimposed.

Example:

> A Web editor at the other newsroom took out a business story from the homepage to make space for a new sports story he was sure would get much more traffic. However, when he checked Chartbeat again, the business story he had taken out was the eighth most-viewed story so far. He decided to put it back. Instead, he took out a story on a girl who was shot dead, saying, "If it does not get any traction in 20–30 minutes, we usually pull it out."[13] Note that online news publishers make money on stories that have an extremely short shelf life; decisions on where to place the story need to be done very quickly to maximize the value of the story.

- **Visual Revenue** (news story placement and advertising analytics): VR determines how interested online audience is in a story that is currently on the news site. It considers when the story has been online too long, not long enough, or whether it was properly placed, and calculates the revenue impact of those decisions around where to place the story and how to preview/change the title of the story, so it gets more audience attention—one of the co-authors knows with the founder of this platform. In 2014 Visual Revenue was acquired by OutBrain, another advertising platform.

Example:

A web editor talked about a story that quoted a football player saying "bad barbecue makes me want to fight." The article was a blog post buried in the sports page and had gone unnoticed by the homepage editors. However, then, out of the blue, Visual Revenue recommended putting it on the homepage. The web editor followed the recommendation, took an underperforming story out and replaced it with the "bad barbecue" story which ended up being the day's most viewed story.[14]

Findings

Question 1: How Do Journalists Use Web Analytics in their News Work?

While journalists are not known to be early adopters of technology, as they adopt new technologies, they fit them to into their existing norms and routines.

- **Newsroom editors discussed what topics were popular on social media at the current moment with the social media manager or assistant managing editor.** Stories that had generated good traffic, based on Web Analytics reporting, get more frequent updates and follow-ups from editors. Topics that have done well in the past also tend to be assigned to reporters, again and again.
- **Selection and "de-selection" of news stories on the home page was impacted by Web Analytics metrics and algorithms (via Visual Revenue).** Visual Revenue, using its own built-in Web Analytics, allows editors to determine which stories to run based their profitability for the publisher.
- **Algorithms are being used to suggest the best titles of a story and its framing**. The researcher observed a Web editor in the act of choosing two possible headlines for the same thing. Visual Revenue randomly exposed readers to one of the two headlines. The first version got a 9% rating while the other version got 42%. The editor decided to go with the second headline based on Visual Revenue's recommendation.
- **While social media can be used to improve stories already online, the observed publications treated it as another traffic delivery mechanism**. The stories promoted the most were those shared on social media as clickbait.
- **What the audience wants is now understood through which stories generate traffic.** Generating significant Web traffic was equated to a job well done by the article's author.

Question 2: In What Other Ways Does Web Analytics Affect Newsrooms?

- Editors no longer ignore audiences, although they appeared to be more interested in what the audience clicked on than what they thought about the stories.
- Newspapers have become online publishers, with the belief that the revenues they generate will be enough for them to stay in business.

- The editors observed for this study professed that they cared more about good journalism than Web traffic. However, their behavior told a different story. Editors looked at their Web traffic dashboards most of the day, and they were deciding the stories to publish based their traffic potential.

Limitations of This Research Study

- Ethnographic observations made by one researcher on three newsrooms in Singapore.

Review Questions

1. What is segmentation and define the steps to go into creating a custom segment in Web Analytics? Do Web Analytics platforms already have some predefined segments out of the box, or does the user should define all the segments they use?
2. Name the two types of reports in Web Analytics.

Chapter 6 Citations

1. Fattah, A. "IBM Big Data & Analytics Hub." www.ibmbigdatahub.com/blog/author/ahmed-fattah. Accessed April 15, 2017.

2. Kaushik, A. "Digital marketing and measurement model: Web Analytics." www.kaushik.net/avinash/digital-marketing-and-measurement-model. Accessed April 15, 2017.

3. Kaushik, A. "Digital marketing and measurement model: Web Analytics." www.kaushik.net/avinash/digital-marketing-and-measurement-model. Accessed April 15, 2017.

4. Angel, G. (2016) *Measuring the Digital World: Using Digital Analytics to Drive Better Digital Experiences*. Upper Saddle River, NJ: Pearson Education, Inc.

5. "Create a filter in Google Analytics." Wikihow. January 18, 2017. www.wikihow.com/Create-a-Filter-in-Google-Analytics. Accessed April 15, 2016.

6. Escalera, C. "Stop ghost spam in Google Analytics with one filter." August 3, 2015. https://moz.com/blog/stop-ghost-spam-in-google-analytics-with-one-filter. Accessed April 15, 2017.

7. Hunter, L. "*New York Times* chief data scientist Chris Wiggins on the way we create and consume content now." July 24, 2014. www.fastcompany.com/3033254/most-creative-people/new-york-times-chief-data-scientist-chris-wiggins-on-the-way-we-create-. Accessed April 15, 2017.

8. Gothwa, A. "All you wanted to know about analytics in e-commerce." February 7, 2015. www.slideshare.net/anjugothwal/all-you-wanted-to-know-about-analytics-in-e-commerce-amazon-ebay-flipkart-44396611. Accessed April 15, 2017.

9. Kaushik, A. "Multi-channel Attribution Modeling: The Good, Bad, and Ugly Models" November 8, 2013. www.kaushik.net/avinash/multi-channel-attribution-modeling-good-bad-ugly-models. Accessed April 15, 2017.

10. Fowler, M. "An appropriate use of metrics." February 19, 2013. http://martinfowler.com/articles/useOfMetrics.html. Accessed April 15, 2017.

11. "Journalism is twerking? How Web Analytics is changing the process of gatekeeping." April 11, 2014. http://nms.sagepub.com/content/16/4/559.abstract. Accessed April 15, 2017.

12. "Journalism is twerking?", p. 568.

13. "Journalism is twerking?", p. 568.

14. "Journalism is twerking?", p. 568.

Understanding and Working with Third-Party Data

CHAPTER OBJECTIVES

After reading this chapter, readers should understand:

- Digital data ecosystems and third-party data
- Data Lakes and Big Data
- Tag Management systems and data collection
- Web Analytics Maturity Models
- Audience analytics using third-party data providers (panel based)
- Additional third-party market research tools available at university libraries for student use
- Geo-location analytics and geo-location case studies
- Introduction to programmatic advertising

We will go into the specifics of the advantages and disadvantages of third-party information in this chapter—specifically, how to evaluate and use data that is acquired from external vendors.

First-, Second- and Third-Party Data

Organizations use Web Analytics to collect first-party data on their digital properties. Below, we describe the characteristics of first-, second- and third-party data.

First-party data is collected by issuing the first-party cookie to the Web browser of a visitor to a website running Web Analytics software. Other applications are running on a site serving first-party cookies as well. Most websites issue first-party cookies for applications and login information that takes place on their website.

Second-party data is the first-party data collected from a business partner (via a first-party cookie) and shared with another party (usually an affiliate). For example, many online banking and credit card customers provide first-party data that is then provided to their business partners (the terms of this arrangement are usually appear in terms of service of the website). Note: there is no such thing as a "second-party cookie," although, as explained, second-party data exists and is always shared with trusted partners—that is how it becomes "second-party" information.

Third-party data is information collected by using a third-party cookie that is issued to a Web browser of a visitor to the website it is issued from. Third-party cookies are issued by various services (many of them are advertising-based) that follow online users across the Internet and collect behavioral information about their activities.

This chapter will focus on the uses of third-party data along with a few third-party market research platforms that are popular with many digital marketers.

Targeting New Customers using Third-Party Data

There is a good reason to collect third-party data on consumers as it seems to be better adapted to target new or potential customers with. Third-party data is particularly useful for the advertisers to determine where to run ads. Moreover, if we step back and look at advertising as means of customer acquisition, then we can make a far-reaching statement—*third-party data could be better suited for acquiring new customers than the first-party data that we already collect via in-house databases and Web Analytics.* Here's why:

- Third-party data vendors are very focused on collecting, aggregating, normalizing, de-duplicating, and summarizing different sets of consumer data into a useable form for marketers. Putting it another way; the data is already cleaned and organized in ways that organizations would find useful.
- Third-party data has a richer selection and range of consumer and customer data than most organizations can collect on their own. Meanwhile, the first-party data gathered by organizations via in-house databases and Web/Search Analytics are not always as well-organized as they could be.

The artful use of third-party data empowers customer acquisition and advertising strategies (that is the main reason third-party data providers are in business). However, third-party data is not usually created to be interoperable across other third-party data providers. When business users combine data collected by one provider with the data provided by another they often run into problems. Here's why:

- Each provider has their own reasons for collecting data—this impacts the context and format of their product offering, possibly making it incompatible with similar datasets offered by alternative providers.
- Third-party data providers want to lock users into using their own data products, so they are not motivated to provide interoperable datasets.
- Most third-party providers are not transparent about how they prepare their datasets, and too often we are not able to find out the actual sample size of the panel.

Just as the bricks of a wall require alignment in the precise dimensions of the building blocks, layering data requires the same precision, but this precision cannot be verified with third-party datasets.

Consequently, our recommendation to readers is to use third-party data sources alongside each other but avoid combining the data into a single metric. However, organizations often end up combining different data feeds because they need select elements in each one that the others do not have.

Managing Third-Party Platforms

Ironically, most of the literature on third-party data platforms was written, provided, and copyrighted by the third-party vendor. Thus, it was difficult to discuss third-party offerings independently of the vendor's claims about the integrity and effectiveness of their products. However, third-party data firms/brokers like comScore and Nielsen collect a lot of useful data. The data is valuable, especially when it is combined with the first-party data such as Web Analytics, customer databases, surveys, and campaign data. Also, third-party data can be combined with second-party data that business partners share with each other. Bridging the gap between the first-party and third-party data source requires the information is merged in some way. Third-party audience analytics is not a complete measurement solution, but when it is supplemented with first-party Web Analytics data the audience readouts give a sense of how much further along the purchase funnel the user/visitor went.

Uses of First-, Second-, and Third-Party Data

Customer lists and Web Analytics (first-party data) have well-established reasons for being used in marketing campaigns and initiatives. However, consumer information (namely, second and third-party data that has been acquired by the data vendors) require more thought and care in their use by marketers, because there is usually no visibility in the details of how that data was acquired and prepared (i.e., "hidden bias"). There are a wide variety of platforms that collect data on us (consumers) and are doing various things with this information. With the complexity of the data being produced by applications, it is necessary to use Tag Management to connect different third-party platforms and customize data collection and services on websites. Figuring out which platforms to use is tough—each platform in the marketing technology stack has its strengths and weaknesses.

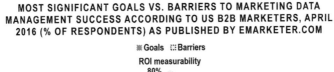

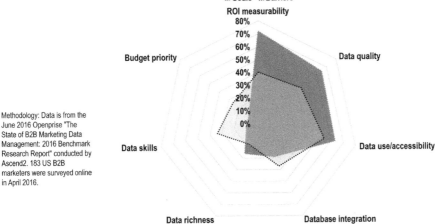

MOST SIGNIFICANT GOALS VS. BARRIERS TO MARKETING DATA MANAGEMENT SUCCESS ACCORDING TO US B2B MARKETERS, APRIL 2016 (% OF RESPONDENTS) AS PUBLISHED BY EMARKETER.COM

Methodology: Data is from the June 2016 Openprise "The State of B2B Marketing Data Management: 2016 Benchmark Research Report" conducted by Ascend2. 183 US B2B marketers were surveyed online in April 2016.

Figure 7.1 Goals vs. barriers to digital marketing data management.
Source: WebMetricsGuru Inc. with data sourced through eMarketer.com.

The marketing technology stack is too vast to compare strengths and weakness of each platform individually. In aggregate, the marketing technology stack allows plug and play capability via third-party Application Programming Interfaces (APIs). Most marketers do not have enough employees with the requisite data skills, or access to the best data for designated marketing goals, to take full advantage of the technologies or make the best platform choices (as shown in the radar chart in Figure 7.1). Making the right platform choices is crucial, and yet it is impossible to test them all in the ways they would be used by an organization once they are purchased. In many of the larger organizations, there is a need to understand and manage how data is processed and stored.

Data is Gold

Customer data may be the most precious thing that organizations have, especially when the capabilities are in place to leverage data.[1] For example:

- "The vast majority of data never gets used. Only 0.5 percent of all data is ever analyzed."[2]
- "Banks have goldmines of data available to them. However, it is not just about the data they collect. It is how they mine it, interpret it and draw insights to provide personal customer experiences, which is deployed across the organization."[3]

While technological improvements allow organizations to collect vast amounts of information, they have not learned how to analyze or use most of it. While the approach any given organization takes with Big Data is unique, they should expect to see increased revenue as an outcome. To gauge success, organizations should be able to drive business decisions with the data and reap the benefits.

Three Organizations Successfully using First-, Second-, and Third-Party Data

The following successful examples of leveraging Big Data are cited in SmartDataCollective.[4]

- **Capital One** created a deal optimization engine to analyze customer demographics and spending patterns. With this data they were able to determine when and where to place offers in front of people; this led to increases in revenue and customer satisfaction.
- **T-Mobile** reduced customer turnover by 50% by examining their usage patterns, geographical usage trends, customer purchases by location, and customer lifetime value. With the massive amounts of data T-Mobile collected on its clients, it was then able to identify its most influential customers and give them extra perks.
- **Starbucks** uses location data, street traffic analysis, demographic info, and data culled from other places to decide where to locate their stores. Armed with this data, Starbucks locations can exist a block away from one another, better serving their audience while remaining profitable.

Tag Management Systems

A tag is just another piece of data-collection code that digital vendors require customers to embed on their pages and mobile apps. Web Analytics platforms collect the data that appears in reports by "tagging" pages and URLs of a site with the necessary code, but the accuracy of the captured data ultimately depends upon how well the tagging is implemented and updated. Adobe and Google (along with several other third-party vendors) have Tag Manager systems. Google Tag Manager (which is free) might be the easiest to deploy and use (although not for all websites).[5]

Keeping tagging up-to-date is difficult enough for site owners. For large sites, it is impossible to keep tagged pages up-to-date without some automation such as a Content Management system (focusing on content changes) or a Tag Management system that keeps track of all the tags on a website. By using a Tag Manager, one master tag is used in place of additional vendor tags. The rest of the vendor tags are stored and updated within in the Tag Manager. Tag Managers make it much easier to build and maintain marketing automation and tracking. Figure 7.2 has examples of JavaScript Tags that are used for Web tracking purposes.

Google Tag Manager handles all the tags on a website and stores them in a data repository, where they can be easily updated and propagated.

```
]
        }
    }];
    </script>

<!-- Google Tag Manager -->
<noscript><iframe src="//www.googletagmanager.com/ns.html?id=GTM-CGSQ"
height="0" width="0" style="display:none;visibility:hidden"></iframe></noscript>
<script>(function(w,d,s,l,i){w[l]=w[l]||[];w[l].push({'gtm.start':
new Date().getTime(),event:'gtm.js'});var f=d.getElementsByTagName(s)[0],
j=d.createElement(s),dl=l!='dataLayer'?'&l='+l:'';j.async=true;j.src=
'//www.googletagmanager.com/gtm.js?id='+i+dl;f.parentNode.insertBefore(j,f);
})(window,document,'script','dataLayer','GTM-CGSQ');</script>
<!-- End Google Tag Manager -->
<meta name="viewport" content="width=device-width">
```

On a website without a Tag Manager, each JavaScript tag must be manually updated and applied which is difficult to manage, especially on large, complex sites.

```
<!-- This site uses the Google Analytics by Yoast plugin v5.3.2 - Universal enabled -
https://yoast.com/wordpress/plugins/google-analytics/ -->
<script type="text/javascript">
            (function(i,s,o,g,r,a,m){i['GoogleAnalyticsObject']=r;i[r]=i[r]||function(){
                        (i[r].q=i[r].q||[]).push(arguments)},i[r].l=1*new
Date();a=s.createElement(o),

            m=s.getElementsByTagName(o)[0];a.async=1;a.src=g;m.parentNode.insertB
efore(a,m)
            })(window,document,'script','//www.google-
analytics.com/analytics.js','__gaTracker');

            __gaTracker('create', 'UA-XXXXXXX-1', 'auto', {'allowAnchor': true,
'allowLinker': true});
            __gaTracker('set', 'forceSSL', true);
            __gaTracker('require', 'displayfeatures');
            __gaTracker('send','pageview');

</script>
<!-- / Google Analytics by Yoast -->
```

Figure 7.2 Comparing Google Tag Manager-managed website code with similar websites that do not run Google Tag Manager.
Source: WebMetricsGuru Inc.

There is a lot of data being produced by applications and users that should be collected for marketing and site optimization purposes. Most organizations do not have the time or expertise to manage and update data collection manually. As an alternative, organizations can use a Tag Management system (TMS); the TMS acts as a data repository to define, store, and update data collection tags on a website, or collection of sites.

- Manage several tags without expertise in JavaScript, to focus on engaging with customers instead of being concerned with conflicts that arise with IT processes.
- Pick the best marketing services solutions and combine them (Google Tag Manager has added templates and support for AdRoll, Marin, ComScore, Bizo, Clicktale, Neustar, Distillery, Turn, Mediaplex, VisualDNA, Quantcast, Criteo and more).[6]

Tag Management Issues

- The Tag Management systems have access to the data collected on the site (which might be a problem for some businesses that do not want to share some of the aspects of their data with a third party).
- Intermixing tags from previous deployments, no longer functional, hampers website performance for end users by slowing down page loads.
- While the TMSs simplify the management of tags, they require coding expertise and access to the website administration to fully utilize them.[7]

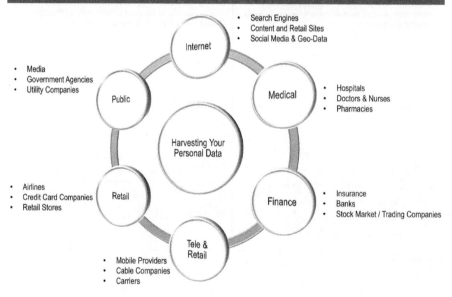

Data Collection Ecosystem

Collectors of digital data that is routinely harvested on individuals

Figure 7.3 Data that is routinely harvested on individuals.
Source: WebMetricsGuru Inc.

There are so many ways to gather audience data that it is mind boggling—and it continues to get faster and more sophisticated every year. The data that is collected by consumers is then anonymized, normalized, de-duplicated, aggregated, repackaged, and sold to advertisers and publishers (and pretty much anyone else willing to purchase it).

Data Lakes

Data Lakes are a customizable, general purpose data store where information is saved in its original format. By placing data into the Lake, it becomes available for analysis by everyone in the organization. The Data Lake is usually formed with a Hadoop cluster with several nodes that holds all the information that populates Salesforce, Marketo, and Adobe Analytics. Marketing data is often trapped in the applications that collect the data. Data Lakes solve this problem by leaving the information intact in Hadoop in an unstructured (or minimally structured) state, ready and waiting to be analyzed. The Data Lake can live in an in-house cloud or a public cloud depends on what best suits the organization of where to house the data.

Data Lake Governance

- The data must be clean, reliable, and available when it is needed.
- Updated campaign codes are required.
- Attribution models in Web Analytics need to be chosen with care.
- The right team is required that has the combination of skills, talents, and a love for data and problem-solving.

Data Lake Issues

While Data Lakes solve some data collection and storage issues, its utility creates other problems.

- **Security and access control:** Captured data goes into the Data Lake with no oversight of the contents. The security capabilities of Data Lakes are still immature.
- **Data quality:** There is an inability to determine data quality, or annotate the findings by other analysts or users that have found value from the same information in the lake. Without descriptive metadata and a way to maintain it, the Data Lake risks becoming a data swamp.[8]

Third-Party Audience Analytics: ComScore MyMetrix[9]

ComScore measures digital and mobile traffic to media properties. Its focus is to gather data for digital advertisers and publishers; although this data could also be used for market research. However, it is a paid solution that is not accessible to the public.

ComScore's suite of measurement products use a "Global Research Panel" comprising more than 2 million people that reside in over 170 countries that provide data readouts of interest to digital advertisers and publishers.

- 2 million+ panel with consistent metric definitions, data collection, and a framework to organize the data.

- Unified Digital Measurement (UDM)™ integrates the panel (2 million+) with global device measurement (maintained with page tagging). Unified UV = total census cookies × cookies per person.
- Constant updates (enumeration) surveys by landline and cellular on a monthly basis with a target of 500 completed surveys per month.
- Panel recruitment by affiliate programs and third parties into two categories (home and "at work") that is merged and de-duplicated to create the ComScore Universe.
- Data capture: For the online panel of 2 million+ (URL, engagement activity, keystrokes and mouse movements and intensity, information parsing, application usage), data stream captures, and many activities on AOL (ISP).
- 85% of users in the panel are identified by the device (single-user machine) and 15% (unmarked and multi-user devices) by biometrics, site affinity and time of day or gender.
- Website audience defined by projecting the panel data activity on a website/ property with census data to the general population at six levels of classification.
- Website properties (entities) appear in the reports if the entity generated at least 30 unique visitors (UV) during the period (month) for US reporting and 15 UV for non-US reporting.

ComScore (and Nielsen, similarly) reports have a lot in common with Web Analytics (first-party data/cookies). However, the comparisons are misleading as the data collection, and counting methodology is entirely different (leading to different numbers on measures/metrics such as visits, pageviews, time spent on site, unique visitors and so on, when the two are compared side by side). From the authors' experience, comScore offers audience analytics on many different channels—each requiring a separate subscription, although they can be combined. Consequently, analysts and stakeholders get the most from comScore by moving back and forth in their reporting between the offerings when they have purchased a subscription that can run into the high six figures, making it more of a corporate marketing solution.

The purpose of these third-party platforms is not absolute accuracy in the numbers. Rather, they provide a means to compare one organization to another (and the industry/world) in a safe way that doesn't violate data privacy. The data is gathered, de-duplicated, cleaned, categorized, organized, and ranked by comScore on any organization that is in its "data dictionary" (company/entity/website). The reports are available to anyone who purchased a subscription. Anyone who has access can generate reports on any organization in the data dictionary (which covers the largest and medium-sized organizations and websites worldwide, which can also choose how comScore organizes the information they collect when they are subscribers). Whatever customers learn from comScore is publicly knowable to everyone else who has a subscription. ComScore is commonly used for corporate marketing and annual reporting. ComScore (and Nielsen) do much pre-processing on the data they collect from their panels; reporting is not often available for a given period until 30–45 days later.

Primary ComScore Operations

- Logging into MyMetrix users can choose between three basic reports: Media Overview, Compare Media, and Month over Month over a current or previous period—usually monthly, but it can be weekly as well.

- The Media Overview report might be the most useful for a media planner since it aggregates data from much of the comScore channel reporting, even for those that a subscriber does not have access to.

Much of the value of this type of third-party data reporting is that comScore (and Nielsen) have already pre-organized the information, and ranked it—saving much work. On the other hand, that pre-organization and ranking comScore did might not suit the particular needs of an organization. Organizations that are subscribers can reorganize their own comScore data by request to better match their needs. There are a lot of specific insights to be gathered from the Compare Media report, especially when there is no access to many of the other comScore offerings such as Video Metrix and Search Metrix. The Compare Media report is an excellent way to populate some of the metrics of a SWOT analysis (Strengths, Weaknesses, Opportunities, and Threats).

Media Metrix Core Reporting

Basic reporting allows subscribers to profile a website audience or find a target audience online (for engagement and cross visiting, covering up to 44 countries) for people counts and not machines.

ComScore offers significant benefits over Web Analytics in some situations. Web Analytics platforms typically contain "analytics spam," including Web-bots and search engine crawlers that are not people. Bots are not going to buy anything or add any value to a website/organization, and can inflate pageview and visit counts (to some extent corrupting the first-party data that Web Analytics collects on a website). One advantage comScore has over Web Analytics is that it gets rid of all the bots—and what is left are unique visitors that comScore and Nielsen have identified.

The Key Measures report compares a given website/media property/entity with its competitors using some basic parameters such as data source, geography, universe, period, target audience, media and measures (metrics) in a ranked category. One example of a parameter is the data source, which can be either multi-platform (i.e., mobile, tablet, PC) or PC only.

ComScore ranks each property/website in a category—subscribers can agree with their categorization or not (if customers disagree with the classification of their Web properties by comScore, they can request for it to be changed by the Data Dictionary group at comScore). Analysts and stakeholders can use the Key Measures report to determine where to purchase advertising. Target audiences can be more complex based on age, gender, income, and the number of children they have. The "media," as ComScore describes the term, are the websites/media properties to run the report on. ComScore provides much flexibility in finding and defining medias in their platform (and getting suggestions on new media based on popular ideas of comScore subscribers). Analysts and media planners/buyers set up advertising (and do market research; a less common use, but a compelling one nonetheless for this platform).

Other Media Metrix Reports

- **Demographics:** Analysts and stakeholders can get the details on the demographics of a media site that is in the comScore Universe (the target audience is defined by age group, gender, household income, region, children (y/n), household size, and race).

- **% Change in Media Trend:** Shows the changes in measures of a particular media (website/media property/entity) over a one-year period.
- **Target Trend:** Shows the changes in demographics of a particular media (website/media property/entity) over a one-year period.
- **Media Trend:** Shows the changes in a particular measure (unique visitors, average minutes per page over a 12-month period.
- **Audience Duplication:** Shows the amount of traffic on a website that is unduplicated, versus the number that duplicated on two or more sites, versus all websites.
- **Source Loss:** Shows where traffic is coming from and leaving to on a particular Internet site/property/media. This is one of the author's favorite reports and is somewhat reminiscent of Web Analytics readouts.
- **Cross Visiting:** Shows the amount of cross-visiting audience across two or more media properties.

There are a few other reports included on the comScore MyMetrix such as Local Markets (covering over 100 DMAs in the United States) and Media Builder (which allows subscribers to build custom media entities if they wish to, instead of the preset definitions of media properties that ComScore provides, by default.

ComScore Plan Metrix

The comScore Plan Metrix uses the same framework as MyMetrix but adds 6,000 audience targets gathered from survey data collected from 12,000 panelists located in the United States who are over 18 years of age. Panelists take a survey once a year and provide personally identifiable information across 22 content categories (such as demographics, lifestyles, interests, product preferences and so on). Plan Metrix reports are anonymized so they can be used for audience psychographics.

Plan Metrix can be used to improve the pervasiveness of advertising campaigns by defining ideal target audiences (based on personas) to find the websites/media properties they visit (so as to advertise there). Plan Metrix could also be an ideal market research platform to better understand the characteristics of audiences (what they like, what they do).

ComScore Plan Metrix Reports

Four reports are available, but they all do different things, so it is best to understand which reports to run depending on the marketing ask.

- **Key Measures:** Understand the target audience's favorite online destinations.
- **Site Audience Profile:** Understand the audience visiting a given website/media property/entity.
- **Consumer Target Profile:** Understand the target audience's interests and online behavior.
- **Cross Visiting:** Understand shared target audiences.

Summarizing Plan Metrix

There is no perfect way to represent the data from Plan Metrix, but it provides much food for thought and provides interesting ideas to develop and test out from the data (given the limitations of comScore's panel, as already discussed).

ComScore Ad Metrix

For online advertisers, ComScore Ad Metrix is a kind of cool platform—the author used Ad Metrix at Monster.com almost a decade ago when the platform was still relatively new. Measuring the impact of online advertising has always been difficult for several reasons, the most common being the ad server counts often don't match up with campaign traffic in Web Analytics platforms. Then there is the viewability issue where often advertising is displayed on the publisher's website, but the viewer may not have seen it (because it appears "below the fold"—below the screen that is in view), therefore advertisers are paying for impressions no one has seen.

Add to that the spambot problem. Lots of ads are being clicked on that appear on publisher's websites generated by robotic means—no humans involved (except those who direct the robots or bots) and yet advertisers are paying for those clicks. As a result, it is difficult to know if the advertising is worth it or not. Until websites figure out another way to monetize their online presence (besides advertising, subscriptions, and memberships), we are pretty much stuck with online advertising of one form or another.

How ComScore Ad Metrix Works

Ad Metrix does not need to use spiders or bots to collect advertising data and measures targeted ads along with cached ads delivered within registration-only and sign-in areas of websites/media properties such as Edmunds.com, where a zip code is required. Also, each display ad view is tied to single panelist and not affected by cookie deletion.

It is not clear how extensive or representative the Ad Metrix reporting is; still, it is better to have this data when there is an opportunity to use Ad Metrix for market research, in the author's opinion.

ComScore Ad Metrix collects advertising creative impressions as defined by IAB codecs and standards along with the URL/page served. ComScore counts validated ad servers serving ads to panelists running comScore's metering software and can collect the data without using Web crawlers or server logs. The advertising creative is assigned to an advertiser when the creative is captured by drawing upon the Media Metrix dictionary structure for assigning advertisers by site and the Ad Metrix product directory structure for product reporting; comScore Ad Metrix does not capture text and video ads. There is no full tracking and attribution solution for digital media.

ComScore Ad Metrix Reports

- **Quick Reports:** Navigator that helps users decide which of the following reports to run.
- **Advertiser:** Provides monthly display advertising of a publisher/advertiser.
- **Advertiser Trend:** Advertiser spend and impression across a defined date range.
- **Advertiser Contacts:** Uses LexisNexis for advertisers and agencies contact information.
- **Publisher:** Reports on display advertising that appears on publishers' websites.
- **Publisher Trend:** Reporting on a month-over-month publisher adverting trends.

- **Demographic Profile:** Demographics of the audience exposed to display advertising on a publisher's website/entity.
- **Creative Summary:** Analyzes advertising creative by size and format.
- **Product Dictionary:** Creates a hierarchical breakdown for advertisers in certain industries (such as CPG) down to a to brand and product level.
- **Media Spend:** Syndicated data on US offline advertising spend.
- **Social Media:** Reports on display advertising that appears on blogs and other social media sites (probably not fully inclusive, may not include LinkedIn, YouTube or Snapchat, etc.).

Ad Metrix data is coming from the same 2 million+ panelists worldwide that comScore collects the rest of its data via the metering software running on each device.

What is the "Use Case" for ComScore Ad Metrix?

Ad Metrix is used to create reporting on hundreds of billions of monthly ad impressions spread across over 170,000 products and advertisers in ten countries (at the time of writing) with up to 24 months of trend data available and includes Facebook creative.

- To find out where (what publishers) an advertiser's ads ran, run Ad Metrix Advertiser, Ad Metrix Advertiser Trend.
- To locate the number of impressions an advertiser ran and how much cost them, run Ad Metrix Advertiser, Ad Metrix Advertiser Trend.
- To find out advertising trends for an advertiser or publisher, run Ad Metrix Advertiser Trend, Ad Metrix Publisher Trend.
- To find out more about an advertiser's creative, run Ad Metrix Advertiser, Ad Metrix Creative Summary.
- To find out what share of an advertiser's budget spent on display adverting, run Ad Metrix Media Spend.

There are more use cases for Ad Metrix, but this is a good start.

Using ComScore Third-Party Data for Marketing to New Segments

Here is an example that comes from one of the students at the Zicklin School of Business at Baruch College in Spring 2016:

> Develop a plan to acquire 15,000 subscribers for *The Wall Street Journal* (Digital). The target demographic is college students, interested in 2016 election. Would like to learn how to use comScore to find out more about the target demographic and determine which sites they visit to run digital advertisement there.

The best way to deal with any marketing task is to break it down into a few talking points, that way it is easier to figure out what data is needed and which reports/data sources can supply it.

- GOAL: Acquire 15,000 new customers who are college students and interested in the 2016 presidential election
  - TACTIC: Use comScore Plan Metrix to find out the demographics of this audience.
  - TACTIC: Use comScore Plan Metrix to find other sites they visit.

ComScore Plan Metrix has three reports (on the face of it) that could inform the marketing ask (Key Measures, Site Audience Profile, and Cross Visiting Report).

Next, develop the Audience Target (which can be saved and reused for other reports in Plan Metrix).

> 18+ yrs. old (Total Audience) AND 18–24 yrs. old AND Attended College, no degree (Edu level) OR Attended graduate school, no degree (Edu level) AND Voted in the most recent mid-term election (political activity) OR Voted in the most recent presidential election (political activity)

Run the Key Measures Report (Plan Metrix)—this is what the report highlighted (to me):

- There were 2.2 million total college students 18–24 years old interested in politics in March 2016.
- Best websites are Quizlet.com, Spotify, Reddit, Pandora, BuzzFeed, Ziff Davis, Gawker Media. Noticed that the website Makebeliefscomix.com has a particularly strong following in this audience. Reddit LifePro Tips and Reddit Sports are also great places where the target audience is concentrated.

Just finding a bunch of websites like Makebeliefscomix.com that accept advertising might supply enough of an audience to fulfill the marketing ask (if we have the right creative and marketing attendant that supports the marketing goals).

Next, run the Consumer Target Profile using the Audience Target already defined and saved—here are some highlights:

- 92% listen to streaming audio files over the Internet on a weekly basis (Pandora, Spotify are good places to advertise); 44% listen to 1–5 streams a day.
- 67% have traveled within the United States within the last six months (probably enough to promote to travel sites for this audience); 48% traveled by air and may have used frequent flyer miles (probably from their parents—gives you more ideas of where to advertise and what the creative should be).
- 59% are interested in adopting a healthy lifestyle (advertise in healthy living—search to find the right venues for this); 45% actively exercise to improve their health (might suggest exercise sites).
- 32% are on Hulu Plus (again, another place to advertise).

Finally, using the Cross-Visiting Report (Plan Metrix) showed that the Wall Street Journal Digital Network shares its "young voter audience."

- 29% go to LinkedIn and 35% go to CBS Interactive, so perhaps both are good places to advertise.

Using ComScore Plan Metrix to Profile a Consumer Audience Visiting a Website

Figure 7.4 Information for advertisers who want to reach specific audiences using comScore third-party data.
Source: WebMetricsGuru Inc.

There is so much to do with comScore beyond what it is typically used (purchased) for; organizations typically use only a small percentage of the platform's potential. Figure 7.4, for instance, was produced based on comScore Plan Metrix data, by the marketing team of an online advertising network. The marketers wanted to show that frequent boat travelers were more likely to see requisite advertising from travel companies specializing in boat trips than their competitors.

ComScore Summary

To sum up—there is a use case for applying the comScore suite of products and reports for market research and even to inform probabilistic and predictive analysis/models though it is more commonly used for media planning.[10] There are some other platforms included in the ComScore suite including Video Metrix, Mobile Metrix, Segment Metrix, MediaBuilder, QSearch, Xmedia, and more that are not covered here, but are worth exploring if they fit an organization's marketing needs.

Other Third-Party Data Tools Useful for Digital Analytics

University students have access to the many additional resources. Here are some the author has found to be useful for Digital Analytics:

- **ABI/INFORM Global:** Find articles from trade journals and magazines, scholarly journals, and general interest magazines covering accounting, advertising, business, company information, industry information, management, marketing, real estate, economics, finance, human resources, and international business.
- **Academic OneFile:** Articles from magazines and scholarly journals from a wide range of subjects.
- **Business Monitor Online (now called BMI Research):** Might be useful to find out about a market in each area.
- **eMarketer:** eMarketer takes data from all over the digital marketing world, recharts and organizes it for reference and publication.
- **Gartner:** Analysis of IT markets for hardware, software, IT services, semiconductors and communications. Reports on IT issues in ten industries including education, banking, retail, healthcare, and manufacturing.
- **Grolier Online:** Useful for definitions of topics along with building citations.
- **IBISWorld:** Reports on more than 700 industries plus specialized analyst reporting.
- **Kanopy:** Might be useful as a source of stock educational videos.
- **American Fact Finder:** Find out details about demographics in a zip code in the US.
- **Business Insights: Essentials**: Good for SWOT analysis of companies, perhaps of industries, also allows keyword search. Provides industry reports that might be useful.
- **Mintel Academic:** Provides overall sector studies and trend analysis.
- **PrivCo:** Information of the filings and financials of private companies.
- **Simmons OneView:** Useful for demographic planning.
- **Statista:** Like eMarketer but has more search capability and numerical data.
- **Warc:** Resource with DATA for many marketing data, trends, and projections.

Combining First and Third-Party Data Case Study: The Informatica.com Data Lake

A Data Lake is a storage repository holding vast amounts of raw data in its native format until it is needed. While a hierarchical data warehouse stores data in files or folders, a Data Lake uses a flat architecture to store data.[11] It is not hard to understand why Data Lakes are so attractive to organizations. Building a modern data warehouse is a very expensive undertaking that doesn't have a high success rate.[12]

Informatica Business Questions

- Which channels are driving the most net new names that eventually convert into customers and revenue?
- Who are all the members of a buying team we need to influence to have the deal go our way?
- What is the value of the different marketing touches eventually leading to not just an opportunity or pipeline but revenue, booked and banked?

Before beginning to improve the quality of analytics to uncover actionable insights, the data and marketing automation in place should be re-examined and, perhaps, reconsidered and replaced when needed. Next, website and Web Analytics need to be set up to connect with the Data Lake, according to Informatica, as quoted below.

> Thus, we switched to the **Adobe Experience Manager** for our whole web stack and ramped up the analytics to where we needed them to be. We looked at lots of web platforms and "marketing clouds" and felt that Adobe was way out ahead in integrating the stack—with high personalization, responsive/mobile capabilities, and all the stuff we would need (metadata capabilities for a robust taxonomy, tag management).
>
> Then we ramped up the analytics to do great visitor tracking, advanced analysis, and track down conversions and affinities. Now we can map visitors to actual product interests on the web, leveraging our product taxonomy in the digital asset management system behind Adobe Experience Manager (visiting web pages and downloading assets for a product like MDM accrues to MDM product interest in the affinity matrix).[13]

The marketing stacks that Adobe and Google have assembled for Digital Marketing Analytics have become crucial—but they are still not very well implemented. Most organizations are learning as they go, and often must re-do a lot of the work.

When Web Analytics collaborates with the rest of the marketing technology stack then you get:

- Tight tracking of all (anonymous and known) visitor journeys.
- Hard-core Web Analytics to page flows, referrers, repeat traffic, conversions.
- Integration with other third-party platforms such as Demandbase for reverse IP mapping, tracking of firmographics like industry, company size.

Once visitors arrive at a website, their visitor session can be categorized using advanced segmentation.

Web Analytics provides the information to stakeholders of where the visitor came from (and where they go to on the site). Behavioral signatures can further categorize visitors based on what they do on the site, then automate the learning to rule-based segmentations (note that Web Analytics is not alone in setting up and utilizing customer segmentation—other platforms can further segment visitor traffic).

Two examples of successful visitor mapping using Web/Data Analytics are as follows:

- A large online retailer transformed their website clickstream data, collected with Adobe Analytics, into more simple analytics readouts that support their strategies for planning, budgeting, product selections offerings, and paid search traffic. The visitor pathing information was copied into an enterprise data warehouse to create a rich data inventory of customer-centric information, transactions, and site activity.[14]
- A global financial services company performed clickstream analysis on 5 billion digital ads each month using Datameer (a Big Data visualization platform). The goal was to improve ad targeting and conversion while avoiding over-targeting certain consumer segments. The analysis determined they were focusing 60% of the ad budget on just 4% of their potential customers! Thus, they reallocated their advertising budget broaden its reach; this led to a 20% increase in conversions.[15]

Efficient tracking of campaigns in Web Analytics requires that campaign codes for all marketing activities be in place. Otherwise, the monitoring will be flawed, uneven, and not that useful. Once the Web Analytics and customer segmentation are in place, organizations can build scalable paid media and SEO programs to attract new visitors (and track them in an actionable way).

- They can create issues-based content that potential customers would care about and distribute the content in multichannel advertising and social media programs (paid search, content display, remarketing, and paid marketing programs on social channels, such as LinkedIn Lead Accelerator).[16]

The next evolution past Web Analytics is Predictive Analytics to score visitors as potential leads and then acting on the information (scoring)—here's where the "Data Lake" comes in.

- Add-on platforms like Lattice Engines, acquired by Apple in 2017, to do predictive scoring can now be added (using the Data Lake). Lattice analyzes people/ companies who buy an organization's product. Lattice examines many hundreds of data points, from the job title, company data including credit ratings, hiring profile, technology profiles, and location, to behavioral data and so on with leads scored as A, B, C, and D, with A being the highest propensity to buy.

Informatica used Lattice as part of their Data Lake and reported that "A" scored leads were six times more likely to buy their product than leads they used to get from their sales teams. Lattice was trained (assisted learning) on 70,000 leads that Informatica had in its customer database. Once trained, Lattice rated each lead, allowing Informatica to focus on the highest rated leads, increasing sales of their products.

Three Pillars of the Digital Marketing at Informatica

Data Lakes support the rest of Informatica's marketing operations stack, but they do not solve all of the issues similar organizations face with their digital marketing and acquisition. Since they are separate applications, Data Lakes just add to the data fragmentation that ends up requiring yet more applications floating in the Lake.

- **Pillar 1: Adobe Analytics** which is part of the Adobe Marketing Cloud (Google Analytics now has a similar cloud offering connected to Google Analytics, but it was not available at the time of this case study in late 2015).
- **Pillar 2: Marketo Marketing Automation** used for tracking known visitors, email, and automating our nurture flows (we chose Marketo).
- **Pillar 3: Salesforce CRM** for tracking the sales opportunities all the way through to revenue, which is a vital part of any big data marketing program.

Additional Pillar Support Applications

- **Dynamic Tag Management via a DTM:** DTM is a CMS for JavaScript, tags, and tracking codes using Adobe Tag Manager (or Google Tag Manager). Adobe's and Google's Tag Managers are powerful (and free) tools, Adobe Tag Manager comes with Adobe Experience Manager and integrates with Adobe Analytics. Google has a similar offering and integrations with Google Analytics and other parts of its Cloud Marketing stack. DTM is used to determine when to fire a tag and what data to collect and where to send it (in Informatica's case from Marketo and Adobe Analytics to Rio SEO, Demandbase, D&B, and Lattice Engines) and it streamlines and automates what would otherwise be a hugely repetitive, manual process.

- **EDW (Enterprise Data Warehouse):** The Data Lake hosts all the unstructured data. There needs to be another place where the output of the Three Pillars (Salesforce, DTM, and Adobe Analytics) resides—the data from the Three Pillars is structured data. Putting structured data directly into the Data Lake might be ideal, but at the time of this writing the Data Lake construct does not have a fast enough response time to serve up data in real time.

- **Data Management Tools:** Informatica used its data management tools to make sure all the information in the Data Lake is properly cleaned (cleaning up information that is incorrect, incomplete or duplicated). Master Data Management (MDM) acts to streamline and automate data management and ensure data quality. The Data Management Tools include Informatica PowerCenter for combining data many different sources, Informatica Data Quality monitoring and automation tools, and Big Data Relationship Management for exposing relationships in the Data Lake such as various accounts, contacts and DUNS numbers from Dun & Bradstreet.

- **Demandbase** (Data Enrichment): Used for reverse IP-lookup to see which companies are visiting Informatica.com along with the company size, and industry segments that are fed to pre-fill forms or to personalize the appearance of the website based on industry. Once the forms are populated and submitted they are fed into Adobe Analytics, Marketo, and ultimately, flow back into the Data Lake.

- **Dun & Bradstreet** (Data Enrichment): Enriches and validate the data with firmographics from Dun & Bradstreet—using the DUNS standard.

- **Rio SEO** (Data Enrichment): Used to identify buying teams within accounts and to track word-of-mouth influencers for Informatica. When a visitor is browsing the site, each page URL has a Rio code. Rio SEO copies the URL of when a visitor visits the page and makes it available to be used in an email to a friend or coworker with a code goes with the link. When an email recipient clicks on the link and arrives on the website, Informatica can tell who the influencer is who sent the email which brought the visitor to Informatica.com.

- **Lattice** (Predictive Analytics/Lead Scoring): Every prospect and account have 300–400 variables attached, used to analyze the companies and prospects of purchasers then generalize the attributes of the buyers to the wider prospect universe for lookalikes (lookalikes are commonly employed on Facebook, LinkedIn, Twitter). Informatica uses two models: one for buyers of their licensed products and the other for purchasers of their cloud products (with slightly different models for North America and Rest of World, so there are four in total). Lattice assigns each lead with two scores depending on how likely they are to purchase each kind of product.

- **Tableau Data Visualization Platform:** Data visualization is the "last mile" of Big Data marketing. Tableau makes it easy to bring together data from different sources into one dashboard.

Programmatic Advertising

Programmatic advertising is automating most of the manual aspects of digital advertising that used to be done more slowly and expensively, such as insertion orders to publisher's websites (both direct and open-auction).

According to Digiday, "programmatic" ad buying typically refers to the use of software to purchase digital advertising, as opposed to the traditional process that involves RFPs, human negotiations, and manual insertion orders. It is using machines to buy ads.[17]

Programmatic technology is one more innovation of the digitization of things. It automates processes, eliminates costs, and allows for more time to be spent on the strategy and the analysis of the data.

Applying Third-Party Data with Programmatic Advertising

Most marketers are still trying to figure out what the term "programmatic" means to a marketer; after all, the term is ambiguous, implying something about building or running a program, or creating programming—and that is not a good definition of what programmatic advertising is.

Buy Side vs. Sell Side

This is confusing since buyers can also be sellers and vice-versa!

- **Buyers/demand side:** Advertisers are trying to deliver the right message in front (eyeballs) of the right person at the right time (targeting) for the best price (return on investment).
- **Sellers/supply side:** Publishers are trying to maximize the money they can make selling advertising space (inventory) to advertisers.

The Buying/Purchase Cycle

The author is not a fan of "canned" models of "buying activity"—not everyone goes through the same process in the same way, we are not all the same in the way we process information. On the other hand, having a model of how consumers behave online when they decide to purchase a product or service is useful because we can make plans and optimize marketing (or so it was thought). As we saw in previous chapters, the consumer buying cycle is not a funnel (except, perhaps, the part of it that happens on a website). However, nothing in this world is perfect. Just because the traditional consumer buying cycle model is deeply flawed, we can still use it at least to get started, because digital marketing and programmatic advertising (especially) needs a plan, a model to base our advertising on—otherwise, how are we supposed to know that someone is getting closer to making a purchase decision?

Media Planning

To run a lot of effective programmatic advertising, marketers need to have the creative ready and know when and where to run it—that was always true of any advertising, but even more so of programmatic. Again, the model is oversimplified but can serve us better than the last one as this model helps to explain why some mediums work better for certain things than others.

Why Programmatic Advertising is Used

Modern technology has changed the way consumers purchase products and services online. Zillions of websites now are on the Web—a lot to wade through (no one can) and/or place advertising on.

- In the past 25 years, we have developed e-commerce—the ease of buying and selling online (just look at Amazon and eBay!).
- The development of precision targeting along with self-service advertising (like Google AdWords) has turned many into digital marketers (whether they realize it or not), although they need to become more sophisticated to take full advantage of what technologies such as programmatic advertising offers.
- Digital and social media platforms have all included sophisticated and powerful analytics (and in some cases, customizable attribution models)

Digital Advertising Types

- **Digital:** Graphic ads appearing next to content on webpages, IM applications, email.
- **Video:** Ads appear in the video before, during, or after the video plays. One of the fastest-growing opportunities online today.
- **Mobile:** Ads used on mobile devices, such as cell phones or tablets are growing quickly.
- **Search:** Ads are placed and ranked by search engines on webpages that show associated results from the user's search engine queries (can be combined with display networks such as Google's).
- **Social:** Produce content that users will share with their social network.
- **Native:** A form of social media advertising that matches the shape and function of the platform on which it appears—looks similar to user's post or newsfeed item but is an ad.

Programmatic can run advertising on any of the channels above (and in some cases on linear television).

Programmatic Advertising Issues

- Requires more expertise from marketers to employ the platform effectively.
- Lack of transparency on where the ads appear (in some cases).

- Not enough creative content to take advantage of the inventory that programmatic allows advertisers to run.
- The cost of an impression can be higher when targeting accuracy is greater.
- Lack of engagement between clients, publishers, and advertisers.

Summary

This chapter examined some of the issues surrounding the tracking and acquisition of customer data.

- Third-party data can be used to enrich first-party data; it is also used for advertising and targeting customers.
- Third-party data platforms and aggregators provide very useful information, but it is tough to intermix data from one third-party platform to another third-party platform, because each platform gathers and processes data in their own way. Using third-party data side-by-side is a much safer practice.
- Data Lakes are a way to store, process and display data on a massive scale relatively quickly and inexpensively. Adobe Web Analytics, Adobe Experience Manager, and Tag Management platforms are combined with other platforms in the marketing technology stack such as Lattice (for lead scoring) and Informatica (for data governance), easily storing and retrieving information from the Data Lake.
- Tag Management systems are databases used to store all JavaScript tags; they also simplify website administration by ensuring managed sites have compliant, up-to-date JavaScript tags.
- Web Analytics platforms capture online information that occurs on a site when properly set up and enabled, but they cannot capture most of the data connected with brands that happen off the site or offline. Web Analytics provide "Intermediate Metrics" that are useful to gauge the progress of marketing initiatives and campaigns.
- ComScore and Nielsen provide excellent third-party audience analytics; they are most often used for advertising and marketing purposes but could also be useful for market research. We examined comScore's MyMetrix, Plan Metrix, and Ad Metrix in depth and provided examples of the types of insights they deliver.
- Third-party data platforms such as comScore can be further extended by using additional platforms most students have access to via university libraries (including eMarketer, IBISWorld, and Reference.com databases).
- Programmatic advertising is briefly introduced and discussed at the end of the chapter. Programmatic is the automation of buying and selling online advertising.

Review Questions

1. How is third-party data different than first-party and second-party data?
2. Is there such a thing as a second-party cookie?
3. Discuss the issues around merging third-party data. Do you think this is a good idea? Why? Why not?
4. What type of analytics does comScore provide? When would use comScore?

Chapter 7 Citations

1. "Five business functions expect to reap the biggest benefit from Big Data." October 14, 2013, www.slideshare.net/SAPanalytics/five-business-functions-expect-to-reap-the-biggest-benefit-from-big-data-at-consumer-products-companies-infographic. Accessed April 15, 2017.
2. Bansal, M. "Big Data: creating the power to move heaven and earth." September 2, 2014, www.technologyreview.com/s/530371/big-data-creating-the-power-to-move-heaven-and-earth. Accessed April 15, 2017.
3. "2015 banking trends slideshare." March 10, 2015. www.mx.com/resources/resources/2015-banking-trends-slides. Accessed April 15, 2017.
4. Oaks, J. "Companies using Big Data successfully." SmartData Collective. July 14, 2015. www.smartdatacollective.com/jessoaks11/330428/4-big-companies-using-big-data-successfully. Accessed April 15, 2017.
5. Gesenhues, A. "Google Analytics launches new set of tools for Tag Manager users." October 15, 2014. http://marketingland.com/google-analytics-launches-new-set-tools-tag-manager-users-104030. Accessed April 15, 2017.
6. Gesenhues, A. "Google Analytics launches new set of tools for Tag Manager users." October 15, 2014. http://marketingland.com/google-analytics-launches-new-set-tools-tag-manager-users-104030. Accessed April 15, 2017.
7. Van Patten, C. "Trigger Google Analytics events within Google Tag Manager." www.vanpattenmedia.com/2014/google-analytics-tag-manager-events. Accessed April 15, 2017.
8. "Gartner says beware of the Data Lake fallacy." July 28, 2014. www.gartner.com/newsroom/id/2809117. Accessed April 15, 2017.
9. "comScore." www.comScore.com. Accessed April 15, 2017.
10. "Probabilistic logic." Wikipedia. https://en.wikipedia.org/wiki/Probabilistic_logic. Accessed April 15, 2017.
11. Rouse, M. "What is Data Lake? Definition from WhatIs.com." http://searchaws.techtarget.com/definition/data-lake. Accessed April 15, 2017.
12. Merrick, C. "9 Reasons data warehouse projects fail." December 4, 2014. https://blog.rjmetrics.com/2014/12/04/10-common-mistakes-when-building-a-data-warehouse. Accessed April 15, 2017.
13. "The Informatica Blog." http://blogs.informatica.com. Accessed April 15, 2017.
14. Benesh, P. "Case study: Clickstream analytics in a competitive world." TDWI. May 6, 2010. https://tdwi.org/articles/2010/05/06/clickstream-analytics-in-a-competitive-world.aspx. Accessed April 15, 2017.
15. "Understanding your customer journey by extending Adobe Analytics." www.datameer.com/wp-content/uploads/2015/09/Multi-Channel-Customer-Journey-Analytics.pdf. Accessed April 15, 2017.
16. "The Informatica Blog." http://blogs.informatica.com. Accessed April 15, 2017.
17. "WTF is programmatic advertising?" Digiday. February 20, 2014. http://digiday.com/platforms/what-is-programmatic-advertising. Accessed April 15, 2017.

8

An Introduction to Social Media Analytics

CHAPTER OBJECTIVES

After reading this chapter, readers should understand:

- Composition of the seven layers of Social Media Analytics
- Origin and history of Social Media Analytics
- Common goals, KPIs and use cases for Social Media Analytics
- Descriptive, predictive and prescriptive analytics for social media
- Differences between Business Analytics and Social Media Analytics
- Challenges to the efficient use of Social Media Analytics
- How to use the Social Analytics Vendor Assessment

Social Media Analytics is the art and science of extracting valuable insights from vast amounts of semi-structured and unstructured social media data to enable informed and insightful decision-making. In this chapter, we examine this new and constantly emerging field that continues to evolve as social media matures. Social Media Analytics is a science as it requires systematically identifying, extracting, and analyzing various social media data using a variety of sophisticated tools and techniques (this book will examine some of the tools and technology to extract and use social media data). However, Social Media Analytics is also an art, which requires analysts, stakeholders, and business owners to align the insights gained via the analytics with business goals and objectives. We should master both the art and science of Social Media Analytics to get full value from it.

Introducing the Seven Layers of Social Media Analytics

In this book, we have posited that the analytics of social media is best understood as a series of data layers. Determining the best social data layer(s) to utilize for business issues is where the art and science of Social Media Analytics merge.

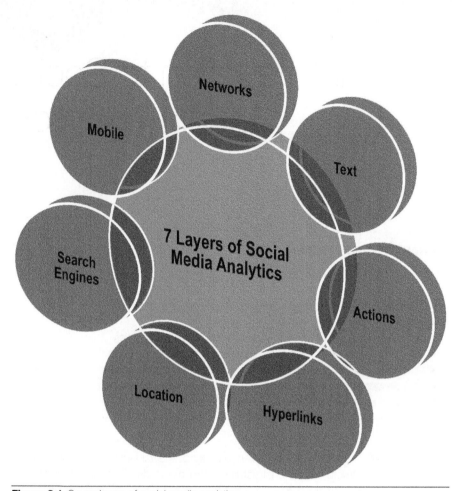

Figure 8.1 Seven layers of social media analytics.
Source: Gohar F. Khan

The science part of social media analytics requires a combination of skilled data analysts, sophisticated tools and technologies, and reliable/cleaned data. Getting the science right, however, is not enough. To effectively consume the results and put them into action, the business must master the other half of analytics; that is, the art of interpreting and aligning analytics with business objectives and goals.

Each layer of social media carries valuable information and insights that can be harvested for business intelligence purposes by using layer-specific Social/Text Analytics platforms as covered in this book. Out of the seven layers, some are visible or easily identifiable (e.g., text and actions), and others are mostly invisible (e.g., social media and hyperlink networks).

The following are seven social media layers that will be discussed in detail in the subsequent chapters.

1. Text
2. Networks
3. Actions (referred to as Intermediate Metrics elsewhere in this book)

4. Hyperlinks
5. Mobile
6. Location
7. Search engines

Definition of the Seven Layers

Layer One: Text

Social media text analytics deals with the extraction and analysis of business insights from textual elements of social media content, such as comments, tweets, blog posts, and Facebook status updates. Text analytics is mostly used to understand social media users' sentiments or identify emerging themes and topics.

Layer Two: Networks

Social media network analytics extract, analyze, and interpret personal and professional social networks, for example, Facebook, and Twitter. Network analytics seeks to identify influential nodes (e.g., people and organizations) and their position in the network.

Layer Three: Actions

Social media actions (Intermediate Metrics) analytics deals with extracting, analyzing, and interpreting the actions performed by social media users, including likes, shares, mentions, and endorsement. Actions analytics are mostly used to measure popularity, influence, and prediction in social media. The case study included at the end of the chapter demonstrates how social media actions (e.g., Twitter mentions) can be used for business intelligence purposes.

Layer Four: Hyperlinks

Hyperlink analytics is about extracting, analyzing, and interpreting social media hyperlinks (e.g., in-links and out-links). Hyperlink analysis can reveal sources of incoming or outgoing web traffic to and from a webpage or website.

Layer Five: Mobile

Mobile analytics is the next frontier in the social business landscape. Mobile analytics deals with measuring and optimizing user engagement through mobile applications (or apps for short).

Layer Six: Location

Location analytics, also known as spatial analysis or geospatial analytics, is concerned with mining and mapping the locations of social media users, contents, and data.

Layer Seven: Search Engine Analytics

Search engines analytics focuses on analyzing search engine data to gain valuable insights into a range of areas, including trends analysis, keyword monitoring, keyword research, search results and search engine marketing (text ads, etc.).

Emergence of Social Media Analytics

Based on Google Trends data, the term *Social Media Analytics* appeared over the Internet horizon during 2008, and interest in it (based on Internet searches for the term) has steadily increased since then. Social Media Analytics was present as a cottage industry, or a business or manufacturing activity carried on in a person's home, as early as 2003 based on the authors' personal experience. In 2008, Google Trends began to detect enough usage of the term "Social Media Analytics" to show up in its trend reporting, and the subject is becoming ever-more popular as we move towards 2020. No doubt, the growth in the development and usage of various social media channels spawned Social Media Analytics, as the means to better understand and harness "social data."

Social media has become one of the main ways people express themselves. Because of this activity, Social Media Analytics is gaining prominence among both the research and business communities.

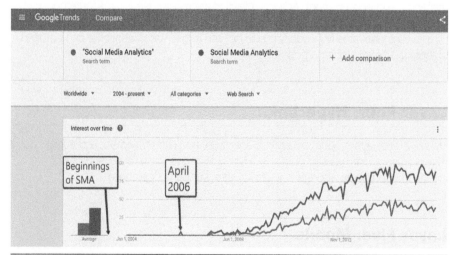

Figure 8.2 Google Trends visualization showing the beginning of the use of the term "Social Media Analytics."
Source: WebMetricsGuru Inc. using Google Trends.

Some Popular Reasons for Using Social Media Analytics

- Measure brand loyalty
- Generate business leads
- Drive traffic to owned media (Facebook pages, corporate blogs, company webpages, organizational microsites, specific mobile applications, etc.)
- Predictive business forecasting
- Demographics and psychographics around specific audiences and topics
- Business intelligence and market research
- Business decision-making

However, it is hard to put a dollar value on the data without accurately tracking every tracking every step in the process of acquiring customers. One of the co-authors was recently interviewed on the issue of Social Media ROI—to read more refer to http://oursocialtimes.com/how-to-measure-social-media-roi/.

Goals of Social Media Analytics

The main purpose of Social Media Analytics is to enable informed and insightful decision-making by leveraging social media data.[1]

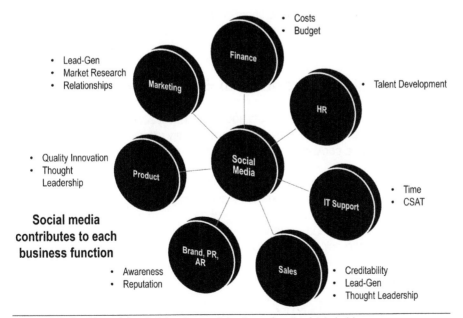

Figure 8.3 Social media's role informing each business function/stakeholder.
Source: WebMetricsGuru Inc.

The following are some sample questions that can be answered with social media analytics:

- What are customers using social media saying about our brand or a new product launch?
- Which content posted over social media is resonating more with clients or customers?
- How can we harness social media data (e.g., tweets and Facebook comments) to improve our product/services?
- Is the social media conversation about our company, product, or service positive, negative, or neutral?
- How can we leverage social media to promote brand awareness?
- Who are our influential social media followers, fans, and friends?
- Who are our influential social media nodes (e.g., people and organizations) and what is their position in the network?
- Which are the social media platforms driving the most traffic to our corporate website?
- Where is the geographical location of our social media customers?
- What are the keywords and terms trending over social media?
- How current is our business with social media, and how many people are connected with us?
- Which websites are linked to our corporate website?
- How are my competitors doing on social media?

Social Media Analytics KPIs

The questions, use cases, and goals that inform social media can be measured using Key Performance Indicators such as share of voice and sentiment score (see a list of suggested KPIs matched to business goals in Table 8.1).

Social Media vs. Traditional Business Analytics

While the premise of both social media and traditional business analytics is to produce actionable business, they do however slightly differ in scope and nature. Table 8.2 provides a comparison of social media analytics with traditional business analytics.

The most visible difference between the two types of information comes from the source, type, and nature of the data that is being mined. Unlike the traditional business analytics of structured and historical data, social media analytics involves the collection, analysis, and interpretation of semistructured and unstructured social media data to gain an insight into the contemporary issues while supporting effective decision-making.[2] Social media data is highly diverse, high volume, real-time, and stored in third-party databases in a semi-structured and unstructured format.

Structured business data, on the other hand, is mostly stored in databases and spreadsheets in machine-readable format (e.g., rows and columns). Thus it can be easily searched, computed, and mined. Unstructured and semi-structured social media data is not machine readable and can take a variety of forms, such as the

Table 8.1 Social media Key Performance Indicators matched to key business goals.

Aligning Business Goals & KPIs (usually Intermediate Metrics, in the case of Social Media) for Business Success

Business Goals	KPI 1	KPI 2	KPI 3	KPI 4	KPI 5
Awareness	Share of voice	Social community growth	Reach, volume of conversations	Sentiment analysis (+/- neutral)	Unique commenters
Engagement	Interactions per follower	Daily active users	% of community interacting	Viral content spread	Hashtag/meme use
Lead Gen	Cost to acquire leads from social	Web referrals via social media	Qualified sales leads via social	Growth of reach in targeted audiences	Number of downloads of select content
Conversion	Downloads via tracked links	Revenue via tracked links	Cost per acquisition (CPA)	Increase % of social conversions	Revenue attribution via Influencers
Customer Support	Cost savings	Decreased time of issue resolution	Sentiment change on support issues	Number of issues resolved	Resolution rate per issue/agent
Advocacy	Number of active advocates	Volume of advocate conversations	Volume of brand advocates conversations	Influence score and reach of advocates	Revenue attributed to advocates
Innovation	Number of ideas submitted related to products or services	Number of ideas that are developed into products or services	Number of bugs that are fixed in developed products or services	Community feedback from development of products or services	Engagement rate in product development forums

Source: WebMetricsGuru Inc.

Table 8.2 Social Media Analytics vs. Business Analytics.

Social Media Analytics	Business Analytics
Semi-structured and unstructured data	Structured data
Data is not analytical friendly	Data is analytical friendly
Real-time data	Mostly historical data
Public data	Private data
Stored in third-party databases	Stored in business-owned databases
Boundary-less data (i.e., Boundary within the Internet)	Bound within the business intranet
Data is high volume	Data is medium to high volume
Highly diverse data	Uniform data
Data is widely shared over the Internet	Data is only shared within organizations
More sharing creates greater value/impact	Less sharing creates more value
No business control over data	Tightly controlled by business
Socialized data	Bureaucratic data
Data is informal in nature	Data is formal in nature

Source: Gohar F. Khan.

contents of this book, Facebook comments, emails, tweets, hyperlinks, PowerPoint presentations, images, emoticons, videos, etc. Thus, it is not analytics-friendly and needs a lot of cleaning and transformation. Another visible difference comes from the way the information (i.e., text, photographs, videos, audio, etc.) is created and consumed. Social media data originates from the public Internet and is socialized in nature. Socialized data is provided for the benefit of humanity; it is created and consumed using various social media platforms and social technologies to maintain social and professional ties (e.g., Facebook, LinkedIn, etc.), to facilitate knowledge sharing and management (Wikipedia, blogs, etc.). Socialized data creates awareness (i.e., Twitter), or to exchange information in the form of text, audio, video, documents, graphics, to name a few.[3]

Social media data is generated by people communicating with each other through social media. Social media is not like the common Business Analytics data, which is structured and formal in nature and is often controlled by organizations and bound within an organizational network or intranet. The value of socialized data is determined by the extent to which it is shared with other social media accounts (e.g., people or organizations): the more it that is shared (i.e., socialized), the greater its overall value. However, it is important to point out that most social media metrics/KPIs are engagement-based and do not yield a tangible Return on Investment (ROI); instead, social media produces intermediate, activity-based metrics that support traditional business metrics (but do not replace them). For example, the value/effect of information can be considered an "Intermediate Metric" and is measured by the growth of followers (e.g., on Twitter or Facebook). On the other hand, most of the common business data and metrics are confined within an organization's databases for use within the organization, and can serve as a source of competitive advantage for that organization.

Types of Social Media Analytics

Like any business analytics, social media analytics can take three forms:

1. Descriptive analytics
2. Predictive analytics
3. Prescriptive analytics

Descriptive Analytics

Descriptive analytics is mostly focused on gathering and describing social media data in the form of reports, visualizations, and clustering to understand a business problem. Actions analytics (e.g., number of likes, tweets, and views) and certain aspects of text analytics are examples of descriptive analytics. Social media text (e.g., user comments), for instance, can be used to understand users' sentiments or identify emerging trends by clustering themes and topics. Currently, descriptive analytics accounts for most Social Media Analytics.

Predictive Analytics

Predictive analytics involves analyzing large amounts of accumulated social media data to predict a future event. For example, an intention expressed over social media (such as buy, sell, recommend, quit, desire, or wish) can be mined to predict a future event (such as a purchase). Alternatively, a business manager can predict sales figures based on past visits (or in-links) to a corporate website. The TweepsMap tool, for example, can help users determine the right time to tweet for maximum alignment with the right audience time zone (see https://tweepsmap.com).

Prescriptive Analytics

While predictive analytics help to predict the future, prescriptive analytics suggest the best action to take when handling a situation or scenario.[4] For example, if you have groups of social media users that display certain patterns of buying behavior, how can you optimize your offering to each group? Like predictive analytics, prescriptive analytics has not yet found its way into social media data.

Social Media Analytics Cycle

Social Media Analytics is a six-step irrelative process (involving both the science and art) of mining the desired business insights from social media data (see Figure 8.4). At the center of the analytics is the company. We want objectives that will inform each step of the social media analytics journal. Business goals are defined at the initial stage, and the analytics process will continue until the stated business objectives are fully satisfied. The steps may vary considerably based on the layers of social media data-mined (and the type of the tool employed). The following are the six general steps, at the highest level of abstraction, that involve both the science and art of achieving business insights from social media data. Interestingly, the steps of the Social Media Analytics cycle are like processes that are used to manage corporations, such as setting goals and objectives that are aligned with the business' vision. Managing a business, which often involves identifying risks and controls, is like performing the same thing with data.

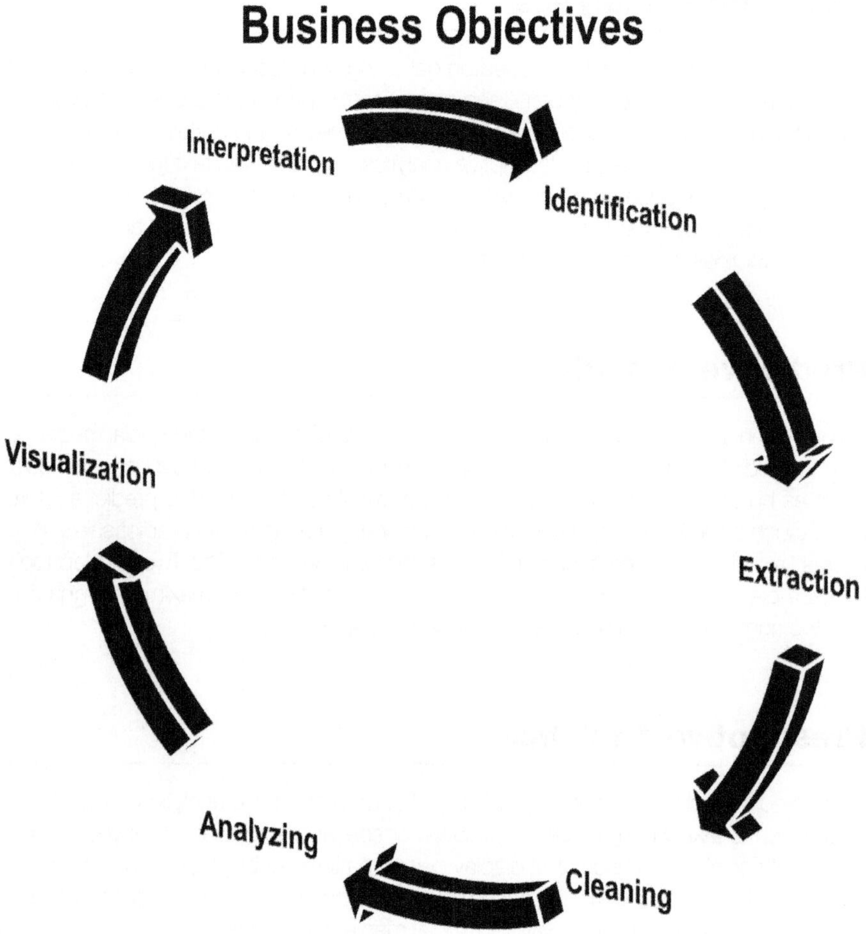

Business Objectives

Figure 8.4 The Social Media Analytics cycle.
Source: Gohar F. Khan.

Step 1: Identification

The identification stage is the art part of Social Media Analytics and is concerned with searching and identifying the right source of information for analytical purposes. The numbers and types of users and information (such as text, conversation, and networks) available over social media are huge, diverse, multilingual, and noisy. Thus, framing the right question and knowing what data to analyze is extremely crucial in gaining useful business insights. The source and type of data to be analyzed should be aligned with business objectives. Most of the data for analytics will come from business-owned social media platforms, such as an official Twitter account, Facebook fan pages, blogs, and YouTube channels. Some data for analytics, however, will also be harvested from non-official social media platforms, such as Google search engine trends data or Twitter search stream data. The business objectives that need to be achieved will play a major role in identifying the sources and type of data to be mined. Aligning social media analytics with business objectives is discussed in a later chapter.

Step 2: Extraction

The type (e.g., text, numerical, or network) and size of data will determine the best method and platform tools that are suitable for the extraction. Small-size numerical information, for example, can be extracted manually (e.g., going to your Facebook fan page and counting likes and copying comments), and a large-scale automated extraction is done through an application programming interface (API). Manual data extraction may be practical for small-scale data, but it is the API-based extraction tools that will help us get most out of various social media platforms. Mostly, the social media analytics tools use API-based data mining.

APIs, in simple words, are sets of routines/protocols that social media platforms (e.g., Twitter and Facebook) have developed to allow users to access small portions of data hosted in their databases. The greatest benefit of using APIs is that it allows other entities (e.g., customers, programmers, and other organizations) to build apps, widgets, websites, and other tools based on open social media data. Some data, such as social networks and hyperlink networks, can only be extracted through specialized tools from platforms like Brandwatch and Crimson Hexagon (for Social Media Analytics data), and several Web scrappers that can extract hyperlinks on webpages.

Privacy and Ethical Issues with Social Media Analytics Data

Two important issues to bear in mind are privacy and ethical issues related to mining data from social media platforms. Privacy advocacy groups have long raised serious concerns regarding large-scale mining of social media data and warned against transforming social spaces into behavioral laboratories. The social media privacy issue first came into the spotlight particularly due to the large-scale "Facebook Experiment" carried out in 2012. In this experiment, Facebook manipulated the news feeds feature of thousands of people to see if emotion contagion occurs without face-to-face interaction (and absence of nonverbal cues) between people in social networks.[5] Although the experiment was consistent with Facebook's Data Use Policy[6] and helped promote our understanding of online social behavior, it does, however, raise serious concerns regarding obtaining informed consent from participants and allowing them to opt out.

The bottom line here is that data extraction practices should not violate a user's privacy and the data extracted should be handled carefully. The policies should explicitly detail social media ownership regarding both accounts and activities such as individual and page profiles, platform content, posting activity, data handling, and extraction, etc.

Step 3: Cleaning

This step involves removing the unwanted data from the automatically extracted data. Some data may need cleaning, while other data can go directly into analysis. In the case of the Text Analytics cleaning, coding, clustering, and filtering of the text data may be needed to get rid of unrelated text using natural language processing (NLP).[7]

Note that coding and filtering can be done automatically using machines or manually done by humans. In Chapter 10, we also cover Text Analytics in detail, including the process of text cleaning. Coding and filtering can be performed by machines (i.e., automated) or it can be carried out manually by humans. For example, Discovertext combines machine learning and human coding techniques to code, cluster, and classify social media data.[8]

Step 4: Analyzing

At this stage, the clean data is analyzed for business insights. Depending on the layer of Social Media Analytics under consideration and the tools and algorithm employed, the steps and approach to take will vary greatly. For example, nodes in a social media network can be clustered and visualized in a variety of ways depending on the algorithm employed. The overall objective at this stage is to extract meaningful insights without the data losing its integrity.

Most of the analytics tools lay out a step-by-step procedure to analyze social data; having background knowledge and an understanding of the tools and its capabilities are crucial in arriving at the right answers.

Step 5: Visualization

In addition to numerical results, most of the seven layers of Social Media Analytics will also result in visual outcomes. The science of effective visualization known as visual analytics is becoming an important part of interactive decision making facilitated by visualization.[9] Effective visualization is particularly helpful with complex and large datasets because it can reveal hidden patterns, relationships, and trends. It is the effective visualization of the results that will demonstrate the value of social media data to top management. Depending on the layer, the analysis part will lead to relevant visualizations for effective communication of results. Text Analytics, for instance, can result in a word co-occurrence cloud; Hyperlink Analytics will provide visual hyperlink networks, and Location Analytics can produce interactive maps. Depending on the type of data, different types of visualization are possible, including the following.

- **Network data (with whom):** Network data visualizations can show who is connected to whom. For example, a Twitter "following-following" network chart can show who is following whom. Different types of networks are discussed in a later chapter.

- **Topical data (*what*):** Topical data visualizations are mostly focused on what aspect of a phenomenon is under investigation. A text cloud generated from social media comments can show what topics/themes are occurring more frequently in the discussion.
- **Temporal data (*when*):** Temporal data visualizations slice-and-dice data on a time horizon and can reveal longitudinal trends, patterns, and relationships hidden in the data. Google Trends data, for example, can visually investigate longitudinal search engine trends.
- **Geospatial data (*where*):** Geospatial data visualization is used to map and locate data, people, and resources. Chapter 11 on Location Analytics provides more details on mapping.

Other forms of visualizations include trees, hierarchical, multidimensional (chart, graphs, tag clouds), 3D (dimension), computer simulation, infographics, flows, tables, heat maps, plots, etc.

Step 6: Interpretation

This step relies on human judgments to interpret valuable knowledge from the visual data. The data should be presented in the right form for the person who is going to read it. It can be as dashboards, for example. Meaningful interpretation is of particular importance when we are dealing with social media data that leave room for different interpretations. Having domain knowledge and expertise are crucial in consuming the obtained results correctly.

Two strategies or approaches used here can be summarized:

1. Producing easily understandable analytical results.
2. Improving analytics analysis and insights capabilities.[10]

The first approach requires training data scientists and analysts to produce interactive and easy-to-use visual results. Moreover, the second strategy focuses on improving management analytics consumption capabilities.[11]

Challenges to Social Media Analytics

Social media data is high-volume, high-velocity, and highly diverse, which, in a sense, is a blessing regarding the insights it carries; however, analyzing and interpreting it presents several challenges. Analyzing unstructured data requires new metrics, tools, and capabilities, particularly for real-time analytics, that most businesses do not possess.

Big Data Volume and Velocity as a Challenge

Social media data is large and generated swiftly. Capturing and analyzing millions of records that appear every second is a real challenge. Capturing all this information may not be feasible. Knowing what to focus on is crucial for narrowing down the

Table 8.3 Examples of Social Media Analytics tools.

TEXT	ACTIONS (Intermediate Metrics)	NETWORK	MOBILE	LOCATION	HYPERLINKS	RESEARCH ENGINES
Discovertext	Lithium	NodeXL	Countly	Google Fusion Table	Webometrics Analyst	Google Trends
Lexalytics	Twitonomy	UCINET	Mixpanel	TweepsMap	VOSON	
Tweet Archivist	Google Analytics	Pajek	Google Mobile Analytics	Trendsmap		
Twitonomy	SocialMediaMineR	Netminer		Followerwonk		
Netlytic	Brandwatch	Flocker		Esri Maps		
LIWC	Crimson Hexagon	Netlytic		Agos		
Voyant		Reach		Geofeedia		
		Mentionmapp		Picodash		

Source: Gohar F. Khan.

scope and size of the data. Luckily, sophisticated tools are being developed to handle high-volume and high-velocity data.

Data Diversity Challenges

Social media users and the content they generate are extremely diverse, multilingual, and vary across time and space. Not every tweet, like, or user is worth looking at. Due to the noisy and diverse nature of social media data, separating relevant content from noise is challenging and time-consuming.

Unstructured Data Challenges

Unlike the data stored in corporate databases, which are mostly numbers, social media data is highly unstructured and consists of text, graphics, actions, and relations. Short social media text, such as tweets and comments, has dubious grammatical structure and is laden with abbreviations, acronyms, and emoticons (a symbol or combination of symbols used to convey emotional expressions in text messages), thus representing a significant challenge for extracting actionable business intelligence.

Social Media Analytics Tools

Social Media Analytics tools are being constantly developed to keep up with the growing need to extract, clean, and analyze the vast amount of social media data. Social Media Analytics tools come in a variety of forms and functionalities. Table 8.3 lists some example tools on each layer of Social Media Analytics. These tools are briefly discussed in several of the following chapters. These tools can be used to measure different layers of social media data, especially when aligned with an organization's business strategy.

Case Study: The Underground Campaign that Scored Big[12]

Background

ESPN is a digital sports leader in the UK, operating websites and apps that deliver a range of multimedia content to sports fans. ESPN.co.uk, the brand's central offering in the region, covers most sports, including football, cricket, rugby, tennis, golf, boxing, F1, and others. Other sport-specific websites under ESPN's stewardship include ESPN FC, which is available in app form, as is the award-winning ESPN UK app.

With a mandate to serve sports fans wherever they are, whenever they want, ESPN's websites and apps carry the latest news, live scores, video, tables, fantasy games, and more. Featuring ESPN's global roster of talents from across the entire sporting spectrum, the brand has enjoyed significant growth in the past 12 months in the primary user engagement metrics and continued to do so. ESPN is a sports television channel in the United Kingdom and Ireland owned by the BT Group under license from American sports broadcaster ESPN Inc. The channel was operated by ESPN from 2009 to 2013 when it was sold to BT and became part of its BT Sports package that focused on international sporting events, predominantly American sports. Programming is available in standard definition and high definition formats.

ESPN FC is the football-dedicated division of ESPN, providing rolling coverage of the world's most popular sport. Formerly ESPN Soccernet, ESPN FC is a multimedia football website that currently has Global, UK, US, and Spanish editions. The site offers news, live scores, fantasy football, blogs, stats, interactive polls and more; ESPN FC showcases the best in world football coverage. Through ESPN FC TV, the website hosts football-related video, utilizing the brand's roster of global football experts, journalists, and contributors, providing insight, analysis and reaction to football around the globe.

The Goal

The World Cup is the most widely viewed and followed sporting event in the world. The 2014 event, held in Brazil, was eagerly anticipated, with major sponsorship from some of the largest organizations on the planet, including Adidas, Coca-Cola, and Visa. Teams—and fans—from all corners of the earth traveled to the country. The world's spotlight was on Brazil. ESPN FC wanted to capitalize on the excitement, enjoyment, and enthusiasm of people all over the planet to hear about the matches taking place in Brazil.

ESPN FC's main goal over the period of the World Cup was to increase awareness of ESPN FC and to drive football fans to www.espnfc.co.uk for the latest news, scores, and team information, helping build the profile of the brand across the globe.

The Challenge

ESPN FC likes to go the extra mile to serve sports fans, anytime and anywhere. With the World Cup being held outside the UK, many of the games were being played at inconvenient times for sports fans in the UK to watch them live on TV, as the matches were being played while people were still at work, traveling home, or very late in the evening. ESPN FC wanted to find a way to get the games to sports fans wherever they were during the World Cup.

The Solution

During the World Cup 2014, ESPN FC estimated that 100 million people would travel on the London Underground. Most Underground stations do not have Internet access, meaning fans were kept in the dark with no access to the scores during vital points in the tournament. With their mantra of "serving sports fans anytime and anywhere," ESPN FC had the ingenious idea of bringing the results of World Cup games to those traveling on the London Underground. Transport for London (TFL) is a local government body responsible for most aspects of the transport system in Greater

London. ESPN FC partnered with TFL to display game results on announcement boards at 150 stations across London—a media first. No brand had ever displayed messages on TFL's boards before.

Influencing the Right Demographic

The ESPN FC and TFL World Cup campaign was aimed at the commuting masses. However, ESPN FC wanted to ensure that they were also reaching the specific demographic segments relevant to their brand. Using the Brandwatch (one of the world's leading social media listening and analytics technology platforms) Demographic feature, ESPN FC could identify which mentions about the campaign were from sales, marketing, and PR professionals, a key audience they were attempting to target. Regarding all positive sentiment about the campaign, 18% came from sales, marketing, and PR professionals, and just 0.4% of negative sentiment came from that industry. Those tweets went on to help influence five other influential people in that sector, each with more than 1,000 followers. Using Brandwatch, ESPN FC could measure that those five tweets alone reached nearly 15,000 followers.

Underground Results

Searching for the online reception of a campaign when there is no Internet reception can be tricky. Using Brandwatch, ESPN FC tracked 3,438 online mentions of the campaign in the first seven days. However, most commuters have no access to Wi-Fi or Internet while on the London Underground, so many remained excited enough about the campaign when returning to street level to share it online. Of the mentions relating to the live coverage, more than 60% of them were positive, a figure much higher than for most marketing campaigns according to Charles Boss, Head of Marketing at ESPN FC UK. To truly understand the effectiveness of this campaign, ESPN FC used Brandwatch analytics to measure how many mentions other London Underground-based projects received over a similar timeframe. Remarkably, the recent decision to introduce euro cashpoints in London Tube stations generated only 218 mentions in the first week, while commuters mentioning Virgin Media's new London Underground Wi-Fi was only slightly better with 473 mentions over seven days. When placed in this context, ESPN FC's World Cup updates were mentioned more than seven times more than these similar campaigns, proving they had the loudest fans and that the campaign was well-received.

The Right Line

Finding out *where* commuters are tweeting can be just as important as *what* they are tweeting. ESPN FC utilized Brandwatch's advanced Boolean Queries to listen to conversations specifically from each Tube line during the campaign. The Central Line proved to generate the largest volume of conversation of ESPN FC's World Cup updates, with 40% of tweets coming from that line, whereas the Northern and Jubilee lines followed with 27% and 23% of the chat. These insights could prove to be invaluable to ESPN FC when planning future social media advertising campaigns on the London Underground. As Charles Boss put it, "Brandwatch was able to demonstrate that the campaign reached a potential 2,363,921 people on Twitter."

Commentating to Commuters

During the campaign, London commuters traveling during the World Cup Final could follow Germany's 1–0 win over Argentina thanks to ESPN FC's live commentary and analysis at Waterloo Station. The game was relayed over the public-address system at London's busiest train station by ex-Chelsea defender Scott Minto and Tottenham Hotspur Assistant Head Coach Steffen Freund. Using Brandwatch's sentiment analysis, ESPN FC could gauge public reaction to the commentary. Of the mentions relating to the live coverage, again more than 60% of them were positive. More significantly, ESPN FC did not receive a single negative mention for their World Cup Final commentary: impressive considering many of those commuting during football's signature game are not the biggest fans of the sport.

Connecting the Dots: The Social Analytics Vendor Assessment

We discussed some of the many tools that are used to understand data from the seven layers of Social Media Analytics. However, deciding which platform best suits our needs is another matter entirely. While the narrative around social media is to consider social data as fuel, as a public commodity that is mined by platforms for us, it is not that simple. One issue that arises with Social Media Analytics is that the tools we use shape the data we get. Each platform captures and stores data in its own way; even when the same information is requested from analogous platforms, the results will often differ. Choosing the right tools and frameworks to work within our organization is crucial to creating successful outcomes.

Filling out the Social Analytics Vendor Assessment

We are presenting readers with a Social Analytics Vendor Assessment created by Demand Metric to help them choose the vendor that best fits an organization's need.[13] The authors call it a "soft-assessment," as results depend on how the assessment is conducted. The assessment does not provide the "right answer," it simply helps the user or reader organize their questions so they can be answered and acted on if desired. Use the accompanying Microsoft Excel matrix to compare Social Analytics vendor solutions based on the requirements of an organization. For each requirement, rank vendors based on their ability to deliver on the organization's needs along the criteria detailed below. At the time this manuscript went to press, we are trying to get permission from Demand Metric to include this assessment spreadsheet in the instructor's guide and supplemental material.

Vendor Evaluation Criteria

1. Does not support
2. Meets requirement
3. Ideal solution

What the Assessment Does

- Logical apples-to-apples comparison between up to three vendors.
- Documents requirements and necessity for each vendor.
- Provides visual report for results in the resulting radar diagram.
- Helps the reader cut through marketing hype and negotiate with various vendors.
- Saves several hours on research and formatting and is reusable in several contexts.
- Focuses vendor demo presentations.

Conducting the Assessment

Use the Vendor Evaluation tab to do the following:

- For each parameter, rank each of the vendors based on the information that the organization or reader currently has. As every organization has different require-ments, the questions can be modified to fit most decision-making criteria.
- In the "Vendor Evaluation" tab, rate each vendor based on your requirements (1—Does not support, 2—Meets requirement, 3—Ideal solution).
- View the "Scorecard" tab to see how the scores translate into a vendor's rating (percentage of total requirements that are ideal solutions).
- Use the data to evaluate which Social Analytics vendor is the best fit for an organization.

The authors are familiar with the Social Media Analytics space and filled out the assessment to give readers an example of how to fill it out—but the example we used should not be taken literally and is just a way of answering the questions the assessment posed based on one's opinion. There is no perfect solution or ultimate right answer. The assessment presented in this chapter is a way to foster dialog between stakeholders and users; out of the dialog, the best answer often emerges.

Hypothetical Situation

Here is a situation that mirrors are a real occurrence that one of the co-authors had. A large computer hardware manufacturer needed to understand how their brand and products were perceived by their target audiences around the world. Which platform best fulfills the organization's various needs?

Stakeholder Requirements
- They need to know about conversations about their products, locations, languages.
- Which conversations are positive, neutral, or negative to their brand?
- Who are the brand's influencers and advocates? The platform chosen should be able to identify and track the influencers.
- Collect problems or issues around specific products or use cases (such as pricing resistance and what to charge for their products).
- Use social data to come up with new products (market research).
- Use social data for customer service.
- Wide coverage of social media platforms that the organizations use to communicate with clients or potential customers.

- The readout from the chosen platform should be as close as possible to real-time data, actionable to employees and analysts in several lines of business (LOBs) within corporate marketing.
- The brand would also like to know what is going on at retailers' locations where their products are being sold. As the brand sells most of its products through affiliate sales channels such as Target, K-Mart, Staples, Office Depot, and Amazon.com, they do not get as clear a picture as they would like in regards what is going on at the point of sale.
- How is the brand doing in their online marketing compared to competitors in social media?
- The brand has a significant amount of textual and image data, both internal and on the Web, and they want to understand the patterns within the data by using Text Analytics.
- The brand uses coupons and social applications to sell their products across various channels; they would like to track the Return on Investment of these initiatives.
- The brand would like to understand the unique opportunities to market their products in specific locations in the main metropolitan centers throughout the world (at the neighborhood and block level).
- The brand owns several analytics platforms that are internally developed or bought, that are used internally to measure various use cases and desires the best integration so the data collected can be reused, if needed, in other applications.
- The brand wants the best platform and the lowest price.

The list of stakeholder requirements is not their entire list of needs! In fact, the organization may have additional requirements that have not been identified yet, and might not be unless a rigorous discovery process occurs before a choice is made, and continues as the platform is deployed. What is already evident is that no platform is going to be able to meet all the identified needs that the stakeholders have. While there are several platforms to choose from, and they each have their strengths and weaknesses, there are also several things that need to be tracked and understood (making it problematic to choose the best platform). Also, most vendors have invested in marketing that tends to obscure their platform's actual capabilities and utility as it pertains to particular organizations needs and data, and we believe that this is common in the Social Media Analytics space.[14]

Vendors Under Consideration
Note: We left the default questions in place for this example, but in many situations, customizing the assessment questions to match the stakeholders' exact requirements will provide better results.[15]

- Platform 1
- Platform 2
- Platform 3

First, stakeholders need to examine each platform by performing research on the Web and speaking to sales and technical support staff at each vendor. Assuming all of that has been done, then the assessment should be relatively easy to fill out.

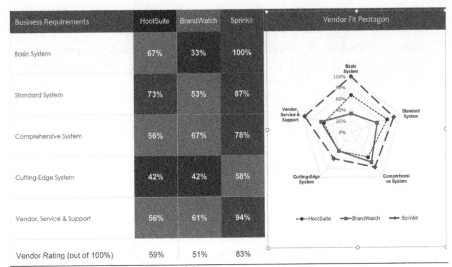

Figure 8.5 Sample Social Analytics Vendor Assessment example.
Note: The grading of this example is hypothetical and was done simply as a quick exercise by one of the authors.
Source: Demand Metric.

Using our example, we ranked each vendor based on our understanding and experience of what the platform offers; each platform has its interface and methods for collecting, processing and storing data.

Review Questions

1. Why it is important for business managers to understand and data-mine social media data?
2. What is Social Media Analytics, and how it is different from traditional Business Analytics?
3. Briefly explain the seven layers of social media data. Support the answer with examples.
4. Explain the Social Media Analytics cycle.
5. What ethical issues should be considered when mining social media data?
6. What are some main challenges to Social Media Analytics?
7. Compare different Social Media Analytics tools available in the market and explain their strengths and weakness.

Chapter 8 Citations

1. Chen, H., R.H.L. Chiang, and V.C. Storey (2012) "Business Intelligence and Analytics: From Big Data to Big Impact." *MIS Quarterly* 36(4): 1165–1188.

2. Bekmamedova, N. and G. Shanks (2014) *Social Media Analytics and Business Value: A Theoretical Framework and Case Study.* The 47th Annual Hawaii International Conference on System Sciences, IEEE Explore.

3. Khan, G. (2013) "Social Media-Based Systems: An Emerging Area of Information Systems Research and Practice." *Scientometrics* 95(1): 159–190.

4. Lustig, I., B. Dietrich, C. Johnson and C. Dziekan. "The analytics journey: An IBM view of the structured data analysis landscape: descriptive, predictive and prescriptive analytics." December 2012. www.analytics-magazine.org/november-december-2010/54-the-analytics-journey. Accessed April 15, 2017.

5. Kramer, A.D.I., J.E. Guillory, and J.T. Hancock (2014) "Experimental Evidence of Massive-Scale Emotional Contagion through Social Networks." *Proceedings of the National Academy of Sciences* 111(24): 8788–8790.

6. Editorial (2014). "Editorial expression of concern: Experimental Evidence of Massive-Scale Emotional Contagion through Social Networks." *Proceedings of the National Academy of Sciences* 111(29): 10779

7. For more details on this process, visit www.linkedin.com/pulse/making-data-science-accessible-text-mining-dan-kellett. Accessed April 15, 2017.

8. Shulman, S.W. "Five pillars of text analytics." Screencast.com. www.screencast.com/t/J1P7R6thJUFR. Accessed 20 Apr. 2017.

9. Wong, P.C. and J. Thomas (2004). "Visual Analytics." *IEEE Computer Graphics and Applications* 24(5): 20–21; Kielman, J. and J. Thomas (2009). "Special Issue: Foundations and Frontiers of Visual Analytics." *Information Visualization* 8(4): 239–314.

10. Ransbotham, S. "Once you align the analytical starts, what's next?" March 31, 2015. http://sloanreview.mit.edu/article/once-you-align-the-analytical-stars-whats-next. Accessed April 15, 2017.

11. Ransbotham, S. "Once you align the analytical starts, what's next?" March 31, 2015. http://sloanreview.mit.edu/article/once-you-align-the-analytical-stars-whats-next. Accessed April 15, 2017.

12. See www.brandwatch.com/case-studies/espn-fc—the original case study is referenced and summarized here. Accessed April 15, 2017.

13. Refer to the Demand Metric website for overall information about the assessment methodology, and specifically to www.demandmetric.com/content/website-vendor-selection-tool. Note: To download this Excel Assessment, one must be a member of the Demand Metric site (however, we may be able to provide university students with a copy of the assessment, based on Demand Metric academic use policy—currently under consideration). We adapted the methodology to focus on Social Media Analytics, which the authors, as members of Demand Metric site, can do.

14. "*Social Media Analytics: Effective Tools for Building, Interpreting, and Using Metrics.*" www.amazon.com/Social-Media-Analytics-Effective-Interpreting/dp/0071824499. Accessed April 15, 2017.

15. Refer to www.lumapartners.com/lumascapes/marketing-technology-lumascape. Accessed April 15, 2017.

9

Leveraging Social Media Content and Analytics

CHAPTER OBJECTIVES

After reading this chapter, readers should understand:

- Social media adoption and use
- Social Media Analytics by channel
- Advantages and disadvantages of the various types and social media channels
- Viral media—what it is, how to measure and use it
- Geo-location and iBeacon technology and uses in Social Media

---

In Chapter 3, we examined the history of social media; in this chapter, we go in much more detail regarding leveraging social media though the use of Social Media Analytics. We considered merging the two chapters, but decided they need to remain separate because the focus of each is different. Social media is such a big part of the fabric of society today that it is almost impossible to imagine our lives without it. Moreover, these days it is more present than ever, and it includes rich analytics and targeting capabilities, some of which we will cover in this chapter. Social media is one of the most powerful technological developments to happen in recent years. Therefore, we will focus on maximizing social media through analytics, which is also called content marketing analytics. Social media has been revolutionary since the start, from email to Internet chats through social networking, and has changed the world— and, even more importantly, how we perceive the world. The rise of "social media" has given us a voice in the world and the result is that social media has merged with marketing and analytics.

There is Wide Social Media Adoption by Age and Gender

Based on Figure 9.1, social media adoption was at ~70% in the United States as of 2015; we think it is closer to 80% today; four out of five people have at least one social media account, and most are at least semi-active on it. Social media is thought to have influenced the outcome of recent elections,[1] thus both the platform and its technologies need to be understood and leveraged.

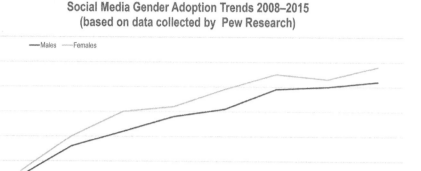

Figure 9.1 Social media adoption trends by gender showing close to 68% of females and 62% of males use social media in the United States as of 2015.
Source: WebMetricsGuru Inc., based on data collected by Pew Internet.

The Complex and Fragmented Ecosystem of Social Media Analytics

The first point we want to make is that the growth of social media and its proliferation makes it imperative to study its analytics. Businesses and individuals now accept the notion that social media is measurable and have even used it to gain an advantage over their competitors. However, many of the "Intermediate Metrics" such as likes, shares, posts, and pins have turned out to be poor proxies for Return on Investment (ROI) unless they are used to measure audience engagement or campaign effectiveness.[2] Unlike Web Analytics and Text Analytics that depend more on the capabilities of specific platforms for data and metrics, Social Media Analytics evolved to focus on online audiences and their activities. Thus, the creation and analysis of digital data need to be considered together, as one unit. Content creation today utilizes a combination of these tools and disciplines that should not be glossed over. During the early period of what we now call "social media" (2003–2011), social media was considered a new phenomenon. Today, social media, marketing, and analytics have fully merged, as shown in Figure 9.2.

Activities in social media differ somewhat, based on the channel. What we have found is a fragmentation has evolved where we cannot understand the activity in a social media channel without the analytics created just for that channel. Much of the data from one channel is incompatible with the others, and even when it has the same terminology—i.e., shares, likes, friends, etc.—this doesn't always mean the same thing and cannot be added together with integrity. When data is gathered through APIs and rolled up into a dashboard platform, the information is useful just for trend correlation and directional purposes, perhaps nothing more. From a Business Analytics perspective, the latter is a challenging situation to be in as we are working with platform tools and metrics that don't add up to a clear Return on Investment. And yet, that is the challenge we face as marketers and students. How does one make sense of all this data? It comes down to what we want to achieve in the first place (our goals). We need to understand the capabilities, technologies,

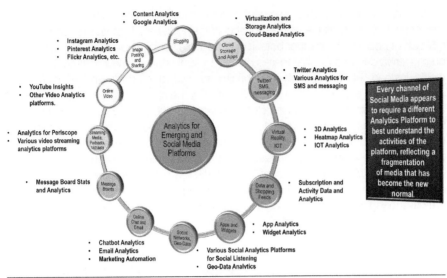

Figure 9.2 Fragmentation of Social Media Analytics platform by channel. Each social media ends up having its set of analytics platforms, making it even harder to get a unified view of social activity around a brand or individual.
Source: WebMetricsGuru Inc.

and limitations of social media platforms, or else our strategies and targets will not be well-informed, and we will miss opportunities because we are unaware of them, or pursue paths and strategies that are unproductive (and perhaps harmful). That's why we included this chapter and placed it at the midpoint of this book. Before we go on, let's make sure we understand social media and what we can do with it.

Investment of Time is High for Social Media because the Data is Unstructured

No matter how much an organization streamlines their business processes, it takes significant amounts of time to do things well. How much time? The amount of time spent working with digital data (Web copy, images, blogs, online video content, social media posts, as well as other forms of information, etc.) is relative; some may think 20 hours a week is a lot, while others disagree. However, the truth is that much of the digital information we are dealing with is what we commonly called "unstructured."[3] Unstructured data takes a lot longer to work with than when the information is structured. When a procedure becomes repeatable (it has been repeated several times and can be performed with little that changes), the time it takes to perform it can be largely decreased and efficiency goes way up. We believe that optimizing process flow is only possible when everything in the process is sufficiently set up and isn't changing much. But that is not a realistic expectation with social media. Our lives do not work like that; real life is much more fluid, and social media reflects the fabric of our lives—it requires interaction and engagement with circumstances that are constantly evolving. We are not seers, everything we need cannot be known and structured perfectly beforehand (even in the age of autonomous bots running off Facebook Messenger). If we are going to engage with the world via social media authentically, it cannot be expected to be fully automated and consequently requires time to create content, along with a significant amount of content curation. While algorithms can help, they cannot eliminate all the work—nor should they! After all, if marketing becomes a bunch of bots talking to other bots, it ceases to be social media at all. So, we are putting forward the notion that there's no way to eliminate the time investment of social media. Instead, let's focus on making the time we spend more efficient (algorithms and streamlined processes can help with this). For the sake of brevity, "unstructured data" is the information one must look at and listen to with one's own eyes and ears to understand (as shown in Figure 1.1 in Chapter 1). In other words, no computer program or algorithm can fully make sense of something complex such art or music *yet* (although the attributes of images,[4] art,[5] and music[6] can be *somewhat* understood via their metadata). Besides, most of what people say online can be interpreted and misinterpreted in many ways (although that can happen with in-person meetings, too). We have found that to understand the "context" of a statement or word; we must directly examine it—bots, algorithms, and other automation can't help much here.[7]

Blogs

When the Internet began, there were various kinds of blogs and bloggers, making it easy for people who wanted to voice their opinion on pretty much any subject to publish it quickly online; and the same for organizations. Blogs and blogging have diversified since they were first created more than 20 years ago; depending on one's interest in the topic, a reader/searcher can find opinions covering a variety of themes such as food, fashion, technology, or anything else of interest.[8] Blogs that are consistent in their topic (and use of certain topic words) tend to do better in search engine results listings[9] (which generate a substantial amount of traffic to many blogs). Blogs utilize RSS Feeds (Really Simple Syndication), alerting search engines and RSS readers of new content/posts that are being produced. Blogs were created in the age of search engines and leverage social media by integrating with Facebook, Twitter, Instagram, Pinterest, and other social sharing applications.

Online Video (YouTube)

According to eMarketer, online video and vlogging are among the most consumable content on the Web and people are increasing the time they spend daily, from 54 minutes in 2014 to a predicted 75 minutes in 2018.[10] Therefore, online video (particularly YouTube) offers many opportunities to marketers for analytics introspection. More people are watching videos online as well—up to 68% of the US population, according to eMarketer. The channels of discovery for new online video content continue to multiply, creating new opportunities and challenges for marketing video content to the right audiences.

Advantages

- **Low production costs**: There are low startup costs to capture video (most digital devices can record and upload digital video directly to YouTube). Limitations on the length of uploaded videos (15 minutes was the limit for low traffic channels) has been relaxed; videos of almost any length can be uploaded and processed within minutes.

- **Extensible:** Sophisticated video editing tools are free or inexpensive and accessible to almost anyone.
- **Social media**: Social media provides a means to gain viewers quickly through social sharing (especially if the video goes viral).
- **YouTube advertising network**: YouTube channel owners are given the opportunity to earn income from their channels by allowing advertising to appear on their uploaded videos through YouTube's advertising network. Also, channel owners can run their advertising to expand the reach and audience of their videos on YouTube. When channel owners run their advertising, they can use a variety of geo-demographic targeting options that YouTube provides.
- **Sponsorship opportunities**: YouTube sponsors some video creators (YouTubers can be influencers and brand ambassadors) by providing an income to produce agreed-upon video content. Brands can also provide YouTube channel owners and videographers with sponsorship opportunities.
- **YouTube production studios**: In some cities, such as New York, YouTube has its own studios that videographers can use or rent to produce and edit their videos.
- **YouTube analytics**: YouTube provides sophisticated analytics to channel owners on their uploaded videos.
- **Advocacy**: Videographers and musicians have additional training and playbook resources that encourage creators to improve their skills and build their audience.

Disadvantages

- **Stiff competition:** With so much new content uploaded every moment, the videographer has a hard time gaining viewership (especially if they have not developed an audience yet).
- **Low attention span**: Viewers need to engage with a video within the first few seconds, or they will not watch the rest, and this may be a reason why video-enabled platforms such as Instagram have become so popular. Consequently, videographers need to be good storytellers to captivate their audiences with their content.
- **Viral sharing**: While many videographers want their videos to go "viral," few ever do. In most cases, videos need to be planned and seeded in various online locations first, which requires spending money on advertising, having a knack for appealing storylines and great timing. Also, most of the videos that go viral are professionally produced (with rare exceptions).
- **Ownership**: YouTube technically owns any video that is uploaded to its platform.
- **Big Brother**: Like most social media platforms, YouTube uses the video data uploaded to channels for its own purposes, including profiling of its users and audiences. The profiling goes well beyond what most videographers are aware of. While YouTube uses the data to improve its services, it also shares some of the information with governmental agencies, commercial brokers, and advertisers.
- **Throttling and network congestion**: As the Internet becomes saturated with video and audio content, it had become challenging to watch the video due to network congestion, especially when videos stall while playing.

Marketing Data Issues

- Third-party software such as VidStatsX and ChannelMeter provide "intermediate" metrics that are not actionable (except perhaps advertising on a highly-trafficked channel, etc.). While YouTube allows users to run advertising that targets demographics and geo-location, the actual channels that are selected are not shared with the advertiser.
- For advertisers, YouTube (Facebook and Twitter are also included) do not share the actual account (channel) information of where your ads will appear; the rationale for that is two-fold.
  - Data: Google, Facebook, Twitter, and LinkedIn consider their "data" as the most important asset they have; they provide targeting for the advertiser, but they are not in the business to building audience lists for advertisers.
  - Privacy: When advertising is run in social media, that advertising is usually matched with a specific user's account, based on the information the social network has on the individual whose account it is (i.e., a Facebook user ID, a Twitter account handle, etc.). Consequently, reviewing to the advertiser exactly where their ads are appearing in social media would be a violation of their users' privacy. If that were not enough reason, social networks regard the data of their members as their most precious asset—they will provide the results of advertising (clicks, impressions, etc.), but not who it was shown to. As a result, marketers who want to build customer lists are frustrated by the privacy policies put in place by social media platforms to protect their membership.

Twitter

Twitter is "short form" communication (essentially a mini blog post of up to 140 characters), and there is little effort needed to post a tweet. Twitter is composed of more than 317 million active users and more than 500 million tweets per day.[11] The tweets themselves—and the hashtags they contain—are the most important part of Twitter because they let users know what trending topics are.

Twitter's Biggest Value May Be as a Data Analytics Platform

The value of Twitter may ultimately reside in the data analytics capabilities[12] it provides regarding member activities on Twitter and how it reflects changes in society, including a deeper exportation into predictive analytics.[13] The one strength Twitter has over other social media platforms is its "open" data nature. All the data on Twitter is accessible to anyone who has API access to it (although large amounts of data can become expensive to collect and store).

Twitter Analytics

While there are hundreds of third-party free and paid services that provide Twitter analytics we are just going to focus in this chapter on Twitter's own analytics platform. Twitter's analytics platform gets constant updates and has continued to evolve. Social media platforms freely provide information surrounding a user's account and audience to the user. What costs money is getting the same kind of data on other accounts, lists of accounts (other than one's own) and industry type, third-party data statistics.

No doubt, the analytics that Twitter provides are useful, but it requires a clear marketing goal, program, and customized metrics to realize the fullest value of the data that is being provided. In December 2013, Twitter added conversion tracking of promoted tweets to allay account owners who are running advertising to drive traffic to their websites. The conversion tracking reveals which tweet(s) drive the most traffic and conversions. Twitter now offers conversion tracking on all tweets, not just the ones that are promoted. Also Twitter has many free tools that do an excellent job of analyzing various elements of the Twitter API stack. But once the data is assembled, analyzed, and visualized, it tends to be treated as a premium item that is purchased (in volume). Today, all the tools needed to track Twitter activity are in place, especially if the user is willing to pay for them. Examples abound, such as Hootsuite, which provides basic reporting on a few metrics, but becomes more expensive as additional third-party data providers along with additional Twitter data and metrics are added.

Facebook

Facebook popularized the concept of "virtual friends" and now is "home base" for many social media users. But just as some of us do not like to hang out at home, Facebook is not always the favorite place for Internet audiences to hang out and share information.[14] Still, people spend more time on Facebook than any other social network. In fact, 16% of college students spend between four and six hours a day on Facebook, while another 34% spend two to three hours a day there.[15] When we compare those numbers with the other social networks, none of the others even come close. Millennials are reading about the stories their friends are posting—and liking some of them, perhaps sharing them when the content moves them—but it is not just millennials; everyone is doing these actions on Facebook because those are the activities the platform is designed to promote. There is so much that happens on the world's biggest social media network that this book cannot cover.

Facebook Analytics

It is hard to talk about Facebook without discussing its analytics and the main audience for it, the advertisers. In fact, the real customer of Facebook is not its members; rather, it is the advertisers who are mining the vast amounts of data generated by the content that members generate and consume. Moreover, it is not just Facebook, every social network that runs advertising is mining the data users generate with their activities in social networks (and outside of them, as well, via third-party tracking cookies). Thus, any time users search on Google, when they next log onto their Facebook accounts, they will see ads tailored to that subjects they recently searched for on Google, and vice versa; the data collected makes it better for advertisers (but not so much for searchers). The way the information can be assembled via analytics and data-brokers can lead to other outcomes that are unexpected, and it goes well beyond Facebook. In fact, the innovation happening in the targeting space is so vast and profound that it is impossible to keep totally update with it in a printed textbook, as new capabilities are frequently being added. In 2016, Facebook introduced a new algorithm "favoring friends" that shared stories rather than *publications* sharing stories.[16] Because of many subtle algorithmic and policy changes, Facebook's organic reach has steadily declined (and, consequently, Facebook's advertising revenue increased), forcing page owners to promote their pages and posts to improve their audience reach (the change is traced back to Facebook's public offering several years ago, creating a need to monetize their platform better to appease Wall Street).

Interest Tracking and Demographics

When sharing content on Facebook, users now can target that message to a specific audience, such as parents of newborns.[17] Even without advertising, Facebook allows users to do basic audience research that is relatively sophisticated. Consequently, any member can research audiences based on location or topic based on the anonymous data from Facebook users that were collected by their activities, likes, and so on.

Local Audience

Facebook continues to add more capabilities to their data tracking of members, including their exact location. Google does the same, in fact, all platforms have that data since mobile devices broadcast their location; in this case, the location is used to broadcast targeted ads within one mile of an advertiser's brick-and-mortar location/store.[18]

Custom Audience

Facebook and Twitter are similar in that they allow a list of email addresses, accounts, or phone numbers to be uploaded to their platforms and used as a basis for targeted advertising both on the platform and outside of them, based on first and third-party cookies. There are other ways of collecting a custom audience, but the concept is very much akin to a "marketing list," and in fact, much of marketing is about the "list" or "Rolodex" a brand/business has. Targeting a specific audience that one already has is more efficient than just serving ads to anyone on the social network (because the audience is already identified and partly understood). However, there are many ways to get that "marketing list" beyond your email list due to the technological capabilities. Today it is possible to geo-sift accounts that are in a specific location and add them to a list of accounts to target—it is also possible to count how often they visit an actual location (visitor loyalty) and qualify them in that way. Triangulating data in a data warehouse also brings up intriguing possibilities to create custom audiences within the data in a data warehouse (or cloud).

Lookalike Audience

Facebook can use a specific audience such as the followers of a Facebook page, or users who have clicked on a Facebook ad and find other, non-connected

Facebook members. Lookalike audiences are used to extend the reach and success of marketing campaigns. The selling point of lookalike audiences is that return on investment metrics tend to be much better.

Mind Control Experimentation

Facebook has been performing research on its users from day one, often unbeknown to them;[19] and in at least one instance, Facebook faced a backlash of negative responses to the research.[20] In 2014, Facebook published a paper detailing emotional experiments the company had conducted on its users. Facebook had tweaked its news feed algorithm to show some users more negative posts than everyone else, just to see how they would react to the posts; and they observed negative contagion of the emotions they promoted. When the news leaked to the media, Facebook COO Sheryl Sandberg apologized for the company's poor communication regarding the project and vowed to set up stringent guidelines for future experiments. Perhaps "spookier" research lies ahead on selected Facebook members, although Facebook promised to be transparent and ethical with its user experiments in the future. When members use Facebook's platform, they must adhere to Facebook's TOS, and in the fine print there are probably clauses allowing this type of experimentation.

Positives and Negatives

Both are well-known; Facebook is the largest social network in the world, but it also collects data on us, filters news (reinforcing filter bubbles), and is fertile ground for fake news.

Positives
- Allows members to stay in contact with family and friends; provides a broad network of weak links linking to up to 1.8 billion members (at the time of publication).
- Allows members to build an audience within Facebook.
- Stringent privacy controls.
- Extensive targeting options for advertisers and publishers.

Negatives
- Fake news.
- Privacy issues.
- Lack of organic search traced back to Facebook's public offering.

Reddit

The name Reddit is a play-on-words of the phrase "read it," and the website content is divided into many categories or "default SubReddits" of discussion that are visible on the front page to new users and site browsers, even without an account. Some examples include Fitness, Food, Science, Space, Art, PhotoShopBattles, GetMotivated, etc. Users earn "Karma" on their profile. When posts and comments are upvoted, the upvotes translate into Karma, thereby boosting the user's standing within the Reddit community. Like many other online communities, Redditors have their language.

Some examples include:

- OP: original poster
- TIL: today I learned
- AMA: ask me anything

Reddit also has a paid subscription model, Reddit Gold, allowing access to secret SubReddits; they also preview features before the wider Reddit community.

The perception of Reddit in the media has changed over time. Several years ago, Reddit was used more for Web traffic generation and link spamming than anything else. Since then, Reddit has transformed into a more legitimate way to obtain information (curated by an enthused community) than most mainstream media (especially during and after the 2016 US election, some have more respect for Reddit than they do for the mainstream press); in fact, some prefer specific SubReddits for accuracy over articles that appeared in the *New York Times* in 2016! In a weird, almost *Twilight Zone* way, much of the mainstream media has become "fake news" in the eyes of many, which has elevated other outlets, including Reddit. Frankly, Reddit is known by its members as a place where unfiltered ideas can be discussed. Since its creation in 2005, Reddit has grown into one of the most influential communities on the Internet and has given birth to interesting collaborative projects that reflect a group character and value system.[21] Examples of Reddit collaboration include:

- **MusicInTheMaking:** Post music collaboration projects.[22]
- **ProjectManagement:** Bridging the gap between engineering and management with concrete data.[23]
- **SideProject:** A SubReddit for sharing and receiving constructive feedback on side projects.[24]

The Reddit community is very active and has had an impact on recent political events like SOPA/CISPA/Pizzagate, but it also has its share of internal social issues, such as grappling with its internal commitment to free speech.

Analytics

There are a few platforms that pull Reddit data and provide visualizations and reports on users or posts.[25] The list below is not comprehensive, and some of the platforms have free and premium account options.

- **RedditInsight:** An interactive analytics suite for Reddit.com using their public API combined with real-time data analysis and d3 visualizations.[26]
- **SnoopSnoo:** Provides user statistics on Reddit accounts and SubReddits.[27]
- **Redditlater:** Provides recommendations to a user on the best time to post on Reddit.[28]
- **RedditMetrics:** Provides information on trending Reddits.[29]
- **Reddit Investigator:** Provides information on a specific Reddit account.[30]

Disadvantages

Reddit is susceptible to being gamed. For example, in 2016 the Nintendo NX controller was leaked on the Games SubReddit, but it turned out to be faked information.[31]

Yelp

Good business reviews boost revenue, while terrible ones can close a venue down. In an age when everyone can be an online critic, online ratings have become vital. However, until now no one knew how important the online star rating could be for a local business' fortunes. In one study, local San Francisco restaurants found that small improvements in their online Yelp ratings significantly impacted their bottom line.[32] The study was done in San Francisco by two economists at the University of California, Berkeley. The economists collected reviews and daily reservation availability for 328 restaurants on Yelp during May 2012. The results of the study found moving from 3 stars to 3.5 stars increased a restaurant's chance of selling out during prime dining times increased from 13% to 34%.[33] Even better, moving from 3.5 stars to 4 stars increased the chance of selling out during prime dining times by 19 percentage points. But star ratings are not always a reliable indicator of the quality of a venue, as some businesses could inflate their star ratings in order to drive more customers to visit their locations. However, ratings are directly impacted by a retail business's quality of products and services in the eyes of its customers; consistently improving the customer's experience should improve a venue's online ratings.[34]

Improving Yelp Online Ratings

In the eyes of consumers, numerical ratings are an objective measure of a business's quality.[35] To improve a venue's online ratings, a business should do the following:

- Register the business venue on Yelp (and other review sites such as TripAdvisor).
- Monitor all relevant review websites (locations and competitors).
- Respond promptly to business reviews to demonstrate to customers that the company cares about the customer's opinion. A one-star improvement in ratings translated into a 5–9% revenue improvement.
- Star ratings matter most to new customers who are not familiar a local business; consequently, improving ratings should yield more new customers.

Positives and Negatives

Positives
- Very helpful for strangers and travelers to find the best local venues based on their current location.
- Provides local venues with a way to engage with customers and build a reputation, especially for new customers.
- Provides actionable analytics (in some cases) that improves the quality of a venue's service or offerings.

Negatives

- There have been several fake reviews and fake reviewers.
- Yelp encourages customers to voice their opinion, but that is not always a positive thing as some customers are impossible to please or are otherwise unreasonable.
- There have been isolated cases of vendors suing customers who left negative reviews or vice-versa. The laws around the liability for negative reviews are not very clear.

Snapchat

Snapchat is one of the top three social media apps among millennials, dominating 33% of the demographic's smartphones right behind Instagram and Facebook (at ~44% and ~75%, respectively). The average user checks Snapchat once a day to find out what their colleagues are doing for that day in a short amount of time, ranging from one to ten seconds. They can add filters as well and draw on their snaps/post text on their snaps.[36] Snapchat is beginning to replace older applications such as Skype, as now users can video chat with friends and call them using Snapchat. Most Snapchat users are between 18 and 34 years of age, and 55% make under $75,000 per year according to eMarketer.[37]

Snapchat Features

- The My Story feature allows users to broadcast multiple Snapchat pictures or videos, for friends' multiple viewings, over a 24-hour period. An example is users will show an event that happened on the commute to work, an even that happened in the morning after arriving at work, lunch, commute home, and arriving home. On Saturdays, Team Snapchat produces various live stories expressing the events of Snapchat users around the world. These stories or compilation of "Snaps," are referred to as an event. Snapchat also allows users to experience a festival or holiday in a different part of the world through their smartphones.
- Snapchat allows users to add specific tags to "Snaps." These tags are referred to as Smart Filters. For example, working in Manhattan, a user can snap friends and add a Geotag by swiping to the left or right on the picture. These Smart Filters are based on the location of the user and differ from place to place; location services need to be on for location filtering to work. Also, anyone can create a tag through Snapchat by paying a small fee. Swiping left on a snap after the time will show the temperature tag. This feature is used to express the weather outside. Swiping left again allows for filters to be added to a picture. Much like Instagram, different lightings, tints, and enhancements can be added to Snaps to add an artistic element to photos.
- Using Snapcash, by typing a dollar sign ($) and an amount of the sign ($20), Snapchat users can transfer funds to one member to another.
- Snapchat also has a private chat option along with a live video chat that is like Facetime, providing an option to save a user's Snaps as photos.

Snapchat is adding new features on a steady basis, and no doubt, by the time this book is published, there will be many more updates.

Analytics

There does not appear to be any platform, at the time of writing, providing free Snapchat analytics for users; the existing Snapchat analytics platforms are designed for brands, marketers, and agencies. Nonetheless, a few platforms have emerged that offer Snapchat analytics.

- **Snaplytics.io:** Provides automation, metrics, followers, and publishing designed and priced for brand advertisers.[38]
- **Delmondo:** Provides Snapchat analytics for brands and media companies.[39]
- **Wicked Society:** Analytics tools for brands, agencies, and influencers using Snapchat for their business marketing.[40]

Pinterest

Pinterest is a big, virtual pin board, an online scrapbook that users can stick any image or video on to and organize anyway they want on a custom "board"—it's similar to stamp collecting but online. Pinterest makes it easy to store and embed photos, videos, and infographics, pinning them up onto a dashboard. The main selling point of Pinterest is its addictiveness. Users spend hours searching for images and re-pinning them, and it is a useful means of generating links back to a website or blog where the content can be further built out and monetized (if desired). Another aspect of Pinterest is that it can use to search for what styles are trending and forecast future products and collections. Pinterest is an excellent resource for inspiration, it gives a good idea of what is immediately attractive visually, structurally, and layout-wise when creative new images and graphics. Users can follow popular celebrities, brands, and bloggers on Pinterest.

Analytics

As listed below, several companies track Pinterest analytics:

- Pinterest offers its analytics platform (called **Pinterest Analytics**) for business users only; this offering will be directed to brand marketing or to an analyst/agency that supports brand marketing. Pinterest Analytics focuses on understanding a user's activity on Pinterest with the purpose of improving it.
- **Tailwind** is another analytics platform that overlaps its functionality with Pinterest Analytics but also includes publishing tools for Pinterest that Pinterest Analytics does not provide (probably because it is already integrated as part of Pinterest).
- **ViralWoot** provides activity tracking on multiple accounts along with the capability to promote specific pins.[41]
- **Curalate** is a brand monitoring and analytics platform that tracks visual imagery across platforms.[42]

Other platforms perform Social Media Analytics that include Pinterest reporting such as Social Report[43] and UnMetric,[44] along with any platform that can access Pinterest's raw data (API).

Research

Pinterest has potential as a market research tool.

- To detect any website where images have been "pinned," enter http://pinterest.com/source/"domain.com."
- Note the boards where pins were posted.
- Study the boards where images came from in the domain in question, and save them (paste many of the pictures from the board in a Word document) for later analysis (look for interesting similarities and trends).
- Discover the list of all the followers of any board that a user is interested in by clicking on the "Followers" link.

Simple investigative approaches yield potentially actionable insights.[45] Pinterest is a platform that has so far been embraced by women more than men (this has shown up in just about every demographic study of the platform).

Instagram

Instagram made it very easy to take almost any photo and make it look semi-professional, and it did it with a very easy workflow—just a couple of taps on your phone. Once edited, it can be posted on Instagram and other social platforms such as Facebook, Twitter, and Flickr, and the appeal of this is magnetic. Also, Instagram has been offering paid advertising for some time (integrated with Facebook advertising), and therefore paid or sponsored posts can appear in targeted users' newsfeeds and on Facebook even without the user following the account.

Analytics

Instagram Analytics from Simply Measured provides a decent basic report for free.[46] Other Instagram analytics tools include Iconosquare and Union Metrics (which also covers Tumblr).

Positives and Negatives

Positives
- Build audience quickly based on images and videos (easily embeddable into Facebook).
- Several filters and enhancements to enhance photos and videos.
- Advertisers can leverage Facebook's extensive advanced targeting and build their Instagram marketing campaigns on top of Facebook's marketing stack.
- Provides the bulk of the public geo-data for third-party data collection platforms such as Picodash.com, etc.

Negatives
- Limited sharing options outside of Instagram.
- Provides the bulk of the public geo-data for third-party data collection platforms such as Picodash.com, etc. There has been a crackdown by Facebook and Twitter on third-party platforms such as Geofeedia.com that some believe have shared too much of a member's information via their geo-filtering.

Viral Media

Without a doubt, almost everyone would like to crack the "viral code" and figure out how to get people who are strangers to share their content massively, but there is no known formula allowing a content creator to "dial in" vital content on demand. For most people, viral marketing is really hit or miss, with a lot more misses than hits. For your content to go viral you need two things to happen:

- A few key people in a network of friends liked the content that was shared and wanted to pass it along to their buddies.
- Enough people (friends and friends of friends) share the content, creating a "network effect" such that it rapidly spreads, almost effortlessly, borne by individuals who liked it and thought it noteworthy (worthy of their attention).

Two Viral Marketing Case Studies

ALS Ice Bucket Challenge

In 2014, the Ice Bucket Challenge went viral. People dumped a bucket of ice and water on someone's head and posted a video or photo on social media to promote awareness of ALS, also known as Lou Gehrig's disease.

The ease of posting and sharing content in social media led to more than 2.4 million tagged videos posted to Facebook during 2014.[47] Because of the Ice Bucket Challenge, the ALS Association received $88.5 million in donations between July 29 and August 26, 2014; the same period during 2013 yielded $2.6 million in grants.[48] In total, 1.9 million new donations were generated by this campaign to the ALS Association. During the ALS Ice Bucket Challenge, each person that took the challenge invited a minimum of three friends to do the same, to take the challenge. To maximize the impact of a viral marketing campaign, targeting well-connected influencers will often produce better results because they have more friends of friends who are well-connected in social media.[49]

The Society of Good Taste Viral Marketing campaign

Mustard company Grey Poupon has always positioned itself as a refined and sophisticated condiment, not something associated with the average Facebook user. To maintain their image online, they made Facebook users apply to join their community. A custom-built Facebook app assessed user's profiles to determine how classy they were based on grammar, misspellings, art taste, education, music selection, movie choices, restaurant check-ins, cities visited, books read, etc. When the Facebook user did not make the cut, Grey Poupon deleted their like. Those who were deemed worthy and accepted into the community received exclusive prizes, such as the "Gravy Yacht"—the classier relative of the gravy boat.

Seeding Content—Make It Go Viral

Most successful viral campaigns do not happen by accident. Viral Content is usually seeded with paid advertising and outreached to targeted lists of people to get the right attention, faster. Viral seeding involves sharing videos in a very targeted and deliberate way to increase their shareability.[50] Various elements of the seeding strategy include targeting influencers, grounding the video content in a common theme the audience can relate to, placing the video on social media, and sending a link to the video on targeted email lists.

Viral Seeding Case Study—Unilever

In April of 2013, Unilever launched a video on YouTube in which several women describe themselves to a forensic sketch artist who cannot see his subject.[51] The same women are then described by strangers whom they met the previous day. The sketches are compared with the strangers' sketches. Interestingly, it is the strangers' sketches that are more flattering and accurate. In a single week, the video had more than 15 million views globally. An article on Mashable about the video was shared more than 500,000 times in 24 hours. One major reason that the video performed so well was that it was based on a universal human truth that every woman could relate to and understand. The content was fresh, deeply emotional, and did not feel like an ad. For content to go viral, a certain "momentum" needs to happen that is not left to chance. In real life, most content that goes viral is planned, developed, seeded, and advertised well in advance, so it has the best chance of being shared.

Predicting What Will Go Viral

In the past, for a video to go viral, it usually had to be shared by a talk show or have a celebrity talking about it. However, some YouTube creators have built those audiences themselves.[52] For example, Roman Atwood has 8 million subscribers on YouTube and counting, while SloMo Guys have had 6.5 million. More professionals are using YouTube as their job and career, which has transformed creators into tastemakers. Also, a marketing professor teaching at the University of Melbourne, Brent Coker, came up with an algorithm to predict when people will share some videos and not others.[53] The algorithm is properly called the BVMP or "Branded Viral Movie Predictor" and has four key elements required for a video to go viral:

- **Congruency:** The themes of a video must be congruent with people's pre-existing knowledge of the brand it is advertising.
- **Emotive strength:** Creating strong emotions is essential if one wants to ensure the video is shared, as emotion is a strong motivator, and there are various levels and intensity of emotions used to gauge emotive strength.
- **Network involvement:** Videos should be relevant to a vast network of people—the larger, the better. The two factors that comprise network involvement are network size and content relevancy to most of the nodes of the network, and this is something that could be precisely defined if one cared to do so.
- "**Paired meme synergy**": Memes are a funny image, video, piece of text, etc. that is copied (often with slight variations) and spread rapidly by Internet users. Paired meme synergy is the "secret sauce" that Brent Coker came up with to explain what the video must express for it to be shared massively. Coker maintains that a video must have at least three of these "paired memes" to be shareable.

Metcalfe's Law

With Metcalfe's Law, the more network nodes (social media accounts, mobile devices, etc.) involved in a social network, the more likelihood the message will spread the costs involved yet remain flat because the network does most of the spreading and bears the costs. Centrally connected social media accounts have a higher likelihood of sharing content with connections than those who are not centrally connected. There are limitations to Metcalfe's Law in the number of connections a typical friend has (n~150). The original Dunbar number was based on the number of people someone could know and meaningfully interact within the real world.[54]

Analytics

Viral marketing does not have dedicated analytics platforms; instead, certain Web Analytics metrics are used to determine content that has gone viral. These metrics are usually provided or calculated based on Web Analytics or Social Media Analytics platforms.

Positives and Negatives

Positives
- The wide audience for content that is viral, hot, topical, unusual.
- Provides a window into the mind of the public, especially via Google Trends (YouTube) and other third-party video aggregators and analytics firms.

Negatives
- Hard to crack the viral code, too unreliable for most marketers to invest in.
- Unrepeatable and not scalable—once something has gone viral, a similar piece of content must be measurably better to do the same.
- While there are general principles around what people share online, tastes are constantly changing, and it is not possible to predict what will go viral in the future with a high degree of confidence.
- Much of the viral spread of media is "seeded," planned and manipulated—it is increasingly becoming a buyer's market, consequently the buyer must have deep pockets. This counters the popular notion that the best content will go viral.

LinkedIn

LinkedIn is known for being the site for job-seekers. It is also a very useful social platform. When a business is focused on reaching other businesses, LinkedIn shines, not only because that is its primary focus, but also due to the metrics it supplies to recruiters and employers. However, it also turns out the same platform that makes it easier for businesses to advertise to each other offers a similar advantage to job seekers to advertise themselves to various companies they want to work with. LinkedIn (now owned by Microsoft) is not as trendy as newer platforms such as Periscope, Snapchat, and Instagram (all of which are used mostly by millennials), but it doesn't strive to be trendy. Also, LinkedIn's targeting capabilities have gradually improved (for example, allowing individuals to target a company or persons working for a company on LinkedIn with advertising).[55]

LinkedIn's Data

The most valuable single asset social networks possess is the data they collect about their members (which they can data-mine), and this is particularly true of LinkedIn and Facebook. In LinkedIn's case, the data is stored in cloud-based repositories via a largely Oracle database backend and can be manipulated by the various data science teams at LinkedIn, but not very well by the ordinary user. LinkedIn makes some of the data available in very limited, specific ways, to users for profiling and targeting purposes.[56] Nonetheless, various teams at LinkedIn have on occasion produced interesting visualizations; they sit on a potential gold mine of insights about the job and professional development that Microsoft hopes to leverage and feed into other Microsoft platforms. Getting back to LinkedIn, some of the more interesting visualizations are new product enhancements are found on their official blog (blog.linkedin.com). Immediately below is a list of a few recent LinkedIn product enhancements that we learned about via the LinkedIn blog:

- Gender disparity in technology industries.[57]
- Publisher analytics.[58]
- Graduate school rankings—LinkedIn has produced a "tool" to rank the outcomes (based on LinkedIn member data) of certain areas of study in graduate school. Unfortunately, at the time of writing, the LinkedIn tool only lists certain professions and doesn't allow users to input new ones.[59]

If there's any single missed opportunity LinkedIn has, it is the way its way its data has remained locked up in a very restrictive user interface. Perhaps LinkedIn's recent Microsoft acquisition will help free up the data so it can be accessed by used in other, more creative ways.

Free vs. Premium LinkedIn Accounts

Most LinkedIn members are using free accounts. It is estimated, based on LinkedIn Premium revenues, that only 2–3% of members have active Premium accounts.[60] However, LinkedIn provides a great deal of pertinent industry career data and training resources, especially to premium members. Consequently, we recommend that students and job seekers upgrade from a free account to the lowest premium membership (currently at $29 per month).

Positives and Negatives

Positives
- Everyone should have a LinkedIn account, even if it is just the free version. Many of our students have found that a strong LinkedIn profile was the easiest way to generate new business connections, interviews, and job offers.
- Excellent platform for business networking.
- Very targeted advertising by career, title, position, company, situation, skill, location, etc. The advertising on LinkedIn tends to be more efficient for specific outcomes such as lead generation.
- While LinkedIn is not primarily a market research platform, it provides a wealth of invaluable profile and company data (describing LinkedIn's data as a "vault" is closer to the truth—it's not easy to get at and use outside of LinkedIn's interfaces, but most features are available for premium members or corporate accounts).

Negatives

- LinkedIn's focus as a business networking platform is too narrow, their data and TOS are restrictive and difficult to work with.
- Microsoft's acquisition of LinkedIn raises questions of the future direction of this platform.

Search Engine Optimization (SEO)

Probably no single marketing avenue has drawn as much enthusiasm (or has been more misunderstood) than Search Engine Optimization. SEO is content and websites that are optimized to engage audiences and search engines. SEO has traditionally been considered "free traffic," but that is not the case, considering the efforts site owners must spend improving website content. While Search Engine Optimization yields long-term benefits, the outcomes cannot be precisely controlled. Search engines monitor their algorithms (which they protect at all costs) and draft policies on what is acceptable search behavior and what is not. Thus, marketers only can do so much to improve their website and user experience to increase their organic search engine traffic, the rest is under the control of the search engine. While Google does not provide an "official" list of the ranking factors and their importance, they have admitted that there were at least 665 search improvements since 2012,[61] but the changes have not been uniformly applied everywhere in the world. Well-known search authority Moz maintains a Google Search Algorithm Change list, claiming that Google makes changes to its search algorithm around 500–600 times a year.[62] One of the main reason Google constantly updates and refines their ranking factors is to frustrate and negate the "black-hat" practices of various rogue SEO firms that exploit weaknesses they detect within Google's algorithms.

The Optimization Process

Another reason for the frequent search engine updates is to improve the quality of search results for searchers. The Internet and search engines are constantly evolving, so the constant changes and improvements seem warranted. Because of these changes, it is much harder to trick or game Google today than it was in the late 1990s, shortly after Google first launched its platform. Having said that, with these changes Google has encouraged search marketers (via its Webmaster Guidelines[63]) to spend their efforts on improving the website content. Google wants to discourage site owners from manipulating the search results (by making it unproductive to do so, leveraging penalties including dropping a website from its search engine index). The SEO process involves matching up the content on a website or blog with the content that audiences are searching for. If the reader is a marketer or content producer, the first thing to consider is finding the right keywords. The next step is ensuring the website or blog is easy to navigate, well-designed, and fast loading (Google does exact website penalties for slower-loading websites and blogs). Taxonomy (how information and navigation are organized) is also part of SEO, as you want to be sure that visitors can properly specify and find what they are looking for; if information on your website is poorly categorized then it makes it much harder to locate the information the searcher is looking for. Eventually Google will figure this out (if Google

Analytics is being used to measure your website) and apply penalties. Most search engines decide how relevant a website is to a search query by looking at the backlinks to other websites or blogs that link to the site. Generating links from social media came to be a replacement; those links are often "not followed," particularly those from Twitter and Facebook. Google has become much more aggressive in re-ranking the web by adding several new "patches" to their search engine, with some of the most popular ones being Panda, Penguin, etc.

SEO Tactics

The marketing initiatives (called "tactics" here) that provide the most value are usually the hardest to do, but not always. The most important SEO tactics are:

- **Keyword research:** This is the most effective single thing marketers can do to improve their search engine visibility. It also takes the least amount of effort; that is why keyword research is usually done first.
- **Content creation:** This is the single most effective tactic, but it is harder to create great content than keyword research.

Local Search

Algorithmic changes may work in some localities better than others, encouraging local marketers to develop search strategies that work in their country or locality.[64] As Google looks at the search and Web history of each searcher, the same search query may yield somewhat different search results depending on the searcher's history.[65] However, let's not forget that search engine algorithms are designed to anticipate what a person would find most interesting and valuable, and give that a higher "score" in the area the algorithm is operating in. Since there are many variations in what people find interesting, search algorithms will almost certainly skew their results, depending on whom they think the searcher is, where they are located, and what they are trying to do at that moment. Consequently, search algorithms are learning from what people are paying attention to via their searches, and they are also self-tuning.

Demographics and Local SEO Process

Local SEO content and keywords can be very successful, as the competition is usually limited to the small number of similar businesses in the same locality.[66] However, how do we measure the impact of SEO on local marketing? It turns out that Web Analytics is an indispensable part of Search Engine Optimization, as the goal of optimization is to bring visitors to designated landing pages. Most analytics platforms now include demographics information; for example, Google Analytics uses the DoubleClick Advertising Network to categorize audience behavior of the visitor's web "cookies" as they are detected. This data collection may include Web behavior over time (such as interests) as well as probable age and gender. Roughly speaking about 65% of all the visitors to a blog being tracked by Google Analytics will have some cookie data that includes demographics and geo-segmentation. However most of the segments Google built for DoubleClick had TV/Cable broadcasters in mind and may or may not be useful for any particular blogger—still, they are better than nothing.[67] Using the demographics reporting in Google Analytics, along with custom libraries, custom dimensions, and various API calls, provides a better understanding of the audience that comes to a website or blog.[68] Additional enhancements to Web Analytics tracking code will yield zip code and neighborhood data readouts of Web visitors who share that information via their browsers, this will usually be a small fraction of the visits to the blog, but if there is enough data, audience planning may be possible.[69]

Positives and Negatives

Positives
- Anyone can improve their website content and potentially gain more visitors from search engines to his or her online sites.
- Most of what works for improving SEO of a website is based on improvements in user design and accessibility. As stakeholders optimize their content to be better for the searcher, their Web referrals from search engines should improve.
- Search engines have invested heavily in the semantic Web and artificial intelligence—they are powered by algorithms and use text analytics to understand the searchers' intent. Platforms such as Google Now and Siri are morphing into personal assistants, keeping track of our travel plans, to-do lists, appointments and other types of semantic information they can gather from our emails, search, and Web history. As a result of this vast evolution of search engines, our lives have been considerably simplified in ways we have yet to quantify fully.

Negatives
- Hard to predict the outcome of SEO efforts—there is no guarantee they will work.
- Depending on Google search too much is perilous as algorithmic changes may suddenly drop an otherwise policy-adhering website to the bottom of the search engine index. Often these occurrences seem arbitrary when they occur and are difficult to fix.
- Difficult to control where or how search listings will show up in search engines.
- Difficult to maintain when new content is constantly being added to a website – becomes more of a process that has been taken over by brands.
- Negative personal and business listings are tough to remove from the search engine index, especially if they point to authoritative websites such as the New York Times or an educational institution (.edu domains are favored by some search engines, especially Google).
- Big Brother—Google knows too much about us. They needed the data to understand better what we want, but many believe they are gathering too much information on us and need to be regulated.

Influence

Opinion seems to be split on how we, as people, are influenced, and how much weight to put on influencers versus how we influence each other. Other studies suggest that the impact of influencers is largely overblown, and often it is our friends that we believe and trust the most, not some distant influential such as the President of the United States. Still, it depends on whom we are talking about. The people we know and are accessible to us might be the most influential, but in politics, for example, it is a different story—the person who holds office is often the most influential. It all depends on the context we seek to consider when discussing who is influential and what/whom they influence.

Role Models as Influencers

Often, we can think of our parents and siblings as "influencers," in other cases it is a mentor or role model, perhaps a celebrity, religious leader, politician, or even a book/author can be influential. However, influencers have a relationship not only to what they influence but also to its value.

Popularity as Digital Influence

Klout (owned by Lithium Technologies) is an example of a platform attempting to measure and score how much influence someone has mainly on Twitter and Facebook (and a few other online channels). Klout measures online influence by using data from various social networks to gauge a specific user's Klout Score, which is a number between one and 100. However, Klout does not track a user's influence beyond the specific social media channels it collects.

Context Determines Influence

Both the Sun and Moon are equally important to us and perceived to be of a roughly equal size, yet the Moon is hardly more than a dust particle compared to the Sun. For most of us, our friends and family are much more influential on our decisions than the President of the United States, or any celebrity.

Analytics

Several platforms measure influence.[70] However, what they actually measure is the popularity on an account within social media.

- **Klout:** Klout is being used for a variety of things, including hiring people for jobs. In fact, it is said that anyone with a Klout Score under 50 has low online influence. Klout does more than provide a score, it also demonstrates the way someone is influential and provides lists of other influencers. Lithium Technologies acquired Klout in 2014.[71]
- **Traackr:** Traackr allows users to record, manage, expand, validate, and scale their global influencer marketing. Influencers are identified by subject and scored on reach, relevance, and resonance. Influencers can be grouped and attached to a campaign.[72]
- **Tapinfluence:** Tapinfluence is an influencer marketing automation solution for brands and agencies.[73] In 2015 they launched TapFusion, a new platform that enables brands to connect with social influencers using its marketplace.[74]

Positives and Negatives

Positives

- Influence is one way to sort through social media and focus on whom is most likely to produce a result in their social network (such as recommending others buy a book we enjoyed, etc.).

Negatives

- The term is incorrect, it's not influence that is being measured, but network popularity. In most cases, it is too hard to qualify what the impact of influencers on changing the behavior or actions other social media accounts they are connected to.
- As social media is a participatory platform, those who are more active in a channel will show up as being more influential. But activity in a social channel, by itself, seems to be a poor predictor of someone being influential.
- Influence metrics are shallow and can be manipulated.

Geo-Location and Hyperlocal Advertising

Most mobile device users can check into locations deliberately using one of their location-based apps, but what is not as well-known is that it is possible to be automatically checked into virtually any location as we transverse the world via our mobile devices (even when it is our desire not to be tracked that way). Hyperlocal advertising is thought by some marketers and analysts to have fundamentally changed marketing.[75] Until very recently, marketers usually didn't know how often advertising was seen by the people whom it was intended for. An advertiser could place an ad on page six of a newspaper and have some idea of how often it might be seen and perhaps read, but we never really knew for sure—it was guesswork and estimation. However, with the latest round of targeting technology, in an age where most consumers have a smartphone and do much of their daily communications and media consumption on it, that's no longer the case. Marketing messaging can be tuned and targeted to an audience in a precise location, perhaps even with a personalized message and then measured for effectiveness—that is not a capability most marketers are fully up-to-date on, which is why we cover it here.

Types of Geo-Targeting

Capture everyone transmitting via his or her mobile devices in a specific area (GPS lat/long), which is termed basic radius targeting as shown in Figure 9.3. Most social media platforms that run advertising now have targeting options that include basic radius targeting including Facebook, Twitter, Instagram, and Snapchat. Radius targeting can also be a great strategy for sending coupons and attracting customers to local businesses nearby.

This approach is useful for tracking activity and interest. In 2014 the co-author conducted studies at the Metropolitan Museum of Art in New York City where 56,000 public social media accounts were tracked over an 11-month period using Geofeedia, a geo-location tracking platform.[76] By default, visitor posts in social media are visible to the world unless users take steps to limit who can view them. Much of the social

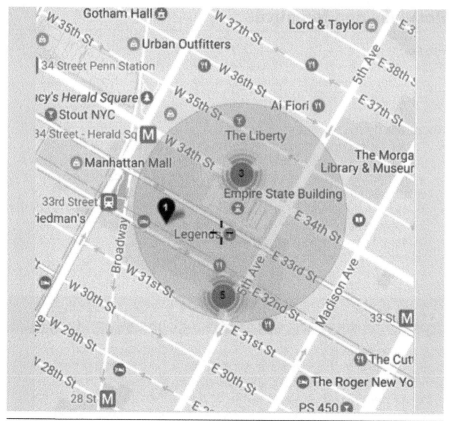

Figure 9.3 Example of radius targeting using a geo-location program called Picodash.
Source: WebMetricsGuru Inc.

media activity of visitors as they moved through the museum was visible (and still is) to anyone who has access to certain data-sifting platforms such as Geofeedia. By treating repeated visitation as evidence of a persistent interest and then looking at the context of the posts, lots of insight can be gleaned along with a marketing list that can also be used for digital advertising. Low-cost tools such as Picodash.com can geo-locate and collect Instagram posts within a basic radius area that covers between a couple of meters, up to several hundred meters. However, the less useful, perhaps, aspect of basic radius targeting is that it like putting out a fish net and catching everything in the area and much of what we capture we do not need or want.

Retargeting with geo-location works much the same as it does on websites except the visits to a specific location are captured then retargeting them with messaging based on their activities (when they were first acquired into the retargeting list). This retargeting is not based on first- and third-party cookies (as it is in websites) but with the mobile device's unique ID (UDID, Unique Device ID) or IDFA (ID for Advertisers). However, using this kind of retargeting takes a certain subtlety, and a familiarity with the customer journey (what the customer, in this instance a museum goer, wants to achieve). Marketers simply haven't learned to think or plan on those terms so the remarketing/retargeting might not always be as effective as it should be.

Contextual local targeting builds upon an existing database of locations corresponding to targeting options such as a shopping mall or school and may even be tied to the geo-demographics of a location (such as income/lifestyle and census data). There are a couple of compelling use case for local contextual targeting including targeting based on political affiliation within a congressional district using what is called "addressable advertising." For example, Democratic presidential candidates for the 2016 presidential election Hillary Clinton and Bernie Sanders used TV ads targeted to New York voters through addressable TV ad services from Cablevision and D2 Media Sales through a partnership between Dish and DirecTV/AT&T.[77] The targeting list was based on likely Democratic primary voters from voting lists during the previous elections that the campaigns provide to Cablevision or satellite providers DirecTV and Dish. That list (usually successfully matched up about 10% at the time) is matched against each vendor's customer database, and the desired ads are served to the matching households. While the cost of such ads is much higher, it comes with a much greater certainty the ads are reaching just the individuals who are targeted. As geo-location applications continue to improve, there will be additional ways to build marketing and advertising on top of these requests, so stay tuned.

iBeacons and Bluetooth transmitters

We are all familiar with the concept of AM/FM radio, but most people are just waking up to other types of broadcast networks based on different frequencies and devices. Bluetooth is a wireless protocol that has been around for more than a quarter of a century and was used initially for wireless printing and device pairing. Bluetooth was used in personal computers and mobile devices to create small, close-location radio networks. Another factoid that is commonly not known is that most smartphones have a built-in AM/FM radio, although it is more commonly used for Bluetooth communications than for radio communications (but it could be and sometimes is). In 2013, Apple came out with the iBeacon protocol built on top of Bluetooth that allows messages to be broadcast based on proximity.[78] One great thing about iBeacons is that the radio transmitters or beacons are inexpensive (a set can be purchased for under $100), and there is software developed by several off-the-shelf vendors that integrate with iBeacons and allow marketers to manage these small networks for information sharing and advertising campaigns.[79] One of the drawbacks of the iBeacon protocol also happens to be one of its strengths. To use iBeacons (to shop in a specific location), a customer must first download an app (application) on their mobile device. The app facilitates communications between the specific iBeacons in a place and the mobile device. However, this is an action not everyone is prepared to do or even aware of, so there is often an adoption issue. However, given that the customer must download and run the application on their mobile device first, communications are automatically "opt-in," which is often not the case with the other kinds of geological tracking we have discussed in this section.

uMesh Networks

uMesh networks are designed to deal with noisy environments such as malls, where overlapping transmitters provide unreliable results. iBeacons have many benefits, but they also have limitations, and it is possible and even common to install several transmitters too close to each other. When this is the case, the wrong transmitter may respond nearby. iBeacons are a noisy medium if care is not taken to set up the transmitters with care.[80] One solution that has recently evolved is the use of uMesh networks of iBeacons that make deployments easier to manage and scale by allowing some additional ways for devices to communicate with transmitters and determine the precise location of the instrument so it can communicate with the right transmitter.

iBeacon vs. Eddystone

In 2015, Google released a competing protocol to iBeacon that has some additional attractive features such as support for iOS and Android devices along with the ability to reach Android devices that have not installed an app that communicated with Eddystone.[81] However, the Eddystone protocol works much better for marketers if there is an app installed. Without an application running to begin with, there are no targeting or personalization options possible at this time, but a URL can still be broadcast (valuable in and of itself). In any case, compared with other geo-location technologies, iBeacon and Eddystone are much less invasive due to the opt-in nature of the platform.

Check-Ins: Active and Passive

Geo-location is a feature that reports on anyone's exact location via their physical devices (latitude/longitude) within a few feet and is usually enabled on mobile devices unless users disable the functionality. However, when one turns off the geo-location aspects of their mobile devices, many of the advanced features built into websites and applications do not work as well. There is an interesting feature of mobile devices running geo-location applications such as Foursquare that most users are unaware of. Active users of most location-aware mobile apps are automatically and passively "checked-in" to locations they are passing by. Thus, even when a user makes no conscious effort to check-in to a location, their movement trails are being tracked and analyzed by servers of the applications collecting this data. The user's collected movements can be used to predict where they are most likely to go soon (or where they visited recently); this type of data has high predictive value for online marketing and advertising. On the other hand, predictive tracking of users' hourly and daily movements be a violation their privacy. Recent developments—such as the blocking of Geofeedia by Instagram, Facebook, and Twitter API access—point to new restrictions on the way a user's geo-data is accessed and used.[82] While Geofeedia did not track passive check-ins (although Facebook, Foursquare, and TripAdvisor do), there are enough deliberate active user check-ins tracked with its platform to alarm the American Civil Liberties Union (ACLU). When the Internet was made up of simple HTML and Flash websites, the needs and capabilities for geo-location were not as present in the ways they are now. As more people bought and used mobile devices, the geo-location services became much more widespread. Many new capabilities came online that were not much in the picture before, such as interacting with customers and fans when they were nearby in real time. Before, we'd never know they were nearby unless notified deliberately (by phone or email), but now, in many cases, all someone should do is show up (thanks to geo-fencing) or check-ins (whether actively or passively). Today many applications such as Uber and Meetup, to name a few, can piggyback off location services with their own iPhone or Android app while other services such as Yelp (checking into locations you are reviewing) are doing the same thing.

Positives and Negatives

One of the coauthors created a table (Table 9.1) that quickly summarizes some of the positives and negatives the various geo-location tracking technologies, but it is not a comprehensive list.

Table 9.1 Positives and negatives of geo-location technologies.

Technology	Positives	Negatives
iBeacon (Bluetooth low-energy (BLE) wireless technology)	• Opt-in, users, must install an app on their mobile device. • Inexpensive technology to implement. • Integrates with Web Analytics (Adobe) and CRM (Salesforce). • Accurate within a few feet.	• Getting users to download an app limits the adoption of this technology. • Uni-directional messaging. • Noise: iBeacons need to be properly deployed.
GPS	• Extensible and widely deployed in devices and business application services. • Inexpensive. • Integrated with sophisticated social media applications such as Geofeedia, WeLink, Picodash.com.	• Not commonly integrated with Web Analytics or Social Media Analytics. • Location placements can be off by several feet. • Databases mapping GPS data to business address listing is not always accurate. • No Z dimension captures latitude and longitude but does not measure altitude/height.
Social Media Geo-location	• Location data is included in metadata of most social media platforms. • A comprehensive set of data provided by people via their mobile devices can be used for advertising (targeting) and market research.	• Users are often unaware they are being tracked. Can opt-out, but often unaware of how. • Public check-in data can be scraped by anyone who knows how.
Near Field Communication (NFC)	• Easily configurable into zones of 150 feet.	• Need to be configured and administered (both hardware and software). • Businesses have not widely deployed NFC. • Not integrated into analytics applications.

Source: WebMetricsGuru Inc.

Advantages

- As it turns out, the data being produced by mobile devices that broadcast their location is more valuable to marketers than anything else they can get their hands on. This is not surprising, as geo-data contains much of the essence of what people are doing along with where they are at a specific point in time.
- Geo-location data is viewed as more actionable than any other kind of data.

Disadvantages

- One of the significant issues around geo-location applications is that many people are unaware of how they are being tracked (and they may not yet have an informed opinion about it).
- iBeacons and other Bluetooth location technologies are excellent ways to engage with the audience in physical locations in real time (such as a retail store), but they-they require a specific application be loaded onto the mobile device to communicate with the iBeacons in the location.[83]

Case Study: Content Analytics Targeting Using LinkedIn and Social Listening Platform

An educational advocacy organization located in the UK wanted to differentiate itself in a crowded market with new training courses for training managers to use with their staff and understand the differences between content consumption of companies in select industries within the UK. The target audience (training managers) had to be segmented based on the size of the business they were working for (1–10, 11–49, or 50–200).

- **Platforms used**: LinkedIn Premium, Excel (macros), Brandwatch Social Listening Platform.
- **Methodology:** Scrape LinkedIn for specific companies' sizes in the UK (using a LinkedIn query with additional filters for company size).
- **Number of profiles of training managers found in the UK only**: Total 151,296 (at time query was run).

LinkedIn can be used to harvest a selection of profiles in the target audience by company size and how long they worked managers were at their current job (see Table 9.2).

Targeted Company Audience by Company Size

Table 9.2 Case study using LinkedIn Premium.

Attribute	Company Size 1–10	Company Size 11–49	Company Size 50–200
Titles	Managing Director, CEO, Director, Partner	Managing Director, Business Development Director, CEO, Founder, Director	Managing Director, Business Development Director, Owner
Avg. Time at a job	~3.1 Years	~10 months	~2.6 years
Services Provided	Business tends to be independent accounting firms providing investment and business advice.	Businesses serve existing account holders, statutory accounts and provides insolvency and debt advice and services.	Business analysis, risk analysis, asset finance, process analysis.
Common Skills	Financial advisers, IR, cash flow, business valuation, internal auditing, etc.	Customer service, relationship building (business development), organizational development, mobile payment systems, business problem solving, sales presentations.	Credit derivatives, digital media, digital strategy, integrated marketing, vendor management, sales operations, salesforce. com, solution selling, SaaS, affiliate marketing, product marketing, brand development, PPC, Web Analytics, SEM, mobile marketing.

(continued)

Table 9.2 (Continued)

Attribute	Company Size 1–10	Company Size 11–49	Company Size 50–200
Top Groups on LinkedIn	Private Equity Investment Group: PrivateEquity.com, Hedge Funds, TED	The Recruitment Network, Financial Times readers' group, Prop Traders, FinTech Startups,	The UK Marketing Network: www.ukmarketingnetwork.co.uk, Payments Strategy, The Institute of Direct and Digital Marketing (IDM),
Top Interests	Traveling, tennis, sailing, swimming, cooking, finance, politics, cars, entrepreneurship	Cycling, smartwatches, mobile devices, etc.	Golf, reading, photography/art, etc.
Top Locations	London, Manchester, Bristol	London, Manchester, Bristol, Leeds	London, Manchester, Newport

Source: WebMetricsGuru Inc.

Strategy

- Create curated content for each group and seed it with influencers—letting it spread on its own, but with some help via advertising.
- Deploy first- and second-party data (from affiliates) to hyper-target content and ads (use programmatic if possible).
- Utilize LinkedIn sponsored ads to hyper-target the audiences we data-mined and their connections (when appropriate). Refresh and reapply as needed.

Findings

- Use LinkedIn to find several thousand profiles of a kind of manager at a particular sized company in a particular geographic location (UK only).
- Take the top 100 Twitter profiles from each group and set up social listening in Brandwatch based on specific topics of interest common to each group.
- Find examples of content that appeals to each group—use these to build a "content playbook" for each group/segment.
- Use Twitter Custom Audiences to target the profiles in each group with new content that is similar to the content they like (very important). The content should direct viewers to act and end up on the customers' website where they can be retargeted (retargeting pixel).

Review Questions

1. Why are there so many different analytics platforms for each social media channel?
2. On average, how much time on a weekly basis does it take to leverage social media effectively?
3. Which social media platform is at the "center" of the social media universe?
4. How is it the exact formula for search engine ranking is so hard to figure out? Be specific in your answer.
5. Which social media channel/platform best facilitates online collaboration?
6. When is it appropriate to "seed" social media content?
7. Name the most popular social media influencer platform?
8. What is a "custom audience" and which social media platforms offer them? How does one create a custom audience?
9. Which platform helps members more easily find new professional opportunities? What other platforms that we discussed in this chapter allow us to do that?
10. What is the most effective SEO tactic? What is the most difficult, but rewarding SEO tactic?
11. What are the two most popular visual social media platforms discussed in this chapter?
12. What are the three types of geo-targeting?
13. How does iBeacon work? Where are iBeacons most commonly used?
14. True or false—second-party cookies are employed in Internet marketing.

The Analytics Selfie

A few years ago, one of the coauthors developed a system to measure the online presence in social media (covered in the Preface). Initially, it was designed for teaching purposes, to measure the progress of students in the development of their own Social Media. The goal was to allow students to visualize their progress a measurement was taken at the beginning of the semester and another measurement at the end of the semester.[84] The idea of a "data selfie" fit in with the idea that we generate data, and, every so often, we may want to take a snapshot of key dimensions of it. Both measurements were compared in a radar chart.

Chapter 9 Citations

1. "Social media accurately calls Trump and Brexit." November 9, 2016. www.brandseye.com/news/accurately-measured-social-media-calls-trump-and-brexit-as-polls-fail. Accessed April 15, 2017.

2. "5 social media metrics you can stop tracking yesterday." https://blog.loginradius.com/2015/05/social-media-metrics-stop-tracking. Accessed April 15, 2017.

3. Stelzner, M.A. "2015 social media marketing industry report." www.socialmediaexaminer.com/SocialMediaMarketingIndustryReport2015.pdf. Accessed April 15, 2017.

4. Grossman, D. "Google's image-captioning AI is getting scary." Popular Mechanics. September 23, 2016, www.popularmechanics.com/technology/robots/a23019/google-ai-captioning. Accessed April 15, 2017.

5. Elgammal, A. "Creating computer vision and machine learning algorithms that can analyze works of art." www.mathworks.com/company/newsletters/articles/creating-computer-vision-and-machine-learning-algorithms-that-can-analyze-works-of-art.html. Accessed April 15, 2017.

6. Langston, J. "What makes Bach sound like Bach? New dataset teaches algorithms classical music." November 30, 2016. www.washington.edu/news/2016/11/30/what-makes-bach-sound-like-bach-new-dataset-teaches-algorithms-classical-music/. Accessed April 15, 2017.

7. Alba, D. "Repeat after me: Humans run the internet, not algorithms." Wired. September 2, 2016. www.wired.com/2016/09/facebook-trending-humans-versus-algorithms. Accessed April 15, 2017.

8. Artale, J. "Evolution of the blogger infographic #1." November 12, 2013. www.jayartale.com/evolution-blogger-infographic-1. Accessed April 15, 2017.

9. Johnson, C.C., E.M. Buchanan, and K.N. Jordan (2014) "Blog Topic and Word Frequency: What Differentiates between High and Low Powered Blogs?", Psychology of Popular Media Culture 3(3): 154–163.

10 "Growth in time spent with media is slowing." eMarketer. June 6, 2016. www.emarketer.com/Article/Growth-Time-Spent-with-Media-Slowing/1014042. Accessed April 15, 2017.

11. "Twitter: number of monthly active users 2010–2016." www.statista.com/statistics/282087/number-of-monthly-active-twitter-users. Accessed April 15, 2017.

12. Mehtap, F. "The future of Twitter is data analytics." June 16, 2015. https://medium.com/@marketing_beans/the-future-of-twitter-is-data-analytics-4b9276e3b954. Accessed April 15, 2017.

13. King, R. "Twitter buys artificial intelligence startup Whetlab." June 17, 2015. www.cnet.com/news/twitter-buys-artificial-intelligence-startup-whetlab. Accessed April 15, 2017.

14. "Time spent with Facebook still growing, but not by much." eMarketer. May 3, 2016. www.emarketer.com/Article/Time-Spent-with-Facebook-Still-Growing-Not-by-Much/1013903. Accessed April 15, 2017.

15. "College students still spend most social time with Facebook." September 8, 2015. www.emarketer.com/Article/College-Students-Still-Spend-Most-Social-Time-with-Facebook/1012955. Accessed April 15, 2017.

16. "Facebook news feed update." Search Engine Watch. June 30, 2016. https://searchenginewatch.com/2016/06/30/facebook-news-feed-update-how-friendmageddon-will-affect-publishers. Accessed April 15, 2017.

17. "Facebook releases smart content tools & improves analytics." December 23, 2014. www.business2community.com/facebook/facebook-releases-smart-content-tools-improves-analytics-01106713. Accessed April 15, 2017.

18. Constine, J. "Facebook launches hyper-local ads targeted to people within a mile of a business." TechCrunch. October 7, 2014. https://techcrunch.com/2014/10/07/facebook-hyper-local-ads. Accessed April 15, 2017.

19. Ong, J. "Facebook introduces new research guidelines, review and training." October 2, 2014. http://thenextweb.com/facebook/2014/10/02/facebook-introduces-new-guidelines-review-process-training-research-practices. Accessed April 15, 2017.

20. Russell, J. "Facebook manipulated 690000 users' news feeds to run a psychology experiment." June 28, 2014. http://thenextweb.com/facebook/2014/06/28/facebook-manipulated-690000-users-news-feeds-run-psychology-experiment. Accessed April 15, 2017.

21. "r/Collaboration." Reddit. www.reddit.com/r/Collaboration. Accessed April 15, 2017.

22. "MusicInTheMaking." Reddit. www.reddit.com/r/MusicInTheMaking. Accessed April 15, 2017.

23. "r/ProjectManagement." Reddit. www.reddit.com/r/projectmanagement. Accessed April 15, 2017.

24. "r/SideProject." Reddit. www.reddit.com/r/SideProject. Accessed April 15, 2017.

25. Aaron, J. "Analytics and sleuthing tools for Reddit." November 28, 2014. http://maximizesocialbusiness.com/analytics-and-sleuthing-tools-for-reddit-16311. Accessed April 15, 2017.

26. "Reddit Insight." www.redditinsight.com. Accessed April 15, 2017.

27. "Snoop Snoo." http://snoopsnoo.com. Accessed April 15, 2017.

28. "Subreddit traffic analysis." Later for Reddit. www.redditlater.com/analysis. Accessed April 15, 2017.

29. "Reddit metrics: Discover fastest growing reddits, Reddit stats." http://redditmetrics.com. Accessed April 15, 2017.

30. "Reddit Investigator." www.redditinvestigator.com. Accessed April 15, 2017.

31. "Nintendo NX controller confirmed fake by 'leaker'." Reddit. March 25, 2016. www.reddit.com/r/Games/comments/4bufes/nintendo_nx_controller_confirmed_fake_by_leaker. Accessed April 15, 2017.

32. Doward, J. "How online reviews are crucial to a restaurant's takings." The Guardian. September 2, 2012. www.theguardian.com/lifeandstyle/2012/sep/02/ratings-boost-restaurants. Accessed April 15, 2017.

33. Doward, J. "How online reviews are crucial to a restaurant's takings." The Guardian. September 2, 2012. www.theguardian.com/lifeandstyle/2012/sep/02/ratings-boost-restaurants. Accessed April 15, 2017.

34. Campbell, C. "Star ratings matter just as much as (if not more than online reviews." Entrepreneur. October 29, 2015. www.entrepreneur.com/article/250838. Accessed April 15, 2017.

35. Fadil, O. and J. Soloff. "Information cascades and online rating games." August 4, 2015. https://arxiv.org/abs/1508.00893. Accessed 15 Jan. 2017.

36. "Infographic: Really cool facts about Snapchat." February 27, 2015. www.didit.com/infographic-really-cool-facts-about-snapchat. Accessed April 15, 2017.

37 York, A. "Social media demographics for marketers." Sprout Social. May 4, 2015. http://sproutsocial.com/insights/new-social-media-demographics. Accessed April 15, 2017.

38. "Analytics for Snapchat." http://snaplytics.io/brand-analytics. Accessed April 15, 2017.

39. "Snapchat and Social Video Analytics by Delmondo." October, 2016, http://delmondo.co/snapchat-analytics-software. Accessed April 15, 2017.

40. "Snapchat Analytics." www.wickedsociety.se/snapchat-analytics. Accessed April 15, 2017.

41. "ViralWoot." https://viralwoot.com. Accessed April 15, 2017.

42. "Curalate." www.curalate.com. Accessed April 15, 2017.

43. "Social Report." www.socialreport.com. Accessed April 15, 2017.

44. "UnMetric." https://unmetric.com. Accessed April 15, 2017.

45. Griteman, R. "How to use Pinterest for market research and trend forecasting." June 9, 2015. http://2060digital.com/blog/how-to-use-pinterest-for-market-research-and-trend-forecasting. Accessed April 15, 2017.

46. "Free social media analytics tools." Simply Measured. http://simplymeasured.com/free-social-media-tools. Accessed April 15, 2017.

47. Adeyeri, E. "Ice Bucket Challenge: what are the lessons for marketers?" The Guardian. August 27, 2014. /www.theguardian.com/media-network/media-network-blog/2014/aug/27/ice-bucket-challenge-lessons-marketing. Accessed April 15, 2017.

48. "The ALS Association is grateful for outpouring of support: Ice bucket donations reach $88.5 million." August 26, 2014. www.alsa.org/news/media/press-releases/ice-bucket-challenge-082614.html. Accessed April 15, 2017.

49. Braiker, B. "The 'Ice Bucket Challenge': A case study in viral marketing gold." Digiday. August 14, 2014. http://digiday.com/brands/ice-bucket-challenge-case-study-viral-marketing-success. Accessed April 15, 2017.

50. Singh, S. and S. Diamond. "How to seed a viral marketing campaign on YouTube." www.dummies.com/business/marketing/social-media-marketing/how-to-seed-a-viral-marketing-campaign-on-youtube. Accessed April 15, 2017.

51. Singh, S. and S. Diamond. "How to seed a viral marketing campaign on YouTube." www.dummies.com/business/marketing/social-media-marketing/how-to-seed-a-viral-marketing-campaign-on-youtube. Accessed April 15, 2017.

52. D'Onfro, J. "YouTube exec explains what makes a video go viral." Business Insider. www.businessinsider.com/youtube-exec-how-to-make-a-viral-video-2015-12. Accessed April 15, 2017.

53. Bullas, J. "4 key elements for a viral video." November 24, 2011. www.jeffbullas.com/2011/11/24/4-key-elements-for-a-viral-video. Accessed April 15, 2017.

54. Carpenter, H. "Why SMBs need social software—Dunbar's number limits Metcalfe's Law." January 19, 2010. https://bhc3.com/2010/01/19/why-smbs-need-social-software-dunbars-number-limits-metcalfes-law. Accessed April 15, 2017.

55. Swant, M. "LinkedIn is now allowing marketers to target ads at specific companies." Adweek. March 1, 2016. www.adweek.com/news/technology/linkedin-now-allowing-marketers-target-ads-specific-companies-169936. Accessed April 15, 2017

56. Accessed from www.slideshare.net/LImarketingsolutions/live-webcast-demy stifying-targeting-on-linkedin?qid=ccf7daa3-8b35-49c8-bfb1-98ae8d6de 9a4&v=&b=&from_search=37. Accessed April 15, 2017.

57. Murthy, S. "Measuring gender diversity with data from LinkedIn." June 17, 2015. https://blog.linkedin.com/2015/06/17/measuring-gender-diversity-with-data-from-linkedin. Accessed April 15, 2017.

58. Yang, A. "New analytics for publishing on LinkedIn: See who's viewed your published post." May 7, 2015. https://blog.linkedin.com/2015/05/07/new-analytics-for-publishing-on-linkedin. Accessed April 15, 2017.

59. Accessed from www.linkedin.com/edu/rankings/us/graduate?trk=li_corpblog_corp_itamar_gradschoolrankings. Accessed April 15, 2017.

60. "How many individuals pay for Premium accounts on LinkedIn?" Quora. www.quora.com/How-many-individuals-pay-for-premium-accounts-on-LinkedIn. Accessed April 15, 2017.

61. "Algorithms: Inside search." www.google.com/insidesearch/howsearchworks/algorithms.html. Accessed April 15, 2017.

62. "Google algorithm change history." Moz. https://moz.com/google-algorithm-change. Accessed April 15, 2017.

63. "Webmaster guidelines: Search console help." https://support.google.com/web masters/answer/35769?hl=en. Accessed April 15, 2017.

64. Shotland, A. "How does Google's local algorithm work in 2016?" Search Engine Land. August 1, 2016. http://searchengineland.com/googles-local-algorithm-work-2016-254579. Accessed April 15, 2017.

65. Pots, K. "Deciphering search ranking credibility and quality: an exploratory analysis." http://essay.utwente.nl/71062/1/KarlijnPots_BA_BMS.pdf. Accessed April 15, 2017.

66. "20+ signals that make your business easier to find in local search engines." February 18, 2013. http://searchengineland.com/20-signals-that-make-your-business-easier-to-find-in-local-search-engines-148496. Accessed April 15, 2017.

67. "About demographics and interests: Analytics Help." https://support.google.com/analytics/answer/2799357?hl=en. Accessed April 15, 2017.

68. Sharif, S. "How a Seattle Business can add street level data in Google Analytics." LunaMetrics. July 8, 2014. www.lunametrics.com/blog/2014/07/08/street-level-insight-google-analytics. Accessed April 15, 2017.

69. Sharif, S. "Using APIs to add insight to Google Analytics." LunaMetrics. June 5, 2014. www.lunametrics.com/blog/2014/06/05/apis-add-insight-google-analytics. Accessed April 15, 2017.

70. "Influencer marketing platforms." www.pfind.com/influencer-marketing. Accessed April 15, 2017.

71. www.lithium.com/sitemap.xml. Accessed April 15, 2017.

72. "Traackr." www.traackr.com. Accessed April 15, 2017.

73. "Influencer marketing software platform." TapInfluence. www.tapinfluence.com/platform. Accessed April 15, 2017.

74. "TapInfluence launches a fully automated platform that could turn influencer marketing into mass media." VentureBeat. September 18, 2015. http://venturebeat.com/2015/09/18/tapinfluence-launches-a-fully-automated-platform-that-could-turn-influencer-marketing-into-mass-media. Accessed April 15, 2017.

75. Vidakovic, R. "How hyperlocal advertising changes everything." Marketing Land. August 18, 2014. http://marketingland.com/hyperlocal-mobile-advertising-changes-everything-92979. Accessed April 15, 2017.

76. Sponder, M. "Merging geo social data & Web analytics at the Metropolitan Museum of Art." SlideShare. November 5, 2014. www.slideshare.net/webmeticsguru/merging-geo-social-data-web-analytics-v6-marshall-sponder-nov-6th-2014-final-submitted. Accessed April 15, 2017.

77. Kaye, K. "Clinton and Sanders aim TV Ads to key households in New York market." April 14, 2016. http://adage.com/article/campaign-trail/clinton-sanders-aim-tv-ads-key-households-york/303532. Accessed April 15, 2017.

78. Mallik, N. "2014: The year that has been for beacons." Beaconstac. December 30, 2014. https://blog.beaconstac.com/2014/12/2014-the-year-that-has-been-for-beacons. Accessed April 15, 2017.

79. "Five ways to use iBeacon you have never thought of." Mobile World Capital. January 28, 2014. http://mobileworldcapital.com/361. Accessed April 15, 2017.

80. Levine, B. "Move over, iBeacons—here come mesh beacons." VentureBeat. December 6, 2014. http://venturebeat.com/2014/12/06/move-over-ibeacons-here-come-mesh-beacons. Accessed April 15, 2017.

81. "Using Eddystone beacons without mobile app." https://neklo.com/eddystone-app. Accessed April 15, 2017.

82. Cameron, D. "Dozens of police-spying tools remain after Facebook, Twitter crack down on Geofeedia." October 11, 2016. www.dailydot.com/layer8/geofeedia-twitter-facebook-instagram-social-media-surveillance. Accessed April 15, 2017.

83. Sjölund, B. "Why iBeacons fail to deliver robust analytics for retail." Walkbase. June 23, 2015. www.walkbase.com/blog/why-ibeacons-fail-to-deliver-robust-analytics-for-retail. Accessed April 15, 2017.

84. Sponder, M. "Connecting data with the Analytics Selfie." ClickZ. July 28, 2014. www.clickz.com/connecting-data-with-the-analytics-selfie/30390. Accessed April 15, 2017.

Advanced Text Analytics and Algorithms

CHAPTER OBJECTIVES

After reading this chapter, readers should understand:

- What Text Analytics is
- Text Analytics processing
- The Text Analytics market through 2020
- Types and use cases of Text Analytics
- Text Analytics use cases
- Future trends in Text Analytics
- Algorithms use in Text Analytics
- Issues with using Text Analytics
- An introduction to specific free and paid Text Analytics platforms
- Choosing the right Text Analytics platform

The world is full of text data (largely generated by the Web-based systems we use to communicate with). Text Analytics is turning text into numbers so we can run mathematical and algorithmic operations, regressions, classifications, neural networks, and Bayesian equations on the transformed data to get insights we might not otherwise get. Note that the algorithms mentioned is this chapter can be and are applied in many other domains besides Text Analytics, all the better for us to examine them with some depth here. Sometimes, we just generate word clouds and other forms of visualizations, and they are not turned into numbers, but we still describe the activity as Text Analytics. We found an excellent introductory article that explains Text Analytics in seven minutes.[1] We believe Text Analytics can be used more widely than it is, but for most organizations it remains a "niche" activity.

Reasons for Using Text Analytics

- Hearing from people provides tremendously valuable insights.
- Text can be utilized alongside statistical measures to build predictive models that are stronger than are possible with either the measures alone or text alone.
- Textual data can give us very useful insights in a variety of use cases such as customer sentiment (VOC), healthcare (patient and hospital), financials (stock

trading is especially hot), voluntary opinion mining (with and without survey data).

- Text Analytics can be used to get customer sentiment in ways customers are reluctant to share voluntarily by mining their textual data.

Process

Most text information is unstructured data for the standpoint of the text analytics process; that is because the processing is done by a software program that is not a sentient, thinking, being, and it cannot understand the world in the way humans do.[2] The Text Analytics process involves many operations:

1. First, the Text Analytics application counts the words in the chosen document, calculating the word distance from a word of interest (such as "wellness" or "illness") and choosing word categories (via pre-processing and employing complex algorithms). The goal at this stage of the process is to produce cleaned text data that has had its sentence structure, punctuation, and word groupings eliminated.
2. Second, the raw text is transformed into a set of information and placed in an internal text table for further processing.
3. Finally, the frequency of the words is counted and then normalized by running mathematical operations on table elements.

All this preprocessing seems like a lot of work, and it is.

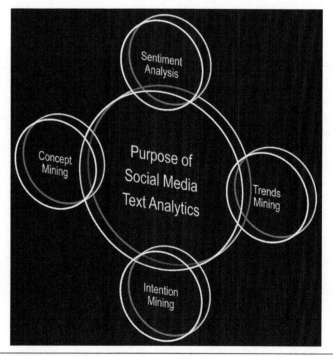

Figure 10.1 Purposes of Text Analytics.
Source: Gohar F. Khan.

Purposes of Text Analytics

Sentiment Analysis

Referring to Figure 10.1, one reason to use Text Analytics is to understand the opinion of others. Sentiment analysis an aspect of Text Analytics that focuses on opinion mining. Sentiment analysis uses computational methods to gather sentiment, opinions, appraisals, and emotions from the text. Opinion mining involves building a system to collect and categorize opinions about a product, service, or event. Automated opinion mining uses machine learning, a type of artificial intelligence (AI), to mine text for sentiment.[3] Sentiment analysis uses the following Text Analytics operations:

- **Polarity analysis:** Identify if the tone of communications is positive or negative.
- **Entity identification, categorization, and emotion tracking**: Identify the emotion and subject of the communications.
- **Context analysis:** Determine the context of social media posts and other forms of customer communication.

Sentiment analysis can be used to understand how others see the world regarding the data being studied. Sentiment analysis works by comparing the words in documents to external tag lists of words (called lexicons) that are classified as positive or negative. However, the meaning and sentiment of the terms can change, depending on the context they are used in. Analysts must make their own determination about text sentiment and meanings, as the software platforms are not able to do this.

- The overall balance of positive to negative words determines the Sentiment Score of a document (this can be done on the sentence level as well). The type of list (lexicon/dictionary) is often subjective and applied arbitrarily by whoever composes the list; these definitions may or may not work well in every situation.
- There has been a lot of misrepresentation involved with sentiment analysis capabilities and interpretations, but there are still excellent and valid reasons to employ it provided there is a good set of data (sample frame) to work with.

Topic and Trends Mining

Another reason to use Text Analytics is to understand what the text in the document is about. Use cases span from scholarly analysis of Shakespeare plays to counterterrorism/threat detection, and everything in-between. We could read a document and form an opinion about topics, but someone else could read the same document and come away with an entirely different set of topics and meanings. Besides, when there are thousands of documents to understand, manually reading large swaths of data is not feasible. Consequently, topic and trend mining are usually performed on large sets of data. Researchers can use deep learning to automatically try to make sense of themes and the trends that lie within a document or set of documents, but that doesn't work too well unless the Text Analytics software is manually trained beforehand on documents that are very close in subject, language, syntax, and form to the documents being analyzed.

Topic and trends analysis uses the following Text Analytics operations:

- **LDA or latent Dirichlet allocation:** Words are automatically clustered into topics, with a mixture of themes in each document.
- **Probabilistic latent semantic indexing:** Given a document, calculates the probability that certain topics are covered within the document. Also, given a certain topic, calculates the likelihood that a word would be used to describe it.
- **Term frequency–inverse document frequency:** TF–IDF counts how frequently a word appears in a document and its importance to the whole set. Frequent words like "the" or "an" are given a much lower weight, but words that show up frequently in certain contexts (say, a story) are given higher weight and used to build classifiers or predictive models, as we will examine shortly.

Examples of Topic and Trends Mining:

- David Rhea, an Assistant Professor of Communication Studies at Governors State University, undertook a qualitative project to determine how viewers of these talk shows disseminate the information they hear. The purpose of the study was to explore how the viewer comes to accept humorous information that they watch on late-night talk shows as legitimate political information. Rhea used NVivo 9 Text Analytics software to process the transcripts of the talk shows and found it easier to organize information than manually coding in a spreadsheet. NVivo helped him code data thematically with just a couple of clicks.[4] However, the method used by Rhea was still manual, and he had to define his topics first (modifying them while he was coding his project in NVivo); this approach works for a small research project, but would not be able to scale to millions of documents.
- In January 2015, Pew Research tested Crimson Hexagon, a text and sentiment analysis platform to analyze Twitter conversations mentioning New Jersey Governor Chris Christie. Crimson Hexagon employs a supervised machine learning approach. Two people trained Crimson Hexagon on more than 250 documents divided into four categories. Each of the four categories in the training set (the categories are manually defined by the people conducting the analysis) had more than 20 posts in them. Finally, once they were happy the training set was accurately categorized for their purposes, Pew Research ran the monitor. Pew used the keyword "Christie" on Twitter posts covering the period between November 4 to December 31, 2014. Crimson Hexagon automatically categorized many thousands of posts with the word "Christie" in it and placed it in one of the four categories that had been defined. The supervised learning model works well when analysts have a good idea what patterns they are looking for, but Crimson Hexagon requires a human analyst to review the analysis and decide on its meanings.[5] Pew Research also used Crimson Hexagon for sentiment analysis[6] around Chris Christie and the Bridgegate incident, demonstrating that Text Analytics platforms are usually able to perform multiple types of analysis.

Intention Mining

Intention mining is what the Google Search Engine does when you enter a search query into Google, and it figures out what you mean based on your query. Google doesn't stop there, it also analyzes queries and webpages for what people did not explicitly say, but what they intended to say, to understand the underlying opinions expressed in the document. Intention mining is a Text Analytics operation that is a big part of Search Engine Optimization. Intention mining can be done in several ways and uses some of the following Text Analytics operations:

- **Topic modeling:** Identify the dominant themes in a vast array of documents or text. The method used to uncover the topics within text include the following:

  - **Named entity recognition:** NER looks at recognizing nouns and could be used to extract persons, organizations, geographic locations, dates, monetary amounts, or the like from text, this works by looking at the words surrounding them.
  - **Event extraction:** Determines the relationships and the events connected with named entities (NER). Establishes the kinds of inferences that can be made from the text.
  - **Latent semantic analysis:** Examines relationships within a set of documents along with the terms they contain; assumes that words that are close in meaning will occur in similar places in the text.
  - **Latent Dirichlet allocation:** Topic modeling that is based on the idea that each text document contains a few topics such that each word in the document is attributable to one of its topics.

- We can take what someone has written and access the probability that it falls into one of the several categories (opinions), which is very close to what Crimson Hexagon and other platforms do in the previous example regarding Chris Christie.
- Use latent semantic indexing to disambiguate the words in a document and try to find the most relevant meanings within it.
- Use unsupervised learning to determine topic segments of based on various characteristics. Techniques such as clustering or dimension reduction are types of unsupervised learning techniques that can take raw data and form groups based on certain characteristics.[7]

Examples of intention mining:

- An analysis of the Bible and the Quran has found that violence and destruction are discussed more frequently in Christian scripture than in the Islamic text. The analysis was done with Text Analytics platform called Odin Text. The Old and New Testaments were studied as well as an English-language version of the Quran dated from 1917. It took just two minutes to complete the analysis and produce a series of data analyzing the words included in the scriptures. The analysis concluded that the Old Testament had more than twice as many violent mentions as the New Testament or the Quran.[8]
- A researcher analyzed 18,000 TripAdvisor reviews from hotels located in Santorini and scored them on cleanliness, value for money, sleep quality, and service and found that mentions of "*bathrooms*" are commonly found in negative reviews, but mentions containing "*service*" were found mostly in positive reviews.[9] Text classifiers were employed to find the most common words around *service* and *bathrooms*. By using Text Analytics, analysts can uncover opinions and feelings about a described experience that are not always explicitly stated.

- Digging down further, the analyst found a clean place, complimentary champagne, delicious food, nice breakfast, and Greek hospitality are the way to a positive review.
- On the other hand, problems with having a restful night's sleep, a shower that doesn't work as it should, and bad odors from the bathroom are likely to lead to a negative review.

Concept Mining

Text mining is the discipline of extracting information from a document. Concept mining attempts to do the same thing using the concepts in the document. Mapping words to concepts is ambiguous. Each word in a document may relate to several possible concepts. For example, the Google Search Engine indexes billions of new documents each day; using concept mining, it will automatically group similar documents together, as representative of a specific idea, along with other documents it has already categorized with the same or similar concept. Google can further refine its content classification by clustering the documents its index by topic; it uses this information to rank search results for a searcher's query better. Examples of concept mining include the following:

- The Dutch National Library has made publicly available more than 80 million historical newspaper articles from the past four centuries, and researchers have been able to search the entire corpus. Using custom developed dictionary software, the researchers could develop a custom dictionary based on statistically relevant words, derived from the frequency of particular words in the document collection and the particularity of those words. Since the words that stood out reflected changes taking place over 400 years, researchers could surmise cultural concept changes (as reflected in language charges) spreading across the entire span.[10]
- Google Books' Ngram Viewer can be used to view the usage terms words or terms over time. For example, comparing the terms "Digital Marketing" and "Web Analytics" went up sharply beginning with 2003 (around the time the Web Analytics Association was formed, so the spike in term usage makes perfect sense) while the term "Digital Marketing" remained relatively flat.[11] Books that cited each term are clustered by decade and can be further searched for occurrences. Google Books' Ngram Viewer covers roughly 200 years.

Text Analytics Market

Text Analytics is a growing market and is estimated to reach $6.5 billion by 2020, growing at a rate of as much as 25% per year from 2013 through 2020. Text Analytics supplies necessary data to Customer Relationship Management (CRM), predictive analytics, and brand reputation management.[12]

Mining Unstructured Data

While text we read has structure and organization based on language/grammar, it is not well organized for text analysis (as mentioned at the beginning of this chapter)— for this, the text must be transformed and placed in a repository where it can be data-mined (see Figure 10.2). Unstructured data takes much more effort to work with than structured data—it is also much more expensive (due to the transformations). Often, organizations merge several types of data using ETL (Extract Transfer Load) in a data warehouse. ETL is a dynamic data rewrite process. ETL was designed to consolidate enterprise information that originated before the era of "Big Data."[13]

Once the data is loaded into the data warehouse, it can be queried with other types of information that have been stored there, such as customer records.

Uses of Text Analytics

Table 10.1 shows some of the more common situations where Text Analytics is likely to be used. Text Analytics tools do not exist independently of the need and use cases

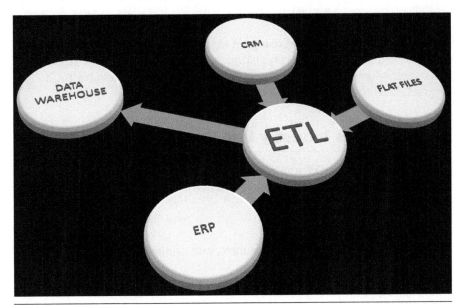

Figure 10.2 Transforming data using enterprise data tools and storing it in a data warehouse.
Source: WebMetricsGuru Inc.

Table 10.1 Common use cases of Text Analytics.

Area	More Common Use Cases
Business	Competitive intelligence, document categorization, HR (voice of the employee), records retention, risk analysis, website navigation
Marketing	Voice of the customer, Social Media Analytics, churn analysis, survey analysis, market research
Analytics	Fraud detection, e-discovery, warranty analysis, medical research
Education	Syllabus classification (compliance analysis), GRE, SAT (writing analysis)
Law Enforcement	Crime and terrorism detection, psychological assessments based on written data (by suspects), fraud detection

Source: WebMetricsGuru Inc.

for them. In every industry, there are different use cases where it makes sense to use Text Analytics platforms. Common situations where Text Analytics is useful include:

- **Tracking customer feelings regarding key topics:** Sentiment regarding a subject within a block of text, scoring it based on the intensity of specific words in the verbatim(s). For example, Facebook analyzed 24,000 confession posts on the social network to find out what millennials thought of their college or university.[14]
- **Tracking customer sentiment around a brand or business:** Text Analytics has been used in industry verticals quite successfully such as healthcare.[15]
- **Enriching news articles with metadata:** *The New York Times* built a robot to help make article tagging easier. Tags and keywords in articles help readers dig deeper into related stories and topics, and provides another way for readers to discover stories. However, adding tags to news stories is very tedious. Tools to automate content tagging can have a big difference to the bottom line. The *Times'* R&D lab developed the new tagging tool; the Editor tool scans text to suggest article tags in real time.[16]
- **Recognizing works of art using an algorithm:** There is a fascinating study conducted at Rutgers University that identified which paintings have had the greatest influence on later artists and whether they can measure a painting's creativity using only its visual features.[17]

Text Analytics Industry Use Cases

At least 80% of enterprise information and new data generated are in text form. Here are some examples of industry specific use cases of Text Analytics.

- **Municipalities** use predictive Text Analytics around call centers to support public welfare initiatives.[18]
- **Financial institutions, manufacturers, and retailers** use text analytics to support a range of applications including marketing, risk monitoring, staff recruitment, and more. In addition, financial institutions use that data to look out for the next "black swan"—a term used to describe the next debacle.[19]
- **Aviation industry** analyzes reports from pilots, mechanics, and other personnel to identify patterns related to airline safety.[20]
- **Finance industry** incorporates customer feedback in efforts to improve service levels and reduce fraud.[21]

Upcoming Trends

Text Analytics has already been widely deployed in enterprise applications for data mining and text extraction.[22] Here's what is coming up next for Text Analytics:

- Multilingual Text Analysis will increase.
- Text analysis will gain recognition as a key business solution capability.
- Machine learning, stats, and language engineering will coexist.
- Image analysis will enter the mainstream
- Speech analytics, with video, will emerge.
- Expanded emotion analytics is arriving soon (already prototyped).
- ISO emoji analytics will be a standard feature on most platforms shortly.

Text Analytics Operations

Turning text into numerical data allows analysts and researchers to run mathematical and statistical operations on the data, as shown in Figure 10.3.

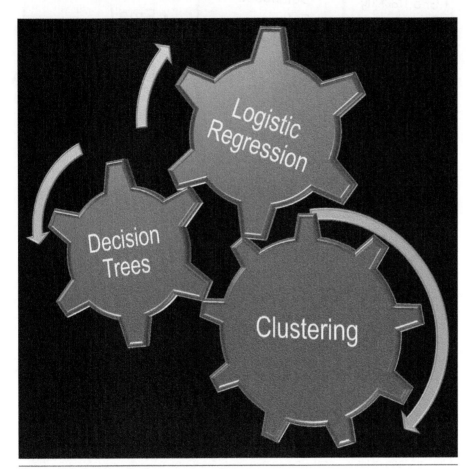

Figure 10.3 Text classification process engine.
Source: WebMetricsGuru Inc.

Working with Unstructured Information

Structured data is organized into rows, columns, and arrays within databases. The data is structured to be easily retrieved and analyzed using statistical and mathematical operations. Conversely, unstructured data is not organized for statistical or mathematical operations. Usually, unstructured data must be structured first, before it can be operated on. Semi-structured data is information that has a combination of structured and unstructured data (such as an email). Emails have a subject line, to and from fields, and a body of text that is usually comprised of unstructured data.

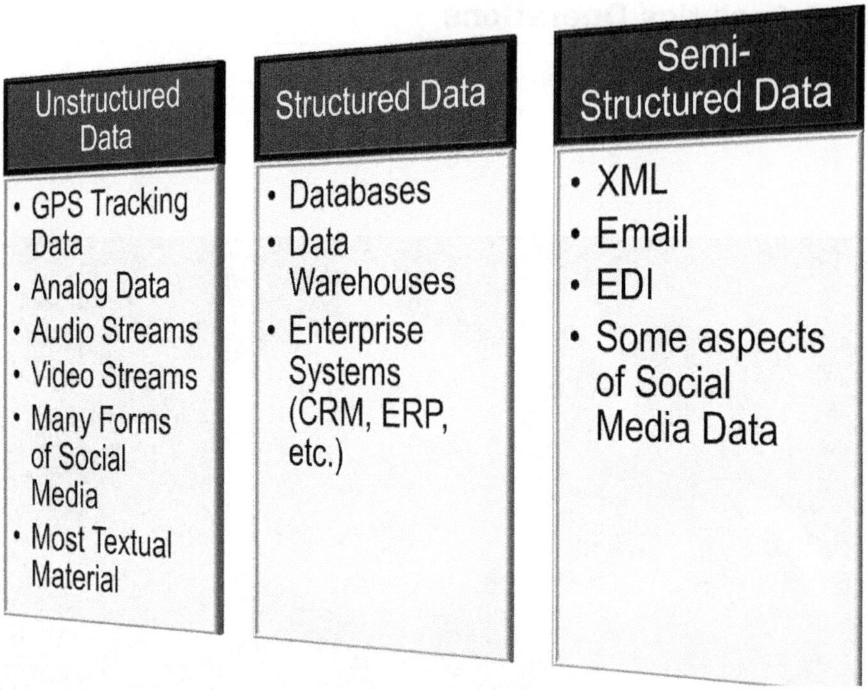

Unstructured Data	Structured Data	Semi-Structured Data
• GPS Tracking Data • Analog Data • Audio Streams • Video Streams • Many Forms of Social Media • Most Textual Material	• Databases • Data Warehouses • Enterprise Systems (CRM, ERP, etc.)	• XML • Email • EDI • Some aspects of Social Media Data

Figure 10.4 Structured, semi-structured, and unstructured data.
Source: WebMetricsGuru INC.

It is extremely complicated to take raw information as shown in Figure 10.4, including raw image data and turn it into useable data. The first part of this chapter gave readers a high-level overview of the Text Analytics process—now we are doing a second pass to take a more detailed look.

The Text Analytics Process (Detailed)

In the process of transforming text to numbers, there are many manipulations on the data, including "tokenization," so we can find "named entities" in the text—many of these steps are shown in Figure 10.5.

- Stop words (such as "the," "of," "and," "a," "to," and so on) are removed.
- All remaining words are made regular by a process sometimes called stemming. Lemmatization is a stemming operation that regularizes words while trying to figure out their part of speech. Caveat: How words get reduced to a stem may differ depending on how the words are used. For instance, the noun "moped" should not be stemmed into the form "mope," while the verb "moped" should.
- Spelling errors are corrected using a dictionary and plurals must be singularized. Idiomatic expressions are resolved.
- Tenses of words are made uniform so that the same word does not reappear many times with minor variations. Comments, such as "nothing" or "what?" or "no comment" or "mpmpmpmpmp," often appearing in the commentary, especially

social media, are removed (however, for sentiment analysis these are retained and analyzed).

- However, word pairs or larger groups of words (e.g. "not good" or "not bad" or "South Gas Works") are noted in sentiment analysis. (Obviously, the kinds of text analysis we do determine if certain words or phrases are retained and analyzed.) Infrequent words are removed, which helps to reduce the overall analytical burden.

Tokenization

Tokens are words taken from a block of text that has been cleaned. This process is called tokenization, and it is often being used to identify people or organizations (named entity extraction). Named entity extraction aims to overcome a problem created when separating words by using blank spaces; IBM SPSS and SAS Data Miner both do this operation.

- For instance, an expression such as 'Mr. Sand' contains two tokens ('Mr.' and 'Sand'), and the computer must recognize that they belong together.

Once we have words cleaned and prepared, we need some further way of reducing the information so it can be analyzed and compared. We should be careful to look at data that can be analyzed easily (into cluster groups, see Figure 10.5).

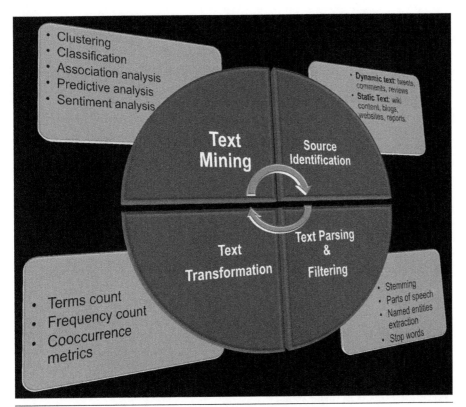

Figure 10.5 How text is transformed into numbers by Text Analytics.
Source: Gohar F. Khan.

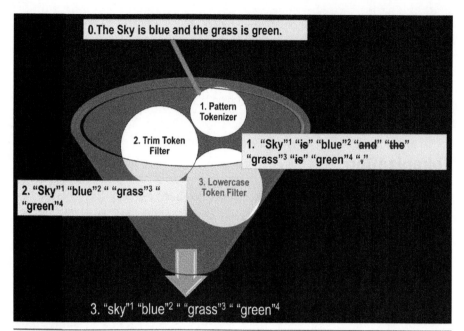

Figure 10.6 Building a CSV analyzer.
Source: WebMetricsGuru Inc.

Turning Text to Numbers, and Numbers into Data

It is very hard to take what people say and turn it into useful information. Humans intrinsically understand many of the structures and meanings of language that computer software does not, making even seemingly simple sentences such as "A dog is chasing a boy on the playground" tough to decode. As text is processed, tagged, entities extracted, sentiment applied, much of the intrinsic meaning we humans take for granted, is lost in translation. Turning text into numbers also involves semantics to derive meaning, involving the ability to disambiguate the meaning of words in various contexts. Even very simple sentences can be difficult for sophisticated software programs to extract the right meaning from, as so much of the meaning of words is "contextual."

Sliding Windows and N-Grams

While searching for information within a document, an "n-gram" or sliding window (of varied character lengths) is used to pick up the occurrences of words and to find "named entities." Sometimes the simplest models are also the most efficient—take the n-gram; it is a method of scanning information much the way our eyes scan. If we want to see what is around us, we should systematically move our eyes in a zig-zag fashion across the area of view, the point where vision is focused would correspond to the n-gram or the window from which we are looking at details. Text analytics works much the same way, zig-zagging across a text document with a window size (n-gram) of a certain number of characters.

- A sliding window (or as it is sometimes called an n-gram window) is one way to address the question of which words occur together.

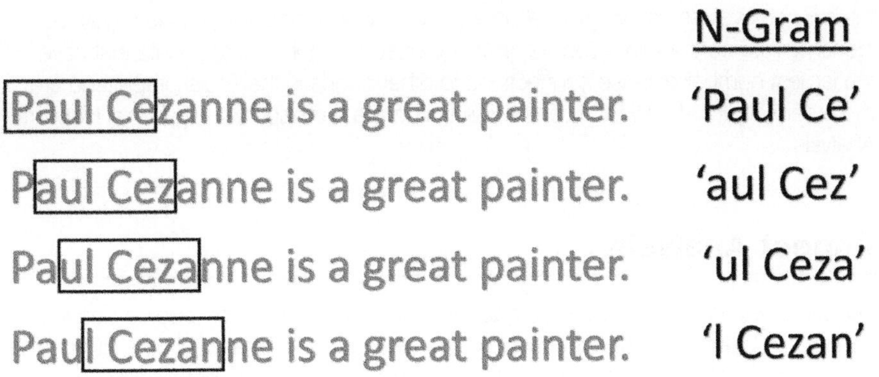

	N-Gram
Paul Ce̲zanne is a great painter.	'Paul Ce'
P̲aul Cez̲anne is a great painter.	'aul Cez'
Pa̲ul Ceza̲nne is a great painter.	'ul Ceza'
Pau̲l Cezan̲ne is a great painter.	'l Cezan'

Figure 10.7 N-gram sliding window text parsing.
Source: WebMetricsGuru Inc.

Think of the sliding window like a box that is a certain length (say seven characters, as illustrated in Figure 10.7) that moves through the text, one word at a time, and which keeps a count of how many times words fall together in that moving box. An approach like this would be useful for analyzing a collection of documents and looking for the strongest themes expressed across this set. (This might be helpful in looking at a single document if it was a long blog post or article.) The sliding window continues this path until it reaches the end of the block of text. As it moves, it keeps count of how many times words fall together in the box.

Similarities Matrix

Turning text into numbers is hard work, and one step in the process of running equations of the resulting data is to organize it into a similarities matrix. A similarities matrix shows how often words occur together. With a sliding window, the text takes a roundabout route to a table but finally appears in one. This chart, in turn, can lead to other, still more compact forms of data representation.

Automated Coding

Statistical platforms such as IBM SPSS and SAS Text Miner can be set up to auto-code verbatim into a table.

Factor Analysis

Factor analysis is a statistical method developed more than 100 years ago to examine responses to questions on intelligence tests that seemed highly related. The factors teased out the ways responses were similar using factor analysis to find common underlying ideas or themes in a set of scaled questions. Factors capture groups of issues around an underlying idea or groups of words that tend to appear together.

Eigenvalue and Factor Analysis

Eigenvalues are the measure of the effectiveness of a factor in a factor analysis. The stronger factor will have a larger eigenvalue (usually a maximum value of 1, but the min/max values can vary). The eigenvalue is used in social media as a way to identify influencers within a social graph. It is used to signify the accounts that have the largest number of close connections to other nodes in the social graph (and are more centrally located) which can be calculated mathematically using Social Network Analysis.

Aspect Analysis

Feature analysis is another term for aspect analysis. Often, when people describe a person, object or event, they mention the distinguishing characteristics such as size, color, texture, price, availability. Text Analytics can extract the aspects or features within the text. Analysts and marketer's opinions about an object or experience, then divide it into aspects and evaluate each individually, summing up the combined score.

Deep Learning and Neural Networks

If there is a large enough sample of text, even if the opinion holders are not clearly segmented, it is possible to forecast the sentiment (and opinions) of opinion holders with increasing accuracy and this what we will examine in this section. Deep learning neural networks are now being used for sentiment analysis with some interesting results. Socher[23] used deep learning to sort words and phrases into categories using distributional semantics. Neural networks and the math that power them have been around for about 30 years and attempt to replicate human biology in machine processing. To that end, neural nets are evolving very quickly—although they cannot curently understand the meanings behind what they are classifying, some day in the not too distant future they may be able to do this.

Counting Words, Centricity and Betweenness

Another way of determining what and who is important in a corpus of text is by looking at the concepts of "centricity" and "betweenness". Counting the number of words in a document is a way to understand the content as well as the words that are occurring more than the average.

- The more the "betweenness" of a word, the more it appears connected with other words that represent different concepts.
- "Centricity" has more to do with the way that betweenness is represented in a network diagram. The idea of centricity has often been used with "influencers'" network mapping.

Predictive Text Analytics

Earlier we covered the differences between describing text (via word clouds) versus making predictions based on what is in the text. Describing relationships (a word map or word cloud) is useful, yet predicting which routes in a map will bring us to our destination more quickly is far more actionable. Text Analytics uses the methods discussed in this chapter such as linear regressions to determine probabilities. By using probabilities, decisions can be made on the probabilities calculated from the text being analyzed.

Simple Models and Linear Regressions

Everyone knows loan calculators that predict monthly payments over time and the impact of making changes to the amount owed minus interest; incidentally, this timeline can be charted linearly because the timeline is based on a model. Regression is used to forecast what is likely to happen and what can be applied to many domains of knowledge and industry with good results. However, regressions do not seem to work too well for many Text Analytics use cases, especially if you have too many variables involved.

Linear Regression

- In a linear regression, there is a variable that is "forecast" or "predicted" termed the "dependent variable" or "target variable"; the dependent variable is usually plotted on the Y axis.
- There is also an "independent variable" or "predictor variable" that is usually plotted on the X axis.
- A simple linear equation can summarize the relationship between the two variables such as $y=3x+25$.
- A constant shows the starting point of the line on the Y axis on the equation chart.
- Since regressions are all about "straight lines" we need a way to tell how close to a straight line the regression is, which is called the "R-squared" of the regression (which measures how well the regression performs).
- The value of "R" is a "correlation coefficient"; correlation is a summary measure that shows how closely two variable falls into a straight-line relationship.

In a linear regression, a change in the value of the independent variable (or X axis), there is a corresponding shift in the dependent variable (or Y axis) which suggests a probabilistic relationship between the two variables.

Examples of Linear Regression
- **Author age prediction from text using linear regression:** Uses blogs, telephone conversations, and online forum posts a common model involving all three corpora together as well as separately and analyzes differences in predictive features across joint and corpus specific aspects of the model.[24]
- **Movie reviews and revenues: an experiment in text regression:** Uses linear regression with metadata around a movie; model attempts to predict a movie's opening weekend revenue.[25]
- **Text analysis in incident duration prediction:** Uses free flow text fields within incident reports of road blockages to predict clearance time, the period between incident reporting and a road's clearance.[26]

Logistic Regression in Text Analytics

Most of the things that dominate life are not linear—life is full of intangibles, even things we enjoy such as art, music, fashion, and sports are not linear in nature, and we should have some other way to make predictions on these. For complex tasks, such as classifying text into a known set of categories, logistic regression is a much better method than linear regression. Logistic regression relates a quantity x to the probability of it being a member of one of two groups and the likelihood of y having a value of 1. For example, logistic regression delivers, for any value of x, the frequency of the word "strange" and the log odds of the word refers to the Marvel Movie *Doctor Strange* (released on November 4, 2016). Logistic regression is often expressed as the odds of something happening or occurring, or not and can consist of several variables that are interrelated to each other and impact the outcome.

Logistic Regression Examples

- **Multiple logistic regression analysis of cigarette users among high school students:** Binary logistic regression analysis was performed to predict high school students' cigarette smoking behavior from selected predictors based on a 2009 CDC Youth Risk Behavior Surveillance Survey.[27] The five predictor variables included in the model were: 1) race, 2) frequency of cocaine use, 3) first cigarette smoking age, 4) feeling sad or hopeless, and 5) physically inactive behavior. The strongest predictors of youth smoking behavior were race, the frequency of cocaine use, and physically inactive behavior.
- **Lying words: Predicting deception from linguistic styles:** In an analysis of five independent samples, a computer-based text analysis program correctly classified liars and truth-tellers at a rate of 67% when the topic was constant and a rate of 61% overall. Compared to truth-tellers, liars showed lower cognitive complexity, used fewer self-references and other references, and used more negative emotion words.[28]
- **Fast logistic regression for text categorization with variable-length n-grams:** Instead of pre-processing text to clean it for Text Analytics, logistic regression was used to automatically tokenize text, even when it was unfamiliar.[29]

Classification Trees

Classification trees are a statistical grouping method that works better for Text Analytics than regression models. One of the most common classification trees used in Text Analytics is the CHAID method that splits the data into groups, then finds smaller groups within those groups that are significant, and keeps on doing that. The original intent of CHAID was to detect an interaction between variables. CHAID stands for "Chi-squared automatic interaction detector" and works s best with "coded" text generated through surveys and questionnaires.

Consider the Response CHAID Tree, in Figure 10.8. The overall response of 10% (from a population of size 1,000) can be predicted by marital status, gender, and pet ownership. Note: CHAID does not work well with small sample sizes as respondent groups can quickly become too small for reliable analysis.

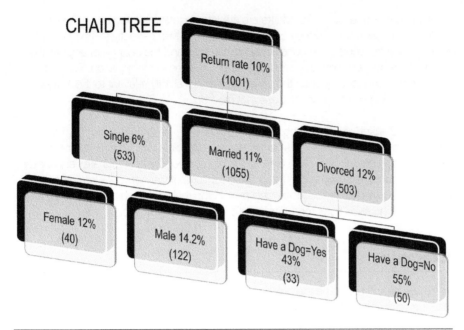

Figure 10.8 Example of a CHAID tree.
Source: WebMetricsGuru Inc.

Example

For a simple introduction to classification trees, see "5 Minutes with Ingo: Decision Trees."[30] Take, for example, a coin sorting system for sorting coins into different classes (perhaps pennies, nickels, dimes, quarters, much like the old coin dispensers that are rarely used these days). Coins usually differ in their diameter, and that can be used to devise a hierarchical tree system for sorting coins. Once we drop a coin into the coin sorter, based on its diameter, it is classified as a penny, nickel, dime, or quarter. The decision process used by the coin changer (or classification tree) provides an easy and common method for sorting a pile of coins, and it can be applied to a lot of different classification problems. Virtually all tree methods behave similarly.

Bayesian Networks

Bayesian network modeling is much more "real world" and realistic than results coming out of a regression network. One of the unique characteristics of the Bayesian networks is that they assemble themselves around the strongest patterns.

Applications

- Bayesian networks are used in a variety of situations such as aeronautics (guidance systems), public safety (nuclear power plants, police protection, etc.), medicine (cancer research, genetics research, etc.), national defense (persons of interest database, etc.). Originally, Bayesian networks were developed for scientists and researchers. Marketers are late in getting started using Bayesian (neural) networks—and they certainly lend themselves perfectly to Text Analytics.

- Bayesian networks have conditional probabilities and the change of any variable in a Bayesian equation impact all the other variables in the equation. Bayesian networks can focus just on the variables that are strictly relevant to the "target" while getting rid of (ignoring) those that are not.

A "Markov Blanket" is a clustering of the most relevant variables that are the main elements of the analysis.[31] Bayesian models are difficult to run. Most software is expensive and hard to learn with a steep learning curve. Feature sets are very uneven across products, and some don't allow modifications of the network while others do, etc. Bayesian Models better model and predict the real world, which is why they are in many situations such as aeronautics, public safety, medicine, etc.

Example

There are known problems that would be very hard to solve without Bayesian math; take the yellow taxi/white taxi problem:

> In a city, there is **an accident involving a white taxi cab**.
>> Someone witnessed the crash and reported the accident was caused by a **white cab**.
>> In this city **85% of the cabs are yellow, and 15% are white**.
>> Police questioned the witness and determined they are **80% accurate in reporting the color of the cab.**
>> **What are the odds the cab was white**?
>> The answer is 41.4%; in a Bayesian network, all the variables impact each other.

- To model the yellow taxi/white taxi problem with Bayesian math; build a network that links the actual color of the cab and the color that the witness saw with each being a network node.

It is beyond this book to cover Bayesian networks in depth; we are simply alluding to them here because they are the best way to solve certain complex mathematical problems. For a simple introduction to naïve Bayesian networks see "5 Minutes With Ingo: Naïve Bayes."[32]

Clustering

Humans take different bits of information and group them in clusters (i.e., "foods we like," "people we like," "jobs we like," and so on). We cluster information when we look at landscapes and group the foreground, middle ground, and background, whereas the landscape is much more complex, and our mechanism to cluster information is central to our ability to process the information and "connect the dots" in our mind and nervous system. Likewise, to derive meaning from textual data, we need to organize text data into groupings and then connect the dots. This paradigm of information retrieval and organization goes back to Marshall McLuhan's theory of media that the medium is the message and the way we organize information profoundly impacts what we see and how we act on it. Some scientists believe that we do not see visual reality as it is. In fact, our brains simplify things to "hide the reality of what we are looking at," by not representing it literally. This is called "unconscious bias"—people tend to judge or process information based on preconceived information that will shape the outcome of newly processed information.[33]

Topic Analysis

There are any number of free Text Analytics tools that organize information, some of them surprisingly powerful, but in a narrow frame of data, limited to a small number of posts that are arranged to be processed by the tool. Topic analysis works best when the information is already cleaned and organized, but sometimes just running any text through topic analysis can reveal interesting patterns for further analysis, such as the cover page of *The New York Times*.[34] The reader can try it by going to http://tweettopicexplorer.neoformix.com/#n=NYTimes and clicking on the various bubbles that are organized by the software into clusters. While the clustering is not based on the meanings of the sentences but rather the words used, it is an advance over simply looking at the text without structuring it.

Word Clusters and Similarity

The utility of word clusters is that they lump together words that reoccur more often than others. Clustering finds patterns of similarities in the sampled data (or the entire corpus being examples) between people or objects, creating groups in which every member of the cluster group is very like the other members, yet different enough from the members of other cluster groupings of words. Clustering of words is based on how closely the words are related (being the most similar). Text clusters are not particularly well suited to organize information in a useful way via similarity because we have first had to define what "similarity" means when we are seeking to organize the textual data for, and that is hard to do.

Ontologies

Ontologies show the relationships of words. Ontologies started becoming popular when Object Oriented Programming (OOP) came into being in the late 1980s as the result of software programming platforms such as Unix and C/C++ that was prevalent at the time. Ontologies and OOP attempt to solve the same problem; provide self-contained data and the descriptors of the data so that it can be operated on as a unit, irrespective of where that operation takes place. Ontologies create a hierarchal order that applies context to words. Context is needed to derive meaning, so ontologies are relevant, especially having the right ones in place for the data being analyzed. Ontologies solve a problem we frequently see in Text Analytics where a word or phrase has multiple meanings, and by using the best ontology, meaning is derived that is more accurate.

The following provides an example of the same words being interpreted differently based on their context in a sentence:

- **Low down payments** are desirable.
- She provided us with the **low down on which payments** to process.
- **Low down payments** are the least of his concerns.

Applying an ontology allows Text Analytics to determine the best meaning for specific words based on the other words they are surrounded by in a sentence.

Clustered Data Types

The information in ontologies on the web can fall within a few categories.

- **Nominal:** Values that are not numerically related and have no fixed scale—here's an example: Northeast =100, Midwest =200, Southwest =300, Northwest =400.
- **Ordinal:** Numerical values that appear not to be related.
- **Continuous:** Values that are numerical and have adhered to a fixed scale; can be an interval and/or ratio-based.

OWL

OWL stands for the Web Ontology Language, and it allows computers (software) to process content within information on the Internet before presenting it back to the reader. OWL is superior for this purpose to XML and other HTML markup languages that do not have the capability to process ontologies in the same way that OWL does.

Advice about the Clusters Used in Text Analytics

- K-means fails for useful text clustering.
- Two-step clustering produces good cluster groupings.
- A small number of cluster groups (3–5) works best.

Hierarchical and K-means Clustering Methods

Many of the high-powered text analytics tools use statistical engines to organize data. This type of software is not intended to be user-friendly. Statistical engines are useful (but not user-friendly) for a wide variety of enterprise data-mining that can handle almost any type of data and run virtually any mathematical operation on it.

Iterative K-means Clustering Algorithm

One of the most popular and useful way to organize information in the "K-means" algorithm.[35] K-means algorithm creates a specific number of groups (K) from a set of objects. It's a popular cluster analysis technique for exploring a set of data.[36]

K-means algorithm works in a similar manner to a simple coin changer that runs for as long as there are coins to sort. Algorithms are simply a set of instructions that are repeated over and over again on a set of data.

The iterative part of the K-means algorithm uses the output of one state of the computation as the input of the next stage, continually re-running the K-means until the output and input no longer meaningfully change.

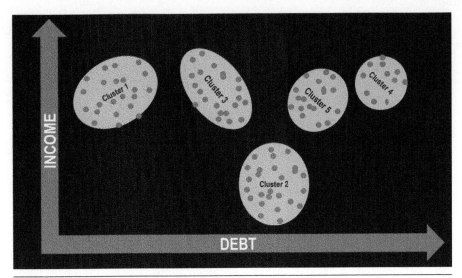

Figure 10.9 K-means clustering example.
Source: WebMetricsGuru Inc.

Many of the algorithms scientists use are based on simple operations; the challenge is to figure out the right algorithm(s) to use and how to organize the input and output. The main problem with using K-means clustering for marketing purposes is that the results often do not seem to be that useful; perhaps it is not the right approach to take (yet many vendors take that approach, which is why we are covering algorithms in this book).

So, analysts and stakeholders run into a familiar problem with Text Analytics that is common with the other types of analytics we discuss in this book. Namely, while the algorithms and platforms are great, the amount of setup for the data to be useable (or useful) is often prohibitive. What we are saying is that K-means clustering works great if organizations are already organized and pre-digested the data, but if they haven't it may end up creating garbage clusters that aren't useful—and may be downright dangerous when used this way.

Choosing the right algorithm and running it effectively, is more of an art than a science at this point—K-means requires enough differences in the data that can be summarized to a few groupings, so it may be that K-means when used by marketers, is simply applied incorrectly by the marketing analysts (or whoever needs the output). Another point that has been made is that clustering data for marketing purposes is not the same as market segmentation: "Clustering is finding borders between groups; segmenting is using borders to form groups."[37]

Effective clustering requires analysts to have "meaningful differences" to form clusters with. But do they have meaningful differences? Are age, gender, and income meaningful differences to form cluster groups with? Not always. Increasingly, these clusters mean less and less—but that is the clustering most industry tools have settled on to build their platform reports; recipe for failure. K-means is a method to define market segments from a set of disparate data, whereas marketers assume the data is grouped in the best way, even when that is not the case, and a better grouping exists, or should be created. The final point is with sampling the right "frame"—what if the data being clustered turns out not to be of significance for the marketing campaign? We could end up with segmentations (based on K-means) that aren't effective.

Cluster Analysis Representation

Once algorithms have been run, and we are satisfied with the results, then the fun part starts. Analysts must represent the data in a manner that makes visual sense to stakeholders, otherwise no one is going to understand the analysis!

Dendrograms

Clustering is not "hierarchal" or time sequenced—we live in a multidimensional world where there is "hierarchy and sequence"; what comes first, second, and third makes a difference, and some things are more important than others (just look at any organizational ORG chart). After clustering the data, we must organize it in a way that makes sense to stakeholders—enter dendrograms, tree clustering and other visualizations.

* Dendrogram and tree clustering diagrams are produced by high-end statistical platforms such as SAS-Text Miner, IBM SPSS, Skytree, and even Google Analytics, etc.

Dendrograms may be an effective way of organizing text data, but are not very popular with stakeholders and marketing executives.

Treemaps

Treemaps are produced by many kinds of software. Treemaps can also be broken down into subgroupings which are also very useful. Statistical platforms produce word Treemaps, but so do many Web and Audience Analytics platforms such as Google Analytics.

Multidimensional Scaling

MDS is a statistical method that produces tables, such as the distances in miles between several cities.[38] High-end statistical platforms like IBM SPSS and SAS Text Miner and RapidMiner can produce MDS charts. While MDS works well for types of comparisons (such as distances in flight routes), it can also be used with Text Analytics (provided the data is manually reorganized by the analyst first).

Word Clouds

Word Clouds are images composed of words, used in a text or subject, where the size of each word indicates its frequency or importance. Many Text Analytics platforms produce word clouds based on an analysis of the text examined.

* **Wordle and Neoformix:** Textual diagrams that shows how many times a word appears in a body of text.
* **Clustering diagram:** Clumping words together in various ways using a statistical method called clustering.

- **Tree diagram (dendrogram):** Analytical visual word map.
- **Word clouds:** Text volume visual representation.
- **Graph layouts of words:** Network of words showing interconnectivity.
- **Heatmaps:** Show concentration of interest in the word map.

Machine Learning: Supervised vs. Unsupervised Learning

There are two classes of machine learning techniques: supervised and unsupervised. In supervised learning, a model is created based on previous observations as a training set using a set of documents tagged by humans to be part of a category. Social Media Analytics tools like Crimson Hexagon work in this way. Once the classifier is trained, it can predict any given document's categories. Supervised learning "classifiers" are developed and used and score the "input" along predefined lines as shown in Table 10.2, below.

Supervised machine learning uses classifiers. When a classifier is fed new text (i.e., blog post, tweet, SMS message, call center record, etc.) to classify, it predicts whether the document belongs to a particular predefined category, and assigns a "label" for the document as well as a confidence score.[39]

SVM

SVM or support vector machine learning models are associated with machine learning algorithms that analyze data for Text Analytics. The SVM algorithm builds a model that assigns new examples into one category or the other, making it a non-probabilistic binary linear classifier.[40] Using SVM for text categorization comes down to an analyst or researcher's judgment call. For a simple video explanation of SVM, watch "5 Minutes with Ingo: Understanding Support Vector Machines."[41]

Table 10.2 Supervised learning example.

Number	COLOR	SIZE	SHAPE	FRUIT NAME
1	RED	BIG	Oval shape with a depression on the top	APPLE
2	RED	SMALL	Globular, heart-shaped	CHERRY
3	GREEN	BIG	Cylinder that is long and curving	BANANA
4	GREEN	SMALL	Elongated oval shape appearing in a grouping that is usually cylindrical	GRAPE

Source: WebMetricswGuru Inc.

Unsupervised Machine Learning

Unsupervised learning is run when we are trying to discover patterns rather than trying to fit the data into the predefined structure. Clustering is an example of "unsupervised learning." Unsupervised data assumes that nothing is initially known, and the software learns as it runs. Unsupervised machine learning differs because it is "not supervised by a human" and does not require a training dataset. Typically, the categories are not even known in advance. Unsupervised learning includes methods such as topic clustering and topic modeling (discussed earlier) and it is used automatically to find groups of similar documents within a collection of records. For example:

- **Analyze several corporate emails as part of a fraud discovery process.**
  At the beginning of the analysis, the analyst has no idea what the emails are about or topics they deal with, but we can use unsupervised machine learning to determine the most common topics present in the emails. Once the common topics are discovered in the email corpus, the analyst can then use K-means clustering algorithm to group the emails into a few distinct clustered categories.[42]

Classification models used in Supervised and Unsupervised Machine Learning

Classification models determine the way information is organized. The classification process involves organizing the text within a corpus of documents into categories for its most effective and efficient use.

- **Discriminant analysis** is used to classify text into clearly defined groups using statistical models.
- **Logistic regression** is like discriminant analysis but works better with data that doesn't clearly fitting into any category.
- **Classification trees** are a form of partitioning, organizing a space and are hierarchical (in some ways like ontologies we just covered in this section), and uses "if–then" rules.
- **Bayesian networks** represent the probabilistic relationships between a set of values and outcomes. For example, given certain conditions, the network can be used to compute the probabilities of the presence of various weather patterns.
- **Custom classifiers** are used when none of the common ways of classifying information are sufficient to classify the information for a task—in this case, creating a custom classification model makes the most sense.

Depending on what we are trying to accomplish, any one or a combination of the classification models mentioned in this chapter could be used.

Visual Text Analytics

Visual information is so much easier to absorb than text, and we are visual beings. Many of the same algorithms we have discussed in this chapter have been adapted and extended to deal with the visual realm (photos, videos, and live streaming).

Decoding Emotions in an Image

The software can decode basic emotions via Text Analytics (with differing accuracy) — now it's being done to images and video streams. Emotient is one of the companies at the forefront of visual emotion tracking, and was acquired by Apple in 2015.[43] Apple likely planned to apply Emotient technology to Siri in later versions of the iOS operating system that runs on iPhones and iPads. Visual Analytics platforms that detect emotion are interesting to experiment with. However, the technologies need to improve and standardize before they can be deployed widely. Emotient had a demo anyone could use with their own computer cam, but once the company was acquired by Apple, the demo was removed. However, Emotient left a video on YouTube showing their emotion tracking demo.[44] There are several other vendors in the same space such as imotions, which still offers a demo, upon request.[45]

Visual Analytics Applications

This space is very dynamic, so there are always going to be new offerings — here are few we found interesting. For example, LaMem allows anyone to upload a photo, and the algorithm will determine how memorable it will be to a normal human viewer.[46]

Recommended Free Text Analytics Platforms

The following is a sampling of the free Text Analytics tools available at the time of publication for readers to experiment with:

- **MeaningCloud:** Install the free MeaningCloud Excel Plugin.[47]
- **Dandelion API** and a Google Spreadsheet Plugin.[48]
- **They Say API:** Paste some text below and then hit the button.[49]
- **PINGAR Demos and API:** Explore the different features of the Pingar API for free.[50]
- **Semantria for Excel:** Allows anyone to utilize sophisticated text analytics technology in free demo.[51]

Recommended Paid Text Analytics Tools

- SAS Enterprise Miner/Text Miner[52]
- IBM SPSS[53]
- ODINText[54]
- Lexalytics[55]
- RevealedContext[56]

Common Text Analytics Terms

- **Natural Language Processing (NLP):** A field of computer science and artificial intelligence that focuses on interactions between computers and human language. Examples of NLP applications include Siri and Google Now.

- **Information extraction:** Extract structured information from unstructured and/or semi-structured data, such as text documents or webpages.
- **Named entity recognition:** Locate and classifying elements from text into predefined categories such as the names of people, organizations, places, etc.
- **Corpus:** Large collection of documents used to infer or validate grammatical rules, perform statistical analysis and test hypothesis.
- **Sentiment analysis:** Use NLP to extract attitudinal information from a piece of text.
- **Disambiguation:** Identify the meaning of words in context using computational means (software). Example: use or develop an algorithm to determine whether when a reference to "Apple" in a verbatim (text) refers to the company Apple or to the fruit.
- **Bag of words:** Commonly used model for text classification; text (a sentence or a document) is represented as a bag of words with word order and word frequency used as a feature for training a classifier.
- **Explicit semantic analysis:** Understand the meaning of a text verbatim through a combination of the concepts found in that text.

Best Practices

- **Speed and scale iteration through software development:** NLP often requires a large set of data, much of it needs to be "cleaned" where multiple query steps feed one another.
- **A centralized location for both types of data and processing:** Most organizations have not figured out how to contain the data they collect so it can be "worked on," even collecting it together so it can be processed is a challenge (since it is often collected and siloed for different reasons and needs).
- **Support for a wide variety of existing and emerging analytics tools:** This point directly addresses our textbook—there are so many new tools and methodologies that are developing, there is no possible way to stay entirely on top of all of them! Today, those toolsets include ETL, SQL, PL/Java, PL/Python, PL/R, Mahout, Graphlab, Open MPI, MADlib, Spring Data, Spring XD, MapReduce, Pig, Hive, Web Analytics, Tag Managers, and others. However, what will the toolset look like five years from now? It is hard to say as new platform tools are constantly being released.

Text Analytics Principles

1. Only work on a clear problem.
2. Be prepared to invest much more time preparing the data for analysis than initially planned.
3. Decide what is important and what is not.
4. Go for the simplest approach that explains what is important.

Faulty analysis leads to faulty conclusions.

Text Analytics Issues

- Raw data needs to be cleared and organized before it will be useful for text analysis. For example, anything in social media might be considered "data," but may or may not be useful.
- Regardless of the data "out there" to collect, unless there is a compelling reason to gather and study it, the data will usually not be collected or examined. That makes it easier to be good at finding and processing information that is valued, and not so good at collecting and examining information that is less valued (or not valued).
- Text Analytics requires a significant investment of time and resources. Software for text analytics ranges in price from free to enterprise level, with "enterprise level" being a secret code for "costing a lot of money." When there are great masses of text, usually there are also great masses of other types of data. One may need to invest in new storage, new hardware, and new software to handle this.
- There may be a need to hire additional people to deal with all the resources necessary to analyze text deeply.
- Even top Text Analytics researchers cannot program machines to correctly tag content in a document 100% of the time. The meanings of words in a document are contextual, so that no matter how much the software is programmed, it cannot handle the variety of ways that people say things.
- There are some newer developments, such as adding emotion detection to text (i.e., Crimson Hexagon detects six emotions on Twitter data in its Buzz Monitors). However, such information, alone, will not be helpful until the data is filtered, cleaned, organized, and analyzed with very specific questions that connect to business goals. After all, programs will most likely take words literally unless there is some method to teach them to realize the entire context of the sentence. As analysts, authors, and professors, we have concluded that the biggest issue with Text Analytics isn't with the tools.

Sentiment Analysis Issues

Confusion Over Number of Emotions

Emotions are not standardized across different sentiment analysis software. Some vendors think people express six basic emotions (love, joy, surprise, anger, sadness, and fear, according to Parrott[57]); others suggest eight or 16 emotions will work better.

Opinions Cannot Be Accurately Extracted

Classifying a document or sentence as positive or negative in emotion does not add much value to analysis if we cannot tell what the opinion-holder feels positively or negatively about.

Choosing a Text Analytics Solution

1. Determine if "knowing more" about a subject is going to make a difference in what actions an organization may take (if yes = proceed; if no = don't use Text Analytics in this context).
2. Determine budget: There are some free tools available, but they are not often that extensible or reliable, so a serious effort with Text Analytics should probably rule out free or low-cost software. Once consideration in platform tool choice is the form of the data that is going to be processed as not all platforms process all file/format types.
3. Determine how much "data cleaning" and "reorganizing" is going to be needed to make sense of the data.
4. Determine the right models and algorithms required to process the data – this is more of an art than a science since there are several ways analyze text (some are more effective for a given situation than others).

Why Many Organizations Are Not Using Text Analytics (Yet)[58]

1. Many organizations do not understand the value of the data in documents, or how to extract it.
2. Researchers too often buy a technology solution when what they need is an insights solution.

Case Study: Tapping into Online Customer Opinions

Founded in 1986, Frequent Flyer Services (Flyertalk.com) has created a unique niche for itself within the travel industry as a company that conceives, develops, and markets products and services exclusively for the frequent traveler. Its focus and distinctive competency lie in frequent traveler programs. Worldwide, these frequent traveler programs in the airline, hotel, car rental, and credit card industries have more than 75 million members who earn an excess of 650 billion miles per year. Flyertalk. com is one of the most highly trafficked travel domains. It features chat boards and discussions that cover the most up-to-date traveler information, as well as loyalty programs for both airlines and hotels. With millions of users generating millions of posts and comments, it wanted to tap into the explosion of customer opinions expressed online. Flyertalk.com knew that the feedback that current and potential customers provide on their website provided a rich source of feedback and was looking for ways to mine it. The answer to the problem faced by Flyertalk.com lies in Text Analytics. The most innovative companies know they could be even more successful in meeting customer needs if they just understood them better. Text Analytics is proving to be an invaluable tool in doing this. Flyertalk.com leveraged Anderson Analytics do the job. Anderson Analytics, a full-service market research consultancy, tackles this issue using cutting-edge text analytics and data-mining software from SPSS that allows the application of scientific, statistical, and pattern recognition techniques to large text datasets. Note that the Text Analytics techniques applied, in this case, are not limited to discussion boards or blogs but can be applied to any text data source, including survey open ends, call center logs, customer complaint/suggestion databases, emails, and social media data, etc. A Text Analytics project is usually part of a much larger data-mining project that would typically involve the identification of some core strategic questions, the allocation of resources and the eventual implementation of findings. However, the focus of this case study is to describe the tactical aspects of a text analytics project and to delineate the three basic steps involved in text analytics:

Step 1: Data collection and preparation
Step 2: Text coding and categorization
Step 3: Text mining and visualization

Step 1: Data Collection and Preparation

Having quality data in the proper format is usually more than half of the battle for most researchers. For those who can gain direct access to a well-maintained customer database, the data collection and preparation process is relatively painless. However, for researchers who want to study text information that exists in a public forum such as Flyertalk.com, data collection can be more complex and usually involves Web scraping. Web scraping (or screen scraping) is a technique used to extract data from websites that display output generated by another program. Many commercially available applications can scrape a website and turn the blogs or forum messages into a data table. Here is how Web scraping works.

The Web Scraping Process
- **Crawl**: Crawl the website and scrape for the topic, ID and thread initiator.
- **Download**: Use topic ID from the first step as part of the URL query string to download messages.
- **Store:** The Web crawls and stores message display pages.
- **Screen scrape**: Screen scraped web pages are extracted, and the data is stored in a structured format.
- **Link:** Link extracted posts with topics from the first step, along with other extracted fields to create the final dataset.

Even with the availability of powerful Web-scraping tools and techniques, text mining a popular blog or a message board like the one at Flyertalk.com presents unique data collection and processing challenges. The amount of free text available on such sites usually prohibits an indiscriminate approach to data scraping. A strategy with clear objectives and a clear data extraction method are needed to increase the reliability of data analysis in the latter stages of the research. In this case, researchers at Anderson Analytics narrowed the scope to just discussion topics within a 12-month period (from August 2005 to August 2006) on the five top forums intended for discussing the hotel loyalty programs of Starwood, Hilton, Marriott, InterContinental, and Hyatt hotels. Specific Web-scraping parameters differ depending on the structure of the target sites. In a discussion board format, the text data tend to follow a simple hierarchy. Typically, each forum contains a list of topics, and each topic consists of numerous posts. Therefore, the Web-scraping process of Flyertalk.com initially retrieves data such as the discussion topics, topic ID, topic starter, and topic start date. Then, by using the topic ID, the Web-scraping application constructs and submits query strings to the Flyertalk.com site to retrieve messages associated with each specific topic. An excellent Web-scraping tool should allow the capture of information that exists in the source data of an HTML page, not just the displayed text. Therefore, hidden information such as the topic ID, date stamp, etc. also becomes available to the researcher. Besides making sure the fields in the final dataset are in the correct format, another problem unique to discussion board text needs to be addressed. It is very common for posters to quote others' text within their posts. These quotes should typically be extracted from the message field and placed in a separate field to prevent double counting and inadvertently adding weight to certain posts. In addition to the text messages posted on the forum, the Web-scraping process should also capture the poster's ID, and "handle," as well as any other available poster information such as a forum, join date, and forum registration information (in this case: location, frequent traveler program affiliation, etc.).

Step 2: Text Coding and Categorization

Text coding and categorization is the process of assigning each text data record a numeric value that can be used later for statistical analysis. Text coding can apply either dichotomous code (flags and many variables) or certain codes (one variable for an entire dataset). Short answers to an open-ended survey question typically use certain codes. However, the amount of text included in most discussion board posts typically requires dichotomous codes. A typical text coding process has the following steps.

Text Coding and Categorization Process
- **Preliminary coding**: Use both computer and human coder to obtain the initial understanding of the data.
- **Initial classification**: Use SPSS Text Mining tool to perform initial categorization on a sample data set (1/100 of the entire dataset).
- **Computer classification**: Information and knowledge gained from the original concept extraction are used by the human coder to assist in computer categorization.
- **Coding and classification refinement**: Categorization and coding are an iterative process. Custom libraries are created to refine the process. Text extraction is performed multiple times until the number of and the details of categories are satisfactory.
- **Coding and extraction rules**: Once the coding result becomes satisfactory, the same coding and extraction rules are used on the entire dataset.
- **Categorization results**: Categorization results are exported for further analysis with tools such as SPSS Text Analysis.

Text coding is usually an iterative process, and this is particularly the case for coding messages on a site such as Flyertalk.com. Text information can be compared to survey answers. The text data on most discussion boards tend to be "user-driven" rather than "provider-driven." Before creating categories, researchers at Anderson Analytics first randomly examine a sample of text messages to gain a basic understanding of the data. This step is required to understand the type of acronyms, shorthand, and terminologies commonly used on the forum of interest. SPSS Text Analysis for Surveys and Text Mining for Clementine are powerful tools. However, the text coding results can be significantly improved if the programs can be "trained" to better understand text information and topics of interest. With a list of industry-specific themes, concepts and words, the researchers at Anderson use tools such as SPSS Text Analysis for Surveys to create a custom dictionary. Then the SPSS Text Analytics applications can be utilized, in conjunction with an SPSS developed dictionary, to extract highly relevant concepts from the text data. In this case, examples of some of the basics in the messages that can be detected by the software include: "rates," "stay," "breakfast," "points," "free offers." The text extraction and categorization processes are repeated with minor modifications each time to fine-tune results.

Step 3: Text Mining, Visualization, and Interpretation

Depending on the needs of any given research project, the coded text data can be interpreted in many ways. In this case, the data is examined via the following methods:

Positive/Negative Comments and Overlapping Terms
The Flyertalk.com data indicates that negative discussions among the posters are centered on the payment process, condition/quality of the bathroom, furniture, and the check-in/out process. The praises seem to be centered on topics such as spa facility, complimentary breakfasts, points, and promotions.

Data Patterns within Different Hotel Brands
By comparing the coded text data of Starwood and Hilton forums, the researchers find that the posters seem to be relatively more pleased with beds on Starwood's board, but more satisfied with food and health club facilities on Hilton's board.

Longitudinal Data Patterns
As this study contains data from a one-year period, data can be analyzed to understand how topics are being discussed on a month-to-month basis. The data in this particular case revealed that the discussion about "promotions" on the Starwood board is especially frequent in February 2006. Cross-checking with Starwood management confirmed that special promotions were launched during that period. Text Analytics is one way to measure the impact of various communication strategies, promotions, and even non-planned external events.

Analysis of Poster Groups
Web mining may clarify the aggregate motivation of some of the most active users of the products. Although it may be difficult to segment posters with only one post, frequent posters can provide a relatively comprehensive set of segmentation variables. In this case, some general motivational themes found were the need for "being in the know," "finding deals," and the desire to "give back."

Conclusion

Companies have discovered that they can compete far more efficiently if they gain a true, 360-degree view of their customers. The feedback that current and potential customers provide in blogs, forums, and other online spaces provides a rich source of feedback. Using Text Analytics to monitor this information helps organizations gauge customer reaction to products and services and, when combined with analysis of "structured" transactional data, delivers predictive insights into customer behavior. This case described how Text Analytics was applied to information posted by users of travel and hospitality services, but the same techniques can be applied to other industries. A company might find, for example, that when it launches a special promotion, customers mention the offer frequently in their online posts. Text Analytics can help identify this increase, as well as the ratio of positive/negative posts relating to the promotion. It can be a powerful validation tool to complement other primary and secondary customer research and feedback management initiatives. Companies that improve their ability to navigate and text-mine the boards and blogs relevant to their industry are likely to gain a considerable information advantage over their competitors. Source: Anderson Analytics, LLC (www. andersonanalytics.com).

Review Questions

1. What is Text Analytics, and why it is useful?
2. Differentiate between static and dynamic social media text.
3. Discuss different social media texts.
4. Explain the four main purposes of social media Text Analytics.
5. Explain the common social media text analysis steps.

Chapter 10 Citations

1. Redmore, S. "Text Analytics in 7 minutes." Lexalytics. April 27, 2016. www. lexalytics.com/lexablog/2016/text_analytics. Accessed April 15, 2017.

2. "5 Minutes with Ingo: Making sense of Text Analytics." YouTube. March 18, 2015. www.youtube.com/watch?v=FsP3Z5ieos8. Accessed April 15, 2017.

3. "What is opinion mining (sentiment mining)?" WhatIs.com. http:// searchbusinessanalytics.techtarget.com/definition/opinion-mining-sentiment-mining. Accessed April 15, 2017.

4. "Identifying the political impact of US talk shows." www.qsrinternational.com/ case-studies/impact-of-us-shows. Accessed April 15, 2017.

5. Hitlin, P. "Methodology: How Crimson Hexagon works." April 1, 2015. www. journalism.org/2015/04/01/methodology-crimson-hexagon. Accessed April 15, 2017.

6. Jurkowitz, M. and P. Hitlin. "Twitter users give Christie negative marks on bridge scandal." January 10, 2014. www.pewresearch.org/fact-tank/2014/01/10/ twitter-users-give-christie-negative-marks-on-bridge-scandal. Accessed April 15, 2017.

7. "Demystifying #MachineLearning part 2." https://mymeedia.com/stages/tech/post/24435859. Accessed April 15, 2017.

8. Bowden, G. "Bible and Quran text analysis reveals 'violence' more common in Old and New Testement." Huffington Post UK." February 9, 2016. www.huffingtonpost.co.uk/2016/02/09/bible-and-quran-text-analysis_n_9192596.html. Accessed April 15, 2017.

9. Kalafatis, T. "Using data science on TripAdvisor reviews (Part 1)." July 19, 2013. www.smartdatacollective.com/themoskalafatis/135106/using-data-science-tripadvisor-reviews-part-1. Accessed April 15, 2017.

10. Huijnen, P. "From keyword searching to concept mining." December 4, 2015. https://pimhuijnen.com/2015/12/04/from-keyword-searching-to-concept-mining. Accessed April 15, 2017.

11. Assessed from Google Books Ngram Viewer and shortened via Bit.ly, http://bit.ly/compareDM-WA. Accessed April 15, 2017.

12. Woodie, A. "Predicting consumer behavior drives growth of Text Analytics." January 16, 2015. www.datanami.com/2015/01/16/predicting-consumer-behavior-drives-growth-text-analytics. Accessed April 15, 2017.

13. Press, G. "12 Big Data definitions: What's yours?" Forbes. September 3, 2014. www.forbes.com/sites/gilpress/2014/09/03/12-big-data-definitions-whats-yours. Accessed April 15, 2017.

14. Nguyen, C. "What 24000 Facebook confession posts tell us about college." June 23, 2015. http://motherboard.vice.com/read/what-24000-facebook-confession-posts-tell-us-about-college. Accessed April 15, 2017.

15. Watcher, B. "Natural language processing in health care: The breakthrough we've been waiting for." July 20, 2015. www.kevinmd.com/blog/2015/07/natural-language-processing-in-health-care-the-breakthrough-weve-been-waiting-for.html. Accessed April 15, 2017.

16. Ellis, J. "The New York Times built a robot to help make article tagging easier." July 30, 2015. www.niemanlab.org/2015/07/the-new-york-times-built-a-robot-to-help-making-article-tagging-easier. Accessed April 15, 2017.

17. Elgammal, A. "Creating computer vision and machine learning algorithms that can analyze works of art." www.mathworks.com/company/newsletters/articles/creating-computer-vision-and-machine-learning-algorithms-that-can-analyze-works-of-art.html. Accessed April 15, 2017.

18. Brown, M.S. "Text & the city: Municipalities discover Text Analytics." January 16, 2014. www.allanalytics.com/author.asp?doc_id=271089. Accessed April 15, 2017.

19. Grimes, S. "Text Analytics 2014: Q&A with Fiona McNeill." The Huffington Post. April 21, 2014. www.huffingtonpost.com/seth-grimes/text-analytics-2014-qa-wi_b_5146419.html. Accessed April 15, 2017.

20. Marshall, P. "NASA applies deep-diving Text Analytics to airline safety." GCN. October 26, 2012, https://gcn.com/articles/2012/10/26/nasa-applies-text-analytics-to-airline-safety.aspx. Accessed April 15, 2017.

21. Rose, S. "3 insurance business applications for Text Analytics." January 9, 2014. www.insurancetech.com/3-insurance-business-applications-for-text-analytics/a/d-id/1314975?. Accessed April 15, 2017.

22. "Text, sentiment & Social Analytics in the year ahead." January 11, 2016. https://breakthroughanalysis.com/2016/01/11/10-text-sentiment-social-analytics-trends-for-2016. Accessed April 15, 2017.

23. Socher, R. "Parsing natural scenes and natural language with recursive neural networks." October 6, 2013. www.socher.org/index.php/Main/ParsingNaturalScenesAndNaturalLanguageWithRecursiveNeuralNetworks. Accessed April 15, 2017.

24. "Author age prediction from text using linear regression—Washington." http://homes.cs.washington.edu/~nasmith/papers/nguyen+smith+rose.latech11.pdf. Accessed April 15, 2017.

25. Joshi, M., D. Das, K. Gimpel, and N.A. Smith. "Movie reviews and revenues: An experiment in text regression." www.cs.cmu.edu/~maheshj/pubs/joshi+das+gimpel+smith.naacl2010.pdf. Accessed April 15, 2017.

26. "Text analysis in incident duration prediction—MIT." http://ares.lids.mit.edu/fm/documents/textanalysis.pdf. Accessed April 15, 2017.

27. Adwere-Boamah, J. "Multiple logistic regression analysis of cigarette use among high school students." www.aabri.com/manuscripts/10617.pdf. Accessed April 15, 2017.

28. M.L. Newman, J.W. Pennebaker, D.S. Berry, and J.M. Richards. "Lying words: Predicting deception from linguistic styles." www.albany.edu/~zg929648/PDFs/Newman.pdf. Accessed April 15, 2017.

29. Ifrim, G., G. Bakir, and G. Weikum. "Fast logistic regression for text categorization with variable-length n-grams." August 24, 2008. http://dl.acm.org/citation.cfm?id=1401936. Accessed April 15, 2017.

30. "5 minutes with Ingo: Decision trees." YouTube. March 25, 2015. www.youtube.com/watch?v=xohJ1Vu-3xY. Accessed April 15, 2017.

31. "Startseite—Fachschaft Informatik." www.fachschaft.informatik.tu-darmstadt.de. Accessed April 15, 2017.

32. "5 minutes with Ingo: Naïve Bayes." YouTube. April 15, 2015. www.youtube.com/watch?v=IlVINQDk4o8. Accessed April 15, 2017.

33. Waugh, R. "Everything you see is illusion, scientist warns—and reality is MUCH weirder." Metro. http://metro.co.uk/2016/04/25/everything-you-see-is-an-illusion-scientist-warns-and-reality-is-much-weirder-5838949. Accessed April 15, 2017.

34. "Tweet Topic Explorer—Neoformix." http://tweettopicexplorer.neoformix.com. Accessed April 15, 2017.

35. "K-means algorithm demo." YouTube. May 2, 2013. www.youtube.com/watch?v=zHbxbb2ye3E. Accessed April 15, 2017.

36. "Top 10 data mining algorithms in plain English." May 2, 2015. http://rayli.net/blog/data/top-10-data-mining-algorithms-in-plain-english. Accessed April 15, 2017.

37. "The difference between segmentation and clustering." Mixotricha. July 17, 2010. https://zyxo.wordpress.com/2010/07/17/the-difference-between-segmentation-and-clustering. Accessed April 15, 2017.

38. Young, F.W. "Multidimensional scaling." http://forrest.psych.unc.edu/teaching/p208a/mds/mds.html. Accessed April 15, 2017.

39. "Text Analysis 101: A basic understanding for business users." January 20, 2015. http://blog.aylien.com/post/104768074963/text-analysis-101-a-basic-understanding-for. Accessed April 15, 2017.

40. "Support vector machine." Wikipedia. https://en.wikipedia.org/wiki/Support_vector_machine. Accessed April 15, 2017.

41. "5 Minutes With Ingo: Understanding support vector machines." YouTube. March 11, 2015. www.youtube.com/watch?v=YsiWisFFruY. Accessed April 15, 2017.

42. "K-means clustering example (Python)." April 27, 2011. http://blog.mpacula.com/2011/04/27/k-means-clustering-example-python. Accessed April 15, 2017.

43. Winkler, R., D. Wakabayashi, and E. Dwoskin. "Apple buys artificial-intelligence startup Emotient. WSJ. January 7, 2016. www.wsj.com/articles/apple-buys-artificial-intelligence-startup-emotient-1452188715. Accessed April 15, 2017.

44. "Emotient facial expression technology demo." YouTube. June 13, 2013. www.youtube.com/watch?v=7BiPZ1gHpEw. Accessed April 15, 2017.

45. "Request demo." iMotions. January 6, 2017. https://imotions.com/requestdemo. Accessed April 15, 2017.

46. "LaMem demo." http://memorability.csail.mit.edu/demo.html. Accessed April 15, 2017.

47. "MeaningCloud text mining solutions." www.meaningcloud.com. Accessed April 15, 2017.

48. "Dandelion." https://dandelion.eu. Accessed April 15, 2017.

49. "API Demo." http://apidemo.theysay.io. Accessed April 15, 2017.

50. "Pingar API Demos." http://apidemo.pingar.com/Default.aspx. Accessed April 15, 2017.

51. "Semantria Sentiment Analysis Tools." www.lexalytics.com/semantria/excel. Accessed April 15, 2017.

52. "SAS Text Miner." http://support.sas.com/software/products/txtminer. Accessed April 15, 2017.

53. "IBM SPSS." www.ibm.com/analytics/us/en/technology/spss. Accessed April 15, 2017.

54. "OdinText." http://odintext.com. Accessed April 15, 2017.

55. "Lexalytics." www.lexalytics.com. Accessed April 15, 2017.

56. "Buyer beware: What Text Analytics providers won't tell you." OdinText. October 26, 2016. http://odintext.com/blog/buyer-beware-what-text-analytics-providers-wont-tell-you. Accessed April 15, 2017.

57. *Emotions in Social Psychology*." www.amazon.com/Emotions-Social-Psychology-Key-Readings/dp/0863776833. Accessed April 15, 2017.

58. "Buyer beware: What Text Analytics providers won't tell you." OdinText. October 26, 2016. http://odintext.com/blog/buyer-beware-what-text-analytics-providers-wont-tell-you. Accessed April 15, 2017.

Geo-Location Analytics

Geo-location analytics deals with mapping, visualizing, and mining the location of people, data, and other resources. All sectors, including business, government, nonprofit, and academics, can benefit from location analytics. Thanks to the GPS (global positioning systems) embedded in mobile devices, providing location-based services, products, and information is becoming a reality. In a recent study, scientists used 6 million geo-located Twitter messages to observe the "heartbeat" of New York City.[1] With the dataset, the scientists could study and map the waking, sleeping, commuting, working, and leisure dynamics of the people living in the city during the weekdays and weekends. Such geo-analytics can be instrumental in better understanding our cities and human behaviors in time and space. Most people are not entirely aware of the extent they are being tracked within social and digital media; existing legislation to define and protect privacy has not kept pace with the technology. Most people who install apps on their phones routinely allow certain default permissions, such as location tracking, to remain active, perhaps without realizing the full extent of the tracking it allows. People are unaware that many companies mine their data as part of their business model and sell the data to third parties (for third-party data). However, many people do not seem to realize that third parties are mining their data. For example, ride sharing platform, Uber, recently rolled out a new feature to its mobile app that lets users track their friends and family in real time while taking Uber rides.[2]

A recent Columbia Business School study of worldwide Internet users, summarized in eMarketer, indicated that 80% of those surveyed would be willing to share their personal data in exchange for cash back, location-based discounts, or other rewards.[3]

Sources of Geo-Location Data

Location information can come from a variety of sources, including the following:

- **Postal address:** Most Business Analytics applications rely on address information of their customers, including city names, locality names, and postal or zip codes.
- **Latitude and longitude:** In geography, latitude (shown as a horizontal line on a globe) and longitude (shown as a vertical line on a globe) are used to find the exact location on Earth.
- **GPS-Based:** GPS is a satellite-based navigation system that can be used to find exact locations, people, and resources. Mobile analytics mostly rely on GPS-based location data. GPS-based location analytics can provide us the most accurate location of social media users. Note: Most GPS providers, especially those for cars, such as Garmin, are dying out because roads are constantly changing and providers have not been able to keep up with it. Alternatively, people prefer to use Google Maps and Apple Maps from their mobile devices because they are free and constantly automatically updated. For example, Google Maps lets users see where traffic is congested and choose alternate routes. Google Maps allows users to download map data to their mobile devices so that users can continue to get directions when there are poor or absent Internet connections.
- **IP-based:** Public IP (Internet protocol) can be used to determine the location of Internet users. An IP address is an exclusive numerical address (like a home address) assigned to a device connected to the Internet. Different regions of the world are assigned a specific block of public IP addresses; hence, it can be used to mine approximate geo-location of Internet users.

Categories of Geo-Location Analytics

Based on its scope, Location Analytics can be broadly classified into two types:

1. Business data-driven Geo-Location Analytics
2. Social media data-driven Geo-Location Analytics

Business Data-Driven Geo-Location Analytics

Business, data-driven Geo-Location Analytics, deals with mapping, visualizing, and mining of location data to reveal patterns, trends, and relationships hidden in tabular business data. The applications of location data vary by country. For example, location-based advertising may be more prevalent in the US and Singapore than Canada, the UK, or Germany (because these markets are less developed in this respect, or, in Germany's case, have strong privacy laws that limit how location-based data can be harvested, shared, and used).

Capitalizing on the data stored in a company database, Location Analytics can map and capture vast amounts of geo-specific data. The geo-data provides information, products, and services that are based on where customers are, as covered in Chapter 9 (such as basic radius targeting, retargeting with geo-location, contextual local targeting, iBeacons, etc.). It is possible to recommend the nearest convenience store, coffee shop, taxi, or even probable social relations by using applications such as Yelp and Foursquare.

In fact, a study by the Location Based Marketing Association (LBMA) and summarized by eMarketer, the most attractive features of location marketing applications are their hyper-precise targeting capabilities.[4]

Applications of Business Data-Driven Geo-Location Analytics

Powerful Intelligence

Simple maps have been widely used, but they are limited in providing insightful details. Using sophisticated mapping techniques, such as clustering, heat mapping, data aggregation (e.g., aggregating data to regions), and color-coded mapping, can generate powerful business intelligence.[5]

Geo-Enrichment

Simple data maps can be enriched with customer data, including demographic, consumer spending, lifestyle, and locations.[6] For example, where do loyal customers spend most of their time?

Collaboration and Sharing

Maps are easy to understand and are excellent communication and collaboration tools. Location Analytics can map business data for collaboration across the organization. It can also be used for information sharing purposes with customers. At the end of this chapter, a step-by-step tutorial is provided to map sample tabular business data using Google Fusion Tables. Using Google Fusion Tables, the reader can map data and display and share the results as maps, tables, and charts.

Social Media Data-Driven Geo-Location Analytics

Social media data-driven analytics rely on social media location data to mine and map the locations of social media users, content, and data; social media location information comes mainly from GPS and IPs. Users also willingly give out their location when they post content via social media sites such as Instagram because it allows them to choose their location on a picture and display it with their post.

Uses of Social Media-Based Geo-Location Analytics

Social media location-based services are becoming a day-to-day reality. Organizations use location-based services for a variety of purposes, including the following:

Recommendation Purposes
Organizations can harvest location data to recommend products, services, and social events to potential customers in real time as they approach certain localities. For example, Tinder recommends possible social relationships based on the location of users and Yelp also has locale and venue recommendations that it provides to users.

Customer Segmentation
Social media location data can be used to segment customers based on their geographic location. Tweepsmap (https://tweepsmap.com), for example, can be used to geo-locate your Twitter followers by country, state, or city.

Advertising
Location-based advertising allows targeted marketing and promotion campaign mostly delivered through mobile devices to reach specific target audiences. Facebook allows members to do this when running Facebook advertising. Geo-targeting accuracy and options have improved, and social media platforms have rich advertising offerings such as Facebook's Local Awareness Advertising that can target potential customers within one mile of a business. Because of geo-location services, a website like Google could recommend the closest resource, based on a mobile search query, so the person can find it and go there efficiently.

Information Request
Based on their current location, customers can apply for a product, service, or resource (e.g., the nearest coffee shop, restaurant, or parking lot).

Alerts
Location data can be used to send and receive alerts and notifications. For example, mobile device users can receive sales and promotion alerts, traffic congestion alerts, speed limit warnings, storm warnings, or text in any traffic or police locations.

Search and Rescue
Geo-tagged location data is vital in search and rescue operations. Geotagging is the process of adding extremely precise location metadata to various media such as a mobile application, tweet, photograph, video, websites, SMS messages, or QR Codes, etc. For example, Agos[7] is a geo-tagging and reporting platform that enables communities to deal with climate change adaptation and disaster risk reduction.

Navigation
Mobile- and GPS-based navigation services and apps assist us in finding addresses. Be-On-Road,[8] for instance, is a free offline turn-by-turn GPS navigation app for Android devices.

Location Analytics and Privacy Concerns

While location-based services bring ease, convenience, and safety to customers and value to businesses, they also raise serious privacy issues related to the collection, retention, use, and disclosure of location information.[9] Tracking, data mining, and storing location information can endanger some fundamental human rights, such as freedom of movement and freedom from being observed. Minch raises several issues arising from location-based services, including the following:

- Should users of location-enabled devices be informed when location tracking is in use?
- Should users of location-enabled devices be permitted to control the storage of location information?
- Should location information as stored be personally identifiable, or should the user have the option to preserve degrees of anonymity?
- What legal protection should a person's historical location information have against unreasonable search and seizure?
- To what extent should users of location-based services be allowed to choose their level of identifiability/anonymity?
- What level of disclosure control should be dictated by government regulation? By the affected individual customers, users, etc.? By other parties?
- What regulatory legislation is appropriate to assure citizens' rights of privacy in an era of location-aware mobile devices? For example, should people get a cut of the money associated with their geo-location services, especially when their personal information gets sold to third-party companies for profit and competitive advantage?

Location Analytics Tools

- **Google Fusion Tables**: Google Fusion Tables is a Web service to geo-tag, store, share, query, and visualize tabular business data overlaid on Google Maps. This chapter provides a detailed tutorial on Google Fusion Tables.
- **Agos**: Agos is a geo-tagging and reporting platform that helps communities deal with climate change adaptation and disaster risk reduction.
- **Tweepsmap**: Tweepsmap maps your Twitter followers by country, state, or city.
- **Trendsmap**: Trendsmap is a real-time tool that maps the latest trends from Twitter, anywhere in the world.
- **Followerwonk**: This tool helps a Twitter user perform basic Twitter analytics, such as, who are their followers, where they located and when they tweet. The tool can be accessed via https://moz.com/followerwonk.
- **Esri**: Esri's GIS (geographic information systems) is software to map, visualize, question, analyze, and interpret data to understand relationships, patterns, and trends (www.esri.com).
- **Geofeedia, WeLink, Picodash, etc.:** Software that filters social media post that is done at a location (latitude/longitude). The range of accuracy is approximately 20 feet; Instagram and Twitter provide a vast amount of data that can be filtered by location. Other platforms such as Facebook provide much less data, because it is secured behind a membership firewall. The tools can be accessed at (www.geofeedia.com, www.welink.com, www.picodash.com). Caveat, privacy laws are beginning to constrain the capabilities of some of these platforms such as Geofeedia.[10]

Geo-Location Based Platforms

A newer variation of Web Analytics looks at geo-location, and the data broadcast from mobile devices. This geodata can function very much like a Web Analytics JavaScript beacon, except devices that are moving through the 3D world are tracked instead of a customer on a website.

Geo-Data Collect Directly from Mobile Devices (Intent-Driven)

Mobile devices provide unique capabilities such as:

- Click to call
- Click to share
- Click to calendar
- Click to website/URL
- Click to drive
- Mobile coupons
- Portable video (with streaming capabilities)
- Downloads
- Bluetooth (iBeacon, etc.)
- Touch sensors
- Virtual reality (with specific headsets/visors)
- Augmented reality (with the use of camera / gyroscope)
- Broadcast of geo-data on device location (lat/long and X, Y, Z axis) to ISPs, mobile device manufacturers, and in some cases, select mobile apps (such as Facebook, Twitter, etc.)

Figure 11.1 Mobile device capabilities.
Source: WebMetricsGuru Inc.

Mobile applications provide a wealth of data, much of it is collected by mobile analytics platforms, even Google Analytics (for apps) can gather and display the data if it has been configured to do so. Much of the scraped data produced by smartphones comes from data aggregators who collect it from social media platforms such as Instagram and Twitter. Facebook and LinkedIn data is much harder to collect, but even little bits of Facebook data can be very illuminating. Based on personal observations by one of the co-authors when using Geofeedia and other geo-location tracking platforms, the amount of traffic gathered in this way is probably in the range of 1–1.5% of actual traffic (people carrying mobile devices that are being tracked in a specific location).[11] Often there is enough traffic (devices) in a specific location that is being examined to provide real business insight.

The information gathered in this way is not anonymous data, as it usually includes social media handles of users along with images and text they post along with a timestamp and exact location within 20 feet. It is unclear what laws govern the privacy of public geo-data. However, the policies and laws around this are likely to change in time—although it is impossible to know yet by how much.

iBeacon and Bluetooth

Locational data can be gathered with precise location up to a few feet with Bluetooth based transmitters and receivers (it sounds like a form of radio, and in a way, it is, because most of the data is broadcasted from Bluetooth transmitters). One feature about iBeacon is that it is relatively inexpensive to set up and deploy, and there are integrated middleware platforms that provide the iBeacons together with campaign management and analytics.

One issue that iBeacon solves is privacy. iBeacons are an opt-in technology and users must first run an application on their mobile device that then broadcasts their location and communicates with the nearest iBeacon transmitter, allowing for a customized message to be sent to the user/customer as they walk by a particular area. iBeacons, although still in an early stage, can provide many uses, it can be expected to be widely deployed soon. iBeacons are an Apple protocol, but it has been widely deployed since launching in 2013; any mobile device running application can communicate with iBeacons placed in a physical location.[12]

Geo-Local Data Collection

This section of the chapter deals with how our activities in the real world are captured and gathered based on our location, which can provide actionable data for many organizations who collect it.

iBeacons

iBeacons are Bluetooth-based radio technology released by Apple in late 2013; since that time, they have become very popular with retail outlets. It is a relatively new technology that extends Location Services in iOS. Adobe Analytics can target in-store shoppers with customized in-app messages, based on all the associated data collected from iBeacons.

Uses of iBeacons

- Adobe Marketing Cloud/Adobe Analytics now offers "Intelligent Location Targeting." iBeacon data is gathered to create the specific content to be sent to the consumers as they enter the radii of iBeacon spots (and track the interaction via Adobe Analytics). The data can also be used to develop specific psychographic and geo-demographic shopper profiles based on in-store behavior.[13]
- Mesh networks (UBeacons) have been made necessary by the dense iBeacon deployments (too many iBeacon transmitters placed too close to each other).[14]
- Deploying iBeacons in museums or galleries can be used to provide more information about the artist or pieces when a visitor is nearby, even when there isn't any Wi-Fi. The possibilities for UBeacon mesh are limitless.
- Determine the best time to go to a local retail store to avoid crowds or even to navigate Black Friday crowds. Black Friday sales simply aren't as relevant as they used to be. That is because most Black Friday sales start then, and end on the following Monday. As most sales also take place online, with purchases shipped to the shopper, it is becoming less attractive to travel to the brick-and-mortar stores. Thus, this type of information may end up encouraging people to shop online (skipping the physical store altogether), or on Cyber Monday.

Near Field Communications (NFC)

NFC is radio-frequency identification technology originally developed in the 1980s (known as RFID), allowing compatible hardware to communicate with passive electronic devices using radio waves; RFID is used for product identification, authentication, and inventory tracking.[15] Near Field Communications creates a cell area with a 150-foot radius (geo-fencing) with mobile devices and is like a "moving Web Analytics" data collection pixel. Mobile devices that are in the radius of a "named" geo-fenced area receive communications about businesses in the location. NFC is a networking technology that several retail stores and even museums/public spaces are experimenting with, including the Brooklyn Museum of Art and the Museum of Natural History/Hayden Planetarium. Only a few years ago, near-field communication was supposed to be the technology to transform the retail shopping experience and bring it up to date with how the online shopping experience is from a data perspective. The issue with NFC technology was that it was not a widely adopted standard available in most mobile devices until recently. Now, Android Pay and Apple Pay utilize NFC technology so that users with an Android/Apple phone can simply tap their devices to a pay screen at a store to pay for their goods. The Android/Apple Pay accounts are connected to the user's bank account.

Privacy Issues with Geo-Data

As a subject ripe for legitimate debate on our privacy rights, geo-data capture should be near the top of the list of things to be concerned about in the era of Snowden, along with violence and terrorism threats.[16] Law enforcement and schools have begun to use geo-location monitoring of localities.[17] At universities, students have been using applications such as Yik-Yak to find out what is happening nearby on campus and send anonymous messaging (and monitoring) of nearby users.[18]

Marketing automation is also becoming more sophisticated, and the raw data that has been collected by default from mobile devices have been surfacing up into application interfaces where it can be selected and used by marketers.

For example, Myrna Arias, a central California woman, got fired after she uninstalled a working app that tracked her exact location 24/7 (even when she was not working). The app—Xora StreetSmart—is intended to let companies manage employees working away from the office. Its creators, ClickSoftware, says it lets firms "see the location of every mobile worker on a Google Map." However, ClickSoftware does not seem to envision the app as a 24-hour tracker, telling potential clients that "field employees" should launch the app "when [they] start their day." However, it is not hard to see how the information could be misused or abused, or just enter a gray area where the legal precedent has not been fully mapped out.[19]

However, there are ways to use geo-location data without giving up one's privacy; for example, users can input their zip code information into some apps rather than enabling location services and still get access to local data.

iBeacons

iBeacons have been successfully integrated with CRM (customer relationship management), email, and Web Analytics datasets. Web Analytics vendors are beginning to configure their platforms to track iBeacons. Facebook started to deploy iBeacons connected with location pages of businesses integrated with Facebook pages for business.[20] In this implementation, the follower of a business page is greeted upon arrival at the site, and hints/messages from page admins are displayed on the Facebook app for the fan as they enter the location. One issue with iBeacons is correctly setting them up, as placing them too close together can provide incorrect responses from the transmitters, and the wrong one may respond first. As with anything else, the more this platform technology is deployed and evolves, the better it will get, and the more experienced users (and particularly retail businesses) it will have.

List Building Becomes Much Better and Easier by Using Geo-Location

An important aspect of marketing involves creating and maintaining a list of contacts. Collecting geo-data makes list building so much simpler and more accurate because marketers can capture people in a certain place and time in the act of doing specific activities. Geo-location analysis is a much better way to get at a customer's mindset than paying attention to what they have said (or not said). However, there is a danger on depending on location capabilities to make up for real customer outreach and marketing; it is easy for marketers to become lazy and complacent in how they deal with their customers. Capturing geo-data is just another way of creating a list of people to target with marketing. Marketing has always been full of wasteful expenditures.[21] However, technology alone cannot make up for poorly thought-out or poorly delivered marketing.

Capturing Public Geo-Data

Most people are totally unaware of just how public their geo-data is (and that can be very dangerous, as other third parties are easily able to mine the location data for a variety of purposes, not all of them benign to the public). For example, more than half of all (redundant) tweets have latitude and longitude metadata that is available at the API level and can be captured by anyone, and it is easy to amass a considerable amount of data with little effort or cost.

Marketers Like Using Geo-Data

Geo-data is considered by senior IT decision makers to be the most actionable (and valuable) of all and is amazingly easy to collect as shown in Figure 11.2. It is easy to

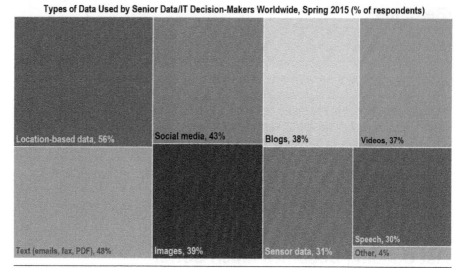

Types of Data Used by Senior Data/IT Decision-Makers Worldwide, Spring 2015 (% of respondents)

Location-based data, 56%   Social media, 43%   Blogs, 38%   Videos, 37%

Text (emails, fax, PDF), 48%   Images, 39%   Sensor data, 31%   Speech, 30%   Other, 4%

Figure 11.2 Types of data used by senior IT decision-makers worldwide—Spring 2015, based on percentage of respondents.
Source: WebMetricsGuru Inc., with data provided by eMarketer.

see why marketers put a high importance on geo-data. Geo-data contains the time, exact location, individuals' identity (social media handle). Also, geo-data often has an image of what the individual looked at or a selfie. Because geo-data is so specific, it is much more actionable than social media data that is not geo-specific. Enterprises have the resources and business reasons to scale this data more than individuals, or smaller businesses could.

Geo-Location Case Studies

Metropolitan Museum of Art

Note: The author conducted this study on his own without any help or collaboration with the Museum.[22] Among the things that this presentation highlighted are:

- There was six times as much activity (verbatim) around the Temple of Dendur than keyword activity with that term used in the verbatim.
- As shown in Table 11.1, there were 16 activities detected using the geo-social data pulled from Geofeedia.com (the platform used at the time to collect the data). Each activity was identified and counted, suggestions for how the Museum could better use its data was presented at ClickZ. 86% of the Metropolitan Museum's visitors only visited once (as shown in Figure 11.3), and the MET knows next to nothing about them, but easily could by using platforms such as Picodash ($8.00 USD for Instagram monitoring), Geofeedia, and Welink.

Ethnographic research and storytelling might be the key to finding patterns in the data that are meaningful.[23]

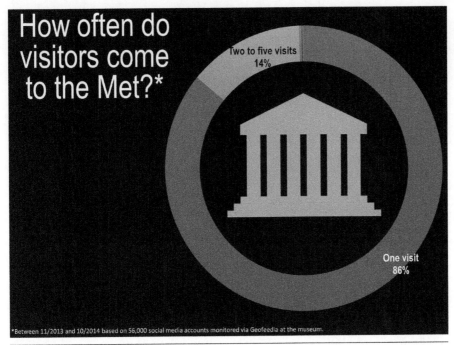

Figure 11.3 Visitation at the Metropolitan Museum of Art between November 2013 and October 2014.
Source: WebMetricsGuru Inc.

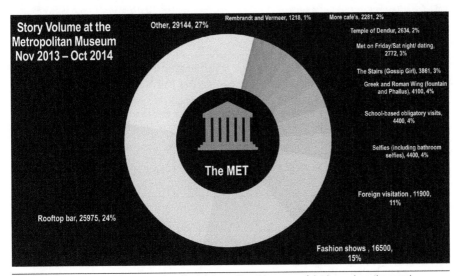

Figure 11.4 Geo-data harvested at the Metropolitan Museum of Art based on themes/stories observed to be taking place at the museum, using a platform called Geofeedia during November 2013 and October 2014.
Source: WebMetricsGuru Inc.

- As long as users and stakeholders have a "story" to search for in the data then that story was much easier to find.
- There were several actionable suggestions, and the key is storytelling that communicates the story and insights from analytics.

Met Stories

The following 16 stories result from ethnographic research done onsite during frequent visits to the museum, along with additional observations that were used to find patterns in the data.

Table 11.1 The 16 data stories observed to be taking place daily at the Metropolitan Museum of Art during the observation period of November 2013 to October 2014.

Stories 1–8	Stories 9–16
1. Temple of Dendur: Family interconnection, picnic area.	9. Come to the Met on Friday and Saturday nights: to be seen dressed for sexual notoriety/dating.
2. Rooftop Bar: Feeling more comfortable in intellectual environments.	10. Upper East Side intellectuals and dilettantes: They come to every Special Exhibit.
3. More Cafes: Cafés are driving more visitors, esp. to the interior of the Met.	11. Name recognition: Van Gogh, Monet, Manet, Renoir.
4. Rembrandt and Vermeer: Popular icons.	12. The Stairs: *Gossip Girl*, perhaps other TV shows such as *Girls*.
5. Children's access: For wide-reaching youngsters in the classroom.	13. Fashion Shows: (at intervals) mostly when these shows are active, otherwise not.
6. Greek/Roman Wing: Visitors display tactile play with fountain and possibly take (or leave) a coin.	14. Foreign visitation: How many visitors from foreign countries?
7. Astor Court: Meditate, contemplate, and see fish in pod.	15. School-based obligatory visits.
8. Greek Wing: Visitors "incidentally" mock phallus.	16. Selfie behavior (next to art, and in bathrooms).

Source: WebMetricsGuru Inc.

Tapping into Geo-data Capture to Make More Efficient Marketing Decisions

Marketers are beginning to think "out of the box" with geo-data and come up with a wish-list of the activities and audiences they can now track at a micro-level of precision.

Some Examples of Geo-Data Tracking[24]

- Retailers can recognize customers based on their cell phone signal when they enter the store and link this to the customer's rewards card and social media accounts.

- Retailers can follow customers through the store by using their GEO coordinates and learn what products the customer prefers and provide a custom offer based on it (in real time).

iBeacon Case Studies

- "Hold the beacon: McDonald's tests wireless offers near stores." McDonald's sales were up by more than 8% when using iBeacon technology in a trial run taking place in 26 stores.[25]
- "San Francisco airport beacons help the blind get around using their phones." The airport has teamed up with Indoo.rs to unveil a Bluetooth beacon system that helps blind passengers find their way through Terminal 2 using only their phone.[26]
- "Virgin Atlantic unveils new airport terminal experience powered by Apple's iBeacon."[27]
- "New York museum uses iBeacons to create a 'digital minefield'." The New Museum used iBeacons as part of an art exhibition. Visitors to the museum donated five dollars to help various countries get rid of hidden land mines and helping to prevent the deaths and injuries which result from them.[28]
- "The Super Bowl kicks off iBeacon season." How iBeacons were used at the Super Bowl 2014. Attendees got popup messages with advertising, offers to buy merchandise and information about NFL exhibits.[29]

Case Study: The "Owl Bus"[30]

Background

The Seoul Night Bus, also known as the "Owl Bus," is the brand name of the Seoul (South Korea) city's intracity buses that run nine routes exclusively from midnight to 5 a.m. Like an owl, animated in the dark with its glowing yellow eyes, the "Owl Bus" was born to make Seoul's public transportation service operate around the clock, carrying the city's late night commuters. As the service is the first of its kind in Korea, policymakers struggled to shape action plans in detail. The biggest task was to address issues such as selection of the routes, ensuring efficient operation, and passengers' safety and convenience. Location analytics and social media help Seoul Metropolitan Government (SMG) to realize the "Owl Bus" project and overcome these challenges.

The Problem

Since the subway line No. 1 opened in 1974 through to the transformation reform carried out in 2004, the SMG has steadily introduced measures to ensure greater convenience and better mobility of the citizens. However, students and workers (such as sanitary workers or small business owners) who return home late at night found it hard to benefit from the pre-existing systems. Most of them suffer from poor working conditions and low salaries, yet they still had to pay the late-night extra charge when taking taxis to return home.

The second issue was the growing inconvenience due to late-night taxis' refusal of passengers and illegal operation. During late night and dawn hours, there are far fewer taxis than people who are trying to hail a cab. Thus, illegal operations are prevalent by taxi drivers demanding special fares, causing serious inconvenience to citizens. Additionally, there are practical limitations in controlling such irregularities. There is a shortage of police officers responsible for preventing such violations, and even if the police catch an offender red-handed, it is hard to obtain evidence to prove the driver's act of refusing passengers or demanding illegal excess fares.

The third issue was related to the public–private consensus regarding the need for new means of transportation to support urban dwellers' economic activities. Seoul, transformed into a global city within just 50 years, is emerging as a prime location in the world economy. As the city's industrial, economic, and cultural activities expand in size and scope, the citizens reached a consensus on the need for a bus service that operates from midnight to dawn. It was also considered that advanced nations such as Germany and the UK have already run such services to promote the safety of citizens and their rights to mobility.

Private bus companies' selective operation on profitable routes was a long-running concern for the SMG. Thus, it shifted from a private to a quasi-public bus operation system. In the new system, Seoul manages the bus routes and revenues while the private companies operate the buses.

The Solution

Since 2012, the SMG has operated the 120 Dasan Call Center and the official blog to listen better to the voices of the citizens, and developed various policy measures based on the information collected through these channels. Along the way, an opinion was received that the late-night taxi service is not only difficult to use but also imposes heavy financial burdens on users. An on-site survey conducted for about six months from October 2012 found it necessary to operate a late-night bus service. Thus, starting from April 19, 2013, the city government operated two pilot routes exclusively for an after-midnight service.

The Role of Location Analytics and Social Media

Social media and Location Analytics played a crucial role in expanding the bus routes and selection of the "Owl Bus" brand name. For three months following the launch of the test operation, the service was extremely well-received by 220,000 people, making it justifiable to raise the number of service routes. The seven new lines were determined by taking into consideration the heavy concentration of individuals on the move during late night hours. During the initial stages of mapping out how to operate the Seoul Night Bus, the issue of selecting bus routes emerged. The municipal government color-coded regions by call volume based on the location data provided by a private communication service provider, KT. Then, it analyzed the number of passengers who get on and off at each bus stop in the heavy call volume regions and connected the dots to lead to the most appropriate routes. The data was used to construct a radial shape network linking outer districts of the city with the hub areas such as Jongno and Gwanghwamun. With news regarding the bus service spreading over social media channels, citizens voluntarily suggested naming the late-night bus. Thus, the city government invited public ideas for the naming of the service and, as a result, the brand name "Owl Bus" and "N (Late Night)," and the character that portrays an owl operating a bus were selected. These symbols have been used to mark bus stop signs, bus route maps, and numbers and distinguish the late-night buses from ordinary ones. With the letter "N" in the bus number, the service began its full operation on September 16, 2014.

Results

The service provides citizens with real-time operation information. Anyone who wants to take the "Owl Bus" can check the arrival time and location of the bus stop in advance through its website or smartphone apps. Given that the service operates late at night, safety measures were critical to protect citizens. Besides the protective partition and speeding prevention device, it was made mandatory to inspect the vehicle before driving. The drivers with proven qualifications are also well-remunerated so that they do not have to take on other vocational activities during the daytime hours and can fully concentrate during night-time driving.

The numbers of "Owl Bus" passengers are constantly rising. A total of 1,735,000 people have taken the buses from September 2009 to June 2013, making the average daily passengers stand at around 7,000. As for economic aspects, passengers are expected to save approximately KRW 6,000 as the "Owl Bus" charges KRW 1,850 per trip while the average taxi fare in the same timeframe costs KRW 8,000. Given that the most of the passengers are students, self-employed small business owners, or workers, the service is expected to help stabilize their household finances.

Most passengers are concentrated in the timeframe from midnight to 3 a.m., when students and workers return home completing their after-school self-study and night duties. As the unfrequented time tends to leave them more vulnerable, the "Owl Bus" is considered to help them move more safely. Notably, the "Safe returning-home service" provided in cooperation with the nearby police stations reinforce the safety.

Income Redistribution for the Economically Disadvantaged

Before the operation of the "Owl Bus," one had to pay up to tens of thousands of KRW to move from the city center to a residential district outside the city. However, they now can complete their journey with just KRW 1,850. The savings will lead to higher disposable incomes; income redistribution effects are expected too. As of 2013, the SMG estimates nearly KRW 14.1 billion worth of economic benefits has been redistributed.

Distribution of the Manual for Other Local Governments to Benchmark

As residents of other cities express their interest in the "Owl Bus" through social media channels, local governments and research institutes have inquired about the process in the run-up to the introduction and requested lectures on the "Owl Bus." With many municipal governments expressing their interest, the Busan Metropolitan Government extended its late-night service. In fact, the operation hours of existing intracity buses and other cities such as Ulsan and Daejun are planning to extend their hours of operation as well.

Resources

- **Budget**: To finance the operation of the "Owl Bus," budget provision was needed to pay for the labor costs and the installation of safety facilities such as protective walls for drivers and a speeding prevention system. However, these expenses were covered by the joint management funds for the shift from private to quasi-public bus operation. Consequently, additional costs were not incurred.
- **Technology**: Information systems connected inside the vehicles such as the Bus Management System, the Bus Information Unit, and Bus Information Tool enable comprehensive control of the bus operations, and dynamic adjustment of intervals while providing users and drivers with real-time operation information.
- **Human resources**: The Owl Bus was introduced without incurring additional costs, and increased operation revenues too. The allocated resources are 45 vehicles and a total of 54 workers; 36 for driving and 18 for management.[31]

Tutorial: Mapping with Google Fusion Tables

Google Fusion Tables is a Web service to store, share, query, and visualize tabular business data overlaid on Google Maps. Tabular data can be visualized and shared in a variety of ways, including charts, maps, network graphs, or custom layout. The state of California, for example, shares government datasets using Fusion Tables, where the data can be viewed, filtered, and downloaded by citizens.[32]

The data formats supported by Fusion Tables include spreadsheets, CSV files, and Keyhole Markup Language (KML, a file format used to display and map geographic data). Google also provides the Fusion Tables API[33] for managing data programmatically and an example library of Fusion Tables.[34]

In this tutorial, we will learn how to configure Fusion Tables to map and share location data online.

Tutorial: Getting Started with Fusion Tables

Step 1: Go to www.google.com/fusiontables/ and click on the "Create a Fusion Table" button. For this exercise, we will use data on the location of police stations in Victoria, Australia, downloaded from https://www.data.act.gov.au/Disaster/ACT-Police-Station-Locations/t6hf-u79n in the KML format.

Step 2: Next, the reader will be asked to upload their data into the Fusion Table. To do so, the reader has four options:

1. Upload from a computer
2. Upload from Google Spreadsheets
3. Create an empty table (for manipulating data later)
4. Search other online publicly available data

In this tutorial, we choose the "from this computer" and click "Browse File" to upload the data. Locate the data that will be uploaded and click the "Next" button.

Step 3: Next, choose the format (i.e., comma separated, tab, colon, or another type) of data being uploaded (in this case KML). Leave the other options on their default settings and click the "Next" button.

Step 4: After the data is loaded, make sure that the right row is selected for the column names (which is usually row 1) and click "Next".

Step 5: Once the data is imported, provide the following details and click "Finish".

  Table—Provide a meaningful table name.

  Allow export—If the reader checks this, other users will be able to export their data into a CSV file.

  Attribute data to—Here the reader can write a message that will be displayed when people view or use their data.

  Attribution page link—Provide the attribution page URL or link, if any.

  Description—Provide a description here that may help the reader remember what the data is about.

Step 6: Now the data is uploaded into the Fusion Table, and the reader is ready to process, visualize, and share it.

Step 7: Fusion Tables auto-detect location data and display a tab called "Map of <location column name>." In this case, the "Map" tab is titled "Map of geometry." Click on "Map of geometry" to see a map of the police stations (Figure 11.5).

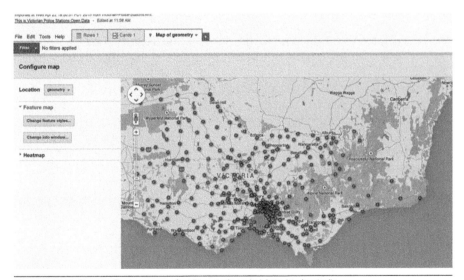

Figure 11.5 Google Fusion map of police stations in Victoria, Australia.
Source: Gohar F. Khan based on mapped data entered Google Fusion Tables.

If the Fusion Table does not automatically detect location information, then the reader needs to configure it manually through the following steps:

1. Click on the "Rows" tab and find the column name that has the location data and clicks on the downward-pointing arrow.
2. Next, click on "Change".
3. On the page that opens, choose "Location" for the type and then click on the "Save" button.

Step 8: Next, double-click on a red placemark to view more information about a police station.

Step 9: Once the map is created, the reader can customize different aspects of it, including creating and customizing charts, creating custom cards, changing marker styles, and apply filters to their data.

Changing marker styles: To modify the marker style (the red dots), use the following steps:

- Ensure that you are on the "Map" tab. Click "Tools→Change map→Change feature styles".
- Click on the "Marker" icon in the left panel and "Fixed" in the right panel.
- Choose a different marker style from the drop-down menu and click "Save".
- The reader can also assign different marker icons to various types of variables by using the "Bucket" option. For example, police stations in the different regions can be marked with different icons.

Filtering data: Filters are variables from the table/data that will be used to filter out data for display. To apply filters to this data, use the following steps:

- Make sure that you are on the "Map" tab. Click on the "Filters" button available at the upper left side of the map.
- Select a filter to apply from the drop-down list (e.g., we chose "Region").

After applying the filter, the reader will be offered all the distinct values for various regions. Users can customize which data appears and how it is displayed.

- Ensure you are on the "Map" tab. Click on the "Tools→Change map", then click the "Change info window" button.
- Click on the checkboxes to add or remove information from the automatic info window template.
- The reader can also customize the overall style and content of the info window template by clicking the "Custom" tab. Once done, click on the "Save" button.

Adding charts: Fusion Tables lets the user add charts to their data so that they compare multiple values at a glance.

- To insert a chart, click on the red plus (+) sign and then click on "Add Chart" from the drop-down menu.
- Once a chart is added, users can choose different variables (e.g., continuous or categorical) to the chart depending on the type of chart you selected (e.g., pie chart, bar graph, line chart, or network chart). A chart type can be changed from the left panel.
- Once the user selects the right type of chart, click on the "Done" button in the upper right-hand corner.

Sharing data: One of the main reasons to use Fusion Tables is to make data available for others to see and download. To share a map, use the following steps:

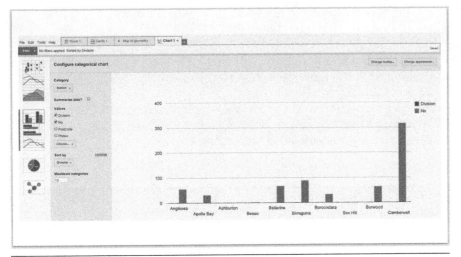

Figure 11.6 Google Fusion charts—configuring charts.
Source: Gohar F. Khan.

- Make sure that reader is on the "Map" tab. Click on the "Tools" menu and then click on "Publish".
- The reader can either share it with a limited number of people through email. Alternatively, the reader can make it available over the Internet for everyone to see. In this exercise, we will make it accessible to the public.
- Click on the "Change" option under "Who has access". A new window will appear. Select the "Public on the web" option and then click "Save".
- Next, the reader will be provided with a link and an HTML code for sharing the data. Copy it and click "Done". The code and the link can be embedded into a blog, a website, or social media platforms. One can always get the link and code by clicking "Tools" and then "Publish".
- In a similar way, the charts that have been created can be shared. Note that to share a chart, the reader must be on the "Chart" tab and then click "Tools→Publish". The reader will be provided with a code and link to share.

Summary

Geo-location data is being abundantly produced and mined for business purposes because it is much easier to target customers and reach them at the precise moment when they are most receptive to the advertising or marketing message. However, geo-location data comes with a price—the vast erosion of the public's privacy. Most people do not know how much of their data is being captured by third parties, or how it is being used (although the data collection is presently legal, in most cases). The legislation is beginning to catch up, but still has a long way to go, as there is a lack of consensus on what geo-location data it is permissible to collect, when, and why.

Review Questions

1. Define Location Analytics.
2. Explain the two main categories of Location Analytics.
3. What are the sources of location data?
4. What are the main applications of business data-driven Location Analytics?
5. What are the main applications of social media data-driven Location Analytics?
6. Discuss privacy concerns related to Location Analytics.

Chapter 11 Citations

1. França, U., H. Sayama, C. McSwiggen, R. Daneshvar, and Y. Bar-Yam (2015) "Visualizing the 'Heartbeat' of a City With Tweets." *Complexity* 21(6): 280–287.

2. Smith, C. "Uber will let you track other people's rides in real time." BGR. May 18, 2016. http://bgr.com/2016/05/18/uber-trip-tracker-family-profile. Accessed April 15, 2017.

3. "Best practices for consumer privacy and personal data: Maximizing value without getting creepy." eMarketer. July 20, 2016. www.emarketer.com/Report/Best-Practices-Consumer-Privacy-Personal-Data-Maximizing-Value-Without-Getting-Creepy/2001804. Accessed April 15, 2017.

4. "Location intelligence, H1 2016: Guidance for US marketers on consumer behavior, data quality and mobile marketing tactics." eMarketer. April 20, 2016, www.emarketer.com/Report/Location-Intelligence-H1-2016-Guidance-US-Marketers-on-Consumer-Behavior-Data-Quality-Mobile-Marketing-Tactics/2001793. Accessed April 15, 2017.

5. Hecht, L. "Location Analytics: The future is where." November 1, 2013. http://insights.wired.com/profiles/blogs/location-analytics-where-the-future-will-be. Accessed April 15, 2017.

6. Hecht, L. "Location Analytics: The future is where." November 1, 2013. http://insights.wired.com/profiles/blogs/location-analytics-where-the-future-will-be. Accessed April 15, 2017.

7. "Rappler Agos." http://agos.rappler.com. Accessed April 15, 2017.

8. "Be-On-Road." www.beonroad.com. Accessed April 15, 2017.

9. Minch, R.P. (2004). *Privacy Issues in Location-Aware Mobile Devices*. The 37th Hawaii International Conference on System Sciences, Big Island, HI, USA. http://scholarworks.boisestate.edu/cgi/viewcontent.cgi?article=1001&context=itscm_facpubs

10. Cameron, D. "Dozens of police-spying tools remain after Facebook, Twitter crack down on Geofeedia." October 11, 2016. www.dailydot.com/layer8/geofeedia-twitter-facebook-instagram-social-media-surveillance. Accessed April 15, 2017.

11. Sponder, M. "Enrich your data to increase converged analytics effectiveness." ClickZ. November 17, 2014. www.clickz.com/enrich-your-data-to-increase-converged-analytics-effectiveness/28712. Accessed April 15, 2017.

12. "iBeacon." Wikipedia. https://en.wikipedia.org/wiki/IBeacon. Accessed April 15, 2017.

13. Akhtar, O. "Adobe Analytics adds in-store messaging capabilities through iBeacon targeting." November 18, 2014. www.dmnews.com/marketing-automation/adobe-analytics-adds-in-store-messaging-capabilities-through-ibeacon-targeting/article/383871. Accessed April 15, 2017.

14. "Move over, iBeacons—here come mesh beacons." Venturebeat. December 6, 2014. http://venturebeat.com/2014/12/06/move-over-ibeacons-here-come-mesh-beacons. Accessed April 15, 2017.

15. "Radio-frequency identification." Wikipedia. https://en.wikipedia.org/wiki/Radio-frequency_identification. Accessed April 15, 2017.

16. "Edward Snowden." Wikipedia. https://en.wikipedia.org/wiki/Edward_Snowden. Accessed April 15, 2017.

17. Ransom, J. "Boston police set to buy social media monitoring software." Boston Globe. November 26, 2016. www.bostonglobe.com/metro/2016/11/25/boston-police-set-buy-social-media-monitoring-software/Vswk24jmuBkuMmPbPY4iYl/story.html. Accessed April 15, 2017.

18. Nelson, L. "Colleges' Yik Yak problem, explained." Vox. November 13, 2015. www.vox.com/2015/11/13/9728368/yik-yak-colleges-missouri. Accessed April 15, 2017.

19. Vincent, J. "Woman fired after disabling work app that tracked her movements 24/7." The Verge. May 13, 2015. www.theverge.com/2015/5/13/8597081/worker-gps-fired-myrna-arias-xora. Accessed April 15, 2017.

20. "About Bluetooth beacons." https://placetips.fb.com/beacons/. Accessed April 15, 2017.

21. Chait, G. "Half the money I spend on advertising is wasted; the trouble is I don't know which half." B2B Marketing. March 18, 2015. www.b2bmarketing.net/en/resources/blog/half-money-i-spend-advertising-wasted-trouble-i-dont-know-which-half. Accessed April 15, 2017.

22. Sponder, M. "Enrich your data to increase converged analytics effectiveness." ClickZ. November 17, 2014. www.clickz.com/enrich-your-data-to-increase-converged-analytics-effectiveness/28712. Accessed April 15, 2017.

23. Sponder, M. "Merging geo social data & Web Analytics at the Metropolitan Museum of Art." SlideShare. November 5, 2014. www.slideshare.net/web meticsguru/merging-geo-social-data-web-analytics-v6-marshall-sponder-nov-6th-2014-final-submitted. Accessed April 15, 2017.

24. Van de Zand, I. "The overwhelming power of analytics in retailing and B2C." SAP Blogs. December 9, 2015. http://blog-sap.com/analytics/2015/12/09/the-overwhelming-power-of-analytics-in-retailing-and-b2c-part-one. Accessed April 15, 2017.

25. Tofel, K.C. "Hold the beacon: McDonald's tests wireless offers near stores." December 18, 2014. https://gigaom.com/2014/12/18/hold-the-beacon-mcdonalds-tests-wireless-offers-near-stores. Accessed April 15, 2017.

26. Fingas, J. "San Francisco airport beacons help the blind get around using their phones." August 3, 2014. www.engadget.com/2014/08/03/sfo-beacons-for-blind-passengers. Accessed April 15, 2017.

27. "Virgin Atlantic unveils new airport terminal experience powered by Apple's iBeacon." May 2, 2014. http://appleinsider.com/articles/14/05/02/virgin-atlantic-unveils-new-airport-terminal-experience-powered-by-apples-ibeacon. Accessed April 15, 2017.

28. Dormehl, L. "New York museum uses iBeacons to create a 'digital minefield'." Cult of Mac. April 1, 2014. www.cultofmac.com/272554/new-york-museum-uses-ibeacons-create-digital-minefield. Accessed April 15, 2017.

29. Elgan, M. "The Super Bowl kicks off iBeacon season." Cult of Mac. February 1, 2014. www.cultofmac.com/264872/super-bowl-kicks-ibeacon-season. Accessed April 15, 2017.

30. "Seoul night bus based on Big Data technology." Metropolis. October 1, 2015. http://policytransfer.metropolis.org/case-studies/owl-bus-based-on-big-data-technology. Accessed April 15, 2017.

31. "Owl Bus based on Big Data technology." Seoul Solution. October 14, 2014. https://seoulsolution.kr/en/content/owl-bus-based-big-data-technology. Accessed April 15, 2017.

32. "Fusion Tables." https://data.ca.gov/category/by-data-format/fusion-tables. Accessed April 15, 2017.

33. "Fusion Tables REST API." https://developers.google.com/fusiontables. Accessed April 15, 2017.

34. "Google Fusion Tables." https://sites.google.com/site/fusiontablestalks/stories. Accessed April 15, 2017.

Social Media Actions Analytics

CHAPTER OBJECTIVES

After reading this chapter, readers should understand:

- Intermediate Metrics (actions) created by social media
- How social media metrics fit in with other Intermediate Metrics produced by Web and Search Analytics
- Various free and paid Social Media Analytics platforms that collect Intermediate (Action) Metrics

In this chapter, we explore social media actions. Actions, (Intermediate Metrics) are the measures that marketers focus on (although Social Media Actions alone, are not enough to establish Return on Investment, ROI). Typical actions performed by social media users include likes, dislikes, shares, views, clicks, tags, mentions, recommendations, subscribing, following, commenting, and endorsements. In social media, platforms actions are a way to express symbolic reactions. For example, Facebook allows users to select emoticons that express certain specific emotions, such as love, related to a Facebook post. Symbolic actions are an easy and fast way to express feelings, unlike written reactions in the form of textual comments. Actions are not just typical responses; they carry emotions and behaviors that can be used in a variety of ways. More importantly, social media actions are social expressions; that can be understood as a user's action (e.g., liking certain content) is visible to (or shared with) other social media users, with their friends. This shareable nature of social media actions makes them very attractive to social media marketers and businesses.

Take as an example Moviefone (an American-based movie listing and information service company), which enabled logins with Facebook and Twitter credentials. Enabling such login services not only allow users to use the Moviefone service conveniently but also lets them connect with their social media friends and share content over the Moviefone site. Enabling social logins led to a 300% increase in site traffic, a 40,000–250,000 increase in referrals per month, and a 40% growth in click-through rate.[1] Also, social logins enable analysts to build better customer profiles by matching precise social actions to specific individuals via their logins.

What are Actions Analytics?

Social Media Actions Analytics deals with extraction, analysis, and interpretation of the insights contained in the actions performed by social media users. Social media actions are of great value to social media marketers because of their role in increasing revenue, brand value, and loyalty. Organizations can employ actions analytics to measure the popularity and influence of a product, service, or idea over social media. However, Actions Analytics are not effective proxies for Return on Investment (ROI), as depicted in Figure 12.1, and they are better suited to measuring the engagement that an audience has with the organization's product or service.

Figure 12.1 Business metrics pyramid of ROI.
Source: WebMetricsGuru Inc.

For example, as illustrated in Figure 12.1, a brand marketer can analyze the popularity of their new product among social media users by analyzing engagement data from social media. By analyzing the Facebook likes and Twitter mentions, they can discern specific answers to their marketing questions.

Common Social Media Actions

Below, we briefly discuss some of the most common social media actions; social media users performed all of them and they are used as social media metrics. Metrics, in simple words, are anything users or stakeholders want to measure. Social media users can be described as followers, fans, and subscribers.

Like Buttons

Like buttons are a feature of most social media sites (e.g., social networks, blogs, and websites) that allow users to express their feelings of liking certain products, services, people, ideas, information, places, or content. These actions are performed by social media users to express a typical positive reaction to the content. Also, the number of likes that a person, product, or feature gets gauges their popularity in social media. Facebook's like button enables users to voice their feelings easily and give your product or service a virtual thumbs-up. In addition to the like button, Facebook implemented reaction buttons so that users can express their feelings with the click of a button rather than commenting.

These reaction buttons serve as emotional faces, for lack of a better term, indicating how people express specific emotions, such as shock or humor, related to the specific post they appear on. Incorporating a "like" button in social media platforms and websites is becoming the norm. Social media platforms display accumulated likes received by content over time. Facebook's like button is the most famous one. The Google+ social networking platform uses a "+1" symbol to express liking. Companies use Google+ and Facebook fan pages to receive likes from customers, but the like button can also be incorporated into a company website or blog.

Recently, Facebook has introduced a range of other buttons, including love, sad, and angry, to allow people to express a variety of emotions; and Facebook users have sometimes wished there was a dislike button provided by the platform. Instead, they can react with an angry or sad type of emoji that Facebook offers. One could argue social media creates more negativity than positivity.[2] However, most social media platforms do not want their members to dislike user content, instead preferring to promote a positive image of the product/services offered by users and advertisers.

Share Buttons

Share buttons or sharing is a feature that allows social media users to distribute the content posted over social media to other users.

For example, the Facebook share button lets users add a personal message and customize whom they share the content with. The share button on WordPress (a blogging platform) allows users to share their blog content across a range of social media platforms. Companies incorporate share buttons into their website to boost their website traffic by channeling visitors from social media sites. Also, social media share buttons can be used to raise awareness for events or causes.

Examples of Social Sharing Buttons

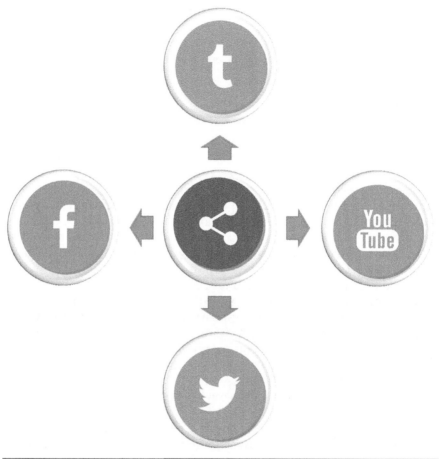

Figure 12.2 Social sharing buttons.
Source: WebMetricsGuru Inc.

Dislike Buttons

Dislike buttons are included in some social media platforms (e.g., YouTube) and allow users to express their negative feelings of disliking certain content (e.g., products, services, people, ideas, information, or places) posted over social media. Similar to like buttons, they are visible to others and accumulated over time. The dislike button, when it is present, is not as prevalent as the like button. Perhaps social media companies do not want people to dislike the content posted on their platforms. Such a practice may go against the core philosophy of advertising, which is used to create a positive mental image of product/services offered by companies and convince them to buy it.

Visitors, Visits, Revisits (Web Analytics Data)

Visitors are a metric that is reported on by Web Analytics platforms. Visitors are measured based on first-party cookies that are captured through a script executed on the Web browser of the visitor; the raw data is sent to a collection server that processes the information into a visitor and visits metrics of the site being measured, as covered in previous chapters. A visitor is a person who visits a website or blog. A single visitor may visit a page or content one or more times (revisits). Visits are also known as sessions. Other related concepts related to a visitor's visit to a website are:

Unique visitor: A person who arrives at the website page for the first time.
Average bounce rate: The percentage of visitors who visit a website and leave the site quickly without viewing other pages.
Session duration: The average length of a visitor's visit or session.

View

Views are the number of times users view social media content (a post, video, graphic, etc.). For example, YouTube measures video views based on a unique cookie/IP address combination. Once a visitor views a video during a visit, viewing the video again does not count as a second view. A slightly different but related concept is the pageview, which is a count of each time a visitor views a page on a company website or blog. Instagram allows members to see how many views they receive on a video or image. Although members cannot see the names of all the people who viewed their Instagram content, they can still see the names of everyone who liked it.

Clicks

Clicks are the actions performed by users by pressing or clicking on the hyperlinked content of a website, image, click-ad, or blog. Through clicks, users navigate the web. Click data can be collected for business intelligence purposes and serve as Key Performance Indicators (KPIs). One of the main reasons to measure clicks is to improve specific website metrics, such as bounce rate, time spent on a site, and the conversion rate, to name a few of the more common metrics that are measured in this manner. Business managers use a technique called clickstream analysis for a variety of business intelligence purposes, including website activity, website design analysis, path optimization, market research, and finding ways to improve visitor experience on the site. The clickstream is the semi-structured data trail/log (such as date and time stamp, IP address, and the URLs of the pages visited) a user leaves while visiting a website. The clickstream includes every click, download, link in/out, search, keyword, time spent, and much more that is recorded using programs such as Web Trends and Google Analytics.

Tagging

Tagging is the act of assigning or linking extra pieces of information to social media content (such as photographs and bookmarks, among others) for identification, classification, and search purposes. Tagging has assumed additional uses, such as tagging individuals (usually friends or connections) within a photo, tweet, or post by adding the metadata of their social media account name (which does not always correspond to their real name). Tagging can be used to raise users' popularity by letting users classify social media content as they see fit. Tagging may take a variety of forms. For example, bloggers can attach descriptive keywords (tags) to their posts to facilitate classification and searching of content, and Facebook users can add tags to anything they post on their status, including photos and comments. Social bookmarking services (such as del.icio.us) let users organize their bookmarks by adding descriptive tags. This practice of collaborative tagging is commonly known as *"folksonomy"* — a term coined by Thomas Vander Wal.[3] These days, almost all prominent companies (e.g., Facebook and Flickr) provide tagging services to their users. Because the contents are tagged with useful keywords, social tagging speeds up searching and finding relevant content. Tagging is also used to share interpersonal relationships and showing a user's followers who they are via tagging pictures. In fact, Instagram users can tag an Instagram company site, friend, follower, or Instagram public page; doing so makes it easier to generate attention and user interaction on the platform.

Mentions

Social mentions are the occurrences of a person, place, or thing over social media by name. For example, a brand name may be referred to in a Facebook comment, blog post, YouTube video, or tweet. Mentions are significant and can indicate the popularity of person, place, or thing. For example, a social marketer may be able to gauge the popularity of a product/service/campaign by mining Twitter mentions data. A Twitter mention is the inclusion of an "@username" in a tweet.

Hovering

Hovering is the act of moving a cursor over social media content. Capturing users' cursor movement data can help understand user behavior on a social media site. Cursor movement/hovering over an ad, for example, can be considered as a proxy for attention. Most people who view an ad do not click on it, thus if we are relying on clicks analytics only, we may lose a vital piece of information (i.e., attention). Traditionally, hovering data has been used in website design and for improvement of user experience. However hovering activity may be useful to marketers for consumer intelligence, but it also presents serious issues regarding a user's privacy.

Two Examples of Issues Surrounding Hovering and Privacy

• Collecting the hovering data of users can infringe on their online privacy even when a user "knows" their online behavior is being tracked. For example, the online learning programs run by many universities are using software to verify the identity of students who are taking an online test or quiz.[4] The verification tracks a student's cursor movement, typing pattern, and gaze to build a profile of the student (via a computer cam) for test-taking purposes, but it is done for regulatory reasons, and to strengthen the reputation and competitiveness of the university program. However, the adoption of such programs has turned out to be very re-pugnant to many people because of the privacy issue. However, as time goes on people have become more accepting of the monitoring activity, even though they may still hold their own reservations about it.

- Third-party data providers such as comScore and Nielsen employ millions of panelists that traverse the Web during their work or leisure, with their precise clickstream tracked with intricate detail. However, concerns about privacy violations led thousands of individuals to sue comScore claiming they were secretly surveilled through its proprietary tracking software. The lawsuit claimed comScore sold panelists' private information to other parties without their knowledge or consent.[5]

Check-ins

Check-ins have been covered in previous chapters; they are a social media feature that allows users to announce and share their arrivals in certain locations, such as a hotel, airport, city, or store. Check-ins are also an Action Analytics metric used to gauge a user's engagement with a location or activity. Many social media services, including Facebook and Google+, provide check-in features. The location of the user is determined using GPS (global positioning system) technology. Check-in data can, for example, be mined to offer location-based services/products. However, there are privacy issues with sharing location data. For example, when a user of a geo-location app such as Foursquare is checking into a location on the other side of the country, it tells friends and followers that the person is on vacation, which could be dangerous—especially if the information gets into the wrong hands.

In other instances, location tracking may be even more invasive, such as police surveillance of public activities around protests, employee movement, and activities both on the job and off the job. While location tracking is usually not illegal, many consider it unethical with many legal challenges that are yet to be resolved. These days, most of the check-in activity is now "passive"; mobile devices automatically register their location via GPS coordinates (often translating to a designated location, such as specific restaurant or museum). This information is collected by various apps and Internet service providers that are connected to the mobile device by wireless, cellular, or Bluetooth networks.

Thus, certain applications can reconstruct a clickstream of a mobile users' movements over a given period, even when they do not check-in to any locations with their mobile devices, and most people are unaware this happening. Google, Facebook, TripAdvisor, Foursquare, and Yelp, to name a few, are collecting information on passive check-ins and our clickstream movements over time. The passive check-in data is used to predict where users are most likely to go next, or where they are likely to have been in the recent past. Passive check-ins have also been used to measure the boundaries of a location, similar to the concept of the "aura" of a landmark such as a restaurant or a museum, etc.

Pinning

Pinning is an action performed by social media users to pin and share interesting content (such as ideas, products, services, and information) using a virtual pinboard platform. Some popular pinning platforms include Pinterest, Tumblr, StumbleUpon, or Digg. Businesses can use these virtual pinboards to share information while connecting with and inspiring their customers. Four Seasons Hotels and Resorts, for example, use Pinterest to curate travel, food, and luxury lifestyle content to inspire customers.

Embeds

Embedding is the act of incorporating social media content (e.g., a link, video, or presentation) into a website or blog. An embed feature lets users embed interesting content into their personal social media outlets.

Endorsements

The endorsement is a feature of social media that lets people share their approval of other people, products, and services. For example:

- LinkedIn lets users endorse the skills and qualifications of other people in their network.
- Celebrities, like Khloe Kardashian, command large sums of money to endorse specific products or services. Also, platforms such as Yelp provide endorsements via a like or a positive review on a product or service.
- Twitter retweets are a form of endorsement; when a Twitter user retweets content that appears in their news stream, it can be considered a tacit form of approval of the tweet.

Uploading and Downloading

Uploading is the act of adding new content (e.g., texts, photos, and videos) to a social media platform. The opposite of uploading is downloading; that is, the act of receiving data from a social media platform. Almost all social media content is created and uploaded by users, which is better known as user-generated content. For some companies, uploading and downloading are the most significant actions to measure. For Instagram and Flickr, which are both photo-sharing platforms, the number of photos uploaded daily matters more than anything else.

Actions Analytics Tools

Currently, no single platform can capture all the actions discussed in this chapter. Certain platforms can be employed to measure social media actions across platforms. Here are a list of popular Actions Analytics tools.

- **Hootsuite:** Hootsuite is an easy-to-use online platform that enables users to manage their social media presence across the most popular social networks. Hootsuite offers different plans depending on business needs and budget: free, pro, or enterprise. In the tutorial later in this chapter, we will employ the free version, which supports up to five social media profiles and has limited analytics information.
- **SocialMediaMineR:** SocialMediaMineR is a Social Media Analytics tool that takes one or multiple URLs and returns the information about the popularity and reach of the URL(s) on social media. The reports include the number of shares, likes, tweets, pins, and hits on Facebook, Twitter, Pinterest, StumbleUpon, LinkedIn, and Reddit.[6]
- **Lithium:** Lithium (www.lithium.com) is social media management tool that provides a variety of products and services, including Social Media Analytics, marking, crowdsourcing, and social media marketing.

- **Google Analytics:** Google Analytics (www.google.com/analytics) is an analytical tool offered by Google to track and analyze website traffic. It can also be used for blogs and wiki analytics.
- **Facebook Insights:** Facebook Insights (www.facebook.com/insights) helps Facebook page owners understand and analyze trends within user growth and demographics.
- **Klout:** Klout (https://klout.com/) measures your influence across a range of social media channels based on how many people interact with your posts. The Klout Score measures a user's influence on a scale from one to 100.
- **Tweetreach:** This tool helps measure the number of impressions and reach of hashtags. The tool can be accessed here: https://tweetreach.com.
- **Kred:** Kred (www.kred.com) helps measure the influence of a Twitter account.
- **Hashtagify.me:** This tool measures the influence of hashtags: http://hashtagify.me.
- **Twtrland:** Twtrland is a social intelligence research tool (http://twtrland.com) for analyzing and visualizing our social footprints.
- **Tweetstats:** Using a Twitter username, Tweetstats (www.tweetstats.com) graphs Twitter stats including tweets per hour, tweets per month, tweet timelines, and reply statistics.

Case Study: Cover-More Group[7]

Visualizing Social Media ROI

The heart of travel insurance provider Cover-More's social efforts is its Social Media Command Center, a unique way to provide customer feedback and performance metrics in an easy-to-understand visual display. Here's how the social media team took control of the cumbersome task of presenting analytics and came out looking like stars.

Cover-More Group

Cover-More Group is an Australian-owned global travel insurance and assistance group with offices in Australia, the United Kingdom, China, India, New Zealand, and Malaysia. Each year, Cover-More provides insurance policies for more than 1.6 million travelers, manages more than 70,000 insurance claims, and helps more than 42,000 customers with emergency assistance.

Goals

Cover-More had three main objectives in building a Social Media Command Center:

- To prove the ROI on social media efforts to stakeholders.
- To provide a snapshot of Cover-More's social media presence to the board of directors.
- To give a real-time feel to reporting and automate the process.

At the board level, Cover-More needed to be able to show a snapshot of how the company's social strategy was progressing, particularly in comparison with competitors. They were also keen to show executives how social media could benefit the business and not just be a risk. However, the social media and e-commerce teams wanted to know how their activities were tracking on a day-to-day basis. Reconciling the reporting needs of executives and practitioners was proving difficult.

Once a month, Lynton Manuel, Cover-More's Social Media Manager, would populate a spreadsheet with data from each of the company's social network profiles, to put the various channels and results in context with one another. The process was inefficient and labor-intensive: dedicating half a day each month to compile a "pseudo dashboard" became the norm. Manuel presented an overview of status, successes, and challenges to the Board of Directors monthly, but the board was most interested in a visual snapshot. Realizing that executives—or anyone within the business that doesn't have knowledge of different platforms—needed a more simplified, visually attractive way to interact with the data, the social media team decided that Hootsuite's Social Media Command Center could be the solution.

Outcomes

The Cover-More social media team needed to bring social media intelligence into the company's nerve center via a large display to inform and impress viewers. So, with the help of the IT department, they set up a 60-inch television in a prominent location where employees, executives, and potential clients could see it. The team decided on what they wanted to display and set up the Command Center using some adjustable Hootsuite widgets via a simple drag-and-drop process. From there, it was just a matter of adjusting the Hootsuite Analytics, Streams, and Monitoring features to customize the display. The team picked specific widgets like Mentions, Sentiment, Exposure, and Sharing, making it quick and easy to choose what information meant the most to them, to the executives, and to prospective and current clients.

By integrating the Social Media Command Center, the social media team could:

- **Show the positive impact of the social media team's efforts to executives.** After the Command Center went live, a senior executive saw the most recent tweets and remarked, "I did not know we had people saying thanks on Twitter. This looks fantastic."
- **Increase employee engagement and morale.** Employees could quickly understand the real-time data, which demonstrated the company's leadership in the social media sphere.
- **Customize the Command Center screen for maximum brand visibility.** The company's graphic designer created a custom background image and style incorporated elements to make sure the Command Center was visually appealing and on-brand.

The Results

The Social Media Command Center was a success, attracted new customers, and helped Cover-More's team to monitor its social media much more efficiently than before.

Tutorial: Analyzing Social Media Actions with Hootsuite

The tutorial assumes that the reader already has their social media profiles configured (such as a Twitter account and Facebook fan page). Below are the step-by-step guidelines to configure and use Hootsuite.

Step 1: To start using the free version, go to http://signup.hootsuite.com/plans-cc/ and click on the "Get Started Now" button available under the free version.

Step 2: Next, provide an email address and name, choose a strong password, and then click on the "Create Account" button.

Step 3: Click on the "Twitter" button available under the "Connect Your Social Network" section. Note that users can choose several social media accounts to manage using Hootsuite. For now, we will only configure Twitter and Facebook.

Step 4: A pop-up window will open asking users to authorize Hootsuite to access the Twitter account. A Twitter username (or email) and password need to be entered, then click on the "Authorize App" button.

Step 5: After authorization, the Twitter account will appear in the added accounts. Next, click the "Continue" button. Note that each user can monitor multiple Twitter accounts using Hootsuite.

Step 6: Click on the "Get Started" button to complete the three simple steps (i.e., adding streams, creating a tab, and scheduling a message) suggested by Hootsuite.

Adding Streams

Step 7: To monitor conversations and actions over Twitter, add additional streams. To do so, click on all the streams to be added for monitoring (e.g., tweets, mentions, and retweets).

Step 8: Streams will start appearing on the Hootsuite dashboard for the user.

Creating a Tab

Step 9: Tabs are used to group stream-based interests or similarities. To add a tab, click on the "+" icon.

Step 10: Name the new tab (e.g., "Followers") and click "Next".

Scheduling a Message

Step 11: With Hootsuite, one can post messages to several social media platforms (e.g., Twitter and Facebook) either instantly or for later. To write a message, click to select the social profile(s) that will post your message (in this case Twitter). Click "Compose Message", and then type message. After writing the message, either click the "Send Now" button or the "Calendar" icon to schedule it for later. This step will complete the initial configuration of Hootsuite.

Hootsuite Analytics

Hootsuite provides two ways to generate analytics reports:

1. Using premade templates.
2. Creating custom-made analytics reports.

Note that the free version has limited analytics abilities and the user will be able to use only a small number of templates.

To use Hootsuite's premade templates, go through the following steps:

Step 1: Click the bar graph icon on the left-aligned launch menu.

Step 2: Choose from several report templates. For example, click on the "Twitter Profile Overview" template.

Step 3: Click on the "Create Report" button. Note that there can be multiple social media accounts configured and then chosen them from the drop-down list. Next, the report will be generated.

Step 4: A report can be printed, saved as a PDF or CSV, and shared with others by using the toolbar available at the top right corner of the report.

Creating Custom Reports

Step 1: Click the bar graph icon on the left-aligned launch menu.

Step 2: Click "Build Custom Report".

Step 3: Click "Custom Report".

Step 4: This will bring users to the custom report page.

Step 5: Click "Upload Image" to upload a logo or an image to brand the report. Selecting and applying a logo is done by locating the image file on the computer, or the Web and clicking "Open". One can also edit the details of the organization and type of header for the report.

Step 6: Under "Details" in the top left corner, enter the title of your report and a brief description. Moreover, under "Email and Scheduling", click the drop-down menu and select the frequency of distribution.

- **Tip:** Users can also have this report emailed to the members sharing this report by clicking on the box, making a check.

Step 7: Next, click on "Add Report Modules" and then click to select the module, adding it to your report. Modules with ENT and PRO are only available to enterprise users.

- **Note:** Modules added to reports can be removed by clicking "Remove" in the top right corner of the module on the report.

Step 8: Complete the information requested by that module to achieve the best results.

Step 9: Click on the "Create Report" button available at the top right of the page. Alternatively, users can click "Save as Draft".

Monitoring and Analyzing Facebook Data with Hootsuite

Step 1: First, add a new tab for the Facebook network. To do so, click the home (Streams) icon on the left-aligned launch menu, and then click on the "+" icon.

Step 2: Name the new tab (e.g., Facebook).

Step 3: Click on the "Add Social Network" button.

Step 4: Select Facebook from the list, and click on the "Connect with Facebook" button.

Step 5: Type the Facebook email (or mobile phone number) and password, and then click "Log In".

Step 6: Next, read Hootsuite's access to the Facebook account message; click to read "App Terms and Privacy Policy" on the bottom left corner, and then click "OK".

Step 7: Read posting permission note, click to select who can see the content being posted to Facebook from Hootsuite, and then click "OK".

- **Note:** Clicking "Skip" will prevent you from being able to post to Facebook from Hootsuite.

Step 8: Read the page permission note, and then click "OK".

- **Note:** Clicking "Skip" will prevent you from being able to manage your Facebook pages from Hootsuite.

Step 9: Click to select the timeline, pages, and groups to import. A check mark indicates that the content will be imported; a plus icon indicates the content will not be imported. When done, click "Finished Importing".

Adding a Facebook Stream

Now that Facebook is added to Hootsuite; it is time to add streams to measure.

Step 1: Click the home (Streams) icon on the left-aligned launch menu, then click the tab hosting your Facebook content.

Step 2: Next, click "Add Stream".

Step 3: Select Facebook and then select a profile that will stream content.

Step 4: Click the "+" button across from the social media stream to add. This process can be repeated for multiple Facebook streams.

Similar steps can be repeated for configuring Twitter, Google+, WordPress, and LinkedIn streams for analytical purposes.

Review Questions

1. Define Social Media Actions Analytics.
2. Briefly, list and define different actions performed by social media users.
3. Why it important to measure actions carried out by social media users?

Chapter 12 Citations

1. Petersen, R. "166 Case Studies Prove Social Media Marketing ROI." BarnRaisers. http://barnraisersllc.com/2014/04/166-case-studies-prove-social-media-roi. Accessed April 15, 2017.

2. Graham, R.F. "Psychologist: Social media causing a 'distancing phenomena' to take place." April 16, 2014. http://washington.cbslocal.com/2014/04/16/psychologist-social-media-causing-a-distancing-phenomena-to-take-place. Accessed April 15, 2017.

3. Wal, T.V. "Off the top: Folksonomy entries." www.vanderwal.net/random/category.php?cat=153. Accessed April 15, 2017.

4. Singer, N. "Online test-takers feel anti-cheating software's uneasy glare." The New York Times. April 5, 2015. www.nytimes.com/2015/04/06/technology/online-test-takers-feel-anti-cheating-softwares-uneasy-glare.html. Accessed April 15, 2017.

5. Scurria, A. "ComScore pays $14m to escape massive privacy class action." June 4, 2014. www.law360.com/articles/544569/comscore-pays-14m-to-escape-massive-privacy-class-action. Accessed April 15, 2017.

6. "SocialMediaMineR." https://cran.r-project.org/package=SocialMediaMineR. Accessed April 15, 2017.

7. "Transforming data into action: Cover-More group." Hootsuite. https://hootsuite.com/resources/case-study/transforming-data-into-action-cover-more-group. Accessed April 15, 2017.

Social Media Hyperlink Analytics

CHAPTER OBJECTIVES

After reading this chapter, readers should understand:

- Hyperlinks (better known as "links") and their impact on Search Engine Analytics and network analysis
- Types of Hyperlink Analysis
- How to use Hyperlink Analytics tools such as VOSON

This chapter discusses hyperlinks, which are the pathways of social media traffic. Hyperlinks are references to Web resources (such as a website, document, and files) that users can access by clicking on them. Hyperlinks can link resources within a document (interlinking) and among documents (interlinking).

Examples of Hyperlinking

- Hyperlinks (usually shortened URLs) within a tweet that links to other resources (e.g., websites) available over the Internet.
- Hyperlinks within a site that link to internal resources such as the homepage, contact us page, about us page, etc.
- Graphics that have embedded hyperlinks.
- QR codes that contain a link to a website page.

Hyperlinks are not merely links between two websites, but serve a more symbolic means.[1] As a website is an official and unique entity representing an organization itself,[2] embedding hyperlinks in an organization's website can be considered an official act of communication between two organizations. Hyperlinks to websites represent not only a reasonable approximation of a social relationship[3] but also serve as a validation or endorsement of the linked organization.[4] Also, incoming links serve to increase the page authority, which helps SEO page rankings.

In conjunction with this, hyperlinks that exist between two organizational websites reflect a sense of validation, trust, bonding, authority, and legitimacy.[5] Websites mostly connect or link to other websites of a similar nature, so hyperlinks can also serve as indicators of content similarity.[6]

Types of Hyperlinks

From a Hyperlink Analytics point of view, there are three types of hyperlinks, as shown in Figure 13.1:

1. In-links (incoming links)
2. Out-links (outgoing links)
3. Co-links and co-citations

In-links

Incoming hyperlinks are links directed towards a website originating from other websites.[7] For example, consider the top-left of Figure 13.1: page A is receiving two in-links from pages B and C. Internet marketers want to get more in-links to their websites because they correlate with higher Web traffic and popularity of the websites. In-links also play a major role in website analytics, as both the quality and number of in-links can impact the search engine ranking of the site.

In-links impact the popularity of social media content. In-links are a measure of site popularity, and the Google PageRank algorithm has been the main mechanism employed to measure this. A study on YouTube viral videos, for instance, found that among other things, in-links play crucial roles in the viral phenomenon, particularly in increasing views of videos posted on YouTube.[8] Studies have also shown that in-link counts strongly correlate with measures describing business performance.[9]

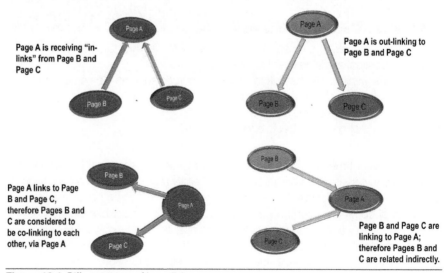

Figure 13.1 Different types of hyperlinks.
Source: Gohar F. Khan and WebMetricsGuru Inc.

Out-Links

Out-links are hyperlinks generated out of a website.[10] As shown in the top-right image in Figure 13.1, page A is sending two out-links: one to page B and one to page C. Website out-links are tracked in the same way as in-links. A website's out-links become the in-links of the websites they point to. Out-links attract relevant and valuable eyeballs.[11]

In the past, out-links (outbound links) were not considered an important factor in SEO ranking, but that position has changed; the consensus is that out-links may count for search engine ranking almost as much as in-links. For example, when a website or page out-links to an authoritative site, it has a positive impact on rankings.[12]

Out-links can damage a site's reputation, drop their search engine rankings, and create exit portals where customers will drop off.[13] However, when out-links are used strategically, organizations may benefit from the outbound links in many ways. Regardless of the quality of a website, it is impractical to include all the valuable information people seek on the site. Providing out-links to valuable content that aligns with a site's business objectives is an excellent way to improve a visitor's experience on the site.

Co-Links and Co-Citations

Co-links are the relationship created by two or more websites or webpages that link to the same website or webpage. Co-links are similar in concept to the idea of "co-citation." Essentially, co-links and co-citations are used by search engines to relate and rank pages on various topics, based on the words they contain (and the words they do not contain but are related to or based on other "common" webpages the pages link to).

Co-links and co-citations are difficult for humans to keep track of, but search engine algorithms do a good job of topic relationships and rank search result pages based on this information. In fact, co-links have been used to compare and map competitive similarity among organizations.[14]

Examples of co-linking and co-citations:

- When *The New York Times* and *The Wall Street Journal* both link to the Wikipedia Twitter account page in various articles being published, the Wikipedia Twitter page becomes a "co-link" to both websites.
- ConsumerReports.com gets a first-page ranking on Google with the search engine query "cell phone ratings," although it does not contain the term "cell phone" or the word "ratings," except in some of the text on the website. Cell phone ratings are not even in the page title, yet they rank well on a competitive query.

Search engines have evolved, via co-linking and co-citations, to rank websites for highly competitive keywords regardless of the presence of website copy containing these keywords anywhere in the title tags, metadata, or the content of the page. Because of the evolution in the application of search engine algorithms, optimizing Web copy for optimal search ranking has become much more complicated to achieve than it once was.

The Importance of User Design (UX) in Search Engine Rankings

Search engines have become more focused on the "searcher experience," resulting in the improved design and execution of webpages. Moreover, Web-based apps are simply mobile-friendly HTML5 code that is executed by a Web server. Thus, they are not distributed in an app store and it is hard to monetize them, but they are among the main UX drivers of an improved searcher experience.

The end goal of UX improvements is to attract visitors to specific websites and convert them into customers. That is not going to happen when website visitors experience technical and aesthetic issues arising on the websites they are visiting.

With the broad adoption of Web Analytics platforms, particularly Google Analytics, search engines determine a visitor's aesthetic satisfaction with the websites they visited using a variety of signals (being fed to highly tuned algorithms) provided by the analytics. Search engines determine a user's satisfaction with a website or page visitor by determining the searcher's intent. A search engine may combine a user's search query with specific Web Analytics metrics such as page load speed, the time spent during a visit to the website, or the bounce rate (to name a few of the more popular "Intermediate Metrics") to determine the search ranking for the user's query.[15]

Search Engines Algorithms Reward Great Website User Design (UX) With Higher Search Engine Rankings

Great websites link to other great websites, and search engines know this. Search engines developed algorithms that reward searcher/user behavior. There are hundreds of ranking factors that search engines use to determine the quality of website/page for a searcher's query or search terms, such as keywords, links, and content (to name a few). Most of these factors are based on the way people process text and images, attention span, and clickstream behavior.[16]

Ranking factor examples:

- By placing keywords near the beginning of the title tag of a page, content creators are practicing good SEO, better known as "white hat SEO." White hat SEO refers to the optimization strategies focusing on a human audience, as opposed to search engines, and that completely follow stated search engine rules and policies. Conversely, "black hat SEO" refers to the use of aggressive SEO strategies that focus only on search engines and not on a human audience, and usually do not obey search engine guidelines.
- Search engines are believed to reward websites owners who employ white hat SEO strategies and practices, as people tend to read content at the beginning of a sentence and the end, but not so much all the words in the middle of sentences; the algorithms that rank page quality are based on average user behaviors. Websites using black hat SEO technologies, such as website cloaking and keyword stuffing, tend to have their search engine ranking drop drastically over a period of a few months. However, certain languages such

as Hebrew are read from left to right, while others are symbol-based (such as Chinese, Korean, Japanese, and Arabic), requiring modifications to search engine algorithms for various countries, languages, dialects, and localities.

- Search engines examine the keywords within the first 250 words of a document as part of a ranking algorithm. The selected keywords have more weight for search engine ranking when used with a white hat SEO strategy than if the content is placed in the middle of a document page (again, based on user behavior). The authors believe the search engine algorithms involved in ranking content are trying to emulate the way people read and process content regarding titles and the first paragraph of a news article. Search algorithms are emulating and automating what people do naturally, which is why the keywords located in the first part of the document are weighted more highly. Eye-tracking studies have confirmed the optimal placements for text and images within a webpage; algorithms have been created to determine and score how page content based on these placements.

- Images are favored by search engines when they have ALT text that details the subject of the image. Search engines favor images that have "snippet" text next to the image that explains the image subject to the reader. Until recently, search engines did not know how to read images and needed the snippet text to determine page content quality. Again, search algorithms are simply approximate the way humans process images but not being sentient, often depend on a written snippet of text to understand the subject and meaning of the image, making it a search ranking factor.

- Many websites run a form of Web Analytics called Google Analytics; Google Analytics provides raw data to Google on user and searcher behavior; the data informs search algorithms on page quality and user engagement. Similarly, more website referral traffic, as measured by Web Analytics platforms, originates from mobile devices than desktop computers. Thus, search algorithms rank mobile friendly websites higher in search results than websites that are not search friendly. Even page load speed is now a ranking factor. The reason for this is obvious and rooted in good UI, or User Interface, design; a slow loading web page frustrates searchers and users—people have a shortage of time and patience, it is best not to aggravate potential or actual customers/users.[17]

- Link anchor text (the actual "link text") is more highly rated by search engine algorithms when it matches the content of the webpages it points to. The use and evaluation of link anchor text are based on the searcher's intent to find relevant information.

The examples provided above confirm that search engines have built their search algorithms around searcher behavior and experience. After all, search engines exist to assist searchers in finding the best content based on their search.[18]

Hyperlink Analytics

Hyperlink Analytics deal with extracting, analyzing, and interpreting hyperlinks (e.g., in-links, out-links, and co-links). Hyperlink analytics reveal the Internet traffic patterns and sources of the incoming or outgoing traffic to and from a website.

Hyperlink Analysis Has Been Used to Study a Variety of Topics

The case study included in this chapter demonstrates the importance of hyperlinks in viral phenomena and shows the valuable insights they carry for viral marketers in formulating viral marketing strategies. By studying hyperlinks, researchers have been able to observe linking patterns and gain new insights in several areas.

Link analysis examples:

- University rankings, blogosphere interconnections, scholarly websites[19]
- Political networks[20]
- Business competitiveness[21]
- Influencer networks[22]

Hyperlink Analysis Limitations

- Fails to provide any real insight into the type or amount of web traffic flowing among sites.[23]
- Usually does not examine internal links within a website between pages.
- Does not measure the effectiveness of navigation within a website.
- Ignores or gives low importance to internal linking within a website.[24]

Types of Hyperlink Analytics

Hyperlink analytics can take several forms, including:

1. Hyperlink website analysis
2. Link impact analysis
3. Social media hyperlink analysis

Hyperlink Website Analysis

Hyperlink website analysis examines the in-links and out-links of a site or set of websites. Hyperlinks (i.e., out-links, in-links, and co-links) of a website are extracted and analyzed to identify the sources of Internet traffic.[25]

Hyperlinked website networks take two forms:

1. Co-links networks
2. In-links and out-links networks

Co-Links Networks

In co-links environment networks, nodes are websites and links that represent a similarity between websites, as measured by co-link counts. With the Webometric Analyst tool, one can construct a co-link network diagram among a set of websites.[26]

In-Links and Out-Links Networks

In-links and out-links hyperlink networks are built based on in-links and out-links from a website or set of websites. In such a network, websites are represented as circular nodes, and the inbound and outbound links show how websites are connected/

interconnected. The VOSON tutorial provided in this chapter demonstrates constructs such as a network using the VOSON hyperlink analysis tool.

Link Impact Analysis

Link impact analysis investigates the popularity of a website address (or URL) regarding citations or mentions it receives over the Internet. In a link impact analysis, statistics about webpages that mention the URL of a given website are collected and analyzed.[27] URLs that are frequently cited on the Web are more popular and topical. Thus, measuring the popularity of URLs is a measure of the importance of a website, page, hashtag, or social media account.

Social Media Hyperlink Analysis

Social media hyperlink analysis deals with the extraction and analysis of hyperlinks embedded within social media texts (e.g., tweets and comments). These hyperlinks can be extracted and studied to identify the sources and destination of social media traffic. However, within social media, both the sources and destinations of social media traffic are visible to most members of a social network that desire to see them (especially on Twitter; most of its data is open to everyone). For example, a Twitter hashtag could be considered a destination of social media traffic.

A good example of the usefulness of the hyperlink embedded in the social media text is the 2014 study by Khan et al.,[28] in which they extracted out-links from Korean and U.S. government agencies' tweets. By extracting out-links and tracing them back to their sender, the authors could construct a map of the out-link structure. According to a comparison of out-links between tweets of the South Korean and U.S. governments, there were some differences in citation (i.e., out-link) patterns. The Korean government tended to cite domestic portals' news services and their blogs (i.e., self-citation).

Although there were social networking services and newspaper sites, most of the related out-links were for portals. On the other hand, the U.S. government showed a more diverse pattern regarding out-link destinations. U.S. out-links were not concentrated in specific sites and tended to go directly to news agencies, not to secondary sources such as portals. These comparisons between the U.S. and Korean governments suggest that social media out-links can carry valuable information and can help explain real-world phenomena and shed light on the disparities in social media use among different cultures.[29]

Hyperlink Analytics Tools

The following are some popular Hyperlink Analytics tools:

- **Webometric Analyst** (http://lexiurl.wlv.ac.uk) is a Web impact analysis tool and can conduct variety of analysis on social media platforms, including hyperlink network analysis and web mentions.
- **VOSON** (www.uberlink.com) is a Hyperlink Analytics tools for constructing and analyzing hyperlink networks. This chapter includes a tutorial on using VOSON for Hyperlink Analysis.

- **Open Site Explorer** (https://moz.com/researchtools/ose) is a link analysis tool to research and compare competitor backlinks, identify top pages, view social activity data, and analyze anchor text.
- **Link Diagnosis** (www.linkdiagnosis.com) is a free online tool for analyzing and diagnosing links.
- **Advanced Link Manager** (www.advancedlinkmanager.com) provides a variety of link analysis capabilities, including the ability to track link-building progress over time, quality domain analysis, backlinks evolution, and website-crawling abilities.
- **Majestic** (https://majestic.com) provides a variety of link analysis tools, including link explorer, backlinks history, and link mapping tools.
- **Backlink Watch**: (http://backlinkwatch.com) is a free tool for checking the quality and quantity of in-links pointing to a website.

Case Study: Hyperlinks and Viral YouTube Videos

Background

Do hyperlinks play a role in the popularity of a video posted on YouTube? YouTube popularity was one of the questions that a research team at Social Listening (a social media consulting company: https://www.sociallistening.co.nz/) set out to explore. The research team knew that the answer lay in extracting and visualizing hyperlinks (particularly in links pointing to a video) network and was looking for ways to get hands on YouTube videos data.

What They Did

- At the first stage of the quest, the research team identified the 100 most viewed YouTube videos. Every video posted on YouTube was automatically assigned a unique ID embedded within the URL of the video.[30]
- At the second stage, to explore the effects of hyperlinks on the viral phenomenon, the team used the Webometrics Analyst platform (http://lexiurl.wlv.ac.uk) — a well-established tool for measuring different aspects of the Web, such as Web impact analysis, Hyperlinks Analysis, and the Web search engine results.[31] Using the IDs text file as an input, through Webometrics Analyst, the search team determined the number of external links and Internet domains pointing to a video. This data was used to construct a two-mode network diagram below for better understanding using UCINET social networking tool.[32]

Results

Most of the videos received URLs from a common set of domains. However, some videos received more links from URLs than others, while other domains sent more links, etc. By studying network maps related to successful viral content, such as a popular video by a celebrity, we can begin to understand the factors and relations that promote the sharing of viral video content.

Conclusion

This analysis shows that apart from the popularity of YouTube network, the most popular videos had a strong in-links network (links received by videos and users) originating from diverse domains over the Internet. This case study demonstrated the importance of hyperlinks and the valuable insights they carry. The study found that in-links may be a factor impacting the viral potential of a video. For example, linking the videos/contents posted on YouTube in several external platforms (e.g., blogs, social network sites, and online discussion communities) may increase the chance of the video going viral.[33]

Tutorial: Hyperlinks Analytics with VOSON

VOSON is a Web-based tool for hyperlink network analysis. To construct and analyze hyperlink networks, VOSON relies on Web mining, data visualization, and traditional social science techniques, such as social network analysis.[34] VOSON is freely available to academics, researchers, consultants, government entities, and others outside of academia. This tutorial is based on the free version.

Creating an Account on VOSON

Step 1: To access VOSON, create an account by visiting www.uberlink.com and clicking on the "create a new account" option available at the top of the page.
Step 2: Create a username and password by filling in the appropriate form, then log into the system. After the account is approved, start using the tool.

Logging in to VOSON

To avoid confusion, note that there are two identical versions of the VOSON System. The first version is from VOSON@ANU, and other is offered from VOSON@Uberlink. Each version is accessed from slightly different locations. So, first, determine the version being subscribed to.

To see which version of VOSON the reader has been granted access to, use the following steps:

- Go to www.uberlink.com and log in with your username and password.
- Click on the "My Account" option available at the top of the website.
- Scroll down to the bottom of the profile to see the version currently subscribed to.
- If it is VOSON@ANU, log in to the VOSON System at http://voson.anu.edu.au/voson-system. If it's VOSON@Uberlink, log in to the VOSON System at https://voson.uberlink.com.au.

VOSON Menus

After logging into VOSON for the first time, users are presented with the following active menu items (many other menus are not active and only become active when they are needed). Details on the description of all menus can be found in the VOSON documentation available at www.uberlink.com/software#voson-system.

Info

>   *User*—only gives basic information on the access privileges and the projects that belong to the user.

Data

>   *Data browser*—this allows users to see the data, where each row is a webpage.
>   *Save database*—use this to save copies of the database.
>   *Add seed sites*—use this to add more seed sites to the database (seed sites are used to create hyperlink networks).
>   *Download*—use this to access the data for viewing in other software; for example, Excel.
>   *Show databases*—this lists all the databases the user has access to. Initially, there are only two databases available: testdb and testdbAN. Users can start with these two databases to get familiar with the tool.

Furthermore, in the VOSON System contains two databases types:

1. VOSON databases
2. VOSON-analysis databases

VOSON databases are the "parent" from which VOSON-analysis databases are created. VOSON databases contain the raw network data; whereas, VOSON-analysis databases are used to conduct network analysis such as crosstabs and network visualization.

Create: *VOSON database*—this menu is used to create a VOSON analysis database.
Help: The Help menu provides two submenus for accessing documentation and information about the software.

Creating a Hyperlink Network

Often, by looking at the pattern and interrelationships of inbound and outbound links to a website (and where they interconnect), a better understanding of the value of a site can be derived.

Step 1: After login, the first thing a user needs to do is to build a database. To create a database, click on the "Data" tab, click "Create" and then click on "VOSON database".
Step 2: Provide the requested information (e.g., database name and description). Leave the other options on their default setting. The default options will perform the following tasks:

*   The crawler will look for inbound links.

    *   For each seed, the crawler stops when it discovers 1,000 in-links.
    *   The crawler will not look for inbound links to each internal page.

- The crawler will look for outbound links.
  - For each seed, the crawler will stop when it discovers 1,000 out-links.
- Then, it will crawl 25 pages without finding a new outbound link (the maximum number of unproductive pages).
- It will crawl only 50 pages (the depth of crawl in pages).
- It will crawl two levels (the depth of crawl in levels), but the text content will not be parsed for analysis (yet).
- The database is now created.

Step 3: Notice that other submenus within the "Data" menu have become active. To create a network, click on the "Data" menu, click on "Create", and then on "VOSON analysis database".

Step 4: Provide a name for the database. Select "Hyperlinks" in the "Link type" and "Page group" in the "Node type" in the drop down boxes, then click "Create database". This database will be used to construct our hyperlink network.

Step 5: Now it is time to add seed sites that will be used to create the hyperlink network. For this tutorial, we used www.uberlink.com as the seed site, but users can use the website address of any website or company URL.

Users can add several additional seed sites, but the total number of seed sites that can be added depends on the subscription plan a user signs up for. To add a new location to the seed list, first click on the newly created database to activate it. Then click on "Data," then on "Add Seed Sites".

A new window will be opened. Type the URL to be analyzed in the box provided. Leave other options on their default settings and click on the "Add" button next to the comment box (which you can use to add comments if you have any).

Now, check the "ready to crawl" box. A pop-up window will alert the user about the status of credit and number of credits needed to perform the crawl. Click "OK" to start the process. Note that the sites will not be crawled immediately; the user will receive an email when the crawling has finished.

Step 6: After having received the email from VOSON informing the user that the data set is ready, click on "Data>Show databases". Now the database has been populated with data (e.g., 31 rows).

Step 7: To check the network properties of the hyperlink network, first click on the database (VOSON-analysis type) to make it active. Then, click on the "Analysis" tab and then click on "SNA".

Step 8: A new window will open summarizing in detail the properties of the network, including the following:

Size—the total number of websites (or nodes) in the network.

Number of edges—the total number of hyperlinks (in-links and out-links) of the websites.

Components—the isolated sub-networks that connect within, but are disconnected between networks.[35]

Density—the number of links in a network.

Number of isolates—the number of nodes that have no connections to other nodes.

Inclusiveness—the proportion of the nodes in the network that are connected.

Step 9: To visualize the hyperlink network, click on the "Analysis" tab, and then "Maps", and then select one of the three available options:

- Minimum spanning tree
- Complete network
- Hierarchy

Depending on the version of VOSON being used, there may be more options. These are network visualization algorithms, and each one will visualize the network differently. We selected the "Complete network," which shows all links and nodes simultaneously.

Step 10: The hyperlink network will appear in a separate window. Users can easily notice the out-links and in-links by looking at the arrowheads. If the arrowhead points to the seed site, it is an in-link, and if it points away, it is an out-link from the seed site to another website. The countries where the hyperlinks are coming from are shown on the right-hand side.

Users can redraw the network based on several parameters shown in the upper part of the window. For example, we configured the node size based on the in-degree (i.e., the number of incoming hyperlinks). The node size will be bigger when a website has more in-links. Clicking on a specific node will display more details about the node.

Step 11: To save the network diagram, click on "download map PNG" and save it on your computer.

Step 12: Users can also export the network data to be used with other network analysis software (e.g., Pajek and GrapML). To do so, click on "Data", then "Download" and then select the format you want to download the data in.

Summary

In this chapter, we examined hyperlink networks and various tools and methods to analyze them. This type of network analysis is important, as it is often used to understand or explain the spread of viral content and identify influential websites and webpages in a hyperlink network. Also, hyperlink networks are the foundation of off-page SEO and a vital part of the original Google PageRank algorithm. We have listed a variety of free and paid tools that can be used for hyperlink analysis and included a case study using VOSON along with an additional analysis of content featuring a celebrity, using VOSON. Readers are invited to explore the various hyperlink analytics tools presented and work through the VOSON tutorial and Connect the Dots exercise using a free Twitter Analytics tool called MentionMapp.

Review Questions

1. What are hyperlinks, and why they are important?
2. Briefly discuss in-links, out-links, and co-links.
3. What is Hyperlink Analytics, and its underlying assumptions?

4. What is hyperlink website analysis?
5. What is link impact analysis?
6. What is social media hyperlink analysis?

Exercise: Connecting the Dots using MentionMapp

1. Sign up for a free account on MentionMapp.com.
2. Enter your Twitter account (or that of a celebrity).
3. Per MentionMapp, who is the most important node(s)? Who is the least?

Chapter 13 Citations

1. Kim, D. and Y. Nam (2012) "Corporate Relations with Environmental Organizations Represented by Hyperlinks on the Fortune Global 500 Companies' Websites." *Journal of Business Ethics* 105(4): 475–487.

2. Garrido, M., and Halavais, A. (2003) "Mapping Networks of Support for the Zapatista Movement: Applying Social Network Analysis to study the Contemporary Social Movements." In M.M.M. Ayers (ed.), *Cyberactivism: Online Activism in Theory and Practice*. London: Routledge.

3. Jackson, M.H. (1997) "Assessing the Structure of Communication on the World Wide Web." *Journal of Computer-Mediated Communication* 3(1).

4. Vreeland, R. (2000) "Law Libraries in Cyberspace: A Citation Analysis of world Wide Web Sites." *Law Library Journal* 92: 49–56.

5. Nam, Y., G. Barnet, et al. (2014) "Corporate Hyperlink Network Relationships in Global Corporate Social Responsibility System." *Quality & Quantity* 48(3): 1225–1242; 4 Vreeland, R. (2000) "Law Libraries in Cyberspace: A Citation Analysis of world Wide Web Sites." *Law Library Journal* 92: 49–56.

6. Chakrabarti, S., M.M. Joshi, et al. (2002) "The Structure of Broad Topics on the Web," from www2002.org/CDROM/refereed/338.

7. Björneborn, L. and P. Ingwersen (2004) "Toward a Basic Framework for Webometrics." *Journal of the American Society for Information Science and Technology* 55(14): 1216–1227.

8. Khan, G.F. and S. Vong (2014) "Virality over YouTube: An Empirical Analysis." *Internet Research* 24(5): 629–647.

9. Vaughan, L. (2004) "Exploring Website Features for Business Information." *Scientometrics* 61(3): 467–477.

10. Björneborn, L. (2001) *Necessary Data Filtering and Editing in Webometric Link Structure Analysis*. Royal School of Library and Information Science.

11. Fishkin, R. "5 reasons you should link out to others from your website." Moz. February 24, 2009. https://moz.com/blog/5-reasons-you-should-link-out-to-others-from-your-website. Accessed April 15, 2017.

12. Aharony, S. "Study—outgoing links used as ranking signal." Reboot SEO Company. February 21, 2016. www.rebootonline.com/blog/long-term-outgoing-link-experiment. Accessed April 15, 2017.

13. Fishkin, R. "5 reasons you should link out to others from your website." Moz. February 24, 2009. https://moz.com/blog/5-reasons-you-should-link-out-to-others-from-your-website. Accessed April 15, 2017.

14. Vaughan, L. and J. You (2006) "Comparing Business Competition Positions Based on Web Co-Link Data: The Global Market vs. the Chinese Market." *Scientometrics* 68(3): 611–628.

15. Thurow, S. "Conversion optimization: Measuring usability in the user experience." April 11, 2014. http://marketingland.com/conversion-optimization-measuring-usability-user-experience-ux-part-1-79557. Accessed April 15, 2017.

16. "The Periodic Table of SEO success factors." http://searchengineland.com/seotable. Accessed April 15, 2017.

17. Lohr, S. "For impatient Web users, and eye blink is just too long to wait." The New York Times. March 1, 2012. www.nytimes.com/2012/03/01/technology/impatient-web-users-flee-slow-loading-sites.html. Accessed 10 Jan. 2017.

18. Fishkin, R. "5 reasons you should link out to others from your website." Moz. February 24, 2009. https://moz.com/blog/5-reasons-you-should-link-out-to-others-from-your-website. Accessed April 15, 2017.

19. Vaughan, L. and M. Thelwall (2003) "Scholarly Use of the Web: What are the Key Inducers of Links to Journal Web Sites?" *Journal of the American Society for Information Science and Technology* 54(1): 29–38.

20. Park, H. and M. Thelwall (2008). "Link Analysis: Hyperlink Patterns and Social Structure on Politicians' Web Sites in South Korea." *Quality & Quantity* 42(5): 687–697.

21. Vaughan, L. and J. You (2006) "Comparing Business Competition Positions Based on Web Co-Link Data: The Global Market vs. the Chinese Market." Scientometrics 68(3): 611–628.

22. Vaughan, L. and J. You (2006) "Comparing Business Competition Positions Based on Web Co-Link Data: The Global Market vs. the Chinese Market." Scientometrics 68(3): 611–628.

23. Ackland, R. (2010). "WWW Hyperlink Networks." In D. Hansen, B. Shneiderm and K.H.M. Smith, *Analyzing Social Media Networks with NodeXL*. New York: Morgan-Kaufmann.

24. Thelwall, M. "Big Data and social Web research methods." www.scit.wlv.ac.uk/~cm1993/papers/IntroductionToWebometricsAndSocialWebAnalysis.pdf. Accessed April 15, 2017.

25. "Image map example from SocSciBot Network." Webometric Analyst. http://lexiurl.wlv.ac.uk/examples/cybermetrics.htm. Accessed April 15, 2017.

26. Thelwall, M. (2005) "Webometrics." In M.A. Drake (ed.), *Encyclopedia of Library and Information Science*. New York: Marcel Dekker, Inc.; Thelwall, M. "Big Data and social Web research methods." www.scit.wlv.ac.uk/~cm1993/papers/IntroductionToWebometricsAndSocialWebAnalysis.pdf. Accessed April 15, 2017.

27. Thelwall, M. (2005) "Webometrics." In M.A. Drake (ed.), *Encyclopedia of Library and Information Science*. New York: Marcel Dekker, Inc.; Thelwall, M. "Big Data and social Web research methods." www.scit.wlv.ac.uk/~cm1993/papers/IntroductionToWebometricsAndSocialWebAnalysis.pdf. Accessed April 15, 2017.

28. Khan, G.F., H.Y. Yoon, et al. (2014). "Social Media Communication Strategies of Government Agencies: Twitter Use in Korea and the USA." *Asian Journal of Communication* 24(1): 60–78.

29. Khan, G.F., H.Y. Yoon, et al. (2014). "Social Media Communication Strategies of Government Agencies: Twitter Use in Korea and the USA." *Asian Journal of Communication* 24(1): 60–78.

30. For example, www.youtube.com/watch? v=kffacxfA7G4 was the URL of a video posted by the user "Justin Bieber" having an ID "kffacxfA7G4." The data was collected for all 100 videos and saved in a text file with one ID per line.

31. Thelwall, M. (2005) "Webometrics." In M.A. Drake (ed.), *Encyclopedia of Library and Information Science*. New York: Marcel Dekker, Inc.

32. To see the image being referenced from the source, refer to http://lexiurl.wlv.ac.uk/images/justin%20bieber%20replies.PNG.

33. Khan, G.F. and Sokha, V. (2014), "Virality over YouTube: An Empirical Analysis." *Internet Research* 24(5).

34. Ackland, R. (2010). "WWW Hyperlink Networks." In D. Hansen, B. Shneiderm and K.H.M. Smith *Analyzing Social Media Networks with NodeXL*. New York: Morgan-Kaufmann.

35. Hanneman, R.A. and M. Riddle "Introduction to social network methods." http://faculty.ucr.edu/~hanneman. Accessed April 15, 2017.

Network Analysis and Social Network Mapping

CHAPTER OBJECTIVES

After reading this chapter, readers should understand:

- Various types of social networks and how they are constructed
- Network analysis tools and their uses

Networks are the building blocks of social media and can carry useful business insights. Network analysis consists of constructing, analyzing, and understanding social media networks. Social Media Analytics can be used for a variety of purposes, and it includes network analysis (i.e., the interrelationship of nodes within a network). The idea behind network analysis is that the structure and interrelationships of a network are as important as who is on the network, perhaps even more important. It is not so far-fetched that the positions of nodes within a network predetermines the quality and tenor of the relationships in that network, and this the main reason to study social media and network analysis in this chapter. Once we understand the type of network we are dealing with, the interrelationships of the nodes gain meaning. Network analysis can be employed to identify influential nodes (e.g., people and organizations) or their position in the network; it can also be used understand the overall structure of a network. Businesses can use network analysis to explore their Twitter or Facebook followers and identify influential members on those networks.

This type of analysis shortens the amount of time it takes to research prospective customers and industry influencers, and provides valuable insights to gauge marketing effectiveness within the networks being examined. Some people on social media are more influential, from a marketing perspective, as they can share information with a large audience of followers, subscribers, and friends, and are considered opinion leaders. For example:

- Celebrities such as Kim Kardashian are paid a substantial amount of money to advertise products on social media because their followers look up to them.
- The Humans of New York Facebook page has been very influential, with more than 18 million followers and over 100,000 people talking about the page at a time.

- Athletes like Kobe Bryant post products on their social media accounts; as followers view the product being used by the celebrity or athlete, they are more likely to use it.
- A tweet by politicians such as Barack Obama or Donald Trump can instantly reach several million followers on Twitter (especially in Trump's case).

However, it is important to highlight that not only famous people are considered influencers nowadays. A lot of "everyday" people are now attracting millions of followers on Instagram, Twitter, YouTube, and other platforms and are chosen as brand ambassadors/influencers. A researcher may be interested in the overall structure of networks to see how certain networks differ or converge. The case study included in this chapter highlights the usefulness of social media networks and how they can be used to answer interesting real-world research questions.

This case study shows how a research team used social media data and proved that the differences in cultural norms (e.g., those of the United States and South Korea) influence social media use patterns in the public sector. Overall, the purpose of network analysis is to do the following:[1]

- Understand overall network structure; for example, the number of nodes, the number of links, density, clustering coefficient, and diameter.
- Find influential nodes and their rankings; for example, degree, betweenness, and closeness centralities.
- Find relevant links and their rankings; for example, weight, betweenness, and centrality.
- Find cohesive subgroups; for example, pinpointing communities within a network.
- Investigate multiplexity; for instance, analyzing comparisons between different link types, such as friends versus enemies.

Example Case Study: Twitter Network Study of US and South Korean Non-Profits—Do Social Media Networks Reflect Social Culture?

Background

Cultural values and norms form an integral part of a society in which "every person carries within him or herself patterns of thinking, feeling and potential acting which were learned throughout their lifetime."[2] Research has shown that culture can have considerable influence on the use of technologies by people with different cultural backgrounds, as different cultures perceive technologies differently.[3] For example, a cross-cultural study of knowledge workers in the U.S. and Japan found that their cultural background played a major role in their predisposition toward and selection of technologies (e.g., telephone and fax).[4]

However, little is known about the effects of various cultural dimensions such as collectivism and individualism[5] on social media use in the public sector. How are differences in cultural norms (e.g., those of the U.S. and South Korea) influencing social media use patterns and strategies in the public sector? The research team at Cyber Emotion Research Center at YeungNam University in South Korea was determined to investigate. The research team knew that network mapping could find the answer. By analyzing various social media networks formed by organizations from different cultures, the team hoped to find ways to leverage those networks. The hypothesis was that cultural differences might be reflected in the structures of social media networks formed among people of various societies.

What They Did

Based on previous research on cultural difference, the team decided to investigate Twitter networks of South Korean and U.S. ministries. South Korea is a hierarchical, collectivistic, and matriarchal society that avoids uncertainty and emphasizes collectivism, whereas the U.S. is a nonhierarchical, individualistic, and patriarchal society that accepts uncertainty and emphasizes individualism.[6] The researchers thought that a cross-cultural comparison of social media networks between South Korean and U.S. governments might provide a better understanding of the diverse patterns of social media use in the public sector. To this end, the research team compiled a list of Twitter accounts utilized by the 40 Korean and 32 U.S. government agencies. The data on Twitter following–followers network was collected. The data was collected by using an in-house software program designed based on the Application Programming Interface (API) provided by Twitter.com.

The program can be used to submit queries to Twitter.com and process results. Once the network data was gathered, NodeXL was used to construct and visualize the networks. With the help of a research assistant, some follow-up telephone interviews were conducted with the manager in charge of the Twitter accounts in selected ministries. The purpose of the interviews was to get a first-hand account of the Twitter communication strategies in the ministries that had dedicated social media staff. As it turns out, market research of this type has many applications beyond traditional marketing.

Results

The results were surprising and showed clear structural differences between the two Twitter networks. For example, South Korean ministries were well-connected in a dense network of follower–following relationships, whereas U.S. government departments tended to be loosely connected. Regarding network density (or the portion of the potential connections in a network that are real connections), the South Korean network (density = 0.86) was substantially denser than the U.S. network (density = 0.26), as shown in Figure 14.1.

This density is a simple but useful measure of group cohesiveness. Figure 14.1 shows that the Korean network had 1,348 (86%) ties, whereas the U.S. network had only 255 (26%). The clustering coefficient (i.e., the degree to which nodes in a network tend to cluster together) was higher for the South Korean network (0.86) than for the U.S. network (0.50), indicating that the South Korean network was more likely to form "cliques."

In other words, Korean ministries tended to be locally embedded in dense neighborhoods (clusters). In fact, unlike U.S. government departments, almost all South Korean ministries followed all the other ministries.

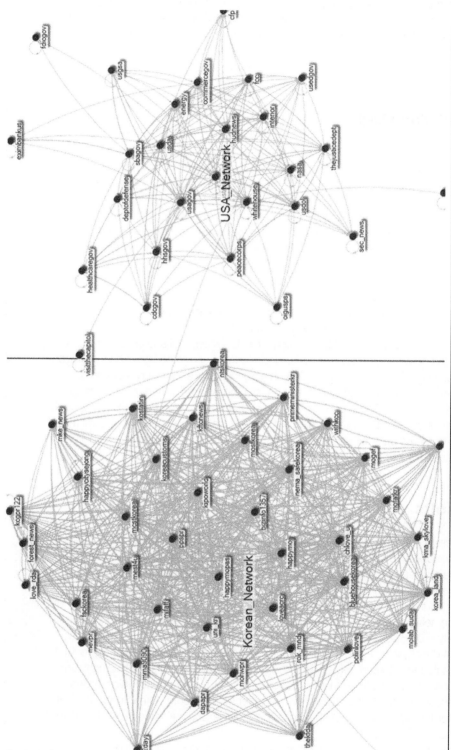

Figure 14.1 South Korean and U.S. ministry social network diagrams compared.

Source: Gohar F. Khan.

Case Study Takeaways

The case study highlights the usefulness of social media network and how it can be used to answer interesting real-world research questions. The research provided some new insights into the effects of cultural values and social norms (e.g., collectivism versus individualism) on the pattern of Twitter networks in the public sector. For example, South Korea is a collectivistic society, whereas the U.S. is an individualistic one.[7]

The dense Twitter network of South Korean ministries may reflect the country's collective norms in the online environment, unlike organizations from individualistic cultures such as the U.S., who were loosely connected and tended to be interested more in engaging in personal communication (e.g., tweets) rather than forming dense networks to pursue collective agendas.[8]

Influencer Marketing Example: Kcore Analytics and Grandata

Influencer marketing employing Kcore Analytics was used by Grandata, an Argentinian corporation integrating financial and telecommunication data. Grandata's marketing goal was to understand key market trends and predict customer behavior. Consequently, Grandata found a strong correlation between high income and social network influence in targeted populations in Central and South America.[9]

By creating a network map and applying Kcore's algorithm to combine first-party information and second-party Telco data, Grandata found a strong correlation between high income and social network influence in targeted populations in Central and South America. Thus, Grandata gained a fivefold increase in their marketing success rate by targeting specific influencers that Kcore's algorithm identified.[10]

Common Social Network Terms

Network

At a very basic level, a network is a group of nodes that are linked together.[11] Nodes (also known as vertices) can represent anything, including individuals, organizations, countries, computers, websites, or any other entities. Links (also known as ties, edges, or arcs) represent the relationship among the nodes in a network.

Social Networks

A social network is a group of nodes, representing social entities such as people or organizations, and links formed by these social entities. For example, links can represent relationships, friendships, and trade relations. Social networks can exist both in the real and online worlds and supplement each other. The online world helps create better connections in our world. A network among classmates is an example of a real-world social network. Moreover, a Twitter follow–following network is an example of an online social media network. In a Twitter follow–following network, nodes are the Twitter users, and links among the nodes represent the follower–following relationship (i.e., who is following whom) among the users.

Social Network Site

A social network site is a special-purpose software (or social media tool) designed to facilitate social or professional relationships. Facebook, Google+, and LinkedIn are examples of social network sites.

Social Networking

The act of forming, expanding, and maintaining social relations is called social networking. Using social network sites, users can, for example, form, expand, and maintain online social ties with family, friends, colleagues, and sometimes strangers.

Social Network Analysis

Social Network Analysis is the science of studying and understanding social networks[12] and social networking. It is a well-established field with roots in a variety of disciplines including graph theory, sociology, information science, and communication science.

Common Social Media Network Types

The following are some common types of social media networks that we come across, and that can be subject to network analytics.

Friendship Networks

The most common type of social media networks are the friendship networks, such as Instagram, Twitter, and Snapchat. Friendship networks let people maintain social ties and share content with people they closely associate with, such as family and friends. Nodes in these networks are people, and links are social relationships (e.g., friendship, family, and activities).

Follower–Following Networks

In the follower–following network, users follow (or keep track of) other users of interest. Twitter is an excellent example of a follow–following network where users follow influential people, brands, and organizations. Nodes in these networks are, for example, people, brands, and organizations, and links represent follow–following relations (e.g., who is following whom). Below are two common Twitter terminologies.

Following are the people whom you follow on Twitter. Following someone on Twitter means:

- You are subscribing to their Tweets as a follower.
- Their updates will appear on your home screen or dashboard.
- That person can send you direct messages.
- You are able to subscribe to tweets to be notified when the account tweets (although you cannot send a direct message unless that person follows you back).

Followers are people who follow you on Twitter. If someone follows you, it means that:

- They will show up in your "Followers" list.
- They will see your tweets in their home timeline whenever they login to Twitter.
- You can send them direct messages.

Fan Network

A fan network is formed by social media fans or supporters of someone or something, such as a product, service, person, brand, business, or other entity. The network formed by the social media users subscribed to your Facebook fan page is an example of a fan network. Nodes in these networks are fans, and links represent co-likes, co-comments, and co-shares. A fan network can be passive (via bought subscribers) or active (an organically generated follower who actively engages with your posts).

Group Network

Group networks are formed by people who share common interests and agendas. Most social media platforms allow the creation of groups where a member can post, comment, and manage in-group activities. Examples of social media groups are Twitter professional groups, Yahoo groups, and Facebook groups. Nodes in these networks are group members, and links can represent co-commenting, co-liking, and co-shares.

Professional Networks

LinkedIn is a good example of a professional network where people manage their professional identity by creating a profile that lists their achievements, education, work history, and interests. LinkedIn members can also search profiles or jobs by specific keywords (i.e., "sports management"). Nodes in these networks can represent people, brands, or organizations. Links are professional relations and in LinkedIn are called "connections" (such as a co-worker, employee, or collaborator). An important feature of professional networks is the endorsement feature, where people who know you can endorse your skills and qualifications. Also, the recommendation feature, where unconnected members of a social network are suggested to a user, is another important characteristic.

Content Networks

Content networks are formed by the content posted by social media users. A network of YouTube videos is an example of a content network. In such a network, nodes are social media content (such as videos, tags, and photos) and links can represent, for example, similarity (content belonging to the same categories that can be linked together).

Dating Networks

Dating networks (such as Match.com and Tinder) are focused on matching and arranging a dating partner based on personal information (such as age, gender, hobbies, common interests, and location) provided by a user. Nodes in these networks are people, and links represent social relations (such as romantic relations).

Co-Authorship Networks

Co-authorship networks are two or more people working together to collaborate on a project. Wikipedia (an online encyclopedia) is a good example of a social media-based co-authorship network created by millions of authors from around the world.[13] A more explicit example of the co-authorship network is the ResearchGate platform: a social networking site for researchers to share articles, ask and respond to questions, and find collaborators. In these networks, nodes are, for example, researchers, and links represent the co-authorship relationship.

Co-Commenter Networks

Co-commenter networks are formed when two or more people comment on social media content (e.g., a Facebook status update, blog post, Yelp restaurant reviews, or YouTube video). A co-commenter network can, for example, be constructed from the comments posted by users in response to a video posted on YouTube or a Facebook fan page. In these networks, nodes represent users, and a link represents the co-commenting relationship.

Co-Like Networks

Co-like networks are formed when two or more people like the same social media content. Using NodeXL (a social network analysis tool), one can construct a network that is based on co-likes (two or more people liking a similar content) of the Facebook fan page. In such network, nodes will be Facebook users/fans and links will be the co-like relationship. Facebook also uses co-likes to suggest other members that they have not yet connected with as a suggested friend. The co-like relationship can be seen on Facebook when people share other's posts.

Co-Occurrence Network

Co-occurrence networks are formed when two more entities (e.g., keywords, people, ideas, and brands) co-occur over social media outlets. For example, one can construct a co-occurrence network of brand names (or people) to investigate how often certain brands (or people) co-occur over social media outlets. In such networks, nodes will be the brand names and the links will represent the co-occurrence relationships among the brands.

Geo Co-Existence Network

Geo co-existence networks are formed when two or more entities (e.g., people, devices, and addresses) co-exist in a geographic location. In such a network, the node represents entities (e.g., people), while links among them represent co-existence.

Examples of geo co-existence networking:

- Visitors to a museum (or any location) use social media applications on their mobile devices to check-in using Facebook or Swarm (Foursquare); other members who have recently checked in are to the museum are shown to the member via the app.
- Shoppers visit brick-and-mortar stores and shop there using a Bluetooth-enabled app that connects to an iBeacon network installed in the location.

Hyperlink Networks

In simple words, a *hyperlink* is a way to connect documents (such as websites). Hyperlinks can be thought of as being in-links (i.e., hyperlinks originating in other websites,[14] bringing traffic/users to your site), or out-links (i.e., links originating in your site and going out.[15]

Types of Networks

From a technical point of view, the networks mentioned above can be classified in a variety of ways, including:

1. based on existence
2. based on the direction of links
3. based on mode
4. based on weights

1. Based on Existence
Based on the way the networks exist online or are constructed, they can be classified as:

1. Implicit Networks
2. Explicit Networks

Implicit Networks
Implicit networks do not exist by default and need to be intentionally built with the help of dedicated tools and techniques. Examples of such networks include keyword co-occurrence networks, co-citation networks, co-commenter networks, hyperlink networks, etc. Constructing and studying implicit networks can provide valuable

information and insights. For example, a Facebook group can be considered an implicit network that is deliberately formed. Another kind of implicit network is when several Twitter users post about an event taking place using the specific hashtag—the members are connected to each other via the hashtags and can view each other's posts that contain the same hashtag.

Explicit Networks

Explicit social media networks exist by default; in other words, they are explicitly designed for social media users to be part of. Most social media networks are explicit in nature. Examples of explicit social media networks include Facebook friendship networks, Twitter follow-following networks, LinkedIn professional networks, YouTube subscriber networks, and blogger networks. In this chapter, we will focus on explicit social media networks.

2. Based on Direction

Based on the directions of links among the nodes, the networks can be classified as:

1. Directed networks
2. Undirected networks

Directed Networks

A network with directed links among nodes is called a directed network, as illustrated in Figure 14.2. Usually, a connection with an arrow is drawn to show the direction of

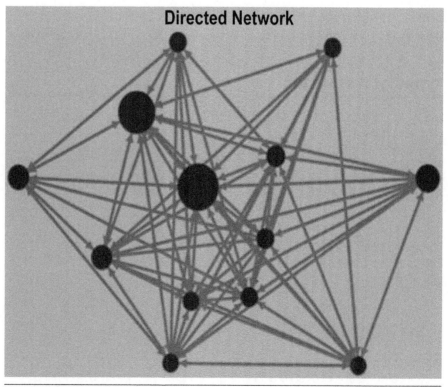

Figure 14.2 Directed network.
Source: Gohar F. Khan. Note: The direction of the links connecting nodes are shown.

the relationship among the nodes. For example, the Twitter follower–following network is a directed network where the direction of the arrow shows who is following whom.

Undirected Network

In undirected networks, the links among the nodes do not have any direction, as illustrated in Figure 14.3. A Facebook friendship network is an example of an undirected network. As an example, Facebook recently added the option to "follow" certain people's posts, similar to Twitter. Moreover, Facebook members can be friends on Facebook, then unfollow some of their friends, so they do not see their former friends' posts on the member's timeline.

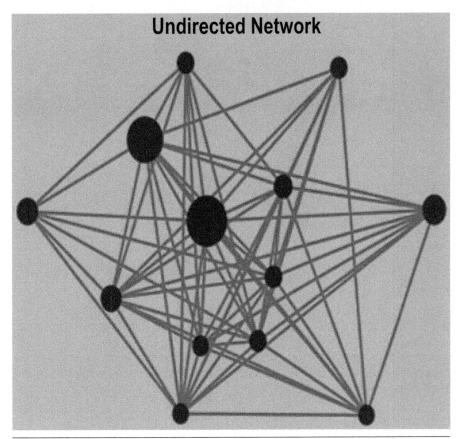

Figure 14.3 Undirected network.
Source: Gohar F. Khan. Note: The direction of the links connecting nodes are *not* shown.

3. Based on Mode

Based on the composition of nodes, networks can be classified as:

1. One-mode network
2. Two-mode network
3. Multimode network

One-Mode Networks

A one-mode network, as shown in Figure 14.4, is formed among a single set of nodes of the same nature. A Facebook friendship network is an example of a one-mode network where nodes (people) form network ties (friendships).

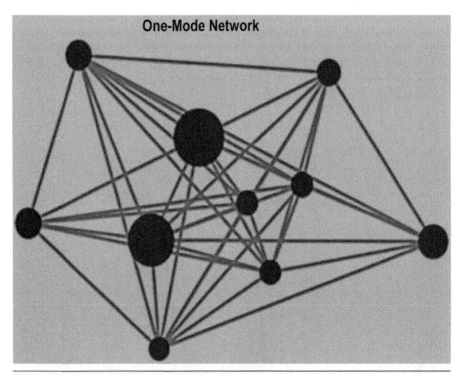

One-Mode Network

Figure 14.4 One-mode network.
Source: Gohar F. Khan.

Two-Mode Networks

Two-mode networks (also known as bipartite networks) are networks with two sets of nodes of different classes.[16] In these networks, network ties exist only between nodes belonging to different sets. For example, consider the two-mode network, where one set of nodes (circles) could be social media users and another set of nodes (squares), as seen in Figure 14.5, could be linked to participation in a series of events. Users are linked to the events they attended.

Multimode Network

A multimode network is also possible where multiple heterogeneous nodes are connected. It can be considered as an amalgam of one and two-mode networks.

4. Based on Weights

Networks can also be classified based the weight assigned to the links among the nodes. There are two types of weighted networks:

1. Weighted networks
2. Unweighted networks

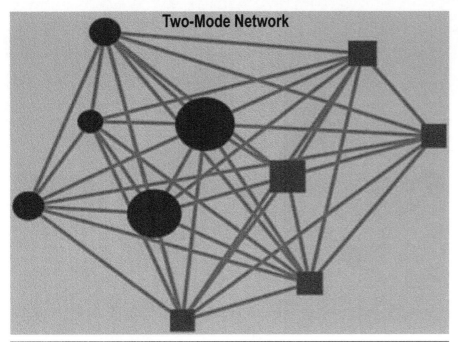

Figure 14.5 Two-mode network.
Source: Gohar F. Khan.

Weighted Networks

In weighted networks, as shown in Figure 14.6, the links among nodes bear certain weights to indicate the strength of association among the nodes. The link (relationship) between, for example, two Facebook friends (nodes) will be thicker if they communicate more frequently. While weighted networks provide rich information, they require sufficient historical data to construct.

For example, Facebook and LinkedIn use proprietary algorithms with weighted networks to condense a user's news feed with a preference towards users the member has interacted with recently. Instagram also changed their algorithm, so images no longer appear chronologically on their newsfeed, but based on the interests of the user. Facebook recently changed their search tab to show pictures/videos of what the user normally clicks on/views.

Unweighted Networks

In unweighted networks, such as Figure 14.7, links among nodes do not bear weights. The links only indicate the existence of a relationship and cannot provide clues about the strength of the relationship. Unweighted networks are easy to construct but may conceal useful information.

Keep in mind that the above-classified types are not mutually exclusive and can exist in a single network. For example, there may exist a directed weighted one-mode network. Alternatively, one could construct an undirected two-mode unweighted network, and so forth.

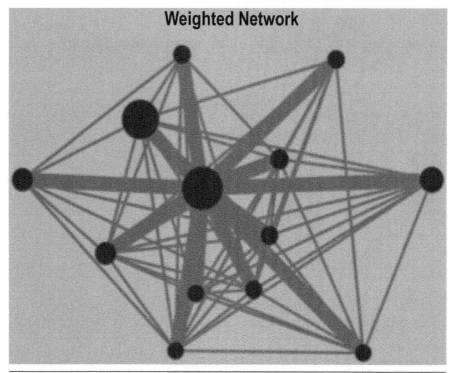

Figure 14.6 Weighted network.
Source: Gohar F. Khan.

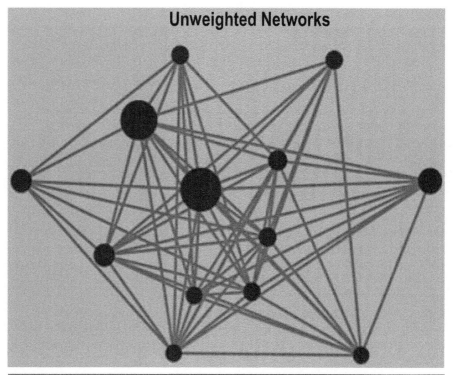

Figure 14.7 Unweighted network.
Source: Gohar F. Khan.

Common Network Terminologies

Let's look at some common network terminologies or properties. Network properties can be divided into two categories:

1. Node-level properties
2. Network-level properties

Node-Level Properties

Node-level properties focus on one node and its position in the network. Some important node properties include degree centrality, betweenness centrality, eigenvector centrality, and structural holes.

Degree Centrality

Degree centrality of a node measures the number of links a node has to the other nodes in a network.[17] In a Facebook network, for example, this will measure the number of mutual friends that a member has.

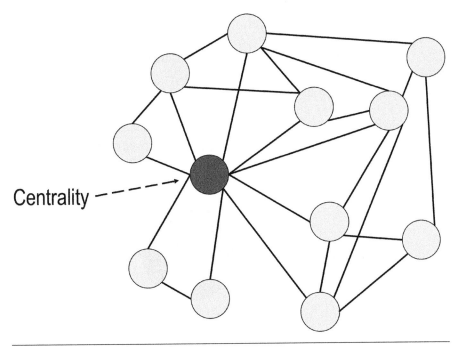

Figure 14.8 Centrality of a network.
Source: WebMetricsGuru Inc.

In a Twitter network, it will equate to the number of followers or following a user has. In a directed network, the degree can be either in-degree (followers) or out-degree (following). In a Twitter network, in-degree (followers) is a more important measure of a node's influence than out-degree (number of individuals a person follows).

Betweeness Centrality

Betweenness centrality is related to the centrality (or position) of a node in a network, as shown in Figure 14.9. The nodes with high betweenness centrality can control the flow of information between connected nodes due to their central position in the network.[18] In a Facebook network, the users who occupy the central position (who have more direct connections to influential friends in the network) are better positioned to control the flow of social media content.

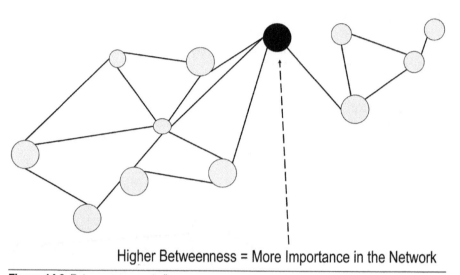

Higher Betweenness = More Importance in the Network

Figure 14.9 Betweenness centrality.
Source: WebMetricsGuru Inc.

Eigenvector Centrality

Eigenvector centrality measures the importance of a node based on its connections with other important nodes in a network. It can provide an understanding of a node's networking ability relative to that of others,[19] as shown in Figure 14.10. The Google

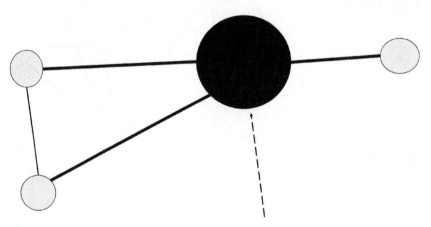

Eigenvector centrality = not all connections are equal and connections to certain nodes are more important than others.

Figure 14.10 Eigenvector centrality.
Source: WebMetricsGuru Inc.

Search Engine has used eigenvectors to rank search results by their relevance to the searcher's query results from the very beginning.[20]

Structural Holes

Structural holes were first put forward by Burt[21], who suggested that certain nodes have an advantage or disadvantage based on their location in a network.[22]

In a social media network, some nodes or users, because of their location in the network, may have an advantage or disadvantage when it comes to spreading information to other nodes in the network.[23] Figure 14.11 shows a simple social network with four nodes and three structural holes; clearly, node one has an advantage in receiving information in that network, that nodes two, three, and four lack.

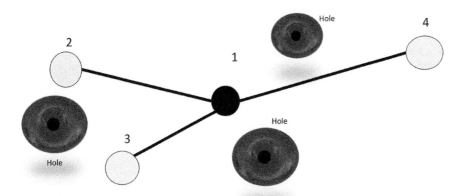

Structural Holes = There are gaps between nodes of a network (such as between node 2 and node 3, or node 4 to node 2, or node 4 to node 2)—information that each node gets may be different as a result.

Figure 14.11 Structural holes.
Source: WebMetricsGuru Inc.

One of the advantages that social media offers is that the most useful information turns out to arise from structure holes (or loose ties) that exist in a network. As an example, in a Facebook or LinkedIn social network, new job opportunities are more likely to come from a friend of a friend, rather than someone in the individuals' closer connections.[24]

Network-Level Properties

Network properties provide insight into the overall structure and health of a network. Important network-level properties include the clustering coefficient, density, diameter, average degree, and components.

Clustering Coefficient

A clustering coefficient is a measure of the extent to which nodes in a network cluster together. In social networks, nodes have a high clustering coefficient, and tend to form with a high density of ties; on average this happens more often than two random nodes forming similar relationships.

Density

The density of a network deals with several links in a network. Density can be calculated as the number of links present in a network divided by the number of all possible links between pairs of nodes in a network (for an undirected network, the number of all possible links can be calculated as $n(n-1)/2$; where n is the number of nodes in a network). A fully connected network, in which each node is directly linking to every other node, will have a density of 1.

Components

Elements of a network are the isolated sub-networks that connect within (but are disconnected between) sub-networks.[25] In a connected component, all nodes are connected and reachable, but there is no path between a node in the component and any node not in the component.[26] The main or largest component of a network is the component with the greatest number of nodes.

Diameter

The diameter of a network is the largest of all the calculated shortest paths between any pair of nodes in a network,[27] which can provide an idea of how long it would take for some information/ideas/message to pass through the network.

Average Degree

The average degree centrality measures the average number of links among nodes in a network.

Network Analytics Tools

- **NodeXL** (an add-in for Microsoft Excel) is the free tool for Social Network Analysis and visualization. It can help construct and analyze Facebook networks (based on co-likes and co-comments), Twitter networks (followers, followings, and tweets), and YouTube networks (user network and comments), among others.
- **UCINET** (https://sites.google.com/site/ucinetsoftware/home) is a social network analysis software application for the Windows operating system. It also includes the Netdraw tool for network visualization. It can be downloaded and used for free for 90 days.
- **Pajek** (http://mrvar.fdv.uni-lj.si/pajek) is a software application for analyzing and visualizing large networks. Pajek runs on Microsoft Windows operating systems and is free for non-commercial use.
- **Netminer** (www.netminer.com) is also a software application for large social network analysis and visualization. The application can be used for free for 28 days.
- **Flocker** (http://flocker.outliers.es) is a Twitter real-time retweets and mentions Networks Analytics tool.
- **Reach** (www.reach-social.com) is an online platform to map hashtag networks and identify the most influential accounts in the Twitter conversation.
- **Mentionmapp** (http://mentionmapp.com) is used to investigate Twitter mentions networks.

Tutorial: Analyzing Social Media Networks with NodeXL

Follow these steps to install and run NodeXL:

Please note: Not everyone may be able to run NodeXL; the program does not appear to work with Office Live or Excel 2016, with Excel 2013 seeming to be the latest version that is verified to work.

Step 1: Go to the http://nodexl.codeplex.com/ and download the latest version of the NodeXL template, then run it.

Step 2: Click "accept" when you are offered the license agreement.

Step 3: If you are asked to accept the "Microsoft Visual Studio 2010 Tools for Office Runtime (x86 and x64)", click the "Accept" button.

Step 4: If you are asked to reboot, click "Yes" to restart the computer.

Step 5: When you are asked "Are you sure you want to install this customization?" click the "Install" button.

Step 6: To open NodeXL after installation, in the Windows Start menu or Start screen, search for "NodeXL", then click "NodeXL Excel Template" in the search results.

After it is opened, you will notice that NodeXL has its menu ribbon available at the top right (see Figure 14.12) and that the first Excel worksheet is called Edges (i.e., nodes). Other default four main worksheets are "Vertices" (i.e., links), "Groups," "Group Vertices," and "Overall Metrics." The Groups worksheet clusters the nodes by common attributes. NodeXL analyzes their connectedness and automatically groups them into specific clusters. The Overall Metrics worksheet shows the overall network measures, for example, density, degree, clustering coefficient, betweenness centrality, etc.

Understanding NodeXL Workflow

The workflow of NodeXL consists of four steps:

1. Importing data
2. Cleaning data
3. Calculating Network Analysis
4. Visualizing the network

We will go through each of the stages in detail.

Note: Because Node/XL does not work on all operating systems and versions, it is uncertain if the following tutorial will work for all readers. Also, we have not included images below because some features of Node/XL have changed or will change from the original version of this tutorial. However, the basic operational steps remain the same; readers can perform the tutorial in order gain valuable insights.

Stage 1: Importing Network Data

The first step in analyzing networks with NodeXL is to import the network data. In NodeXL, network data can be imported from a variety of sources and formats, including Pajek files, UCINET,[28] other spreadsheets, and comma separated value (CSV)

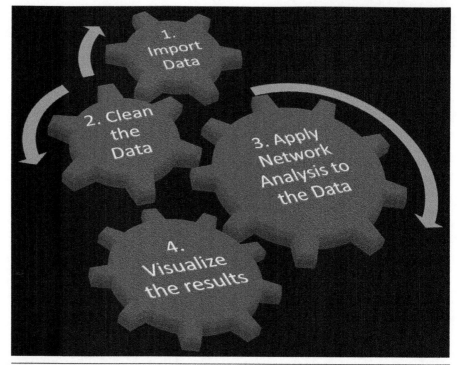

Figure 14.12 NodeXL workflow stages.
Source: Gohar F. Khan and WebMetricsGuru Inc.

files, and directly from social media sites. You can also start creating your network by manually typing a list of the edges in the network into the NodeXL sheet. With NodeXL social imports/plug-ins, data from a variety of social networks can be directly imported, including Facebook, Twitter, YouTube, Flickr, email, Exchange, wikis, and surveys. Social importers are regularly updated, and new social importers are made available on the NodeXL website. To add new social importers, use the following steps:

Importing Third-Party Data Importers
Step 1: Download the installation zip file from the NodeXL social importer website: http://socialnetimporter.codeplex.com.
Step 2: Unzip it and save it to your desktop (or any other location). After unzipping it, you will find the following four items:
FacebookAPI.DLL
FacebookAPI.pdb
SocialNetImporter.DLL
SocialNetImporter.pdb
Step 3: Now open the NodeXL template and then go to "Import>Import Options>Browse". Locate and select the unzipped files you have just downloaded and then click "OK".
Step 4: Close and restart NodeXL. You should now see the "Facebook Import" option in the NodeXL> Import menu.

Note that email, wiki, and VOSON, can be accessed and installed in a similar fashion by going to "NodeXL>Data>Import menu>Get third-party Graph Data Importers". In this tutorial, we will import data directly from a Facebook network.

Importing a Social Media Network Directly
Step 1: Open the NodeXL template and then click on "File>Import". Note that there are a variety of options to import data from. For this exercise, we will use a Facebook fan page network.
Step 2: Then click on "Import from Facebook Fan Page Networks".
Step 3: Next, you will be provided with the "Import from Facebook Fan Page Networks" dialog box. To import the network, NodeXL should be authorized. Click on the "Log in" button available at the bottom of the dialog box. Provide your Facebook username and password in the Facebook login window, then click "Log In".
Step 4: Once you are connected to Facebook, you will be able to provide your Facebook fan page name or ID in specified field. The ID or name of the fan page can be found in the fan page URL.

In this tutorial, we will extract data from the Centre for Social Technologies Facebook fan page. Select all the other desired options provided in the "Import from Facebook Fan Page Networks" dialog box, such as network nodes (e.g., users will become nodes in the network), type of network relations (e.g., likes and comment will become links among the nodes), and edge creation options. You may also change the limit on the number of posts to include or specify a date for data extractions. Depending on the size of the activity on the fan page, choosing several options may cause it to take a long time to extract the data. Once you are ready, click the "Download" button to extract the network.

Stage 2: Cleaning the Network Data
After the network data is downloaded, sift through the NodeXL worksheets and verify and clean the data if necessary. If the data looks good, proceed to the analysis stage.

Stage 3: Network Analysis
Step 1: Calculate the network properties by clicking on the "Graph Metrics" option available at the top of the NodeXL window.
Step 2: In the "Graph Metrics" window, select all the network measures of interest (e.g., overall graph metrics, degree, betweenness centrality, clustering coefficient, etc.) and then click on the "Calculate Metrics" button.

The network measure will be calculated and added to the NodeXL worksheets. You can explore, for example, the overall network measures in the "Overall Metrics" worksheet of the NodeXL. You can see that the network has 293 nodes and 1,216 edges (or links among the nodes). From the network density and diameter, it is evident the network is very sparse.

Step 3: Next, click on the "Show Graph" button to visualize the network.

Stage 4: Visualizing the Network
Step 1: The constructed network will be displayed. However, the network is basic and does not carry much information.
Step 2: To make the network more constructive or informative, click on the "Autofill Columns" button available at the top of the NodeXL window.
Step 3: With the "Autofill Columns" functionality, you can alter the node and edge appearance (e.g., size, shape, color, opacity, or label) per the network properties, such as degree centrality, betweenness centrality, clustering coefficient, and page rank. For example, node size can present importance (betweenness centrality),

edge size can represent the strength of relationships among the nodes, and color of a node can be coded as gender.

Step 4: Click on the "Autofill Columns" and resize the vertices (fans) according to their in-degree centrality (so that the size of the node will represent importance in terms of the number connections a person has). Also, set "Vertex Shape" to gender and color (in our dataset, gender is coded as 1=male and 2=female). To do so, click on the "Options" arrow and set 1= Disk and 2= Solid Square. Next, select the "Edge" tab, and adjust the width of the edge per the number of comments/likes, so that the width of the link represents the strength of the relationships among the nodes regarding the number of comments/likes received. Set "Edge Label" to "Edge Type" to display the type of relationship among the nodes, such as Liker, Commenter, Post Author, Co-Liker, etc. Next, click the "Autofill" button to redraw the network.

Now the network conveys more useful insights. There are three important male fans (circle nodes with a bigger size) in the network that drive most of the network activity, and that liking accounts for most network activity.

Further Adjustments

Several useful adjustments can be performed to the network with the NodeXL template; below, we briefly discuss some of the relevant options.

Adjust layout: with the help of "Adjust Layout," you can adjust the layout of the network (i.e., where each node in the network will be located) using a variety of different algorithms available at the "Adjust Layout" dropdown list. These include a force-directed Fruchterman-Reingold layout algorithm for automatically grouping tightly connected nodes together, as well as circles, grids, and spirals.

Apply dynamic filters: Dynamic filters trim parts of the network and then recalculate network metrics and layout based on the remaining nodes and edges. With dynamic filters, edges and nodes can be selectively hidden or shown, depending on the attributes of the network. For example, the in-degree filter will hide less important nodes.

Graph options: Graph options allow further customization of the network layout, such as changing edge color, arrow size, and curvature.

Saving the Network

Saving the diagram: To save the network diagram to your computer, right-click on the network diagram and then click on "Save Image of File>Save Image".

Saving the network data: The network data can be saved in its native NodeXL format for future use ("File>Save"), or it can be exported into a different format to be used in various network analysis tools (such as UCINET and Pajek files). The "Export" menu is available at the top left a corner of the NodeXL window (below "Import").

Summary

In this chapter, we learned that there are many types of networks and they can intermix, making social network analysis challenging and rewarding. The relationships of network nodes are more important than any other single factor in determining the influence and importance of that node in a network. The information in this chapter was presented to make network maps more interesting and meaningful to readers than they might otherwise be.

Review Questions

1. What is a network?
2. What is the purpose of Network Analytics?
3. Briefly differentiate among social networks, social network sites, social networking, and social network analysis.
4. Briefly explain the different types of social media networks.
5. What is the difference between explicit and implicit networks?
6. What is the difference between one mode, two-mode, and multimode networks?
7. Differentiate between weighted and unweighted networks.
8. Briefly define relevant node-level properties, such as degree, betweenness, eigenvector centralities, and structural holes.
9. Briefly explain important network-level properties, such as clustering coefficient, density, diameter, average degree, and components.

Chapter 14 Citations

1. Perer, A. and B. Shneiderman (2008) *Systematic Yet Flexible Discover: Guiding Domain Experts through Exploratory Data Analysis*. 13th International Conference on Intelligent User Interfaces, New York.

2. Hofstede, G. (1991) *Cultures and Organizations: Software of the Mind*. London: McGraw-Hill.

3. Hofstede, G. (1984) "Cultural dimensions in management and planning." *Asia Pacific Journal of Management* 1(2): 81–99; Hofstede, G. (1991) *Cultures and Organizations: Software of the Mind*. London: McGraw-Hill; Simon, S.J. (2000) "The Impact of Culture and Gender on Web Sites: An Empirical Study." SIGMIS Database 32(1): 18–37.

4. Straub, D.W. (1994). "The Effect of Culture on IT Diffusion: E-mail and FAX in Japan and the U.S." *Information Systems Research* 5(1): 23–47.

5. Hofstede, G. (1984) "Cultural dimensions in management and planning." *Asia Pacific Journal of Management* 1(2): 81–99.

6. Hofstede, G. (1984) "Cultural dimensions in management and planning." *Asia Pacific Journal of Management* 1(2): 81–99; Hofstede, G. (1991) *Cultures and Organizations: Software of the Mind*. London: McGraw-Hill.

7. Hofstede, G. (1984) "Cultural dimensions in management and planning." *Asia Pacific Journal of Management* 1(2): 81–99

8. The Korean–U.S. case study is compiled from the study by Khan et al. Complete research can be accessed from Khan, G.F.H. Young, and H.W. Park (2014) "Social Media Communication Strategies of Governments: A Comparison of the USA and S. Korean Governments." *Asian Journal of Communication* 24(1): 60–78.

9. "Case study: Marketing." KCORE LAB. www.kcore-analytics.com/case-study-marketing. Accessed April 15, 2017.

10. Marone, F. and H.A. Makse. "Influence maximization in complex networks through optimal percolation." Nature." 6 Aug. 2015, www.nature.com/articles/nature14604. Accessed April 15, 2017.

11. Wasserman, S. and K. Faust (1994) *Social Networks Analysis: Methods and Applications*. Cambridge: Cambridge University Press.

12. Hanneman, R.A. and M. Riddle "Introduction to social network methods." http://faculty.ucr.edu/~hanneman. Accessed April 15, 2017.

13. Biuk-Aghai, R.P. (2006) *Visualizing Co-Authorship Networks in Online Wikipedia. Communications and Information Technologies, 2006*. International Symposium.

14. Björneborn, L. and P. Ingwersen (2004) "Toward a Basic Framework for Webometrics." *Journal of the American Society for Information Science and Technology* 55(14): 1216–1227.

15. Björneborn, L. (2001) *Necessary Data Filtering and Editing in Webometric Link Structure Analysis*. Royal School of Library and Information Science.

16. Latapy, M., C. Magnien, et al. (2008). "Basic Notions for the Analysis of Large Two-Mode Networks." *Social Networks* 30(1): 31–48.

17. Hanneman, R.A. and M. Riddle "Introduction to social network methods." http://faculty.ucr.edu/~hanneman. Accessed April 15, 2017.

18. Liu, X., J. Bollen, et al. (2005). "Co-Authorship Networks in the Digital Library Research Community." *Information Processing & Management* 41(6): 1462–1480.

19. www.analytics-magazine.org/november-december-210/54-the-analytics-journey. Accessed April 15, 2017.

20. "Feature column from the AMS." www.ams.org/samplings/feature-column/fcarc-pagerank. Accessed April 15, 2017.

21. Burt, R. (1992). *Structural Holes: The Social Structure of Competition*. Cambridge, MA: Harvard University Press.

22. Hanneman, R.A. and M. Riddle. "Introduction to social network methods." http://faculty.ucr.edu/~hanneman. Accessed April 15, 2017.

23. Nooy, W.D., A. Mrvar, et al. (2005). *Exploratory Social Network Analysis with Pajek (Structural Analysis in the Social Sciences)*. New York: Cambridge University Press.

24. "How strong and weak ties help you find a job." Facebook Research. March 31, 2016. https://research.fb.com/how-strong-and-weak-ties-help-you-find-a-job. Accessed April 15, 2017.

25. Hanneman, R.A. and M. Riddle. "Introduction to social network methods." http://faculty.ucr.edu/~hanneman. Accessed April 15, 2017.

26. Wasserman, S. and K. Faust (1994) *Social Networks Analysis: Methods and Applications*. Cambridge: Cambridge University Press.

27. Wasserman, S. and K. Faust (1994) *Social Networks Analysis: Methods and Applications*. Cambridge: Cambridge University Press.

28. Note: Pajek and UNINET are social network analysis tools with their own network data formats and mechanisms.

Mobile Analytics

CHAPTER OBJECTIVES

After reading this chapter, readers should understand:

- The basic facts of Mobile Analytics
- Types of mobile apps
- Deciding what type of mobile app to develop/use

A whole book could be devoted to Mobile Analytics; consequently, we decided to take a brief, high level treatment of Mobile Analytics in our textbook. Mobile applications are becoming an integral part of our lives; this chapter is a brief introduction to Mobile Analytics. Mobile applications (or apps) are special-purpose software developed to perform certain tasks on the go (some are free, but many are not). Each app has a precise function and runs on specific mobile devices, such as smartphones, tablet computers, and smartwatches. Mobile devices use a type of operating system called a mobile operating system (or mobile OS); popular mobile operating systems include Android (Google), iOS (Apple), Windows (Microsoft), and BlackBerry 10.

Specific apps are developed for each mobile OS. Most apps (but not all) are made available online for download through application distributors (or app stores); such as the Apple Store, Google Play, and the Amazon apps store. According to Statista.com, as of June 2016 there were 4.2 million apps available for download in the Apple Store and Google Play alone. App stores also provide opportunities for users to comment on and rate apps, as well as create them.[1]

What is Mobile Analytics?

Mobile data is constantly generated by our mobile devices, and there are two main methods to view and analyze this data:

1. Mobile Web Analytics
2. Apps Analytics

Mobile Analytics

Mobile Analytics focuses on characteristics of the mobile devices and the activities that originate on them, whereas traditional Web Analytics focuses on the activities that occur on HTML websites. Mobile analytics platforms are designed to track the actions and behaviors of visitors to websites or apps originating from visitors or app users. Mobile Analytics is both similar and different to traditional Web Analytics in its scope and methodology. However, in some cases, using traditional Web Analytics to visualize mobile device activity can be misleading. For example:

- A web referral in traditional Web Analytics is generated from a website domain or page within a domain; whereas, in Mobile Web Analytics, the referral originates from a mobile device, which is not the optimal way to visualize the activity.
- Showing activity from a specific app or mobile web application would be much more helpful, but traditional Web Analytics was not designed to collect and represent this relationship (although attempts have been made to broaden the scope of Web Analytics to include more activities than it was originally created to track).

Organizations collect and analyze a variety of mobile user data, including views, clicks, demographic information, and device-specific data (e.g., the type of mobile device used to access the website). However, all websites should be mobile-friendly for several reasons.

Reasons to Make Websites Mobile-Friendly

1. Search engines rank mobile-compatible websites higher in search results than websites that are not mobile-compatible. Since 2015, mobile compatibility has been a Google Search Engine ranking factor and, overall, most of the referral traffic arriving on websites originates from mobile devices.[2] Similarly, searches that originate from desktop and laptop computers is also taken into consideration by Google's search ranking algorithms.[3]
2. Many websites have been designed to work on desktops or laptops rather than mobile devices; thus creating frustration in the user experience while use is attempted on mobile devices.
3. There is evidence that searches performed on a mobile device are highly correlated to customers who are willing to visit a local business and make a purchase the same day.[4] Mobile devices are portable and broadcast their location; they are optimized to take advantage of this information via services such as Yelp, Foursquare, and Google Now. It should come as no surprise that a mobile search engine query or API-issued request from a mobile app such as Yelp provides better conversion results than desktop and laptop searches when it pertains to a local retail purchase.

Thus, when a business fails to create a mobile-friendly website experience for visitors, they are most likely leaving money on the table and losing business.

Mobile App Analytics

Today, most organizations, big or small, are using mobile apps to drive sales, improve brand affinity, and make purchases possible with a few swipes. For instance, Virgin Atlantic allows customers to search, book, and board their flights with swipes on their smartphones. Companies also need to have a thorough understanding of their customers and their characteristics. Mobile App Analytics focuses on the understanding and analysis of mobile app users' characteristics, actions, and behaviors.

Purpose of Apps Analytics

The main purpose of Apps Analytics is to measure and analyze user behavior, improve user experiences, drive revenue, user engagement, and loyalty. Some sample questions that can be answered with App Analytics are provided below:

- Who are our users?
- Which countries are they coming from?
- What actions they are taking?
- How do our customers navigate in the app?
- What are our in-app payments and revenue?
- How long do they stay on our app?
- How many daily active users (DAU) do we have? (Note: DAU is considered an important business metric because it provides better insights related to how well the app is performing.)
- Which operator, operation system, and devices do they use?
- What item is purchased the most?
- Which countries were top performers regarding in-app purchases (IAP)?
- Which application version leads to more sales?
- How often do our users open the app?
- How many users started a specific number of sessions?
- How do our applications versions compare to one another?

Based on the types of questions being asked, the answers will vary depending on what app analytics are being performed.

Types of Apps

Apps can be mainly classified in two ways:

1. App development
2. Type of app

App Development
There are three classification methods[5] that mobile apps are developed and deployed across:

1. Native apps
2. Web-based apps
3. Hybrid apps

Native Apps (Mobile Apps)

Mobile or native apps are specifically created for and installed on mobile devices by downloading them from the iPhone or Android app store. Obviously, as native apps are executable code, run directly by the microprocessors on the mobile device, they can only run on compatible devices that can run that code (hence, the term "executable" is used). For example, apps for Android-based mobile devices are created in the Java programming language, and iOS apps are developed in Objective-C and Cocoa programming (a programming language native to Apple devices).

When a business wants to create an app that can run both on Android and iOS, they need to develop two separate versions of the app. As previously mentioned, native apps are made available for download in app stores (such as Google Play and the Apple Store). One way to distinguish native apps from the other types is that these apps can only be accessed through specific mobile devices. Tinder (a social networking app) and Uber (a taxi-sharing app) are examples of native apps whose program must first be downloaded and installed from the app store. Both Apple and Google run their own app stores and the keep track of the most updated version of the app. App users are notified when a new version of the app is available on the app store. Frequently, updated apps are automatically downloaded and installed on mobile devices where the app is installed.

Web-Based Apps

Web-based apps look like native apps, but are websites that are optimized for mobile access. For example, TouchStyle (a fashion design app) is a Web-based app for the iPad that is accessed with Safari. Web-based apps are created using standard web coding techniques (such as JavaScript or HTML5) and are accessed using Internet browsers, and are hence not available in app stores. The advantage of developing Web-based apps is that they can be accessed from any mobile device and are less costly to establish and maintain. However, regarding performance, Web-based apps are not as fast and usable as native apps. Moreover, Web-based apps are simply mobile-friendly HTML5 code that is executed by a Web server. Thus, they are not distributed in an app store, and it is hard to monetize them. It should be noted that Web-based apps should execute similarly on mobile and desktop devices.

Hybrid Apps

A hybrid app combines the functionalities of both native and Web-based apps. Like native apps, they are available in the app stores; and like Web apps, they are developed using standard Web programming languages (e.g., HTML) and then packaged up into native applications. Packaging or wrapping it into a native container makes it possible for a hybrid app to access native platform features.[6] The Facebook app, for example, was initially a hybrid app, but later was changed to a native app so it could take advantage of features of the various mobile devices it runs on. The advantage of hybrid apps is that they can be used on any mobile device, including Android, iOS, Windows, and BlackBerry. This way, businesses can get the advantages of native applications while keeping the cost of development down.

Classifying Apps by Type

Mobile apps have been created with the purpose to assist users in pursuing many different tasks, and there are dozens of possible categories that apps fall under. For example, the Google Play store lists at least 27 different app categories; only a few of the most common categories are discussed on the following pages.

- **Transaction-oriented apps** are designed to carry out virtual business transactions (such as purchasing a product or depositing money into an account) with customers. For example, eBay's app allows the user to buy, sell, and manage products using their mobile devices. The Venmo app is a digital wallet,[7] which allows users of the app to send and request money from friends, but they must also be a Venmo user to do so. Transaction-enabled apps provide functionality like an electronic commerce website's shopping cart system. Mobile transaction applications such as Vemno and Square fall into this category. Square helps millions of sellers run their business by including secure credit card processing and other point of sale solutions.[8]
- **Ads-oriented apps** are designed to generate revenue using advertising banners that are embedded in the app. Owners provide the app for free with the hope of generating revenue by linking the user to the advertiser's website. However, it should be noted that advertising can appear within any of types of apps listed in this section. For example, the YouTube app requires users trying to watch a video to view several seconds of advertising before proceeding to the content. However, there are ways to ensure users do not see ads or commercials on YouTube Finally, apps such as Pandora and Spotify each have a free version that requires users to view advertising and premium versions that are free of advertising.
- **Information-oriented apps** are designed primarily for providing information. Companies, organizations, and sometimes ordinary people deploy these apps to help users find information about things such as products, services, and facilities. These apps do not have virtual transaction abilities. Examples of information-oriented apps include Find-My-iPhone (locate an iPhone), Toilet-Finder, MyCar (for locating cars), and MapFactor (a navigation app).
- **Networking-oriented apps** such as Instagram, Twitter, and Tinder are designed to make it easier for users to connect with each other. These apps may have a common purpose, but they often appeal to different demographics. Millennials tend to use Instagram, Tinder, and Snapchat while the older population are easier to reach on Twitter and Facebook, etc. Meanwhile, organizations can use these apps to generate more attention by using selected features, such as hashtags.
- **Communication-oriented apps** are used to facilitate communication among users. Users can exchange text messages, pictures, and carry voice and video communication. WhatsApp, Snapchat, Group Me, and Facebook Messenger are examples of communication-oriented apps.
- **Entertainment-oriented apps** such as Netflix and Hulu are created for entertainment purposes, such as watching popular network programming. Gaming apps, such as Angry Birds and Candy Crush, are free but are monetized through in-app purchases.
- **Education-oriented apps**—many apps are created for educational purposes, such as learning a new skill, language, or subject. For example, Quizlet is an app that allows users to use commercially available study sets, or create their own to study with.
- **Self-improvement apps** are used to track their progress for a variety of purposes, including improvement of health, habits, skills, and abilities. Nike+, for example, is an app for tracking users workouts and fitness progress. Also, My Fitness Pal is a free online calorie counter and diet plan and has millions of users.

Characteristics of Mobile Apps

The best way to differentiate mobile apps from desktop-based applications is through its features. The following are some main features that distinguish mobile apps from desktop-based applications.

- **Always on:** An app is always on and connected to the Internet; this makes it possible to push information and content to users as it becomes available. For example, the Starbucks app sends users promotions when they are near a Starbucks (and, as Starbucks locations are numerous and widespread, there are many opportunities to be alerted by the app). The Weather App and Yahoo's Weather App send alerts to users when there is a high probability that it is about to rain or snow. It should be noted that many apps remain active even when a user closes out of them; however, notifications from the apps can be manually turned on or off.
- **Moveable:** Unlike the desktop applications, mobile apps go where the user goes. Thus, it stays with the user 24/7, and users can access it anywhere and anytime.
- **Location awareness:** Thanks to the GPS (global positioning system) embedded in mobile devices, apps are always aware of the user's location. The location awareness ability of apps is of great interest to social marketers, as it can be used to send target ads and promotions based on users' current locations. For example, Groupon helps users to find the best deals for restaurants and entertainment in their specific locations.
- **Focused:** Being focused on one theme/issue is one of the key features of mobile applications that distinguishes it from desktop-based applications or websites, which have a wider scope. There are always a narrow set of activities that apps are designed to carry out. For example, the Google Maps app is a subset of Google (and is fully integrated into Google's desktop website), but it is presented as a standalone application for mobile devices.
- **Personalized:** Mobile apps can provide personalized experiences based on a user's preferences. Users get to control what content they see and how it is shared. They can also control what exactly the app does, and how it performs (specifics depend on the app).
- **Short-term use:** Unlike desktop applications that are used for longer sessions (with some exceptions, such as video-streaming apps such as Netflix or Hulu), mobile app usage is characterized by frequent but short-term use ranging from several seconds to several minutes.
- **Inexpensive:** Most apps cost only a few dollars or are free.
- **Easy to use:** Last but not least, mobile apps are extremely easy to use and navigate.

Developing Apps

App development is beyond the scope of this book. However, when it comes to developing a mobile app, organizations have three options:

- **Do-it-yourself:** Hire a programmer/developer to develop one for the user or organization, which is usually very expensive. Google's software development kit (SDK) for mobile analytics is a great place to start.[9] This way the user can cut some of the development expenses; however, it requires a lot of technical resources.

- **Outsource app development:** If it is beyond the programming skills of an organization or individual to create an app, they can hire a company to develop a custom app for the user. However, by outsourcing app development, users lose control over the app and increase the development costs.
- **Open-source:** Users can create the business app through open-source platforms. For example, OpenMEAP™ is a case of an open source application platform that enables businesses with no technical skills to easily create, manage, and deploy mobile apps. Alternatively, business users could deploy the PhoneGap open source platform to create their app for free.[10]

Mobile Analytics Tools

Some leading mobile analytics tools are listed below:

- **Google Mobile Analytics** is a platform for analyzing and tracking mobile application data.[11]
- **Count.ly** is a mobile application analytic tool.[12]
- **Mixpanel** is a mobile analytics platform that is favored by developers for mobile clickstream analysis.[13]
- **Flurry** (Yahoo!) measures and analyzes activity across an app portfolio to answer marketing questions and optimize a user's mobile app experience.[14]

Case Study: Mobile Analytics to Optimize Process

About Airbnb

Airbnb is a trusted community marketplace for people to list, discover, and book unique accommodations around the world—online or from a mobile phone. Whether an apartment for a night, a castle for a week, or a villa for a month, Airbnb connects people to unique travel experiences, at any price point, in more than 33,000 cities and 192 countries. Airbnb is succeeding in the collaboration economy because they provide more affordable prices than most hotels. Also, Airbnb provides a variety of rental properties that appeal to many different types of travelers. Airbnb partnered with social influencers like the Kardashians, by giving them complimentary homes to rent when they travel and in return have them promote/advertise Airbnb to their large followers on social media.[15]

The problem

Travelers love Airbnb for the high number and wide variety of interesting spaces available to rent. Airbnb needed an analytics solution to help them optimize the process host properties go through as their rental spaces are listed.

The Solution

Airbnb built their Web Analytics tool from scratch when they developed their website. However, when it came time to launch their iPhone app, they turned to Mixpanel[16] to develop the app.[17] Airbnb had Mixpanel set up and track the events taking place on their iPhone app in just a couple of hours by importing Mixpanel's iPhone library into their app. Finally, Airbnb added custom tracking calls to all the events they wanted to analyze.

The Outcome

Airbnb did not just optimize their first-time listing and booking flows, they also used Mixpanel to measure where their customers spent the most time within the app, their most frequent actions, and the percentage of people who passively browsed vs. managed a booking. Airbnb used Mixpanel's event tracking and funnel analysis to optimize the listing process for first-time hosts. Funnel analysis involves tracking a series of events that lead towards a defined goal. Based on the drop-offs they found in the Mixpanel funnel analysis, Airbnb revamped host listing process on their app, resulting in a 400% increase in conversion rate.[18]

Review Questions

1. Explain the two main categories of Mobile Analytics.
2. What is the purpose of Apps Analytics?
3. Explain the different classes of mobile apps.
4. What are some key features of mobile apps?
5. Explain the different app development options.

Exercise: Connecting the Dots—the Mobile Application Type Assessment

With the Mobile Application Type Assessment tool,[19] we will explore and help the reader who is developing a mobile application decide what type of app best fits their needs. With this assessment tool, readers will be able to evaluate if their organization should begin development on a native smartphone application (native) or a browser-based mobile application (Web).

1. In the "Questionnaire" tab, answer the questions as they relate to your organization.
2. Check the "Results" tab to view your overall assessment and recommendations for your mobile

Many of our students (and readers) are working for organizations that are developing their own mobile applications. The assessment should be filled out by putting ourselves in the shoes of application stakeholder. Based on the way we filled out the Mobile Application Type Assessment, there is a stronger case to develop a Web application rather than a mobile application. Readers can download and complete the same assessment we did, and come up with a better understanding of which type of mobile app to develop.

For readers who are employed by corporations and startups (and perhaps nonprofits), developing a successful mobile app requires sophisticated business processes and executive buy-in. Use this assessment to audit the mobile marketing competencies of the organization so as to understand the current level of process maturity. In this evaluation, the reader is required to identify a way to evaluate their organization's current mobile marketing capabilities.

The Mobile Marketing Maturity Assessment, available via Demandmetric.com,[20] evaluates an organization's capability across seven key mobile marketing perspectives: Strategy, Resources, Results, Promotion, Execution, Follow-Up, and Measurement. For each of these different areas, the reader is required to select the level of process maturity they believe that they have.

Once the reader has gone through the mobile marketing audit, they will be able to determine what the level of process maturity exists in their organization for each of these categories. In this resource, we also provide readers with an overall mobile marketing effectiveness score and an overall mobile marketing maturity index.

Mobile Marketing Maturity Results

One of the authors filled out the self-assessment based on what he knew about his university's mobile marketing capabilities and discovered there is a stronger case for developing a Web-based app versus a native app. The results suggest that some universities may have a long way to go before they can deploy and support practical native or Web mobile applications.

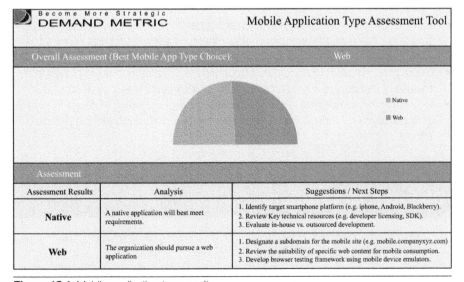

Figure 15.1 Mobile application type results.
Source: WebMetricsGuru Inc. using a Demand Metric Assessment.

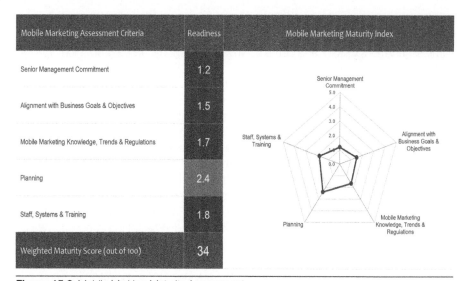

Mobile Marketing Assessment Criteria	Readiness	Mobile Marketing Maturity Index
Senior Management Commitment	1.2	
Alignment with Business Goals & Objectives	1.5	
Mobile Marketing Knowledge, Trends & Regulations	1.7	
Planning	2.4	
Staff, Systems & Training	1.8	
Weighted Maturity Score (out of 100)	34	

Figure 15.2 Mobile Marking Maturity Assessment.
Source: WebMetricsGuru Inc. using a Demand Metric Assessment.

The Mobile Marketing Maturity Assessment is another tool provided by Demandmetric.com that helps stakeholders determine their readiness to develop and market a mobile application. Demand Metric members can download the Mobile Marketing Maturity Assessment from the demandmetrics.com site, but the authors will seek permission to include it as a download for this book.[21]

Some of the Mobile Marketing Maturity Recommendations

Some of the following points emerged based on how the assessment was filled out:

- Obtaining buy-in from senior management is paramount, along with preparing a business case and scorecard for mobile marketing and present action plans to executives.
- Conducting research was indicated to determine if customers would benefit from the use of mobile and if it is profitable (from an ROI perspective, to do so).
- Reviewing the competitive landscape to identify opportunities (i.e., this suggests a similar analysis to Porter's Five Forces that many marketing students in business school).

Chapter 15 Citations

1. "App stores." Statista. www.statista.com/statistics/276623/number-of-apps-available-in-leading-app-stores. Accessed April 15, 2017.
2. "Make sure your site's ready for mobile-friendly Google search results." https://support.google.com/adsense/answer/6196932?hl=en. Accessed April 15, 2017.

3. "Google and mobile-friendly websites 2016." Search Infuse. May 17, 2016. www.searchinfuse.co.uk/google-mobile-friendly-websites-2016. Accessed April 15, 2017.

4. Lee, J. "Google: Local searches lead 50% of mobile users to visit stores." May 7, 2014. https://searchenginewatch.com/sew/study/2343577/google-local-searches-lead-50-of-mobile-users-to-visit-stores-study. Accessed April 15, 2017.

5. Korf, M. and E. Oksman. "Native, HTML5, or hybrid: Understanding your mobile application development options." https://developer.salesforce.com/page/Native,_HTML5,_or_Hybrid:_Understanding_Your_Mobile_Application_Development_Options. Accessed April 15, 2017.

6. Korf, M. and E. Oksman. "Native, HTML5, or hybrid: Understanding your mobile application development options." https://developer.salesforce.com/page/Native,_HTML5,_or_Hybrid:_Understanding_Your_Mobile_Application_Development_Options. Accessed April 15, 2017.

7. "Venmo." https://venmo.com. Accessed April 15, 2017.

8. "Square." https://squareup.com. Accessed April 15, 2017.

9. "Google Analytics for mobile apps." Google Developers. https://developers.google.com/analytics/solutions/mobile. Accessed April 15, 2017.

10. "PhoneGap." http://phonegap.com. Accessed April 15, 2017.

11. "Google Analytics for mobile apps." Google Developers. https://developers.google.com/analytics/solutions/mobile. Accessed April 15, 2017.

12. "Countly." https://count.ly. Accessed April 15, 2017.

13. "Mixpanel." https://mixpanel.com. Accessed April 15, 2017.

14. "Flurry analytics." Yahoo Developer Network. https://developer.yahoo.com/analytics. Accessed April 15, 2017.

15. Chung, G. "Inside Kim Kardashian's $30 million Airbnb." Celebuzz. www.celebuzz.com/2016-08-30/kim-kardashian-new-york-city-airbnb-kanye-west-mtv-vmas-2016. Accessed April 15, 2017.

16. "Mixpanel." https://mixpanel.com. Accessed April 15, 2017.

17. Vilcsak, A. "Airbnb—case study." Mixpanel. https://mixpanel.com/case-study/airbnb. Accessed April 15, 2017.

18. "Mixpanel office hours—Airbnb." YouTube. May 7, 2015. www.youtube.com/watch?v=-OYAqGAGlwg. Accessed April 15, 2017.

19. "Mobile Application Type Assessment tool." Demand Metric. www.demandmetric.com/content/mobile-application-type-assessment-tool. Accessed April 15, 2017.

20. "Mobile Marketing Maturity Assessment." Demand Metric. www.demandmetric.com/content/mobile-marketing-maturity-assessment. Accessed April 15, 2017.

21. Demandmetric.com has a policy of providing free access to their tools to educational institutions, and the authors will request permission to include it in this book in a downloadable portal (perhaps Dropbox).

16

Aligning Digital Media with Business Strategy

CHAPTER OBJECTIVES

After reading this chapter, readers should understand:

- The need to align social media content and campaigns with business goals
- How to perform a social media audit from several perspectives
- Steps that can be taken to minimalize the business risk arising from the deployment and use of social media

---

This chapter introduces Social Media Analytics and business alignment concepts, social media alignment matrices, the role of the chief information officer (CIO) in facilitating the alignment, and the steps needed to formulate a social media strategy. Having Social Media Analytics can be helpful as a tool ready to mine data, but that is simply not enough. Analytics should be strategically aligned to support existing and future business goals. Without a well-crafted and aligned social media strategy, the business will struggle to get the desired outcomes from analytics.

Reasons for Aligning Social Media with Business Goals and Use Cases

- Improve search engine rankings of a business's website
- Listen to and communicate with customers (increase customer satisfaction)
- Gain audience insights and provide market research (Social Media Analytics)
- Drive influencer marketing and communicate with influentials
- Provide customer support and advocacy services

Aligning social media objectives and goals with the organization's objectives should be the starting point of any Social Media Analytics initiative. In fact, the marketing strategy may fail without that alignment. Aligning Social Media Analytics with business objectives is analogous to the well-known Chinese yin and yang philosophy, where two seemingly opposing forces (in this case, social media and business) complement each other, as shown in Figure 16.1.

Figure 16.1 Aligning Social Media Analytics with business goals (yin and yang philosophy). *Source*: Gohar F. Khan.

Table 16.1 provides example scenarios for aligning social media with business objectives. If the business goal is to understand customer sentiments expressed over social media, the Social Media Analytics should be designed to facilitate this aim. It may require, for instance, tools and skills for extracting and analyzing tweets or comments posted on a Facebook fan page. Alternatively, when the objective is to identify important social media customers and their position in the network, the focus should be on social media networks.

Social Media Analytics Alignment Matrix

Several factors determine the alignment of Social Media Analytics with business goals. The factors impacting the alignment include the availability of technical, financial, and administrative resources appropriate to achieve the business goals. Aligning information technologies with business objectives has been a widely studied field. However, aligning Social Media Analytics with business objectives may require a comprehensive approach to the strategic alignment model suggested by Henderson and Venkatraman.[1]

Table 16.1 Aligning analytics with business objectives.

Example Business Question	Layer of Interest	Data Source	Tool Example
Is the social media conversation about our company or service positive, negative or neutral?	Text Analytics	Tweets, Comments, Retweets, Reviews	Discovertext, Lexalytics, Semantria, Brandwatch
Which content posted over social media is resonating with my customers?	Actions Analytics	Likes, Shares, Mentions, etc.	Google Analytics, Hootsuite
Who are the most influential network nodes and what is their position in the network?	Network Analytics	Fans, Followers, Network, etc.	NodeXL, Netlytic, Mentionmapp, etc.
How is our mobile app performing?	Mobile Analytics	Total Sessions, New Users, Time Spent, etc.	Count.ly, Mixpanel, Google Mobile Analytics
Where are our customers on social media located?	Location Analytics	Geo-Map, IP Address, GPS, etc.	Google Fusion Tables, Followerwonk, Tweepsmap, Picodash, etc.
What social media platforms are driving the most traffic to our corporate website?	Hyperlink Analytics	Hyperlinks, In-Links, Co-Links, etc.	VOSON, Webometrics Analyst, etc.
Which keywords or terms are trending?	Search Engine Analytics	Trending Topics	Google Trends, etc.

Source: Gohar F. Khan.

Figure 16.2 Social Media Alignment Matrix.
Source: Gohar F. Khan.

In this book, we used a simplified Social Media Analytics alignment matrix, as provided in Figure 16.2. On the Y axis of the matrix is "resource availability," which refers to the availability of financial, technical, administrative, and leadership resources for Social Media Analytics. On the X axis of the matrix is the impact of Social Media Analytics alignment regarding its potential to achieve business goals (or its potential to generate economic value and return on investment). Depending on the two variables (i.e., resources availability and its potential), an organization's Social Media Analytics alignment with business goals can fall into four possible quadrants.

When the alignment resides in the "highly aligned" quadrant of Figure 16.2, leadership, financial, administrative, and technical resources are available within the organization to leverage and (sustain) Social Media Analytics. Also, the potential is high in regard to achieving business goals. For instance, mining the layers of social media data is technically and financially demanding, but rewarding to the organization. Moreover, the Social Media Analytics alignment efforts reside in the "not aligned" quadrant when its potential to achieve business goals and the organization's resource availability is low.

Overall, an organization's analytics efforts ought to focus on highly aligned and high-impact alternatives. Nevertheless, the business goals and availability of resources will play a major role in determining the depth of the analytical efforts and resulting quadrant in the matrix. For instance, using Facebook's built-in analytical tools is financially and technically less challenging than using a sophisticated Facebook analytics tool, such as SocialBakers, Quintly, and Razorsocial,[2] which may require technical and financial resources, but are more helpful to achieve the stated business goals.

The alignment matrix visualized in Figure 16.2 is very flexible. We can replace the variables at both the axes with any other variables of interest. For example, by placing the criticality of Social Media Analytics (the extent to which the analytics is critical to

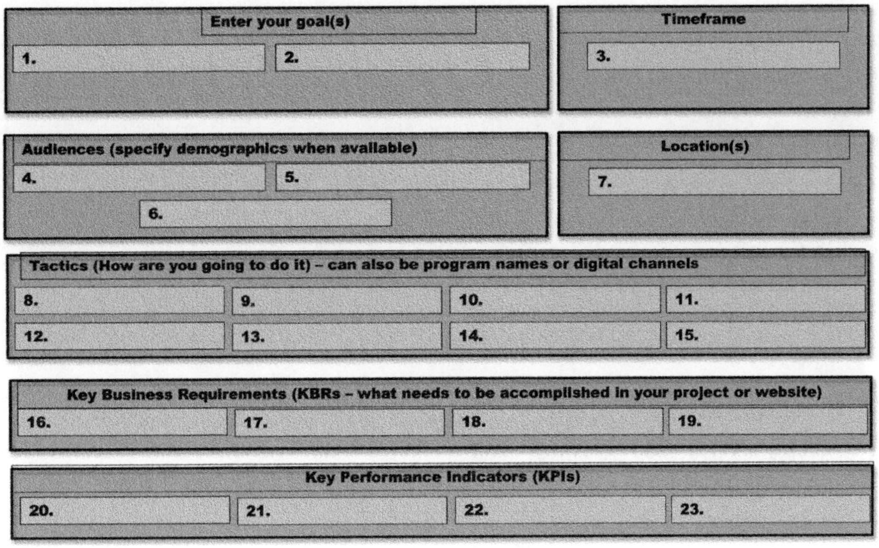

Enter your goal(s)		Timeframe
1.	2.	3.

Audiences (specify demographics when available)		Location(s)
4.	5.	7.
6.		

Tactics (How are you going to do it) – can also be program names or digital channels

8.	9.	10.	11.
12.	13.	14.	15.

Key Business Requirements (KBRs – what needs to be accomplished in your project or website)

16.	17.	18.	19.

Key Performance Indicators (KPIs)

20.	21.	22.	23.

Figure 16.3 Social Media Analytics strategy alignment process.
Source: WebMetricsGuru Inc.

the business) on the Y axis and sensitivity of the analytics (e.g., regarding security, privacy, or ethics) on the X axis and determine the extent of your alignment. The Social Media Analytics alignment matrix will assist in the formulation of the business strategies needed to achieve the business goals, as illustrated in Figure 16.3.

Senior IT executives, particularly the CIO, play a major role in envisioning and creating aligned Social Media Analytics strategy. The CIO is the person in charge of managing and aligning information communications technologies (ICTs) to achieve business-wide goals. The role of CIO has evolved from a technical guru to an informed leader, communicator, and strategic thinker. For a sustained strategic IT–business goals alignment, a CIO should possess the following skills and competencies:[3]

Strategic thinking and evaluation:

- Business and policy reasoning
- IT investment for value creation
- Performance assessment
- Evaluation and adjustment

Systems orientation:

- Environmental awareness
- System and social dynamics
- Stakeholders and users
- Business processes
- Information flow and workflow

Appreciation for complexity:

- Communication
- Negotiation

- Cross-boundary relationships
- Risk assessment and management
- Problem-solving

Information stewardship:

- Information policies
- Data management
- Data quality
- Information sharing and integration
- Records management
- Information preservation

Technical leadership:

- Communication and education
- Architecture
- Infrastructure
- Information and systems security
- Support and services
- IT workforce investments

Formulating a Social Media Strategy

The purpose of formulating a social media strategy is to create business rules and procedures that align social media with stated business goals (such as reaching out to a target market to increase the business's awareness and popularity with that audience). Planning an aligned social media strategy should follow a strategy formulation process like that used by IT management, as suggested by Luftman et al.,[4] although some additional steps are needed to account for the unique nature of social media technologies.

Steps in Formulating a Social Media Strategy

The following steps will lead to the formulation of a sound social media strategy.

- **Get hold of an executive champion:** For any organizational strategy development and implementation, the sponsorship of a senior-level executive is crucial. The most important factor for success in Social Media Analytics is not technology, but leadership and top management commitment. Success is possible only when the transformation is steered through strong leadership, setting in the right direction, building momentum, and ensuring the disciplined execution of an inspiring vision and ambitious plans (i.e., Steve Jobs comes to mind with the way he promoted Apple products in his product launch videos). A social media executive champion will be someone with charisma and the power to enforce social media strategy in the organization. It usually is the head of the department or the government chief information officer (GCIO). Enlisting the support of a champion is crucial for social media efforts to be fruitful.

- **Build a cross-functional team:** The first step in formulating a social media strategy is to create a cross-functional team with senior management members from all the departments, including the IT department. Ideally, this team should be led by a CIO. Having a cross-functional team will make sure that all the stakeholders have their say and have ownership of the Social Media Analytics initiative.
- **Assessing organizational culture:** Is the organization ready to embrace Social Media Analytics? What are the organization's assumptions and beliefs about Social Media Analytics? Embracing social media in all aspects of the business requires organizational cultural transformation at all levels. Corporate culture refers to the shared values, attitudes, standards, and beliefs of the members of an organization. By first seeking to understand the current state of the corporate culture, it becomes much easier to determine how to improve it. Understanding a corporate culture and transforming it is a very complex task and is beyond the scope of this book. A roundtable with the team members may provide some clues on the organization's social media readiness. Perhaps the age of members is a factor; note that organizations with younger management tend to use social media more effectively, and are thus more open to using it than senior execs. Also, a variety of organizational culture assessment and change tools are available on the market that can be used to access and highlight the need for a cultural shift. For example, The Organizational Culture Assessment Instrument (OCAI) is a free tool for diagnosing organizational culture (developed by Professors Robert Quinn and Kim Cameron) and Culture Builder Toolkit prepared by Corporate Culture Pros.[5] The bottom line is that with the cultural assessment, business users and stakeholders may want to ensure that their organization is ready to embrace social media and that it has the necessary vision and will to leverage it (i.e.: by targeting specific users attention and building a following via social media).
- **Review the current social media presence:** Before formulating a social media strategy, stakeholders need to document their current social media use and presence (i.e., by using some of the platforms in previous chapters of this book). Start by asking team members about their current social media status and by conducting a search for social media pages representing their organization. The best way to do it would be to arrange small, interactive seminars. The objective is to find out all the officially sanctioned and unauthorized social media outlets, including blogs, wikis, fan pages, and Twitter pages that use the organization's name. For example, they may use topsy.com to search for social media profiles representing the organization. They can also employ a SWOT (Strength, Weakness, Opportunities, and Threats) analysis to determine their current social media landscape. Documenting the status will determine a baseline, and help stakeholders streamline their organization's social media presence.
- **Determining business objectives:** Once we measure and understand the baseline social media presence, the next step is to create a list of the targets and goals to achieve through that social media presence. With a clear idea of what stakeholders want to accomplish with social media, they are likely to put together a sound social media strategy. Clearly defining business goals and objectives is important, as different social media goals require different sets of actions and tools. In a worst-case scenario, having teams with divergent views and goals in mind will make it next to impossible to get anything done. Making sure everyone is on the same page is one of the keys to a successful business enterprise. Below are some commonly identified objectives.

Some Possible Social Media Business Tactics

- Attract customers by driving traffic with high-quality content on social media platforms, such as LinkedIn that links back to corporate websites.
- Share news, alerts, and updates through social media platforms, including Twitter, Facebook, and YouTube (i.e., statistics show millennials are more likely to check social media platforms for the news rather than mainstream media news sites).
- Implement a participatory platform (e.g., blog) where customers can submit ideas and suggestions, providing them with the opportunity to participate in business strategy-making.
- Increase awareness about products/services by disseminating information on social media platforms.
- Provide customer service and resolve issues.

Each department may have different goals and objectives to be achieved through social media platforms, so creating a broader social media policy will make sure each department has its say. The social media engagement matrix introduced earlier can be used here to determine the ease of achieving an objective against its impact.

Aligning Social Media Goals with Business Goals

As mentioned earlier, aligning social media goals with business goals is vital. First, each goal must be specific, realistic, and measurable. Next, each goal should be brought into line with the existing business goals and strategy. If the organizational goal is to network with customers via social media platforms, the social media strategy should be aligned with this objective.

Developing a Content Strategy

Establishing a social media presence is the easy part; sustaining it is the real challenge (i.e., the problem of getting new followers as well as keeping them). Developing a sound content strategy will make sure stakeholders know what to post and when to post, and how to post the right content. Content strategy is tied to the business goals, and only the content that supports the goals should be developed and posted. Organizations should know how to target a specific audience by using the correct form of social media and tweak their content to fit the demographics and psychographics of the target audience.

A sound content strategy should at the minimum answer the following questions:

- What type of content should we post to social media; for example, news, updates, alerts?
- How often should we post the content? Daily or weekly?
- Who will create the content?
- Does the organization approve the content?
- Who will respond to follow-up suggestions and comments?
- How will the feedback be handled?

Platform Strategy

A successful platform strategy should detail the type of social media platforms that are being utilized to achieve business objectives. The platforms being used should be matched to the business goals and objectives. For example, if the aim is to share news, alerts, and updates, choose existing mainstream social media platforms, such as Twitter, Facebook, and YouTube. However, if the goal is to crowdsource ideas, a custom-built Web 2.0 or Web 3.0 platform may be needed; the strategy goals and objectives will determine what type of resources that are required.

Resource Considerations

Social media is the place for organizations to interact with their consumers. It increases the touchpoints throughout the customer journey. It is crucial to understand the desired level of social media engagement, as it will determine the kind of resources (technical, human, and financial) that are required. For example, if the goal is to establish an idea-generation platform to solicit creative ideas in-house, the purpose-built platform may be necessary. Bear in mind that creating and sustaining a Facebook fan page requires planning, along with human, financial, and technical resources. Facebook pages should contain posts, updates, and answers to customer complaints. Extraction and analysis of data (tweets or comments) should be used for better decision-making. Facebook business pages will also display how quickly they typically respond to customer's messages. However, Hootsuite and Buffer are among the platforms that can help business users create and distribute their content. Both platforms can send out tweets at certain, preconfigured times. While it may sound easy to create an engaging social media presence, in practice it is time-consuming and repetitive. That is why organizations form dedicated teams to tackle all the work associated with maintaining a successful social media presence.

Establish a Social Media Security Policy

A social media ownership plan and policy should outline the rights and responsibilities of employers and employees. Security plans cover social media ownership regarding both accounts and activities such as accounts themselves, individual and pages profiles, platform content, and posting activity. Policies related to social media clarify issues related to personal and professional use, trade secrets, intellectual property, confidentiality, etc. Courtney Hunt[6] has done an excellent job of providing social media ownership guidelines. The guidelines touch on the following areas related to social media ownership.

- **Organizations accounts and profiles:** This part of the ownership plan deals with all the social media accounts and activities, such as accounts themselves, individual and page profiles, platform content, and posting activity. Ideally, all the organization's social media profiles should be owned by the organization.
- **Individual profiles:** The individuals' personal social media profiles; businesses should provide employees with comprehensive social media guidelines for how they are permitted to use social media while working for the company. Employees should consider setting their social media profiles to be private to protect their

image/reputation (especially in the age we live in, where privacy barely exists). Employees are representations of the company and what they do outside of work, although personal, can be a direct influence on the company's image. One can never be too careful about content posted on social media.

- **Contact information:** Social media allows people to have multiple contact addresses (e.g., email), and this policy should specify which communication medium the employee should display on their personal profile. A good practice is that employees include both a personal and a professional address.
- **Contacts:** This policy should specify the rules for social media contacts made during the employment period (e.g., through LinkedIn). For example, business owners might specify that the contacts made are joint property, but that employees can keep their contacts after leaving the organization. However, organizations should have a contact management system to capture the valuable contacts or leads, such as Salesforce.
- **Comments:** Ownership strategy should also provide policies and guidelines on whether and how employees can comment on a variety of social media platforms. For example, when commenting, employees should make it clear whether they are commenting on behalf of the organization or expressing their personal thoughts.
- **Posting:** What should and should not be posted to the social media platform is covered here. Clearly defining posting rules can help avoid issues with trade secrets, intellectual property, confidentiality, defamation, etc.
- **Groups:** Organizations may establish policies and guidelines about the kind of groups employees can join or be members of. Allowing employees to join groups that promote business goals is encouraged.
- **Privacy settings:** By setting guidelines for social media privacy settings, agencies may encourage employees to set their social media privacy settings in the best interest of the both individuals and the organization.

A paper published by Socialfish.org on the risks connected with social media provides further useful guidelines on the structure and characteristics of a sound social media policy.[7]

Select Success Metrics

Success metrics such as likes, shares, tweets, retweets, followers, and following, will help stakeholders evaluate their social media strategy's effectiveness. Defined metrics should be put in place to measure the success of social media in the organization. Metrics will help determine whether social media is making a difference in the business. Depending on the type of social media engagement, success metrics may vary. For example, if the prime objective of the social media use is to engage customers in dialogue, the number of comments may be utilized as a metric. Alternatively, if it is to promote awareness, then the number of likes, shares, and pageviews may provide some indication.

Use Analytics to Track Progress

Social Media Analytics should be used to evaluate social media presence and determine how the organization is performing. For example, Google Analytics can provide useful Web metrics, such as visits and conversions. Hootsuite Pro also offers advanced analytics and reporting for social media measurement needs. The important thing to note is that the analytical tools should be properly configured to match the organization's success metrics and business goals. Organizations almost always have a vast amount of internal and external data at their disposal, but it is not always captured in a usable form. For instance, customer call center complaints from the Macys.com retail site that are initiated by customers, but not cross-referenced to their website visits where their issues first occurred. It is probably best to perform an audit to understand better what data exists in the organization, where it is located, who owns the data, and how to access it.

Social Media Strategy Implementation Plan

A strategy implementation plan is an essential part of the social media strategy formulation process. This plan lays out strategies and tactics to put the strategic plans into action. The strategy implementation process can vary from organization to organization and depends on a variety of factors, including support from senior executives and involvement of members from key departments. Four major barriers to strategic implementation are:[8]

- 85% of executive teams spend less than one hour per month discussing strategy
- 60% of strategic plans are not linked to budgets
- 25% of managers have incentives linked to strategy
- 5% of the workforce understands the strategy

The best way to go is to select team members from key departments who understand the purpose of the plan and the steps involved in implementing it. Establish a mechanism to discuss progress reports and let team members know what has been accomplished. Communicate the plan throughout the organization and clearly specify ownerships, deadlines, and accountabilities.

Periodic Review

In the face of rapid technological, business, and social changes, the social media strategy should be periodically reviewed. The review will make sure that the initial assumption made about the external and internal factors (e.g., technology, vision, budgets) are still relevant.

Protecting Business and Data Security

The rise of social media and its pervasive use introduces new challenges for marketers. Persistent challenges to privacy, security, data management, accessibility, social inclusion, governance, information security, cyber-warfare, and fake news sites have arisen. It has become important to protect online assets in much the same way that offline, brick-and-mortar operations have traditionally been guarded. For example, damage caused by the Sony Pictures hack in late 2014, allegedly perpetrated by North Korea, ran into several million dollars for the movie studio.[9]

The risk is defined as the possibility of losing something of value, such as intellectual or physical capital. A comprehensive definition of risk is provided by National Institute

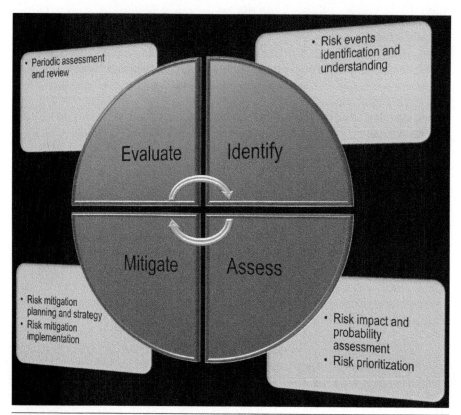

Figure 16.4 Social media risk-management framework.
Source: Gohar F. Khan.

of Standards and Technology (NIST), which states that "risk is a function of the likelihood of a given threat sources exercising a particular potential vulnerability, and the resulting impact of that adverse event on the organization" (http://nvlpubs.nist. gov/nistpubs/Legacy/SP/nistspecialpublication800-30r1.pdf). Here we will focus on the risks associated with social media usage and define it as the potential of losing something of value (such as intellectual property, information, reputation, or goodwill).

Social media-related risks need to be managed properly, both from the strategic and technological point of view. Organizations need a set of proactive social media risk-management strategies.

A simple but effective way to proactively manage social media risks is through the social media crisis management loop (Figure 16.4), which includes four iterative steps:

1. **Identify:** Potential risks are identified.
2. **Assess:** Risks are assessed and prioritized regarding the probability of occurrence and impact on the organization.
3. **Mitigate:** Risk reduction strategies are formulated and implemented.
4. **Evaluate:** Periodic assessment and reviews are carried out.

Below, we discuss each step.

Risk Identification

- Risk identification is the process of identifying social media threats (such as friend-ing fake social media accounts, fake news, and malware) regarding vulnerabilities and exploits that could potentially inhibit the organization from achieving its objectives. At this stage, the goal is to determine potential accidental or malicious risks that can come from within or outside the company. Examples of common (but not necessarily malicious) social media-related security breaches are hacking, information leaks, phishing (defrauding an online account holder of financial information by posing as a legitimate company), and impersonation. Phishing and hacking are examples of malicious outsider attacks.

Two examples of malicious security breaches:

- A Snapchat employee in the payroll department fell for a phishing attack and ended up exposing information on several current and former employees.[10] In response, Snapchat contacted affected employees and offered two years of identity-theft monitoring and insurance. Additionally, Snapchat improved its security education efforts for employees.
- A growing number of incidents at hospitals across the country have revealed PHI, PII, and other sensitive information. Three incidents were caused by a phishing attack, unauthorized access to a database, and an improper mailing, revealing the cost of human error in breaches.[11]

Well known social media platforms (such as Facebook, Twitter, and YouTube) are at high risk for security breaches. According to a study based on surveys and interviews with 99 professionals and 36 companies,[12] the main social media risks identified are the following:

- Damage to reputation and trust
- The release of confidential information
- Legal, regulatory, and compliance violations
- Identity theft and hijacking
- Loss of intellectual property
- Loss of privacy
- Social engineering attacks

While not exactly a social media platform, 500 million Yahoo! accounts were breached in 2014, but the public did not find out about it until the news was announced in February 2016.[13] The theft included names, email addresses, telephone numbers, dates of birth, and in some cases, encrypted or unencrypted security questions and answers. Yahoo believed the theft (the largest security breach ever to have taken place in the history of the United States) was state-sponsored (i.e., by Russia, China, Iran, etc.). Let's not forget to briefly mention the political upheaval, security hacks, and fake news (spread via social and mainstream media) that dominated the 2016 US presidential election occurred at an extremely high visibility level that had never been seen before.[14] The implications are that no computer system is fully immune from being hacked, and soon we are likely to see even more privacy violations at every level, similar to what occurred in 2015 and 2016, leading up to and during the election.[15]

Risk Assessment

Risk assessment is "the process of assessing the probabilities and consequences of risk events if they are realized."[16] The risk evaluation process determines the likelihood of a social media risk event that could impact the organization economically and socially. The potential risks identified in the earlier step are priorities and ranked based on the probability of occurrence and impact on an organization.[16]

Probability (P) is the likelihood of occurrence of a risk event and can take a value from 0 to 1. Probability can, for example, be assigned to risks events as follows:

- **Certain to occur (P=1):** The risks with a P value equal to 1 are the risks that will certainly happen. In other words, they have a 100% chance of occurring.
- **Extremely sure to occur (P=> 95 <1):** The risks, for example, with a probability value greater than 0.95 and less than 1.0 can be considered as "extremely sure to happen" risks. In other words, they have a 95–100% chance of occurring.
- **Almost sure to occur (P= > 0.85 <= 0.95):** The risks with a probability value greater than 0.85 and less than or equal to 0.95 can be considered as "very likely to occur" risks. The can be said to have an 85–95% chance of occurring.
- **Very likely to occur (P=> 0.75 <=0.85):** These are the risks with a 75–85% chance of occurring.
- **Likely to occur (P=> 0.65 <=0.75):** These are the risks with a 65–75% chance of occurring.
- **Slightly likely to occur (P=> 0.55 <=0.65):** These are the risks with a 55–65% chance of occurring.
- **Evenly likely to occur (P=> 0.45 <=0.55):** These are the risks with a 45–55% chance of occurring.

As shown in Table 16.2, stakeholders can assign other probabilities similarly.

The impact of a risk event can be characterized as:

1. Severe
2. Significant
3. Moderate
4. Minor
5. Minimal

Table 16.2 Risk probability and prioritization assessment.

Probability (P)	Chance of occurrence	Priority
P=1	Certain to occur	High Priority Risks
P=> 0.95 <1	Extremely sure to occur	High Priority Risks
P=> 0.85 <= 0.95	Almost sure to occur	High Priority Risks
P=> 0.75 <=0.85	Very likely to occur	High Priority Risks
P=> 0.65 <=0.75	Likely to occur	High Priority Risks
P=> 0.55 <=0.65	Slightly likely to occur	Medium Priority Risks
P=> 0.45 <=0.55	Evenly likely to occur	Medium Priority Risks
P=> 0.35 <=0.45	Less than an even chance	Medium Priority Risks
P=> 0.25 <=0.35	Less likely to occur	Low Priority Risks
P=> 0.15 <=0.25	Not likely to occur	Low Priority Risks
P=> 0.00 <=0.15	Certainly sure not to occur	Low Priority Risks

Source: Gohar F. Khan, based on Mitre methodology.

A risk event is considered severe if it has devastating economic, technological, political, or social impact on the organization. Moreover, a risk is deemed minimal if its impact is minimal or negligible.

Based on the incidence and probability, social media risks can be prioritized as:

1. High
2. Medium
3. Low

- **High priority hazards:** Risks that will have a severe impact on the organization. These are risks that need immediate attention and should be managed carefully.
- **Medium priority risks:** Medium-probability risks that have a considerable impact the organization.
- **Low priority risks:** Low probability risks that have a low impact on the organization.

Risk Mitigation

The risks prioritized and ranked in the earlier stage should be physical, technically, and procedurally managed, eliminated, or reduced to an acceptable level. Depending on the nature of the risks, different strategies should be used. The accidental risks posed by employees (e.g., posting copyrighted material online or tweeting confidential information) can be eliminated by a training and awareness program. It also helps to have a sound social media policy in place to minimize risks. Hacking attacks are another type of security risk that is mitigated using updated antivirus systems and by creating an extra layer of security. In fact, that is why so many jobs have a firewall of what sites can be accessed at work—several ban all social media sites.

Measures to Decrease Risk

- **Risks management governance:** New governance structures, roles, and policies are created within the business for properly managing social media risks. These activities may involve identifying and empowering a social media risk management manager, developing a business-wide risk-management strategy, the identification of actions and steps needed to implement the strategy, and determining the resources required to mitigate the risks.[17] This risk assessment should include IT, finance, public relations, human resources, legal, and communications. These components play a major role in identifying and mitigating social media risks.
- **Training and awareness:** Provide education and spread awareness on legal issues such as copyright, intellectual property, defamation, slander, and antitrust issues.
- **Social media policy:** Create a sound and easily accessible social media policy that outlines the related rights and responsibilities of employers and employees. As of 2013, 72% of U.S. companies did not have a social media security policy for employees.[18]
- **Secure social media platforms:** Secure social media platforms to minimize the impact or likelihood of the security risk from occurring.

Security measures are set up at the platform level (i.e., Facebook sets up its security protocols), but some programs can scan social media accounts, such as

Facebook pages, for malicious words in visitor posts. When malicious words are detected, the posts are automatically flagged and hidden from view until the page owner examines them.

Creating Strong Passwords
The following techniques will help secure various social media platforms:

- Password should be at least ten characters long.
- Password should contain a combination of uppercase and lowercase letters, numbers, and symbols.
- Password should not include personal information such as phone numbers, birthdays, name, etc.
- Password should not contain common words (such as "and," "or," "but," "the," etc.).
- Password should not use alphabetical sequences (such as "abcd1234") or keyboard sequences (such as "qwerty").
- Password should not be reused across websites; for example, the Twitter account password should be unique to Twitter.
- Password should be memorized and kept in a safe place if written down.

Securing Facebook Accounts
Two-step authentication: Many organizations are following this model. Facebook's two-step authentication (or login approval, as Facebook calls it) is an excellent way to secure your account. It provides an extra layer of security that uses a phone to protect user accounts. For example, if an account is compromised or someone figures out a user password, they will still not be able to access the account unless they have physical access to a security token such as a four-digit pin. Each time the user logins in from an unknown browser or computer, they will need to provide a security code to access their account (unless the device is listed as secure). The security code is only given to the user through their phone via a text message or through a third-party code application installed on a smartphone, such as the Google Authenticator application.

- *Steps*: Login to your Facebook account → Go to "Account Settings" → "Security Settings" → "Login Approvals" → "Getting Started". Clicking on the "Getting Started" button will take you through a step-by-step process to enable the two-mode authentication. Note that the codes cannot be texted to a landline or Google Voice, so you will need a mobile phone to configure the authentication properly.

Trusted contact: The trusted contact is an account recovery feature provided by Facebook to help members access their account securely through their friends when they have trouble accessing their account. Members select three to five friends to be trusted contacts who can be reached independently of Facebook (e.g., phone or email). In the case of emergency, members can contact their trusted contacts and Facebook will provide each of them a security code with instructions on how to help the member. The member can then use the codes to recover their Facebook account.

- *Steps*: Login to your account → "Account Settings" → "Security Settings" → "Trusted Contacts" → "Choose Trusted Contacts".

Review your login history: It is a good practice regularly to review your account login history and location.

- *Steps*: Login to your account → "Account Settings" → "Security Settings" → "Where you are Logged In". Your location is estimated with your public IP address. Bringing your cursor over the location will display the IP used to access the account. Make sure the IP address is associated with the organization. The page will also provide information about other devices used to access the account (e.g., Chrome on Windows 7 or Android-based device). If you notice any unfamiliar devices or locations, you can end the session by clicking on the "End Activity" button.

Login notification: Enable your Facebook login notification so that you can be notified through email or text message when your account is accessed.

- *Steps*: Login to your account → "Account Settings" → "Login Notification" → "Email" and "Text". The notification email provides detailed information about the login, including the IP address used, location, time, and type of device used to access the account.

Disable or revoke third-party apps: Your information (e.g., friends list and profile) is available to third-party applications running on Facebook. Third-party apps are developed by other companies but have access to Facebook via its application programming interface (API). While third-party apps improve your Facebook experience (e.g., if you allow access to the WordPress app, your Facebook updates will automatically appear on your wordpress.com blog), some of them may be vulnerable to attacks or may handle your account information insecurely. Here is how to disable the vulnerable apps:

- *Steps*: Login to your account → "Account Settings" → "Security Settings" → "Apps" → "Edit" → "Disable Platforms".

Securing Your Twitter Account

Use login verification: Like Facebook, Twitter also provides two-step authentication known as login verification. After enabling the login verification feature, you will need both your password and your phone to log in to your Twitter account. When you log in to Twitter.com, you will receive a text message with a login code or a push notification.

- *Steps*: "Settings" → "Security and Privacy Settings" → "Send login verification requests to my phone" → when prompted, click "Okay, send me a message" → if you receive the verification message, click "Yes". Before using this feature, make sure that you verify your emails, add a phone number, and check that your carrier is Twitter-supported.[19]

Revoke third-party apps: Like Facebook, Twitter also provides access to third-party apps. While these apps make your Twitter experience more convenient, as mentioned earlier, some of them may be vulnerable to attacks or may handle your account information insecurely. Here is how to disable them:

- *Steps*: Log in to your account → "Settings" → "Apps" → you will be provided with a list of apps that have access to your account → "Revoke Access".

Use strong passwords: As already discussed.

Securing Your Blog

The following are some techniques to secure your blog.

Two-step authentication: *Steps*: Go to your blog and click on your avatar (or profile picture if you have uploaded one) available in the upper right-hand corner of the window → "Account Settings" → "Security" → "Two-Step Authentication".

Disconnect third-party applications: *Steps:* "Account Settings" → "Security" → "Connection Applications" → click on any unwanted applications that you want to remove → "Remove App Connection".

Back up your blog: You can back up your blog's content (including posts, pages, comments, custom fields, terms, navigation menus, and custom posts), which then can be restored in case of emergency. Here is how to do it:

- Step 1: Go to your blog by typing its address into your Internet browser.
- Step 2: Click on the "WP Admin" option, this will bring you to the blog's "Dashboard".
- Step 3: Once in the Dashboard click on the "Tools" available at the lower left corner of the dashboard, and then on "Export". There are two export options: "Export" and "Guided Transfer". Select the "Export" option.
- Step 4: You will be offered a "Choose What to Export" option. Click on the default "Select All Content" and click "Download export file". Save the file in a secure location. It can be restored when needed.

To restore the blog content you have exported earlier, use the following steps:

- *Steps:* "WP Admin" → "Tools" → "Import" → from the available systems select "WordPress" → "Choose the file" you have saved to your computer → "Upload File and Import".

Risk Evaluation

Social media risk management is a rigorous process that requires professional stakeholders who are kept informed. In the face of rapid technological, political, and social change, social media risks should be periodically reviewed. The continuous evaluation and monitoring efforts will make sure that the initial assumption made about the external and internal risks are still relevant.

Summary

This chapter covered the some of the essential elements of aligning business goals with social media and introduced the social media alignment matrix. Also, we discussed a way to evaluate the risks involved that are connected with Social Media Analytics using the Mitre framework. To reduce risk, organizations should take stringent steps to protect passwords, personal and business accounts, and infrastructure from various security threats, including network and computer hacking.

Review Questions

1. What are some common social media risks?
2. Explain the four steps in social media risk management.
3. Explain common social media risk mitigation strategies.

4   Explain different techniques to secure social media accounts.
5. What is the goal of aligning Social Media Analytics with business objectives?
6. Explain the social media alignment matrix.
7. Briefly, explain the role of CIO in aligning analytics with business objectives.
8. What is the purpose of a social media strategy?
9. Explain the steps needed to formulate a social media strategy.

Chapter 16 Citations

1. Henderson, J.C. and N. Venkatraman. "Strategic alignment: Leveraging information technology for transforming organizations." http://didattica.cs.unicam.it/lib/exe/fetch.php?media=didattica:magistrale:abit:ay_1516:henderson_venkatraman_1993_strategic_alignment_leveraging_information_technology_for_transforming_organizations.pdf. Accessed April 15, 2017.

2. Cleary, I. "Facebook analytics tools: 7 alternatives to Facebook Insights." August 19, 2016. www.razorsocial.com/facebook-analytics-tools. Accessed April 15, 2017.

3. Dawes, S.S. (2008). "What Makes a Successful CIO?" *Intergovernmental Solutions Newsletter*, GSA Office of Citizen Services and Communications. 21.

4. Luftman, J.N., C.V. Bullen, et al. (2004). *Managing the Information Technology Resource: Leadership in the Information Age*. New York: Prentice Hall.

5. "OCAI online." www.ocai-online.com. Accessed April 15, 2017.

6. Hunt, C. "Social media ownership: Recommendations for employers." http://denovati.com/2014/02/social-media-ownership. Accessed April 15, 2017.

7. Dreyer, L., M. Grant, and L.T. White. "Social media, risk, and policies for associations." SocialFish. www.socialfish.org/wp-content/downloads/socialfish-policies-whitepaper.pdf. Accessed April 15, 2017.

8. Kaplan, R.S. and D.P. Norton. "The strategy-focused organization." http://iveybusinessjournal.com/publication/building-a-strategy-focused-organization. Accessed April 15, 2017.

9. Musil, S. "Sony Pictures hack has cost the company only $15 million so far." CNET. February 4, 2015. www.cnet.com/news/sony-pictures-hack-to-cost-the-company-only-15-million. Accessed April 15, 2017.

10. King, H. "Snapchat employee fell for a phishing scam." CNN. February 29, 2016. http://money.cnn.com/2016/02/29/technology/snapchat-phishing-scam. Accessed April 15, 2017.

11. Bailey, M. "The latest in phishing: March 2016." Wombat Security. March 16, 2016. https://info.wombatsecurity.com/blog/the-latest-in-phishing-march-2016. Accessed April 15, 2017.

12. Webber, A. "Guarding the social gates: The imperative for social media risk management." www.slideshare.net/Altimeter/guarding-the-social-gates-the-imperative-for-social-media-risk-management. Accessed April 15, 2017.

13. Snider, M. and E. Weise. "500 million Yahoo accounts breached." USA Today. September 22, 2016. www.usatoday.com/story/tech/2016/09/22/report-yahoo-may-confirm-massive-data-breach/90824934. Accessed April 15, 2017.

14. Gallagher, S. "Did the Russians 'hack' the election? A look at the established facts." Ars Technica. December 12, 2016. http://arstechnica.com/security/2016/12/the-public-evidence-behind-claims-russia-hacked-for-trump. Accessed April 15, 2017.

15. "2015–2016 US politics hacking." www.thompsontimeline.com/tag/2015–2016-us-politics-hacking. Accessed April 15, 2017.

16. "Risk impact assessment and prioritization." www.mitre.org/publications/systems-engineering-guide/acquisition-systems-engineering/risk-management/risk-impact-assessment-and-prioritization. Accessed April 15, 2017.

17. Garvey, P.R. (2008) *Analytical Methods for Risk Management: A Systems Engineering Perspective.* New York: Taylor & Francis Group.

18. "73% of companies do not have employee social media policies." April 9, 2013. http://leaderswest.com/2013/04/09/study-68-of-companies-dont-share-the-purpose-of-social-media-with-employees. Accessed April 15,. 2017.

19. "Updating your email address." Twitter Help Center. https://support.twitter.com/articles/15356. Accessed April 15, 2017.

Applying Digital Analytics to a Social Network

Author: Adi Andrei, CEO of Meritwork

Meritwork—Building Trust on the Internet

Meritwork is an online services marketplace that makes heavy use of different types of digital analytics to fulfill its mission.

Platform Vision

Initially, we wanted to find a way to lower the very high barrier of entry most self-employed and entrepreneurs encounter when starting a new venture, entering or creating a new market. At the same time, we were all frustrated by how hard it was to find service providers (like an accountant, graphic designer, massage therapist, Web developer, etc.) that we could trust without having to go through a few people and lose quite a bit of time and money in the process. So we started to look into why these things were happening and what we could do about it.

Per a study commissioned by the Freelancers Union in 2014, 53 million Americans are independent workers.[1] This is around 35% of the total workforce, and the number is expected to grow significantly in the coming years. We see a similar situation developing around the world, and this is being driven by multiple factors.

On one side, technology has revolutionized the ability to work from anywhere. This has led to the rise of co-working and increasing preference in many professionals for location-independent jobs. At the same time, in recession economies or unstable economic times, companies tend to hire less full-time employees, preferring the use of contractors. Not to mention that traditional job security is more and more a thing of the past, even in cultures like Japan where it used to be a given that you will work only for one corporation that will take care of you for the rest of your life. Another factor that strengthens this trend is the newly discovered desire of an increasing number of people to find more meaning in their work. Per a study by yougov.co.uk—a market research organization—more than a third of working British adults say their job is not making a meaningful contribution to the world.[2] This was also true for 35% of Germans and 24% of U.S. workers.

Despite all this, becoming an independent worker or starting a small business has not proven an easy goal to achieve. UK government researched showed that while in 2006, a third of the working population—11 million people—were seriously considering dumping the rat race to join the ranks of the self-employed or had already taken steps to do so, by 2011 less than a million had done so. Not from lack of trying, but because of the difficulties they encountered. And by far, the most difficult thing to achieve when you don't have an established reputation is the ability to find and maintain clients for your business and to achieve sustainability. Everyone is unique and has something to offer that is of use to or needed by someone else. The question is how to connect the two, the service provider and potential customer?

While there are many online avenues for individual or small business service providers to market themselves, they all share a common trait, which is that you don't know how much you can trust such a provider until after they have done the job. If you are looking for a lawyer, accountant, computer programmer, massage therapist, car mechanic or any other service—your options are usually unlimited—just try a Google search. Unfortunately, the knowledge about the *level of trust* you can assign to any potential candidate is minimal, since the existing review-based systems are easy to game and fake five-star reputations are surprisingly easy to achieve.[3] This makes it tough for people who are just starting up in their endeavor and do not have an established reputation, as well as for people who are looking for reliable and trustworthy services. A much better alternative is to ask people you know—friends, family, coworkers—if they can recommend you someone they used in the past and that they trust. While this approach will result in the highest amount of confidence and quality recommendations, it is also the most "expensive" in terms of the time and energy you need to put into contacting your acquaintances and asking them for a recommendation.

With Meritwork, we believe we found a way to make this process seamless, such that finding a provider you can trust is as easy if not easier than doing a Google search. You see, Meritwork is not just a services marketplace—it is also a social network. Think of it as LinkedIn meets Yelp.

A Network of Trust

Meritwork is a social network where new connections are being created when you use someone's service or provide a service for someone on the platform. Unlike other networks, recommending someone on Meritwork implies a certain responsibility, because it is equivalent to recommending a service provider to other people you know in real life, and the experience they will have with this provider will reflect on you. This makes "fake reviews" a total no-no, and the cost of creating a fake reputation is so much higher than any reward you may get out of it to the point of being completely impractical and "suicidal" as far as your ability to use the platform goes.

In many ways, this is an implementation of the "word of mouth" concept, which works well in small communities where everyone is a first- or second-degree network connection. With Meritwork, this concept is now being brought online and made available in the context of the whole world, without losing its effectiveness.

Marketing Yourself on Meritwork

As a service provider on Meritwork, you don't need to worry about marketing costs, competing against big-budget advertisement or fake reputation competitors. All you need is to focus on doing an excellent job and bringing in as connections people you trust and people who trust you (because you used their services or did good work for them in the past). Then, automatically, these people's networks of friends, providers, or customers become second-degree connections to you and therefore potential clients.

Suppose you are a student who just graduated. You have no experience, and it is hard to launch in the job market. Or you could be still in school, or already have a job, but you would like to leverage something else you like to do or are good at and earn some extra money. With Meritwork you can do this. Once you connect with a few people, you will be put in front of their networks—your second-degree connections now—as a service provider for the services you are offering.

All these connections know that you are not just another stranger, but there is someone else in between that knows both of you, and therefore they have reason to trust you will do an excellent job—much more than if you were just another Amazon or Google search result. This also protects your reputation in the case of a mishap or getting a bad review, which happens to everyone; no matter how good you are, there is always someone who will not like you. With Meritwork, your reputation will not be ruined by such an anomaly. But if you consistently do lousy work and get bad reviews, then it will be ruined very fast. This creates a much-needed balance where the main motivation of the provider is to do a good job, but without the fear that a single bad review will ruin them.

Another side effect of the network-based approach is that you yourself are now connecting people and facilitating transactions without any conscious effort on your side. We intend to distribute a part of our profits to reward these silent facilitations such that even if you did not provide a service during a period of time, the fact that services have been provided based on your recommendations would result in the member being rewarded for it.

Creating Your profile

To provide services using Meritwork, you need to create a profile, add a picture, and say some things about yourself. Then you can add the services you would like to offer to your profile. Or, if you prefer to see what is available in the community, you can see the front-page for market intelligence, search for services, look for people you may know, and then come back to add services and complete your profile.

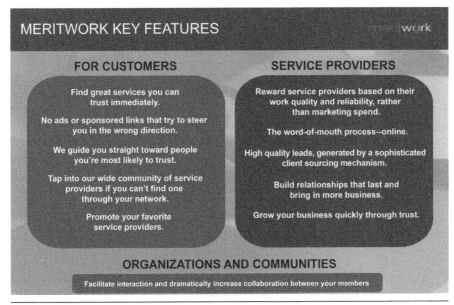

Figure 17.1 Meritwork features.
Source: Meritwork.com.

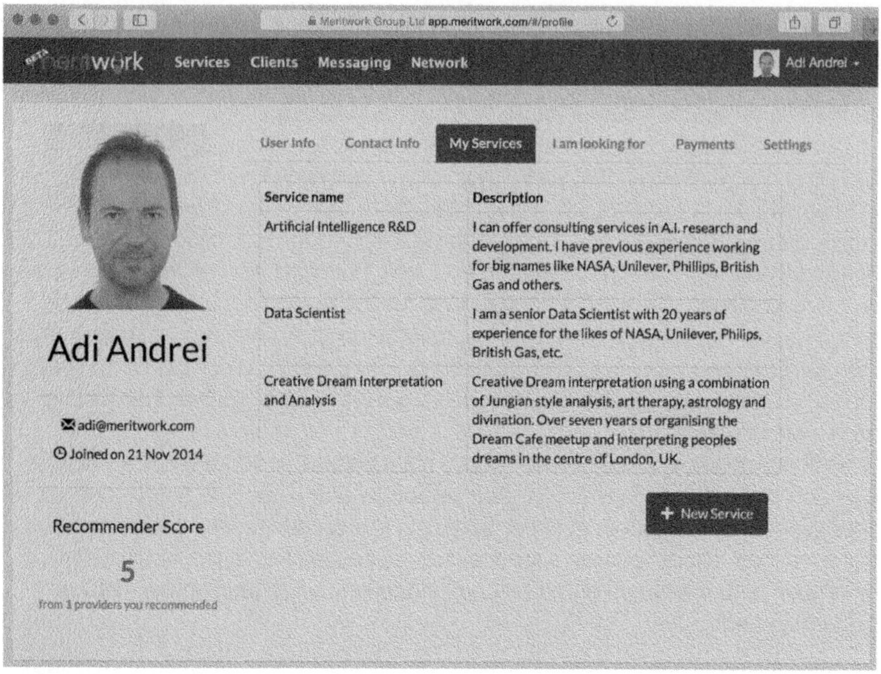

Figure 17.2 Meritwork profile view.
Source: Meritwork.com.

Adding services

A user can offer as many different services as they like. For each added service, they can specify details such as qualifications, what they normally charge for it, and if they are open to negotiation, barter, etc., as well as the location where they are providing the service (e.g. dog walking in New York, or website design anywhere in the world). The more details they provide, the more information the Text Analytics will match them with potential clients.

They can also add specific questions that people must answer before requesting an offer. For instance, when a member offers their psychotherapy services, the prospective clients will have to respond to questions such as what the purpose of the session is (self-development, depression, mental health issue, and if they are taking any medications, etc.). You are free to create your own questions based on your own professional needs.

Adding Connections to Your network

Trust is based on having connections which can lead you to trusted providers or potential clients.

There are a few different ways you can add connections:

- You can search on Meritwork for people you know and ask to connect with them (by going to their full profile page).
- You can invite people to Meritwork using email or Facebook. Once they join they become part of your network.

But you also create connections by:

- Providing a service to someone.
- Having someone provide a service for you.

You can also disconnect from existing connections any time you feel that a particular connection is creating difficulties for you—like let's say they keep getting bad reviews, this will result in a lowering of your recommender score so you may want to stop recommending them to your network or unfriend them.

Searching for Services

This is the main feature potential customers will use to find service providers. It should be as easy and intuitive as typing your query in the search box. The results are sorted in order of relevance as well as inherent trustworthiness, as shown in Figure 17.3.

Creating an Ad for a Service You Are Looking For

If using the search did not bring the results you were looking for (likely at the beginning, when there are not many people on the platform) you can post a "looking for" advert (aka public request) describing the kind of service you are looking for, and then service

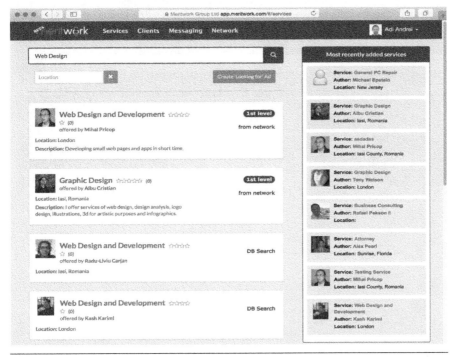

Figure 17.3 Meritwork search results view.
Source: Meritwork.com.

providers looking for clients will contact you with their offers which you can then accept, reject, or negotiate. Just as with creating services, the more details you add, the better the chance you will be contacted with meaningful offers.

Searching for Clients

Searching for clients is like searching for services, but instead of looking at the services offered, we look at the "Look for ads" section, also known as "open requests" that other people posted and are waiting for service providers to contact them with offers. If you have added services to your profile, potential clients and their ads will be shown when you go to the Clients page, preempting your search, so-to-speak, based on the information you put in the description of your services.

Market Intelligence

The first thing you see after your login, right below the search box is some top-level real-time market intelligence: what the most needed, or the most offered occupations are on Meritwork at the moment. This information can be provided in regards to your network, your location, or the whole world.

As you go down the page, you see your feed, with up-to-date information about what is going on in your network, new service available or requested, system messages, etc.

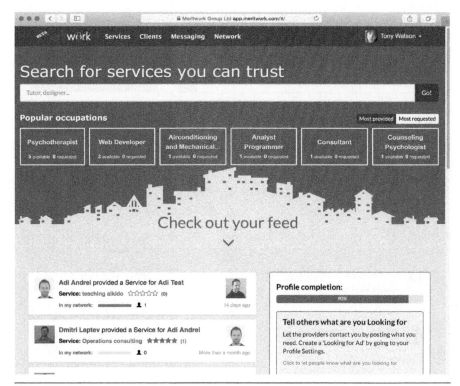

Figure 17.4 Meritwork market intelligence view.
Source: Meritwork.com.

Making Transactions and Communicating on Meritwork

Central to transacting on Meritwork is the integrated messaging platform. You can use it to make, and request offers for services, negotiate, chat, ask for more details, send and pay invoices, give reviews, recommend people to your network, and ask for recommendations.

One important feature of Meritwork is that you can also contact the person in-between, the one that knows both you and the service provider, to ask them for more details about the provider if necessary.

Meritwork in the Current Technological and Economic Landscape

Unlike some of the other so-called "sharing economy" businesses that act more like temp agencies or employers, Meritwork's role is only that of a facilitator for providers and potential customers to find each other, communicate, and transact. Unlike most social networks (like Facebook, LinkedIn, Twitter, Instagram, etc.) where your first-degree connections are the target audience for your activity, in Meritwork, the most important audience are second-degree connections—the people you don't know directly, but you both have someone in common.

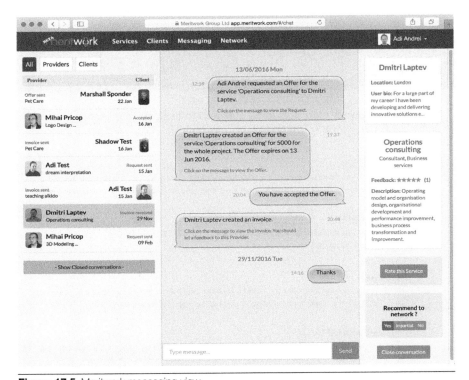

Figure 17.5 Meritwork messaging view.
Source: Meritwork.com.

The relationships (connections) developed by a member on Meritwork carry more significance and more responsibility than on other platforms—bringing in more rewards and real-life value. One side-effect of this is the positive reinforcement cycle where developing significant relationships attracts more and more significant relationships and so on, which leads to a certain self-sustainability for the service provider and a kind of relationship-based material security that trumps whatever was left in the modern day (from the old idea of "job security"[4]).

Meritwork is free to join, search, offer, or request services. We are considering charging a small monthly subscription fee ($7) if you had any customers that month. For those under the age of 22, using Meritwork is completely free of charge, regardless of the amount of business, in order to help the young generation.[5]

Suggested Use Cases for Meritwork

- Anyone who needs professional services and wants a personal recommendation.
- Professional service providers—for example, Web developers, accountants, graphic designers, tutors, copywriters, massage therapists, etc.
- People looking for work or exploring a way to make extra money selling their services online.
- People who have a business but no website and cannot afford to spend on advertising.
- Any organization or community looking to facilitate interaction and increase collaboration between its members.
- Larger businesses looking to connect with self-employed and small service providers as a flexible way to access potential human resources, and as a source of external innovation

HOW IS MERITWORK *DIFFERENT?*

What sets Meritwork apart from other business-to-customer connection sites like Fiverr, Upwork, Thumbtack, or TaskRabbit?

TRUST

We rely on the social network of our users to find trusted connections. You are immediately exposed to potential clients that have reasons to trust you because you are connected through someone they know.

FAIRNESS

No ads, no sponsored result, no paid promotions.
You cannot pay your way to the top on Meritwork.

AFFORDABLE

A small monthly subscription of £7 is much more affordable than the 8–25% commissions our competitors charge. We also offer Meritwork free of charge to those aged 21 and younger.

MEANINGFUL

We help people make the transition into meaningful work. Keep your current job for as long as needed, but continually grow a business you're passionate about on the side through personal connections.

Figure 17.6 Meritwork value propositions.
Source: Meritwork.com.

The Role of Digital Analytics in Meritwork

Without the combination of network algorithms and Text Analytics algorithms, Meritwork would not be possible.

Text Analytics

The Text Analytics play a major role in finding either services or potential clients that are relevant to your query. A complex multilayered search mechanism is employed every time you type something in the search box. The autocomplete algorithm has about four levels of search. Once you click the search button, another ten-level process is employed. At each level, the algorithm searches for matches in a more and more relaxed context until the number of matches goes over 30 or it has exhausted all the avenues. If your keywords are not found in the name of a service, they are searched among job categories, occupations, service descriptions, and provider bios. If actual words cannot be found, we look for their synonyms and so on. For the search to be fast (milliseconds), we make heavy use of n-grams. Stemming is also being employed across the whole spectrum (refer to Chapter 10 for more details on n-grams and stemming).

Network Algorithms

Network analytics are essential in selecting and presenting results in order of possible, potential trustworthiness. Network algorithms can search for services and potential clients in a member's extended network—something technologically very challenging using conventional means.

Once results that are relevant from a text analytics point of view are found—whether in your extended network or the whole platform, they are sorted in order of trustworthiness. This involves another multilayer approach:

- People in your network—your first-degree connections—show up on top.
- Second-degree connections are sorted based on the feedback and reviews they received, but also based on the reputation level of those who recommend them.
- People in your interests groups show up next.
- People not in your group and not connected to your network show up based on relevance as well as feedback and reviews.
- On top of this, we may use location filters or geo-location based distance.

Every time something is shown in regards to your own network, graph search algorithms, as well as a graph database, are used to filter this information from millions of user records quickly, then aggregate it and present it to you. When location filters are being employed, geo-location is used—if permitted—to identify your current GPS coordinates and filter the information based on distance from your present location. A similar multilayer approach is being employed when looking for potential clients, but instead of searching for offered services, the algorithms are applied to public requests or ads.

Web Analytics

Although the main purpose of Web Analytics is to report and optimize Web usage by measuring Web traffic, we also use it as a tool for business and market research in order to improve the effectiveness of the app. Web Analytics helps one to estimate how the traffic goes at different times of the day, by tracking information about the number of visitors of the app and the number of page views (refer to Chapters 5 and 6 for more details on Web Analytics).

On Meritwork, every event is tracked and countered so we can improve the overall experience in time. For example, you can look for services in two ways: directly from the home page, but with no filtering options, or by going to the dedicated services page and searching for posts using the given tools. By tracking both possibilities, we can improve the user's experience in time.

Another example of the opportunity to improve the user experience is to track different lists of events of how the user gets to make a certain action or event on the app, and compare to how the Meritwork's team wanted this to be done (refer to Chapter 5, where site pathing is covered in more detail). The idea is to improve the app based on the user's preferences, and by using Web Analytics, we can do that in time.

Review Questions

1. Write in your own words: what is Meritwork?
2. Create a full profile (you can delete it later after the semester is over), add at least one (or more) service you can provide and one or more services that you would like someone to provide for you.
3. Join the group created by your instructor.
4. Have at least one transaction:

   - Ask someone to provide a service for you, or make an offer to someone who is interested in your services
   - It can be just "pretend," it does not have to be a money-based transaction or to do the service. Just go through the process of negotiating a price or exchange, all the way to creating and sending an invoice.
   - If you have a real transaction, that is even better.
   - Output a screenshot of the conversation.

5. Do a comparative analysis for how you would you achieve a similar result using another platform (physical or digital, i.e., Facebook, newspaper, Google, etc.). Consider the following:

   - How long it takes to find relevant results
   - How do I pick a service and why?
   - Communication/negotiation
   - Payment
   - Trust level comparison

6. How relevant could Meritwork be for you (assuming lots of people are on it)

   - as a service provider?
   - as a service consumer?

7. How intuitive is the interaction? What other features do you think would be useful to have on the platform, or how we could make it more engaging for users like yourself?

Chapter 17 Citations

1. Horowitz, S. and F. Rosati. "53 million Americans are freelancing, a new survey finds." September 4, 2014, https://blog.freelancersunion. org/2014/09/04/53million/. Accessed April 15, 2017.

2. Dahlgreen, W. "37% of British workers think their jobs are meaningless." August 12, 2015. https://yougov.co.uk/news/2015/08/12/british-jobs-meaning less. Accessed April 15, 2017.

3. Hill, K. "I created a fake business and bought it an amazing online reputation." Fusion. September 15, 2015, http://fusion.net/story/191773/i-created-a-fake-business-and-fooled-thousands-of-people-into-thinking-it-was-real/. Accessed 29 Jan. 2017.

4. James, G. "How to achieve true job security." Inc. April 3, 2012. www.inc.com/ geoffrey-james/how-to-achieve-true-job-security.html. Accessed April 15, 2017.

5. Bingham, J. "Young becoming new economic underclass in UK." The Telegraph. October 30, 2015. www.telegraph.co.uk/news/uknews/11963750/Young-becoming-new-economic-underclass-in-UK.html. Accessed April 15, 2017.

Index

Note:
Page numbers in **bold** type refer to **figures**
Page numbers in *italic* type refer to *tables*
Page numbers followed by 'n' refer to notes

Index 389